Reconstructions

Reconstructions

*New Perspectives
on the Postbellum United States*

Edited by Thomas J. Brown

OXFORD
UNIVERSITY PRESS

2006

OXFORD
UNIVERSITY PRESS

Oxford University Press, Inc., publishes works that further
Oxford University's objective of excellence
in research, scholarship, and education.

Oxford　New York
Auckland　Cape Town　Dar es Salaam　Hong Kong　Karachi
Kuala Lumpur　Madrid　Melbourne　Mexico City　Nairobi
New Delhi　Shanghai　Taipei　Toronto

With offices in
Argentina　Austria　Brazil　Chile　Czech Republic　France　Greece
Guatemala　Hungary　Italy　Japan　Poland　Portugal　Singapore
South Korea　Switzerland　Thailand　Turkey　Ukraine　Vietnam

Copyright © 2006 by Oxford University Press, Inc.

Published by Oxford University Press, Inc.
198 Madison Avenue, New York, New York 10016

www.oup.com

Oxford is a registered trademark of Oxford University Press

Library of Congress Cataloging-in-Publication Data
Reconstructions : new perspectives on the postbellum United States /
edited by Thomas J. Brown
p. cm.
Includes bibliographical references and index.
ISBN-13 978-0-19-517595-0
ISBN 0-19-517595-6
1. Reconstruction (U.S. history, 1865–1877)
I. Brown, Thomas J., 1960–
E668.R425 2006
973.8—dc22　　2005055479

1 3 5 7 9 8 6 4 2

Printed in the United States of America
on acid-free paper

To graduate seminars in History

CONTENTS

CONTRIBUTORS

Thomas J. Brown is associate professor of history and associate director of the Institute for Southern Studies at the University of South Carolina. He is the author of *Dorothea Dix, New England Reformer* (1998), coeditor of *Hope and Glory: Essays on the Legacy of the Fifty-Fourth Massachusetts Regiment* (2001), and editor of *The Public Art of Civil War Commemoration: A Brief History with Documents* (2004).

Leslie Butler is assistant professor of history at Dartmouth College. Her monograph *Cultivating Democracy: Victorian Men of Letters and Transatlantic Liberal Reform*, is forthcoming from the University of North Carolina Press.

Michael W. Fitzgerald is professor of history at St. Olaf College. He is the author of *The Union League Movement in the Deep South: Politics and Agricultural Change during Reconstruction* (1989) and *Urban Emancipation: Popular Politics in Reconstruction Mobile, 1860–1890* (2002), as well as many essays on Reconstruction politics.

Heather Cox Richardson is associate professor of history at the University of Massachusetts, Amherst. She is the author of *The Greatest Nation of the Earth: Republican Economic Policies during the Civil War* (1997), *The Death of Reconstruction: Race, Labor, and Politics in the Post–Civil War North, 1865–1901* (2001), and *Race, Riots, and Rodeos: The Reconstruction of America after the Civil War* (forthcoming).

John C. Rodrigue is associate professor of history at Louisiana State University. His *Reconstruction in the Cane Fields: From Slavery to Free Labor in Louisiana's Sugar Parishes, 1862–1880* (2001) received the Kemper and Leila Williams Prize from the Louisiana Historical Association and the Historic New Orleans Collection. He is a coeditor of the forthcoming volume in the Freedmen and Southern Society Project collection *Freedom: A Documentary History of Emancipation, 1861–1867* entitled *Land and Labor, 1865*.

Mark M. Smith is Carolina Distinguished Professor of History at the University of South Carolina. His major publications include *Mastered by the Clock: Time, Slavery, and Freedom in the American South* (1997), which received the Avery Craven Prize of the Organization of American Historians and the annual book prize of the South Carolina Historical Society; *Debating Slavery: Economy and Society in the Antebellum American South* (1998); *Listening to Nineteenth-Century America* (2001); *Stono: Documenting and Interpreting a Southern Slave Revolt* (2005); and *How Race Is Made: Slavery, Segregation, and the Senses* (2006).

Michael Vorenberg is associate professor of history at Brown University and the author of *Final Freedom: The Civil War, the Abolition of Slavery, and the Thirteenth Amendment* (2001) as well as many essays about emancipation and the Constitution in the era of Reconstruction.

Stephen A. West is associate professor of history at the Catholic University of America. His monograph *From Yeoman to Redneck in Upstate South Carolina, 1850–1915* is forthcoming. He is a coeditor of a future volume in the Freedmen and Southern Society Project collection *Freedom: A Documentary History of Emancipation, 1861–1867* entitled *Land and Labor, 1866–1867*.

Reconstructions

INTRODUCTION

Once likened to a dark and bloody ground, scholarship on Reconstruction now thrives less as a form of combat than as a collective building on a solid foundation. The making of that foundation is one of the most familiar chapters in the history of American historical literature. Many historiographical essays have recounted the rise and fall of the view of Reconstruction associated with William A. Dunning, one of the few renderings of the national past developed so systematically and comprehensively that it is customarily called a school of interpretation.[1] The Dunning school studies that began to appear around the turn of the twentieth century featured assiduous research and an impressive breadth of attention to political, social, and economic transformations. But the critical perspective of the work was often badly distorted by

---

[1] Bernard A. Weisberger, "The Dark and Bloody Ground of Reconstruction Historiography," *Journal of Southern History* 25 (November 1959): 427–447. Other accounts of the rise and fall of the Dunning school include A. A. Taylor, "Historians of the Reconstruction," *Journal of Negro History* 23 (January 1938): 16–34; Francis B. Simkins, "New Viewpoints of Southern Reconstruction," *Journal of Southern History* 5 (February 1939): 49–61; Howard K. Beale, "On Rewriting Reconstruction History," *American Historical Review* 45 (July 1940): 807–827; T. Harry Williams, "An Analysis of Some Reconstruction Attitudes," *Journal of Southern History* 12 (November 1946): 469–486; John Hope Franklin, "Whither Reconstruction Historiography?" *Journal of Negro Education* 17 (Autumn 1948): 446–461; Vernon L. Wharton, "Reconstruction," in *Writing Southern History: Essays in Historiography in Honor of Fletcher M. Green,* ed. Arthur S. Link and Rembert W. Patrick (Baton Rouge: Louisiana State University Press, 1965), 295–315; Richard O. Curry, "The Civil War and Reconstruction, 1861–1877: A Critical Overview of Recent Trends and Interpretations," *Civil War History* 20 (September 1974): 215–238; Eric Foner, "Reconstruction Revisited," *Reviews in American History* 10 (December 1982): 82–100. Surveys of Reconstruction historiography since the mid-1980s are cited in the essays in this collection.

the same racial prejudice that had shaped partisan characterizations of Reconstruction as a sordid era of misrule and disorder. Only in the mid–twentieth century did scholars begin to build on participants' defenses of Reconstruction and identify its promise and collapse as, in the words of C. Vann Woodward, "the moral core of national history."[2]

Woodward's classic explorations of the southern response to the upheavals brought by defeat and emancipation illustrate the immediacy of postwar reform initiatives for intellectuals eager to trace the roots of public controversies and point toward historical bases for progressive solutions. These motives inspired landmark revisionist books on Reconstruction by W. E. B. Du Bois, John Hope Franklin, and Kenneth Stampp, among other luminaries, and shelves of valuable monographs.

The revisionist line of formulation reached a climax in the scholarship of Eric Foner. His *Reconstruction: America's Unfinished Revolution* (1988) not only presented a synthesis of social and political history wide-ranging enough to complete the displacement of the Dunning school; it also mediated skillfully between revisionist interpretations and the postrevisionist critiques that had argued since the 1960s that Reconstruction reforms were less substantial than either the Dunningites or the revisionists claimed.

Foner's work maximized the leverage offered by a close concentration on the process of adjustment to the end of slavery. Placing Reconstruction at the center of American history, he stressed that the experiences of former slaves constituted a key stage in the redefinition of the fundamental idea of freedom. That transformation was in part a grim change. Despite the strivings of ex-slaves for the economic self-sufficiency that earlier generations of Americans had considered essential to independence, national emancipation policy reconceptualized autonomy as a right to compete in labor markets for the reward of social mobility. Leaving freedpeople acutely vulnerable, the shift converged with a hardening of class stratification in a consolidating industrial capitalism that resisted protective labor regulation as antithetical to laissez-faire principles but drew readily on the coercive power of the state to suppress workers' protests. Foner was equally sensitive, however, to the inspiring strands of his story. He pointed out that the rapid American extension of voting and office-holding rights to freedmen was unique in the hemispheric dismantling of slavery. That step, the centerpiece of a restructuring of the constitutional order, was more than vindicated by the achievements of Reconstruction governments. Setting the political emergence of African Americans alongside their establishment of churches and rebuilding of families, Foner offered a stirring depiction of a community that

---

[2] C. Vann Woodward, *Thinking Back: The Perils of Writing History* (Baton Rouge: Louisiana State University Press, 1986), 52.

persevered through the violence of opponents and the halfheartedness of allies and formed a steadfast force for American social progress.[3]

This volume examines the directions that scholarship has taken in the years since the appearance of Foner's synthesis. Publications have continued to proliferate, but our review of the field is prompted less by the sheer quantity of new research than by the distinctive challenges of writing on a historical subject framed for so long in terms of a continuous argument that has culminated in such distinguished contributions to American literature. Even leading specialists wondered whether the postbellum era would remain a dynamic field for original interpretation of the national past after Foner's *Reconstruction* exhausted the potential energy built up in the long struggle to supplant the Dunning school.[4] Almost twenty years later, this collection of original historiographical essays shows that the aftermath of the Civil War continues to stimulate compelling new writing and offer opportunities for fresh understanding of a pivotal transition.

The organization of the book reflects a confidence that established frameworks of Reconstruction scholarship will support additional interpretive approaches. A survey of this sort might have offered essays centered on themes that have recently increased in prominence, such as religion (which about half of the contributors discuss) and gender (which almost all address). The following chapters instead adopt more traditional building blocks for analysis of Reconstruction, including the experiences of former slaves, the social and economic remodeling of the South and the North, the trajectory of national politics and international relations, and the revision of the Constitution. The essays on intellectual life and on Civil War remembrance similarly orient themselves around longstanding historiographical landmarks.

This design readily covers the important new studies of Reconstruction, often from more than one angle. For example, Stephen West and John Rodrigue both assess new research on labor arrangements in the post-emancipation South, in the first essay as a structural element of the regional economy and in the second as an expression of the aspirations of freedpeople. The most pervasive interpretive trends cut across the treatment of many different topics. The rise of cultural history in the last two decades links Stephen West's and Heather Cox Richardson's discussions of writing on the construction of race, Mark Smith's observations about the permeability of the foreign and the domestic as categories of

---

[3] Eric Foner, *Reconstruction: America's Unfinished Revolution, 1863–1877* (New York: Harper and Row, 1988). See also Foner, *Nothing but Freedom: Emancipation and Its Legacy* (Baton Rouge: Louisiana State University Press, 1983); Foner, *The Story of American Freedom* (New York: Norton, 1998); and relevant essays collected in Foner, *Who Owns History? Rethinking the Past in a Changing World* (New York: Hill and Wang, 2002).

[4] See, e.g., Michael Perman, "Eric Foner's *Reconstruction*: A Finished Revolution," *Reviews in American History* 17 (March 1989): 73–78.

public affairs, Michael Vorenberg's use of the concept of popular constitutionalism, Leslie Butler's account of the revitalization of intellectual history, and Thomas Brown's attention to narratives and performances of Civil War remembrance. But our goal is not to outline a new synthesis that marshals the methods and concerns of cultural history as effectively as Foner integrated social and political history. The collection is marked more by eagerness to canvass different approaches to Reconstruction than zeal to demonstrate the potential of any particular innovation to realign the field.

To acknowledge the richness of the revisionist legacy is not to suggest that debate over it has ended. Michael Fitzgerald's contribution to this volume most thoroughly describes a line of analysis that looks toward a balancing of revisionism with further development and modification of critiques raised by outstanding postrevisionist scholarship. Reasoning that advances in civil rights and the parallel acceptance of revisionism have reduced scholars' sense of an imperative to rehabilitate the racial egalitarianism in Republican policies, he anticipates what he describes as an "ethical recalibration of Reconstruction studies" that downplays the idealistic strand of the era. Conversely, John Rodrigue points out that the effort to enlarge upon revisionism can turn into a challenge to it. His essay shows that recognition of black agency in Reconstruction has produced a literature that generates a creative tension with the narrative of black community consolidation by highlighting the diversity and often the divisions among African Americans. These examples underscore scholars' continued appreciation that Reconstruction is a great historical subject because of the opportunities it offers to explore themes of race. Similarly, much recent scholarship has found an electric connection between race and gender after emancipation that is comparable to the well-established emphasis on the end of slavery as a crucial moment in both race relations and labor relations.

The keynote of the book is less the contestation or elaboration of revisionism than the recognition of additional approaches to Reconstruction as an extraordinarily fertile field for historical writing. Emancipation and race remain central in current work, but other themes have gained in urgency. Nationalism, a subject that David Herbert Donald observed a quarter-century ago had been "surprisingly neglected" in scholarship on the crisis of the Union, is a case in point.[5] Nationalism has been a subject of tremendous intellectual interest over the past two decades, and Reconstruction is one of the prime sites for its investigation in United States history. In many cases scholars have reinforced the revisionist tradition by exposing racial ideologies embedded in the postbellum concept of the nation. But the research has also followed other leads, such as the crosscurrents between war and society, and has produced important historical literature on such new topics as the rise of the American flag to its position as the foremost icon of national identity. Understanding of postwar state-build-

[5] David Herbert Donald, *Liberty and Union* (Lexington, Mass.: Heath, 1978), 273.

ing, previously focused on race relations and industrial regulation, has similarly been enriched by a burgeoning scholarship on the innovative entitlement programs for Civil War veterans and their families.

The attention to work on nationalism and state-building, subjects that have engaged political scientists, constitutional theorists, sociologists, literary critics, and other specialists, illustrates the variety of perspectives that the collection describes. This effort to widen the scope of thinking about Reconstruction is perhaps the most striking common theme in the essays, which were written without any concerted plan of argument. The contributors advance a succession of proposals to open borders between Reconstruction scholarship and the fields of intellectual history, legal history, western history, diplomatic history, and other disciplinary categories.

The attempt to achieve a more comprehensive view also shapes the approach of the collection to the problem of periodization. Several essays underscore the importance of recognizing that Reconstruction began almost immediately upon secession, though for want of a better term the book must often use "postwar" and "postbellum" to refer to the period opening in 1861 and continuing beyond 1865. Over half of the essays emphasize that fundamental adjustments to the consequences of the war continued after the 1877 date traditionally used to mark the end of Reconstruction. As many historians have previously observed, conventional distinctions between Reconstruction and the Gilded Age contribute to an incomplete picture of the aftermath of the war. Altogether the collection discusses more than three dozen works with titles that bracket dates beginning during the war or at its end and extending beyond 1890, most often to 1900 or to the years just before or after World War I. Books that adopt similar periodizations include some of the most widely acclaimed historical publications of recent years, such as David Blight's *Race and Reunion* (2001) and Steven Hahn's *A Nation under Our Feet* (2003).[6] This pattern indicates that historians might profitably supplement intensive examination of the 1860s and 1870s by thinking of the postbellum era in wider terms.

Reconsideration of themes and periodization in the study of Reconstruction is the broadest way this book seeks to assist scholars working in the field. The contributors also point out gaps in the information presently available and clarify conflicts in interpretation. Several of the essays identify sources that invite further investigation, and many describe research designs that are especially promising for particular topics. These discussions of needs and opportunities for new scholarship underscore that the purpose of the volume is more to offer suggestions than to draw conclusions.

---

[6] David W. Blight, *Race and Reunion: The Civil War in American Memory* (Cambridge, Mass.: Harvard University Press, 2001); Steven Hahn, *A Nation under Our Feet: Black Political Struggles in the Rural South from Slavery to the Great Migration* (Cambridge, Mass.: Harvard University Press, 2003).

The book addresses the reading as well as the writing of history. The topic of Reconstruction is an excellent case study in the relationship between the publications that research specialists routinely call "the literature" and the subset of work that deserves more frequent recognition as literature. The essays explore this relationship by situating exemplary historical writing within the development of disciplinary fields. For example, Leslie Butler examines the enduring vitality of George Fredrickson's classic *The Inner Civil War* (1965) and uses it as a starting point for tracing shifts in the study of intellectual history that have since shaped different—but comparably creative and powerful—books about the reverberations of the war.[7] While Butler's essay documents the rejuvenation of a field, Michael Vorenberg and Mark Smith indicate that transformations of constitutional history and diplomatic history could yield analogously fruitful work on Reconstruction.

The chief consideration in the overview offered here is not the breadth of a publication in topic or in readership, but the depth of meaning its author locates in Reconstruction. The revisionist focus on Reconstruction as a mirror for continuing struggles over freedom and equality has illustrated that depth frequently involves an element of timeliness. Recent work has continued to find vantage points that respond to the interests of a changing society, for example by turning from the status of workers to the place of consumers in postwar industrial capitalism and from the course of race relations to the formation of ethnic identities and the variety of black experiences and viewpoints. Several contributors note that the end of the Cold War and American efforts to replace regimes in Afghanistan and Iraq have sharpened interest in the attempt to reconstruct the social and political order of the South.

If the collection directly aspires to contribute to reading and writing on Reconstruction, it less obviously aims to foster the attention of public history to the topic. For all of its triumphs, the scholarship of the past forty years has had uneven success in reaching the general public. Dunningite stereotypes retain remarkable popular influence, in part because of the challenges of teaching Reconstruction successfully in schools but in large part because of the imbalance in presentation of the topic in other forums. Creditable histories have not yet found adequate outlets to counter more widely the hoary fictions of a subjugated white South that are perpetuated by novels and films like *Gone with the Wind* and by some strands of contemporary political discourse. Here again Eric Foner has blazed a trail toward a better informed public understanding, as the curator of a museum exhibit on Reconstruction, a member of a superb team of consultants for a documentary film on Reconstruction, and an advocate of legislation to establish a National Park Service site focused on Reconstruction in

---

[7] George M. Fredrickson, *The Inner Civil War: Northern Intellectuals and the Crisis of the Union* (New York: Harper and Row, 1965).

Beaufort County, South Carolina, scene of the Port Royal Experiment.[8] This volume originated in support of the last of these initiatives, an important complement to the recent efforts of the National Park Service to expand the thematic contextualization of the Civil War battlefield parks that figure so prominently among the landmarks of American heritage.

The collection illustrates the rewarding partnership that has begun to flourish in recent years between the production of research publications and the practice of public history. On the most basic level, the essays contribute to the process by which planning for the proposed National Park Service project might draw on up-to-date scholarship. The survey can help not only to inform the overall interpretations presented to visitors but also to connect broad ideas to specific sites. Residences of the era, for example, take on fresh significance when seen in light of scholarship ranging from studies of household economies to readings of marriage as an ideological template for the integrity of the restored Union and the dilemmas of contract in the post-emancipation order. At the same time, the book exemplifies the leadership role of outstanding museums and historic preservation venues in stimulating new scholarship. The public history initiative in Beaufort County created the impetus for this undertaking, extended generous logistical support, introduced the contributors to extraordinary local historians and interested citizens, and offered abundant inspiration in the evocative Sea Islands. Discussed in draft form by the contributors in the former Beaufort office of the Freedmen's Bureau, these essays share a sense of hopeful adventure as well as an awareness of the challenges in this field. As a point of reference for such attempts to imagine new beginnings, Reconstruction will always remain an eminently usable part of the American past.

[8] Eric Foner and Olivia Mahoney, *America's Reconstruction: People and Politics after the Civil War* (New York: HarperPerennial, 1995); Elizabeth Deane, Llew Smith, and Patricia Garcia-Rios, prods., *Reconstruction: The Second Civil War* (WGBH Productions, 2004); Page Putnam Miller, "OAH Supports National Park Service Study Interpreting the Reconstruction Era," *OAH Newsletter*, August 2002, 14.

1

"A GENERAL REMODELING OF EVERY THING"

Economy and Race in the Post-Emancipation South

STEPHEN A. WEST

The first day of 1865 dawned cold and clear over the upper piedmont of South Carolina. The sun shone brightly, but it did little to lift the spirits of Emily Harris, the wife of a middling slaveowner who had departed eight months earlier to enter the Confederate cavalry. During his absence, Emily Harris struggled to manage the family's farm and oversee its slaves in the straitened circumstances of wartime, and the new year appeared to offer no prospect of improvement. "The war goes on with unabated fury," she wrote in the farm journal she kept during her husband's absence. "Many are willing to unite again with the hated Yankees rather than continue the hard and seemingly hopeless struggle." Her comments echoed the same gloom and apprehension she had recorded a few weeks earlier. "I go forth into the 'shadowy future' but not without a fear. I can see no more beyond the next crop. After that there will have to be a general remodeling of every thing, *Every thing.*"[1]

Emily Harris's bleak assessment was, if anything, overly optimistic: the war ended before the family's 1865 crop could be planted, let alone harvested. The final victory of Union armies spelled the end of the Confederacy and the end of slavery, and indeed inaugurated "a general remodeling of every thing." The Harrises and their ten former slaves were among the millions of southerners who would struggle, in the years after the Civil War, to shape the contours of life in a society no longer defined by racial slavery. This essay will evaluate recent scholarship on those struggles and their results, with a special focus on two areas. The first is how historians have understood the emergence of new economic relations after the Civil War. The peculiar institution had shaped—and

[1] Philip N. Racine, ed., *Piedmont Farmer: The Journals of David Golightly Harris, 1855–1870* (Knoxville: University of Tennessee Press, 1990), 357, 351.

its destruction thus reshaped—every aspect of the southern economy, from the plantation belt to the upcountry, from the role of towns and industry to the place of commerce and finance. If plantation slavery was at its heart a labor system, its growth in North America had proceeded, since the colonial era, with the development of practices of racial subordination and ideologies of racial difference. The transformation of those ideas and practices, then, is the second area of scholarship to be examined by this essay. The end of racial slavery hardly created a colorblind society, but the color line would be drawn in new ways, and to different purposes, in the post-emancipation South.

To discuss scholarship in both of these areas is to confront the powerful legacy of C. Vann Woodward. Indeed, after a fashion, each has its own Woodward thesis. According to the dates in its title, Woodward's seminal *Origins of the New South, 1877–1913* (1951) was not a book about Reconstruction at all. But with his Beardian insistence on the "newness" of the postwar economy—the fall of the planter class, the emergence of sharecropping, tenancy, and the crop lien, and the rise of a new middle class—Woodward set the stage for decades of debate among historians about the extent of change between the antebellum and postbellum eras, and Reconstruction as the crucial link between the two. In *The Strange Career of Jim Crow* (1955), Woodward argued likewise for the essentially new character of race relations in the postwar South. Debate over this Woodward thesis centered on his contention that the twenty-five years after 1865 represented a period of relative tolerance and fluidity that gave way to the "stiff conformity and fanatical rigidity" of legalized segregation after 1890.[2]

For a generation, controversy over these Woodward theses drove a great deal of scholarship. Increasingly, however, many historians found those debates rigid in their terms and narrow in focus, and by the late 1980s, complaints about the staleness of the "change versus continuity" framework may have come to outnumber actual uses of it. Since that time, a growing number of historians have moved beyond the established contours of the Woodward debates—in some cases, by bringing new interpretive approaches to bear on established questions; in others, by turning their attention to topics that had been previously neglected. The proliferation of scholarship has produced no overarching interpretations with the same power as Woodward's work—a testament in part to Woodward's originality, but also to the sheer quantity and variety of new research. The goal of this essay is not to impose a false coherence on the last generation of work, but to survey it in order to identify important trends and opportunities for fur-

[2] C. Vann Woodward, *Origins of the New South, 1877–1913* (Baton Rouge: Louisiana State University Press, 1951); *The Strange Career of Jim Crow*, 3rd rev. ed. (New York: Oxford University Press, 1974), 44. On Woodward's legacy, see John B. Boles and Bethany L. Johnson, eds., *"Origins of the New South" Fifty Years Later: The Continuing Influence of a Historical Classic* (Baton Rouge: Louisiana State University Press, 2003).

ther research—including a number of areas where historians have perhaps not done enough to go beyond the Woodward debates.

Given the questions of periodization that arise in writing about Reconstruction, a few words are in order about the chronological boundaries of this essay. For present purposes, I am conceiving Reconstruction as a period marking the transition between slave and free society: as a period, in other words, when white and black southerners established many of the social and economic relations that would define the region for decades to come. The fifteen years or so after 1865 by no means determined the precise shape of what would follow, but they laid much of the groundwork from which later developments and struggles would proceed. With that understanding in mind, this essay discusses a number of works that focus primarily on the late nineteenth or early twentieth centuries, but that treat the years after the Civil War in a substantial way, as a means of understanding what came afterwards. Omitted, however, are works that neglect, or treat only in passing, the period between 1865 and 1880.

Reconstructing the Plantation Economy

For historians interested in the postwar history of southern agriculture, share-cropping has long been an irresistible subject. The relationship has been understood as a vivid example of the region's distinctiveness and a cause of its poverty that endured through the first half of the twentieth century. During the 1970s and 1980s, a growing number of economic and social historians turned their attention to understanding how and why the sharecropping system arose in the wake of slavery's destruction. Roger Ransom and Richard Sutch, Robert Higgs, Jonathan Wiener, Michael Wayne, Gerald Jaynes, and many others debated whether this system arose from the imposition of former slaveowners, from the demands of former slaves, or from the invisible hand of the market.[3]

In his 1988 synthesis, Eric Foner presented what probably remains the closest thing to a consensus on the origins of sharecropping. Left to their own devices,

[3] Important contributions include: Roger L. Ransom and Richard Sutch, *One Kind of Freedom: The Economic Consequences of Emancipation* (New York: Cambridge University Press, 1977); Robert Higgs, *Competition and Coercion: Blacks and the American Economy, 1865–1914* (New York: Cambridge University Press, 1977); Jonathan M. Wiener, *The Social Origins of the New South: Alabama, 1860–1885* (Baton Rouge: Louisiana State University Press, 1978), and "Class Structure and Economic Development in the American South, 1865–1955," *American Historical Review* 84 (October 1979): 970–992; Michael Wayne, *The Reshaping of Plantation Society: The Natchez District, 1860–1880* (Baton Rouge: Louisiana State University Press, 1983); Gerald David Jaynes, *Branches without Roots: Genesis of the Black Working Class in the American South, 1862–1882* (New York: Oxford University Press, 1986).

neither former masters nor former slaves would have selected it as their preferred economic arrangement. Many freedpeople wished to acquire land and become independent proprietors; many planters wished to reinstitute the discipline of the slave gang. Sharecropping emerged, in Foner's words, as a "compromise not fully satisfactory to either party": freedpeople failed to secure land but escaped "gang labor and day-to-day white supervision," while planters grudgingly surrendered some degree of oversight in order to stabilize their work force. Although struggles over the exact nature of the relationship would continue throughout Reconstruction and well beyond, it quickly became one of the chief forms of organizing labor in the vast cotton belt that stretched from the Carolinas through Texas.[4]

For many historians during the 1970s and 1980s, their interest in sharecropping was driven by the wider debate over the degree of change or continuity between Old South and New. Although much of this discussion—often framed as a question of whether the postbellum plantation system was or was not capitalist—focused on developments after 1877, the events of Reconstruction were nonetheless crucial to it. Jay Mandle and Jonathan Wiener took the lead in depicting the Civil War and Reconstruction as a revolution that went at most halfway, freeing slaves but failing to break up and redistribute the large landholdings of the planter class. The result was a labor-repressive economy that emerged in full force after Reconstruction, in which black sharecroppers were bound to their landlords by debt and by a legal system firmly in the landlords' hands. This "plantation mode of production," as Jay Mandle called it, had essential continuities with the Old South, and remained in place until it was destroyed by the New Deal and World War II.[5]

Such arguments faced a stiff challenge from other historians, including Harold Woodman and Barbara Fields. Without denying the exploitative character of agricultural labor in the postbellum South, they emphasized the newness of the relations through which that exploitation took place. Sharecroppers, as Woodman pointed out, were hardly bound laborers in any literal sense, since they moved with a frequency equal to or greater than that of their northern counterparts. If the sharecropping contract, the crop lien, and the furnishing system did not qualify as "mature capitalist social relations," according to Fields, even less did they represent continuity with a slave system whose "ultimate sanction [was] direct force, resting on the master's ownership of the slave's person." The Civil War and Reconstruction, whatever their limitations, marked an irrevers-

[4] Eric Foner, *Reconstruction: America's Unfinished Revolution, 1863–1877* (New York: Harper and Row, 1988), 174.

[5] Jay R. Mandle, *The Roots of Black Poverty: The Southern Plantation Economy after the Civil War* (Durham, N.C.: Duke University Press, 1978).

ible break with slavery. The lack of land redistribution was not a cause of the Old South surviving in the New, but rather represented an essential step in constituting ex-slaves as a proletarianized class of free laborers.[6]

The participants in these debates from the 1970s and 1980s have continued to pursue them in more recent years. Jay Mandle has repeated his argument for the persistence of a plantation mode of production, rooted in authoritarian and paternalist social relations and based on the immobility of plantation laborers.[7] William Cohen has modified somewhat his own conclusions, presented in a 1976 journal article, that white southerners succeeded in imposing "involuntary servitude" on African Americans through vagrancy, antienticement, and other laws passed during Presidential Reconstruction and after Redemption. In his 1991 monograph *At Freedom's Edge*, Cohen finds that these laws clearly reflected planters' desires to restrict black mobility but did not prove especially effective, as black southerners "clung tenaciously to that most important of rights, the right to move."[8]

More recently, Harold Woodman has extended his analysis of the legal foundations of the postbellum economic order in his *New South—New Law* (1995). Befitting the title—and in keeping with his earlier work—Woodman's emphasis is again on the essentially new character of postwar relations of labor and credit; he also explores how freedpeople contested the legal definition of these relations and put them to unexpected uses. The crop lien, for example, received its first statutory definitions during Presidential Reconstruction, from white-only legislatures concerned with providing planters a basis of credit to resume their operations. Freedpeople, however, seized upon the crop lien as a means to secure advances from merchants and thus set the stage for a three-way battle over control of crops and credit. Although the legal tide turned strongly against freedpeople after Redemption, Woodman nonetheless concludes that the repressive system of sharecropping and crop lien laws did not constitute "little more than slavery with a new name." The law defined croppers as "part of a rural proletariat on the pattern of the industrial proletariat in the North," with a legal

[6] Harold D. Woodman, "Comment," *American Historical Review* 84 (October 1979): 997–1001; Barbara Jeanne Fields, "The Advent of Capitalist Agriculture: The New South in a Bourgeois World," in *Essays on the Postbellum Southern Economy*, ed. Thavolia Glymph and John J. Kushma (College Station: Texas A&M University Press, 1985), 73–94, and "The Nineteenth-Century American South: History and Theory," *Plantation Society* 2 (April 1983): 7–27 (quotations at 24 and 22).

[7] Jay R. Mandle, *Not Slave, Not Free: The African American Economic Experience since the Civil War* (Durham, N.C.: Duke University Press, 1992).

[8] William Cohen, "Negro Involuntary Servitude in the South, 1865–1940: A Preliminary Analysis," *Journal of Southern History* 42 (February 1976): 31–60, and *At Freedom's Edge: Black Mobility and the Southern White Quest for Racial Control, 1861–1915* (Baton Rouge: Louisiana State University Press, 1991), xvi.

right to their wages, but no ownership of the means of production and no claim to the prerogatives of management.[9]

The view of Civil War and Reconstruction as setting off a capitalist transformation of the slave South—what might be called the Marxist revision to Woodward's Beardian thesis—has been widely influential during the past fifteen years. It underlies the published work of the Freedmen and Southern Society Project, whose two documentary volumes on reconstruction in the Union-occupied South are titled *The Wartime Genesis of Free Labor* (1990 and 1993). Its influence is clear as well from such titles as Joseph Reidy's *From Slavery to Agrarian Capitalism in the Cotton Plantation South* (1992) and Julie Saville's *The Work of Reconstruction: From Slave to Wage Laborer in South Carolina, 1860–1870* (1994).[10]

Acceptance of this interpretation, nonetheless, is hardly universal. Alex Lichtenstein, for example, contends that these historians, influenced by Eugene Genovese's "model of slavery as a precapitalist or 'seigneurial' social formation[,] . . . naively conclude that its negation through abolition automatically entailed a transition to free labor." Like Wiener and Mandle, Lichtenstein sees that transition as coming only in the 1930s and 1940s; unlike them, however, he views black sharecroppers and tenants before that time less as bound laborers than as peasants. "To use the term 'peasant' for emancipated slaves and their descendants," he writes, "calls attention to the permanent, household, and non-waged character of much of their agricultural labor, the persistence of their debilitating vertical ties to the landed class, and the highly individualist and deeply rooted relationship tenants and sharecroppers maintained with the land." Lichtenstein is certainly right to emphasize such issues as the family organization of labor, and the means of resistance and forms of cohesion among black agricultural workers. But it is not clear how such a notoriously imprecise category as "peasant" will advance the study of those important questions.[11]

---

[9] Harold D. Woodman, *New South—New Law: The Legal Foundations of Credit and Labor Relations in the Postbellum Agricultural South* (Baton Rouge: Louisiana State University Press, 1995), 93, 105.

[10] Ira Berlin et al., eds., *Freedom: A Documentary History of Emancipation, 1861–1867*, ser. 1, vol. 2, *The Wartime Genesis of Free Labor: The Upper South*, and ser. 1, vol. 3, *The Wartime Genesis of Free Labor: The Lower South* (New York: Cambridge University Press, 1993, 1990); Joseph Reidy, *From Slavery to Agrarian Capitalism in the Cotton Plantation South: Central Georgia, 1800–1880* (Chapel Hill: University of North Carolina Press, 1992); Julie Saville, *The Work of Reconstruction: From Slave to Wage Laborer in South Carolina, 1860–1870* (New York: Cambridge University Press, 1994).

[11] Alex Lichtenstein, "Was the Emancipated Slave a Proletarian?" *Reviews in American History* 26 (March 1998): 124–145 (quotations pp. 132, 139), and "Proletarians or Peasants? Sharecroppers and the Politics of Protest in the Rural South, 1880–1940," *Plantation Society in the Americas* 5 (Fall 1998): 297–331. For the argument that white and black sharecroppers possessed a "peasant mentality" and placed a "high social value on indolence," see Ronald Seavoy, *The American Peasantry: Southern Agricultural Labor and Its Legacy, 1850–1995* (Westport, Conn.: Greenwood Press, 1998), 4.

Although debate over the Woodward thesis has not disappeared, it no longer plays as important a role in driving new historical research as it did a generation ago. At heart, the discussions Woodward inspired about change and continuity focused more on the extent than the process of change, and often led historians to look past the immediate postwar years to evaluate the sharecropping and tenant farming system of the cotton South as it existed in more settled form into the twentieth century. By contrast, the last fifteen years have seen a proliferation of local studies that often eschew generalizations about the region as a whole to explore how the particularities of antebellum slavery and wartime experience shaped the reconstruction of the plantation economy after the war. These works are too numerous to be characterized individually here, but taken as a whole, they display three tendencies in theme or approach that are important to recognize: first, a focus on crop regions outside the cotton belt, and labor regimes other than sharecropping; second, an emphasis on the intersection of grassroots politics with struggles over land and labor; and third, the use of gender as a category of analysis in examining the shift from slave to free labor.

Through the 1980s, historians' predominant focus in examining the reconstruction of plantation agriculture was on developments in the cotton belt, and especially the emergence of sharecropping. Since then, however, studies of the tobacco, rice, and sugar regions have equaled or exceeded in number those on the cotton South.[12] Especially interesting as points of comparison are the sugar- and rice-growing regions, where sharecropping and tenancy never took hold on a wide scale. In his study of Louisiana's sugar country, John Rodrigue examines how wage labor, introduced during Union occupation by federal officials, became the basis for reconstructing plantation agriculture under planters' centralized management. In contrast to studies of the cotton belt that portray former slaves as rejecting gang labor in favor of independent proprietorship, Rodrigue emphasizes that "freedmen of the sugar country repudiated neither wage labor nor their old work routines." For freedpeople, the wage system provided a means to pursue "both a measure of personal autonomy and a sense of

---

A number of sociologists and other nonhistorians have continued to argue for the noncapitalist character of agriculture in the postwar South. See, for example: Susan Archer Mann, *Agrarian Capitalism in Theory and Practice* (Chapel Hill: University of North Carolina Press, 1990); Larian Angelo, "Wage Labour Deferred: The Recreation of Unfree Labour in the US South," *Journal of Peasant Studies* 22 (July 1995): 581–644; Daniel Gaido, "A Materialist Analysis of Slavery and Sharecropping in the Southern United States," *Journal of Peasant Studies* 28 (October 2000): 55–94. These works offer little in the way of evidence or interpretation about the postbellum South that will be new to historians familiar with the works discussed earlier.

[12] The cotton belt has by no means been ignored; see, for example, the works by Joseph Reidy and Julie Saville cited in note 10, and Jonathan M. Bryant, *How Curious a Land: Conflict and Change in Greene County, Georgia, 1850–1885* (Chapel Hill: University of North Carolina Press, 1996). See also the works cited in notes 25–26 here.

collective self-determination"; for planters, it provided a means to slowly restore sugar production in the region, although output did not match antebellum levels until the 1890s.[13]

Julie Saville and Leslie Schwalm explore how postbellum developments took a decidedly different course in the lowcountry of South Carolina and Georgia, where rice and long-staple cotton were the chief crops. Several features distinguished the region. One was the task system of labor, which allowed slaves a significant degree of control over their time and work, and which freedpeople were loath to surrender after emancipation. The lowcountry, moreover, had been a stronghold of secessionist sentiment before the Civil War; in the face of Union occupiers, planters fled the area in much greater numbers than did their counterparts in more Unionist southern Louisiana. After the war's end, returning landowners found that it was one thing to secure legal recognition of their titles to land, but another to claim effective possession from freedpeople who had occupied their plantations and in some cases claimed the land under General William Sherman's Special Field Order 15. Although few former slaves secured ownership of land in the immediate aftermath of the Civil War, their resistance complicated the return to plantation agriculture.[14]

The amount of noncrop work required in rice cultivation—to maintain canals, ditches, and trunks—ill suited it to a decentralized system of sharecropping or tenancy; ex-slaves, however, resisted planters' efforts to reduce them to full-time wage workers. By the late 1860s, the lowcountry was marked by the widespread emergence of a labor renting system, whereby freedpeople agreed to work two or three days a week for a landlord in exchange for "the right to reside on and cultivate particular tracts of plantation lands," as Saville explains it. This arrangement, she stresses, did not leave freedpeople outside the labor market for the rest of the week; many were compelled into additional wage labor to secure provisions or farm supplies. Over the long run, however, this system provided only a shaky basis for plantation agriculture. In his discussion of Georgia's lowcountry, J. William Harris emphasizes that production of neither rice nor long-staple cotton approached antebellum levels. Some planters sold small tracts to freedpeople as a means of generating income and securing access to at least occasional labor. The combination of a stagnating plantation system and freedpeople's persistent petty accumulation contributed to the growth of a relatively large class of landowning black farmers; in parts of the Georgia lowcountry, Harris finds that over half of black farm operators owned land in 1880.[15]

[13] John C. Rodrigue, *Reconstruction in the Cane Fields: From Slavery to Free Labor in Louisiana's Sugar Parishes, 1862–1880* (Baton Rouge: Louisiana State University Press, 2001), 3.

[14] Leslie A. Schwalm, *A Hard Fight for We: Women's Transition from Slavery to Freedom in South Carolina* (Urbana: University of Illinois Press, 1997).

[15] Saville, *Work of Reconstruction*, 133; J. William Harris, *Deep Souths: Delta, Piedmont, and Sea Island Society in the Age of Segregation* (Baltimore: Johns Hopkins University Press, 2001).

Other recent studies examine the tobacco belt of Virginia and North Carolina, which bore a greater resemblance to the cotton South than did either the Atlantic rice coast or the Louisiana sugar bowl. Unlike sugar and rice, tobacco could be grown effectively on small plots as well as on centralized plantations, and was thus amenable to farming by tenants and croppers. Nonetheless, several historians of the postbellum tobacco belt have not focused exclusively or even primarily on sharecropping and tenancy; without denying their importance, they have instead emphasized the variety of relations under which landowners mobilized the labor of freedpeople.[16] In parts of Granville County, North Carolina, for example, Laura Edwards finds that laborers outnumbered sharecroppers and tenants by a factor of five to one in 1870, and at least two to one in 1880; "[a]gricultural waged work," she concludes, "grew in tandem with other forms of labor."[17]

In another study of Granville County, Sharon Ann Holt deemphasizes the importance of sharecropping and tenancy in a somewhat different way, arguing that even freedpeople who entered into such relations engaged in many other productive activities and economic roles. Beyond their "contract work" as tenants or sharecroppers, freedpeople undertook seasonal and other occasional wage labor, and also raised money through the sale of butter, chickens, garden crops, and other goods. Holt perhaps relies too much on the contrast between this "household economy" and freedpeople's contract work, and does not analyze the relative contribution of, and the substantial differences among, the activities she combines in the former category (the differences between wage labor and petty production being the most striking). But in emphasizing the variety of economic activities that freedpeople undertook, her book points to issues that might be usefully explored in other settings.[18]

In addition to looking beyond sharecropping and the cotton belt, many recent works on the reconstruction of plantation agriculture share a second charac-

---

[16] An exception is Lynda J. Morgan, who concludes that sharecropping "evolved fairly rapidly in the tobacco belt, making for a speedier transition than that which occurred in Lower South cotton districts"; see *Emancipation in Virginia's Tobacco Belt, 1850–1870* (Athens: University of Georgia Press, 1992), 187.

[17] Laura F. Edwards, *Gendered Strife and Confusion: The Political Culture of Reconstruction* (Urbana: University of Illinois Press, 1997), 88. See also Jeffrey R. Kerr-Ritchie, *Freedpeople in the Tobacco South, Virginia, 1860–1900* (Chapel Hill: University of North Carolina Press, 1999), and James R. Irwin, "Farmers and Laborers: A Note on Black Occupations in the Postbellum South," *Agricultural History* 64 (Winter 1990): 53–60.

[18] Sharon Ann Holt, *Making Freedom Pay: North Carolina Freedpeople Working for Themselves, 1865–1900* (Athens: University of Georgia Press, 2000). Although the concept of a "household economy" has been used in the study of peasantries around the world, and bears some resemblance to Lichtenstein's argument for considering sharecroppers and tenants as peasants, Holt does not make more than passing reference to that literature.

teristic: their emphasis on the importance of freedpeople's grassroots political activity in shaping the evolution of new labor arrangements. Another essay in this volume considers the significance of these studies for the understanding of Reconstruction-era politics, but it is worth emphasizing here how this approach stands in contrast to earlier discussions of the postbellum economy. Economists like Ransom and Sutch, Jaynes, and Mandle recognized the importance of freedpeople's own aspirations and actions in shaping new relations, but tended to focus on their economic aspects and the process of bargaining; the same was true of the work of many social historians, like Wiener and Wayne.

More recent works, by contrast, examine not just the process of freedpeople's contracting with employers and landlords but also how former slaves shaped and pursued their goals through collective organizing. This has been an important theme in local studies on the cotton belt as well as the rice and tobacco regions, and is explored for the South as a whole in Steven Hahn's Pulitzer Prize–winning synthesis *A Nation under Our Feet* (2003). According to Hahn, freedpeople's wartime and post-emancipation struggles drew upon forms of political practice that they had developed under slavery—such as the use of rumor, for example, in the so-called Christmas Insurrection Scare of 1865, when white southerners' fears about a possible uprising by freedpeople influenced the process of contracting for the 1866 agricultural season. Like Julie Saville, Hahn also explores how former slaves organized quasi-military companies in 1865 and 1866 as a means both to resist planters and to enforce conformity in their own ranks. With black men's enfranchisement, more formal political organizations like the Union League proliferated throughout the South. In attending the meetings of these groups, freedmen laid claim to control of their time and freedom of movement—issues at the heart of postwar struggles between planters and freed laborers.[19]

As a number of local studies emphasize, freedpeople's grassroots organizing could lead to different outcomes in different places. Michael Fitzgerald, for example, assigns the Union League an important role in the emergence of sharecropping in the cotton South. Many freedmen, he argues, successfully used local leagues as a means to resist planters' efforts to impose coercive and centralized management. But the dispersal of freedpeople onto individual family plots rendered them vulnerable to Klan violence, which destroyed the Union League and left such decentralized farming the norm in the cotton belt. In Louisiana's sugar parishes, by comparison, John Rodrigue finds that centralized plantations facilitated freedpeople's political organizing, which in turn "galvanized freedmen's efforts to gain a measure of control over their working lives."[20]

[19] Steven Hahn, *A Nation under Our Feet: Black Political Struggles in the Rural South from Slavery to the Great Migration* (Cambridge, Mass.: Harvard University Press, 2003).

[20] Michael W. Fitzgerald, *The Union League Movement in the Deep South: Politics and Agricultural Change During Reconstruction* (Baton Rouge: Louisiana State University Press, 1989); Rodrigue, *Reconstruction in the Cane Fields*, 78.

Freedpeople's organizing did not cease with Republicans' loss of office. Hahn, for example, explores how freedpeople, both before and after Redemption, undertook collective attempts to emigrate to Liberia, Kansas, and elsewhere; although the number of successful emigrants was small, many more freedpeople participated in emigrationist meetings and organizations. Several recent studies of Reconstruction stretch the chronological boundaries of the period by closing with a look at the 1886–87 southern campaign of the Knights of Labor. In Louisiana, an 1887 strike by Louisiana sugar workers ended in the "Thibodaux massacre," the slaying of dozens of workers by white vigilantes under the eyes of state militia. Rodrigue uses this event to underscore how the end of Reconstruction "placed legitimate, state-sponsored coercion at the planters' service" and also produced state sanction of planters' extralegal use of violence.[21] In the tobacco belt of North Carolina, the Knights operated as a labor organization and a force in electoral politics before meeting a less bloody if equally decisive defeat—a victim, according to Laura Edwards, of planters' hegemony over cultural assumptions about labor and household relations in the postbellum South.

Edwards's work is representative as well of a third trend in post-emancipation studies—the emphasis on exploring the history of freedwomen and family and gender relations. Historians have long recognized that one of planters' complaints after emancipation was that freedwomen and children withdrew from the sort of regular field labor they had performed as slaves; one of the benefits of the sharecropping system, from the landlord's perspective, was that the assignment of plots of land to individual families served as at least a partial means to "recover" that lost labor. In her study of the South Carolina low-country, Schwalm challenges the notion that black women—who had been the "backbone of the field labor force" as slaves—withdrew into their own families and households after emancipation. Women participated alongside men in the groups of ex-slaves who confronted returning planters in 1865 and 1866. Freedwomen continued to work in the rice fields, Schwalm finds, but "increasingly rejected *full-time* field labor," contracting as fractional rather than full hands to devote more time to labor within their own families. Holt argues that historians who write of "freedwomen as if they were not working" overlook the crucial importance of women's labor to the household economy. Their activity—if in many cases invisible to landlords—was not apart from the market, since they produced eggs, butter, quilts, and other goods that they sold for income outside the family.[22]

Other recent work has taken as its starting point the emphasis of antebellum historians on the central importance of the plantation household, which in the slave South served as the locus of relations of production and reproduc-

<hr/>

[21] Rodrigue, *Reconstruction in the Cane Fields*, 188.
[22] Schwalm, *Hard Fight for We*, 45, 206; Holt, *Making Freedom Pay*, xi.

tion. "War and emancipation," Laura Edwards writes, "shook the antebellum Southern household to its foundations, destabilizing the configuration of private and public power it supported." Although Edwards's ultimate interest is in how this "gendered strife and confusion" played out in political culture, she sees it as rooted in the reorganization of material relations set off by emancipation. Former slaveowners clung to the personal authority they had once exercised over slaves who labored as household subordinates, while "the central challenge freedpeople faced was severing the ideological tie between dependence and the need to labor for others." That challenge bore especially heavily on freedwomen who worked as domestic servants and faced the demands of white employers that they continue to labor, in Schwalm's words, as "'Jill[s]-of-all-trades' . . . at the beck and call of the planter family." Freedwomen's forceful resistance produced "the servant problem" complained of so bitterly by many elite white women.[23]

Although the plantation mistress has figured prominently in discussions of the slaveholding southern household before the war, her role on the postbellum plantation has received far less attention. The most thorough treatment is Jane Turner Censer's *Reconstruction of White Southern Womanhood* (2003), which examines the experience of elite white women in North Carolina and Virginia. Much of Censer's account focuses on the reconstruction of these women's economic roles: their legal rights to property, their ownership and management of plantations and businesses, and their growing "domestication" as they faced the need to maintain respectable homes without the slave labor they had once commanded. Censer adopts a generational approach missing in many post-emancipation studies to argue that younger women—those who came to adulthood only after 1865—proved most adept at adjusting to life after slavery.[24]

The emphasis in recent scholarship on gender and grassroots politics will surely continue in the future. Since much of the literature of the past fifteen years has focused on rice, sugar, and tobacco-growing regions of the postbellum South, one promising opportunity for historians is perhaps to head back to the cotton belt—which, after all, was home to the great majority of freedpeople involved in plantation agriculture. To what extent did developments there resemble what historians have found in studying other regions of the South?

Some reassessment along these lines is clearly already under way. Nancy Bercaw, for example, examines gender and family relations in Mississippi's cot-

---

[23] Edwards, *Gendered Strife and Confusion*, 8, 19; Schwalm, *Hard Fight for We*, 209.

[24] Jane Turner Censer, *The Reconstruction of White Southern Womanhood, 1865–1895* (Baton Rouge: Louisiana State University Press, 2003). See also Laura F. Edwards, *Scarlett Doesn't Live Here Anymore: Southern Women in the Civil War Era* (Urbana: University of Illinois Press, 2000), and Marli Frances Weiner, *Mistresses and Slaves: Plantation Women in South Carolina, 1830–80* (Urbana: University of Illinois Press, 1997).

ton-growing Delta region. Although historians' discussions of sharecropping have largely assumed the nuclear family as its basis, Bercaw finds that such households were not the norm in 1865, because of both wartime dislocations and antebellum patterns of slavery in what had still been a cotton frontier. Family formation during the late 1860s was driven not just by freedpeople's efforts but also by federal and state policy regarding marriage and dependency, and by planters' efforts to limit former slaves' access to the means of subsistence and economic livelihood. Similar forces were at work elsewhere. In her forthcoming study of southwest Georgia, Susan O'Donovan demonstrates how planters evicted black women, especially those with small children, from their plantations in 1865 and 1866, compelling many to seek the support of male kinfolk. Freedpeople's families thus became both the primary means of relief to the needy and the primary units of agricultural labor to cotton planters.[25]

More generally, the time may be ripe for historians of the cotton belt to rethink prevailing interpretations about the development and importance of sharecropping after the Civil War. The consensus arrived at a generation ago dated its emergence to the late 1860s and portrayed it as widely in place by the 1870s. Even though most historians were careful to acknowledge the use of wage labor on cotton plantations, they devoted the great bulk of their attention to the tenants and croppers who farmed their own family plots. In keeping with studies on the tobacco region, however, several recent works on the cotton belt call that approach into question. J. William Harris's *Deep Souths* (2001), the most comprehensive of recently published works on the cotton South, examines both the well-established cotton belt of Georgia's eastern piedmont and the still-emerging plantation area of the Mississippi Delta. Using data from the 1880 census, Harris finds that in both areas, more black household heads worked as farm laborers than as sharecroppers or tenants. Other examinations of the Mississippi Delta and of western Tennessee reach similar conclusions.[26]

The work of compiling these findings is laborious, and beyond noting the high percentage of laboring households, these historians have generally said

---

[25] Nancy Bercaw, *Gendered Freedoms: Race, Rights, and the Politics of Household in the Delta, 1861–1875* (Gainesville: University Press of Florida, 2003); Susan O'Donovan, *Slavery's Legacies* (Cambridge, Mass.: Harvard University Press, forthcoming).

[26] Robert Tracy McKenzie has explored this point in *One South or Many? Plantation Belt and Upcountry in Civil War–Era Tennessee* (New York: Cambridge University Press, 1994), and two articles: "Freedmen and the Soil in the Upper South: The Reorganization of Tennessee Agriculture, 1865–1880," *Journal of Southern History* 59 (February 1993): 63–84, and "Rediscovering the 'Farmless' Farm Population: The Nineteenth-Century Census and the Postbellum Reorganization of Agriculture in the U.S. South, 1860–1900," *Histoire Sociale/Social History* 28 (November 1995): 501–520. See also James R. Irwin and Anthony Patrick O'Brien, "Where Have All the Sharecroppers Gone? Black Occupations in Postbellum Mississippi," *Agricultural History* 72 (Spring 1998): 280–297.

little about their place in the rural economy. They are surely, however, deserving of more study, because they have the potential to change in fundamental ways our understanding of the rebuilding of the plantation economy after the war. If Harris is right that "the most common image of white-owned cotton plantations" with "black sharecroppers raising the crops . . . is incorrect" as of 1880, then we clearly need to know more about when and why the shift occurred, and about the labor relations that prevailed beforehand. The presence of a large number of wage laborers in the rural South would also have implications for the debate about the capitalist nature of postbellum agriculture, and could move it beyond its familiar focus on how to categorize sharecropping and share tenancy.[27]

In investigating these laboring households, several lines of inquiry seem potentially fruitful. One would be to study the demographics of rural black households in search of differences between those that operated farms as sharecroppers or tenants and those that did not. To the extent that sharecropping and tenancy were family systems of labor, households with fewer laborers—that is, working-aged, able-bodied adults and children—were probably less likely to find work under such arrangements. Into the 1870s, according to some local studies, perhaps 10 to 15 percent of rural black households were headed by women, who no doubt continued to experience difficulties in an economy organized around the labor of nuclear families.[28]

Some members of these laboring families found employment as domestics in the households of white landowners and as farm laborers employed by the month or year to cultivate acreage directly controlled by landlords. They likely also served as a reserve work force that could be drawn on as day laborers during harvest and other moments of peak demand for field labor, and throughout the year to perform the kind of noncrop work—such as digging ditches, tending the landowners' livestock, and building and repairing fences and other structures—that freedpeople had effectively resisted performing as part of their share contracts immediately after the war. In all of these ways, the labor of such families would have been essential to the economy of the South's plantation districts,

Like earlier works that emphasized the prevalence of tenancy and sharecropping, these studies rely heavily on the federal manuscript census of 1880, but they use it in a different way. Previous historians matched entries on the agricultural schedule of the census to the population schedule, to determine the race of farm operators; these studies also reverse the process in order to determine if black households listed on the population schedule appear as farm operators, and discover that many did not.

[27] Harris, *Deep Souths*, 30.

[28] On the number and occupation of black women who headed households in one cotton belt county, see Orville Vernon Burton, "African-American Status and Identity in a Postbellum Community: An Analysis of the Manuscript Census Returns," *Agricultural History* 72 (Spring 1998): 213–240.

even if the majority of cotton and tobacco in these areas was grown on plots tended by croppers and tenants.

Also deserving of further study is the extent to which sharecroppers and tenants in the cotton South engaged in the kinds of waged and other productive work that Holt associates with the "household economy" in her study of North Carolina's tobacco belt. In examining that activity in other parts of the South, it would be useful to attend to regional variations in freedpeople's access to towns, merchants, and markets for their produce. Differences in antebellum patterns of slavery are also important to bear in mind. If it is true that these activities drew on the independent production and marketing in which slaves had engaged, then historians may find differences among places where such practices had been more or less widespread, or followed different patterns, before the Civil War. Susan O'Donovan suggests, for example, that independent production was less common on the newly settled plantations of southwest Georgia. Finally, there is the question of sharecroppers' and tenants' opportunities for wage earning beyond their contract work. They likely engaged in the kind of day labor described earlier, performing harvest labor or noncrop work for their own landlords or other neighboring farmers. Holt suggests that the year-round needs of tobacco cultivation allowed little time for substantial periods of work off the farm, but those who grew cotton may have found themselves with more opportunities for seasonal labor in timber, turpentine forests, railroad construction, and other pursuits. Exploring such work would help us develop a finer appreciation of the extent to which contract work on their own crops did not exhaust the economic lives of sharecroppers and tenants.[29]

In assessing recent scholarship on the southern plantation economy after the Civil War, it is worth emphasizing how much of this work continues to be done in the form of local and community studies. Many of the advantages and disadvantages of this approach are well known. It allows historians to make intensive use of voluminous census, tax, Freedmen's Bureau, and other records that are organized geographically; it emphasizes regional variations and peculiarities; it is well suited to the scope of a dissertation or first book. On the other hand, such projects are usually at least implicitly comparative but seldom explicitly so, and it is standard to lament the lack of synthesis that would allow for an examination of broader patterns.

There are also some kinds of questions that are not well suited to the format of the community study. Law and political economy, at both the state and national levels, are subjects that have received some scrutiny, but could clearly bear a good bit more. Harold Woodman's work on the law of sharecropping, tenancy, and liens is a fine example of such a study; another is Peter Bardaglio's

---

[29] For a later example of such activity, see Theodore Rosengarten, *All God's Dangers: The Life of Nate Shaw* (New York: Knopf, 1974).

Reconstructing the Household (1995), which examines the law of marriage, family relations, and sex. In her study of the little-known Bankruptcy Act of 1867, Elizabeth Lee Thompson explores how thousands of debt-bound white southerners—including vocal critics of the national government—happily availed themselves of the protections offered by Reconstruction-era federal courts.[30]

One area that could reward further study is the legal basis of free labor in the southern states. Robert Steinfeld, Karen Orren, Christopher Tomlins, Amy Dru Stanley, and others have examined the roots of the wage labor relationship in the older law of master and servant, and debated how and when lawmakers and judges fashioned a modern understanding of free labor, shorn of the more coercive aspects associated with a status relationship of dependency.[31] Their studies have for the most part focused on the North; the widespread presence of slavery, and its violent and abrupt destruction, added further complications in the South. Laura Edward's *Gendered Strife and Confusion* (1997) and James D. Schmidt's *Free to Work* (1998) provide a start, but there is much more work to be done in the statutes and case law of the southern states during Reconstruction and Redemption.[32]

Adopting a comparative or international approach provides another alternative to the community study, but the difficulties of such work make it more admired than emulated. Several recent studies, however, show the potential rewards. In a 1990 article, Steven Hahn compares southern planters to their counterparts elsewhere to emphasize the degree of change between Old South and New. Where the landed elites of Brazil and Germany shaped the terms of emancipation and continued to wield considerable national influence thereafter, southern planters saw slavery destroyed in a bloody civil war and suffered a loss of federal power that was hardly compensated by their control of state and

[30] Peter W. Bardaglio, *Reconstructing the Household: Families, Sex, and the Law in the Nineteenth-Century South* (Chapel Hill: University of North Carolina Press, 1995); Elizabeth Lee Thompson, *The Reconstruction of Southern Debtors: Bankruptcy after the Civil War* (Athens: University of Georgia Press, 2004).

[31] Robert J. Steinfeld, *The Invention of Free Labor: The Employment Relation in English and American Law and Culture, 1350–1870* (Chapel Hill: University of North Carolina Press, 1991); Karen Orren, *Belated Feudalism: Labor, the Law, and Liberal Development in the United States* (New York: Cambridge University Press, 1991); Christopher L. Tomlins, *Law, Labor, and Ideology in the Early American Republic* (New York: Cambridge University Press, 1993); Amy Dru Stanley, *From Bondage to Contract: Wage Labor, Marriage, and the Market in the Age of Slave Emancipation* (New York: Cambridge University Press, 1998). Despite the differences among them, all of these studies make clear that the legal creation of free labor in the North took considerable time, and that labor law retained some of its more coercive aspects well into nineteenth century. This should serve as a caution to historians who want to contrast "genuinely" free labor in the North to a "labor repressive system" in the South.

[32] James D. Schmidt, *Free to Work: Labor Law, Emancipation, and Reconstruction, 1815–1880* (Athens: University of Georgia Press, 1998).

local governments after Redemption.[33] Given historians' recent attention to the differing paths of crop regions within the South, Rebecca Scott's comparative work on sugar-growing in the Americas provides a useful illustration of how widely developments could diverge even among plantation economies devoted to the same crop. Compared to the centrally managed plantations of post-emancipation Louisiana, more decentralized systems of farming developed in Cuba and especially in Brazil, permitting freed slaves more access to land and more opportunities to avoid full-time wage work. Pursuing another recent theme in literature on the Reconstruction-era South, Scott also emphasizes how those different labor regimes shaped, and were shaped by, the possibilities for freedpeople's political activity.[34]

Beyond the Plantation Belt

The slave plantation hardly accounted for the whole of the antebellum southern economy, nor was it the only part to feel the effects of Civil War and emancipation, which extended as well to agriculture outside the plantation belt and to the role of commerce, towns, and industry. These areas, however, have seen nothing like the outpouring of scholarship that has characterized study of the plantation belt during the past fifteen years. There are of course good reasons for this difference: plantation slavery dominated the region's economy before the war, and was destroyed in one of the most dramatic social upheavals of American history. The result has been not just fewer works but less innovation in the study of other areas of the southern economy, so that scholarship on them has moved only fitfully beyond the familiar terms of the Woodward debates—with some notable exceptions.

One of those exceptions is the study of the southern upcountry, where commercial agriculture rose dramatically during the decades after the Civil War. In

[33] Steven Hahn, "Class and State in Postemancipation Societies: Southern Planters in Comparative Perspective," *American Historical Review* 95 (February 1990): 75–98. Roger Ransom provides a reminder of the importance of slaveholders' national power in a recent counterfactual study that asks what would have happened if the Confederacy had won its independence in the Civil War. Faced with declines in the profitability of cotton agriculture and in slave prices by 1880, he speculates, southern slaveholders might have used their power in the Confederate government to work out a plan of compensated emancipation. See Roger L. Ransom, *The Confederate States of America: What Might Have Been* (New York: Norton, 2005).

[34] Rebecca J. Scott's *Degrees of Freedom: Louisiana and Cuba after Slavery* (Cambridge, Mass.: Harvard University Press, 2005) appeared in print too late to be considered fully in this essay, but it develops themes she explores in "Defining the Boundaries of Freedom in the World of Cane: Cuba, Brazil, and Louisiana after Emancipation," *American Historical Review* 99 (February 1994): 70–102, and "Fault Lines, Color Lines, and Party Lines: Race, Labor, and Collective Action in Louisiana and Cuba, 1862–1912," in Frederick Cooper, Thomas C. Holt, and

his 1983 *Roots of Southern Populism*, Steven Hahn updated Woodward's portrait of the "unredeemed farmer" of the New South by drawing on a wider historiography about republicanism and the market economy; in doing so, he extended the analysis and recast the terms of discussion so thoroughly that his account became an essential starting point for scholarship on the subject. Focusing on the upper piedmont of Georgia, Hahn depicted the yeomen of the antebellum era as pre-capitalist petty producers, devoting much more of their energy to food crops than cotton. The Civil War, however, swept away a wider political economy based on plantation slavery, which had sheltered the upcountry from the forces of capitalist development. After 1865, new railroad networks and a proliferation of crossroads merchants incorporated the upcountry into the national market economy; yeomen drawn into cotton production to recover from wartime debts and destruction found it hard to escape in the face of mounting merchants' bills and falling cotton prices. The results were apparent by 1880 in rising levels of cotton production and white farm tenancy, and fueled the dissatisfactions that led to Populism.[35]

Several features distinguished Hahn's book from a number of other works on the nonplantation South that appeared at about the same time.[36] One was its wide sweep and its focus on republican ideology in linking the history of the antebellum yeomanry to the Populist rebellion of the 1890s. Another was how it meshed with, and contributed to, the wider view of a capitalist transformation that followed the destruction of slavery; Hahn situated the yeomanry in the slave society of the Old South and explored how some of the same postwar changes that remade the plantation belt—the rise of the crop lien and the furnishing merchant, the spread of tenancy and sharecropping—transformed the upcountry as well. In becoming the standard work on the nonplantation South, however, *Roots of Southern Populism* suffered a curious, if not uncommon, fate. Historians who accepted Hahn's interpreta-

Rebecca J. Scott, *Beyond Slavery: Explorations of Race, Labor, and Citizenship in Postemancipation Societies* (Chapel Hill: University of North Carolina Press, 2000). Historians can also look forward to Peter Kolchin's study of emancipation in the United States and Russia, a follow-up to his *Unfree Labor: American Slavery and Russian Serfdom* (Cambridge, Mass.: Harvard University Press, 1987); in the meantime, they might consult his "Some Thoughts on Emancipation in Comparative Perspective: Russia and the United States South," *Slavery and Abolition* 11 (December 1990): 351–367.

[35] Steven Hahn, *The Roots of Southern Populism: Yeoman Farmers and the Transformation of the Georgia Upcountry, 1850–1890* (New York: Oxford University Press, 1983).

[36] Among works that discuss the Reconstruction period are Paul D. Escott, *Many Excellent People: Power and Privilege in North Carolina, 1850–1900* (Chapel Hill: University of North Carolina Press, 1985); Robert C. Kenzer, *Kinship and Neighborhood in a Southern Community: Orange County, North Carolina, 1849–1881* (Knoxville: University of Tennessee Press, 1987); Lacy K. Ford, "Rednecks and Merchants: Economic Development and Social Tensions in the South Carolina Upcountry, 1865–1900," *Journal of American History* 71 (September 1984): 294–318.

tions and findings incorporated them into their own work, or used them as a starting point to examine other topics, without necessarily investigating the particulars any further. As a result, his work has received its closest scrutiny from those who disagree with it.

Several challenges are especially important as they relate to the immediate postwar years. Frederick Bode and Donald Ginter have argued that levels of landlessness were substantially higher in the antebellum upcountry than Hahn allowed, thus precluding "any interpretation portraying whites as having 'fallen into tenancy' under Reconstruction." Robert McKenzie likewise questions whether a "proletarianization" of the yeomanry occurred in postwar Tennessee; tracking farm households from one decennial census to the next, McKenzie finds no "widespread dispossession . . . of smallholding farmers" between 1860 and 1880, and argues instead that population growth was a greater cause of the rise in landlessness among white farmers.[37]

Other historians have challenged Hahn's depiction of the yeomanry's views on property and market relations. Shawn Kantor and J. Morgan Kousser argue that small farmers opposed postwar fence laws because of their individual calculations of self-interest, and not because of the producerist ideology and defense of local custom that Hahn emphasized. Robert McKenzie, Bradley Bond, and other historians have seen, to varying degrees, a stronger "market orientation" among the yeomanry of the southern upcountry and other nonplantation areas than did Hahn. Although a good bit of this work has focused on the antebellum period, it has clear implications for later developments as well: if small farmers had engaged in commercial agriculture enthusiastically and extensively before the Civil War, then it is hard to see them as having been forced into it unwillingly afterward, or to view that opposition as the basis of the agrarian revolt at century's end.[38]

Although the lines of debate on these questions have been clearly drawn for some time, there is a good deal more research that might be done to explore them. It would be useful, for example, to know more about the place of white tenants and laborers in the Old South, and how they experienced the transformations of the Civil War. If Hahn's critics are right in saying that he under-

[37] Frederick A. Bode and Donald E. Ginter, *Farm Tenancy and the Census in Antebellum Georgia* (Athens: University of Georgia Press, 1986), 147; McKenzie, *One South or Many*, 115.

[38] Shawn Everett Kantor and J. Morgan Kousser, "Common Sense or Commonwealth? The Fence Law and Institutional Change in the Postbellum South," *Journal of Southern History* 59 (May 1993): 201–242; A reply by Hahn, and a rejoinder from Kantor and Kousser, appear in the same issue of the *Journal of Southern History*. See also Kantor, *Politics and Property Rights: The Closing of the Open Range in the Postbellum South* (Chicago: University of Chicago Press, 1998). On market production among small farmers in Mississippi, see Bradley G. Bond, *Political Culture in the Nineteenth-Century South: Mississippi, 1830–1900* (Baton Rouge: Louisiana State University Press, 1995).

emphasized the extent of landlessness among white farmers in the antebellum upcountry, the discussion of numbers alone explains neither where they fit in the web of agricultural class relations nor how those relations changed over time. Historians might also differentiate among those farmers conventionally labeled "yeomen," a category usually drawn to include small slaveowners as well as nonslaveowners. For the former, the loss of slave property and labor entailed a particular set of challenges; whatever their antebellum status, those who successfully emerged as small landlords may have done so with distinctive views on issues like the crop lien and the fence law. Finally, a generational approach would enable historians to appreciate how, even if many individual smallholders were not dispossessed, they may have found it harder to perpetuate landownership to their children—a finding that might in turn refine our understanding of the growth of white farm tenancy.

If these are important issues to pursue in the context of existing scholarship, the greater opportunities for new research may lie in looking beyond those debates altogether. Groundbreaking as it was, Hahn's work is now more than twenty years old, and scholarship on the yeomanry could surely benefit from new approaches. Particularly striking is the lack of work on the history of women and gender relations. Laura Edwards provides one of the few available discussions of gender roles among what she calls "common whites," but—useful as her work is—that rubric tends to obscure the relationship between gender norms and postbellum economic changes by grouping together landless and smallholding rural white households. Those seeking to study the Reconstruction period in more detail will certainly look to build upon Stephanie McCurry's work on gender relations in the household of antebellum yeomen, and will also find useful Sharon Ann Holt's discussion of the "household economy." Although Holt's focus is on freedpeople, she observes that women's production of eggs, butter, and other goods for sale was common in white farm households as well—a point reinforced in recent works by Melissa Walker and Lu Ann Jones on the twentieth century.[39]

Historians may also find it profitable to study in greater depth the economic roles and experiences of freedpeople in agriculture outside the plantation belt. To date, most studies of the transition from slavery to freedom have concentrated on black-majority counties in the cotton, rice, and tobacco regions. While there is a good reason for this focus—such counties were home to the majority of black southerners—many areas outside the plantation belt had large black

---

[39] Stephanie McCurry, *Masters of Small Worlds: Yeoman Households, Gender Relations, and the Political Culture of the Antebellum South Carolina Low Country* (New York: Oxford University Press, 1995); Melissa Walker, *All We Knew Was to Farm: Rural Women in the Upcountry South, 1919–1941* (Baltimore: Johns Hopkins University Press, 2000); Lu Ann Jones, *Mama Learned Us to Work: Farm Women in the New South* (Chapel Hill: University of North Carolina Press, 2002).

populations as well. In the Georgia upcountry, for example, slaves accounted for roughly 25 percent of the antebellum population. Although few historians of the nonplantation South can be accused of ignoring freedpeople, their work generally has not been informed by the kinds of questions that have guided more recent studies of the plantation regions. How did gender and family relations among former slaves, and their grassroots political activity, evolve in the different conditions that prevailed outside the plantation belt, and intertwine with struggles over land and labor?

Scholarship on the economic reconstruction of the upcountry, like that on the plantation belt, has generally taken the form of community studies. Although there are certainly more communities to be studied—the history of Appalachia, for example, has long stood as a subdiscipline that receives too little wider attention—historians would also do well to think about ways to transcend that approach altogether. One might be to frame studies around the larger commercial and financial networks that penetrated both the plantation and nonplantation regions of the South: to look, in other words, at the wholesalers, banking firms, and railroads that connected rural and small-town merchants to the national economy. An older but still valuable work along these lines is Harold Woodman's *King Cotton and His Retainers* (1968), which treated both black belt and upcountry, as well as the antebellum and postbellum periods. A very different and more recent study is Scott Nelson's *Iron Confederacies* (1999), which concentrates on the period of the Civil War and Reconstruction to chart the formation of new railroad networks that stretched from Virginia to Georgia. Nelson explores not only the impact of these railroads on places along their routes but also the history of the workers who built and maintained them, and the politics of railroad development and Klan violence. Nelson's emphasis on the involvement of northern capitalists—including Tom Scott of the Pennsylvania Railroad—recalls C. Vann Woodward's discussion of the "colonial economy" of the New South.[40]

Don Doyle pursues another of Woodward's points—his discussion of the rising "new middle-class society" of the New South—by examining the established port cities of Charleston and Mobile, and two interior towns that grew rapidly after the Civil War, Atlanta and Nashville. Concentrating on what he calls the "business classes" of each place, Doyle finds a difference between the conservative and sometimes backward-looking ethos among leaders in the older cities and an entrepreneurial spirit in the newer ones. He also emphasizes how those differences were conditioned and reinforced by the circumstances of

[40] Harold D. Woodman, *King Cotton and His Retainers: Financing and Marketing the Cotton Crop of the South, 1800–1925* (1968; reprint, with new introduction, Columbia: University of South Carolina Press, 1990); Scott Reynolds Nelson, *Iron Confederacies: Southern Railways, Klan Violence, and Reconstruction* (Chapel Hill: University of North Carolina Press, 1999).

the new economy. The new railroad networks that made Atlanta and Nashville regional hubs for commerce and finance drained trade away from the coastal cities, which stagnated economically and provided fewer opportunities for the ambitious or innovative.[41]

The urban working classes of the South receive attention in recent works by Eric Arnesen and Tera Hunter, who bring to bear the methods and concerns of labor historians in charting the transition from slavery to freedom. Arnesen examines the New Orleans waterfront to address a perennial question of American labor history—how racial divisions affected workplace relations and organizing. Competition between white and black dock workers dated to the antebellum era and intensified during and immediately after the Civil War, as the city's black population swelled with the arrival of rural immigrants—a common phenomenon in the urban South. Nonetheless, according to Arnesen, by 1880 black workers had formed their own trade unions and forged alliances with white workers that would shape the New Orleans waterfront into the early twentieth century. Focusing on Atlanta, Tera Hunter examines a very different segment of the labor force with her look at domestic service—a form of work that was dominated by slaves before the war, and that employed the great majority of the city's wage-earning black women afterward. Hunter examines how domestic work was transformed in the years after emancipation, as black women resisted "living-in" with their employers and laundering emerged as a form of outwork that freed them from regular supervision (a development with some parallels to changes in postwar agriculture).[42]

Although both Hunter and Arnesen pursue developments into the early twentieth century, they see the period of the Civil War and Reconstruction as a crucial part of the stories they tell. The same cannot be said, for the most part, of historians of industry in the New South. It is conventional to date what C. Vann Woodward called the "industrial evolution" of the South to the 1880s, and many histories of the region's leading industries—cotton textiles, timber, and mining—take that decade as their starting point, and treat the period before as background, to be briefly summarized. Measured by later employment and production figures, industry during Reconstruction indeed appears of minor importance compared to what would come later. But historians might find a good deal more significance in the period by regarding it not as background to later events but rather as terrain on which to explore some of the same themes that have guided the study of postwar agriculture.

[41] Don H. Doyle, *New Men, New Cities, New South: Atlanta, Nashville, Charleston, Mobile, 1860–1910* (Chapel Hill: University of North Carolina Press, 1990).

[42] Eric Arnesen, *Waterfront Workers of New Orleans: Race, Class, and Politics, 1863–1923* (1991; reprint, Urbana: University of Illinois Press, 1994); Tera W. Hunter, *To 'Joy My Freedom: Southern Black Women's Lives and Labors after the Civil War* (Cambridge, Mass.: Harvard University Press, 1997).

In this regard, two sectors of industry may have special potential for further study. One is the manufacture of tobacco products. Although it would be eclipsed by the machine production of cigarettes later in the century, the manufacture of chewing tobacco had long been important in Richmond, Petersburg, and a number of other upper South cities, relying to a large extent on the labor of hired slaves before the Civil War. Postwar developments have received brief treatment from Steven Tripp and Lynda Morgan, but there is much more to be learned about relations between former slaves and their employers, the evolution of workplace routines and resistance, and how those post-emancipation struggles affected the later tobacco industry, which continued to employ large numbers of black men and women into the twentieth century.[43]

The timber industry of the deep South also offers promising opportunities for the historian willing to piece together a story—of corporate interests, labor history, and the spread of cotton agriculture—that for the moment remains rather fragmented. Although timber production did not soar until the 1880s, the foundations were laid in the 1870s, when northern and British speculators began amassing huge tracts of forest—sometimes in conjunction with railroad building, and also by the purchase of federal and tax-delinquent land. The very qualities that are often cited as making the timber industry hard to study—the seasonal nature of labor and the transient character of logging crews in search of new timber—may hold some of the keys to its importance. To freedmen, logging and sawmills offered opportunities for seasonal work and extra income, but planters were more likely to regard them as a threat to their control of labor. In nonplantation areas, hard-pressed yeomen also turned to work in the forests, as Mark Wetherington finds in his study of Georgia's wiregrass region. Logging operations during the 1870s and 1880s in some cases opened up land that became the South's new cotton frontiers. This was the case, as Wetherington explores, in southeast Georgia, and also in the Mississippi Delta, where some of the best cotton land of the twentieth century lay in swamps and forests in 1865.[44]

Race in the Post-Emancipation South

The destruction of slavery transformed not only the southern economy but also the ideas and practices of racial subordination that had intertwined with human bondage over two centuries. In understanding this transformation, historians

---

[43] Steven Elliott Tripp, *Yankee Town, Southern City: Race and Class Relations in Civil War Lynchburg* (New York: New York University Press, 1997). On the tobacco industry after 1880, see Richard Love, "The Cigarette Capital of the World: Labor, Race, and Tobacco in Richmond, Virginia, 1880–1980" (Ph.D. diss., University of Virginia, 1998).

[44] Mark V. Wetherington, *The New South Comes to Wiregrass Georgia, 1860–1910* (Knoxville: University of Tennessee Press, 1994); see also Jeffrey A. Drobney, *Lumbermen and Log Sawyers:*

were for a generation also heavily influenced by the work of C. Vann Woodward. In *The Strange Career of Jim Crow*, Woodward made a powerful argument not just for change between the Old South and New but also for differences within the postbellum era. The first twenty-five years after the Civil War—the periods of Reconstruction and Redemption—were not a golden era of racial harmony and integration, Woodward insisted, but did represent at least a time of relative tolerance and flexibility in comparison to what would follow after 1890, when Jim Crow finally received its firm legal basis.

The challenges to this Woodward thesis are by now as well known as the argument itself. Howard Rabinowitz, Joel Williamson, and others questioned Woodward's account of the timing of Jim Crow's emergence, arguing that segregation existed in many realms of postwar life earlier than Woodward had acknowledged, often by practice or local ordinance if not by state law. Rabinowitz emphasized as well the ways in which freedpeople were not merely the passive victims of a Jim Crow system imposed by white southerners; they led the way in establishing racially separate churches and accepted the segregation of certain government services where separate access represented an advance over earlier practices of exclusion. In his *Reconstruction*, Eric Foner conceded something to both sides. "[S]eparation, not integration, characterized Reconstruction social relations," Foner wrote, maintaining nonetheless that "if Reconstruction did not create an integrated society, it did establish a standard of equal citizenship and a recognition of blacks' right to a share of state services that differed sharply . . . from the state-imposed segregation that lay in the future."[45]

The Woodward thesis has continued to provide a starting point for historical scholarship during the past fifteen years. In separate studies of Charlotte, North Carolina, Thomas Hanchett and Janette Greenwood reinforce Woodward's view of the 1870s and 1880s as a period of fluidity and "forgotten alternatives." Hanchett finds little residential segregation before the 1890s, while Greenwood emphasizes the cooperation of the black and white "better classes" on temperance and other public issues during the 1870s and 1880s. Barbara Welke, on the other hand, arrives at a bleaker assessment of the period before 1890 in her study of lawsuits brought by African Americans to challenge their exclu-

Life, Labor, and Culture in the North Florida Timber Industry, 1830–1930 (Mercer, Ga.: Mercer University Press, 1997).

[45] Foner, *Reconstruction*, 372. Among the most important contributions to the debate over this Woodward thesis are: Joel Williamson, *After Slavery: The Negro in South Carolina during Reconstruction, 1861–1877* (Chapel Hill: University of North Carolina Press, 1965); Howard N. Rabinowitz, *Race Relations in the Urban South, 1865–1890* (New York: Oxford University Press, 1978); John W. Cell, *The Highest Stage of White Supremacy: The Origins of Segregation in South Africa and the American South* (New York: Cambridge University Press, 1982). For Woodward's reflections, see his *Thinking Back: The Perils of Writing History* (Baton Rouge: Louisiana State University Press, 1986), chap. 5.

sion from first-class railroad cars. Although some black women succeeded in these cases, they did so not by challenging racial discrimination, but rather by claiming access as women to what had conventionally been designated first-class ladies' cars, separate from male-dominated smokers. And their very success, Welke argues, encouraged the shift from a gendered to an explicitly racial system of segregation.[46]

With time, debate over the Woodward thesis came to concentrate largely on questions about the timing and causes of segregation. This focus had a special vitality for historians who experienced at firsthand a civil rights movement that challenged the law and practice of racial separation in twentieth-century America. It is, nonetheless, a somewhat narrow approach to some of the questions Woodward raised in *The Strange Career of Jim Crow*. Part of his goal was to call attention to the "philosophies," "ideas," and "attitudes" (as he variously characterized them) that underlay practices of racial subordination, and to insist that they were not "immovable 'folkways' and irresistible 'mores.'" To that end, Woodward devoted a good deal of the early chapters of *Strange Career* to emphasizing not only the theme of change over time but also the variation in racial views among white southerners. Woodward's comments, to be sure, did not always go much beyond broad generalizations—as, for example, when he counterposed "an aristocratic philosophy of paternalism and *noblesse oblige*" to the "hot breath of cracker fanaticism." Nonetheless, his work stood a world apart from that of Ulrich B. Phillips, who had declared the "central theme of Southern history" to be "the common resolve . . . that it shall be and remain a white man's country."[47]

Other historians of postbellum society have also explored the racial "philosophies," "ideas," and "attitudes" of white southerners. Perhaps the most influential is Barbara J. Fields. In her 1982 essay "Ideology and Race in American History"—part of a festschrift to Woodward—Fields argued that race, as an ideological construct, is at once a product of the social relations in which people find themselves and a means by which they make sense of that reality. In Fields's view, "white supremacy"—the rallying cry for a succession of Democrats, from the nineteenth and into the twentieth century—was "a slogan, not a belief."

[46]Thomas W. Hanchett, *Sorting Out the New South City: Race, Class, and Urban Development in Charlotte, 1875–1975* (Chapel Hill: University of North Carolina Press, 1998); Janette Thomas Greenwood, *Bittersweet Legacy: The Black and White "Better Classes" in Charlotte, 1850–1910* (Chapel Hill: University of North Carolina Press, 1994); Barbara Y. Welke, "When All the Women Were White, and All the Blacks Were Men: Gender, Class, Race, and the Road to *Plessy*, 1855–1914," *Law and History Review* 13 (Fall 1995): 261–316, and *Recasting American Liberty: Gender, Race, Law, and the Railroad Revolution, 1865-1920* (New York: Cambridge University Press, 2001).

[47]Woodward, *Strange Career*, 109, 49, 51; Ulrich B. Phillips, "The Central Theme of Southern History," *American Historical Review* 34 (October 1928): 30–43 (quotation at 31).

This is not because it meant nothing, but rather because it meant different things to different classes in white society; those meanings, for Fields, are to be sought in the circumstances, experiences, and overall outlook that conditioned the "particular variety of racialist ideology" of each class.[48]

During the past twenty years, one of the most noteworthy developments in the study of race has been its confluence with scholarship of gender, which historians have likewise understood as a social construct that often poses, historically, as a product of natural differences. Increasingly, historians have produced studies that examine the intersection of gender and race and their significance for post-emancipation society.[49] These inquiries have led in a number of different directions. Three topics seem especially important to note here: first, the legal regulation of family and sexual relations between black and white persons; second, white vigilantism and its relation to gender and racial norms; and finally, the politics of white manhood in the post-emancipation South.

Since the colonial era, the racialization of slavery had involved a good bit of policing of family and sexual relations, as officials tried to make the line between free and slave at least approximate that between white and black. The end of slavery did not bring an end to those regulations, as Peter Bardaglio describes in *Reconstructing the Household*. South Carolina, the only Confederate state that did not regulate interracial marriages before the Civil War, banned them in its 1865 black code, and other states took steps to strengthen their prohibitions during Presidential Reconstruction. Although southern Republicans subsequently overturned some of these laws, Democratic Redeemers restored them, in some cases by writing them into state constitutions. "Racial amalgamation," Bardaglio writes, "quickly became one of the most volatile legal and social issues as white anxiety over black male sexuality reached unprecedented heights."[50]

Several studies explore in more detail the changes that occurred in sexual relations between black men and white women—and white southerners' anxieties about them—in the wake of slavery's destruction. Martha Hodes argues that consensual liaisons were sometimes tolerated in the Old South but assumed a new sig-

[48] Barbara J. Fields, "Ideology and Race in American History," in *Region, Race, and Reconstruction: Essays in Honor of C. Vann Woodward*, ed. J. Morgan Kousser and James M. McPherson (New York: Oxford University Press, 1982), 143–77 (quotations at 156 and 158); see also her "Slavery, Race and Ideology in the United States of America," *New Left Review* 181 (May/June 1990): 95–118.

[49] Although she does not treat the Reconstruction period in detail, Glenda Elizabeth Gilmore, *Gender and Jim Crow: Women and the Politics of White Supremacy in North Carolina, 1896–1920* (Chapel Hill: University of North Carolina Press, 1996), is noteworthy for its influence on many of the historians discussed hereafter.

[50] Bardaglio, *Reconstructing the Household*, 177; see also Mary Frances Berry, "Judging Morality: Sexual Behavior and Legal Consequences in the Late Nineteenth-Century South," *Journal of American History* 78 (December 1991): 835–856.

nificance after emancipation, as many white southerners "conflated the recently won political and economic authority of black men" with sexual transgressions against white women. In the midst of this "sexualization of Reconstruction politics," as Hodes calls it, the nightriders of the Ku Klux Klan targeted not just Republican voters and leaders but also black men accused of any of a wide range of offenses involving white women, from rape to disrespectful behavior. Hodes's study thus provides an important reminder that such violence did not arise only after 1880, the year when many studies of postbellum lynching begin.[51]

Diane Sommerville complements many of Hodes's findings in *Rape and Race in the Nineteenth-Century South* (2004), arguing that the "rape myth"—white southerners' "hysterical fear of black men as rapists"—was a distinctly postbellum development. In the Old South, she argues, white slaveholders and judges often acted to ensure procedural fairness and secure acquittal for black men charged with sexually assaulting white women. Emancipation and Reconstruction brought several crucial changes. White masters lost the financial incentive they once had to protect their slaves. In the political sphere, Democrats not only inflamed fears that black men sought social equality through sexual relations with white women but also undermined faith in the ability of Republican-controlled courts to mete out justice in cases of rape. Those developments, Sommerville writes, prepared the way for the "spasm of lawlessness and lynching" at century's end, when the image of the "black beast rapist" firmly took hold in justifications of mob violence.[52]

Hannah Rosen's dissertation and forthcoming book, *The Gender of Reconstruction*, highlight a different aspect of racial violence—the sexual assaults committed by white rioters, Klansmen, and other vigilantes against black women during Reconstruction. In a published essay drawn from the larger work, Rosen explores the role of sexual violence in the Memphis Riot of May 1866, when at least five freedwomen were raped by white rioters. "As white southern men struggled to reclaim the power and privilege that white manhood had signified in a slave society," Rosen writes, "they turned to black women's gender and sexuality as a site for reenacting and reproducing racial inequality and subordination."[53]

Several recent works examine the intersection of whiteness or white manhood with the practice of politics after the Civil War. Dismissing the idea that

---

[51] Martha Hodes, *White Women, Black Men: Illicit Sex in the Nineteenth-Century South* (New Haven: Yale University Press, 1997), 148, 165. A notable exception to the tendency to commence studies of postbellum lynching around 1880 is George C. Wright, *Racial Violence in Kentucky, 1865–1940: Lynchings, Mob Rule, and "Legal Lynchings"* (Baton Rouge: Louisiana State University Press, 1990).

[52] Diane Miller Sommerville, *Rape and Race in the Nineteenth-Century South* (Chapel Hill: University of North Carolina Press, 2004), 223, 17.

[53] Hannah Rosen, "The Gender of Reconstruction: Rape, Race, and Citizenship in the Postemancipation South" (Ph.D. diss., University of Chicago, 1999), and "'Not That Sort of

"white racial animosity and anxiety [were] . . . inevitable," Jane Dailey explores how white members of the Readjuster party in Virginia were able to blunt Democrats' race-baiting and forge a coalition with black voters that for a few years ruled the state. According to Dailey, white Readjusters embraced the liberal notion of a dichotomy between public and private, accepting the equality of white and black men in politics while rejecting "social equality" in the private sphere of marriage, family, and sexual relations. For their part, Virginia Democrats fought back with appeals to white manhood that focused on the threat posed by black school officials to white female teachers and children. Drawing a short line from mixed school boards and schools to mixed marriages and mixed-race children, Democrats exposed the instability of the public/private dichotomy, Dailey argues, and undermined white support for the Readjusters.[54]

Focusing on the career of an individual rather than a political party, Stephen Kantrowitz explores the "reconstruction of white supremacy" through a study of South Carolina's "Pitchfork Ben" Tillman, who served as a paramilitary Red Shirt during the 1870s before becoming governor in 1890 and later a United States senator. Like other white supremacist leaders, Kantrowitz argues, Tillman mobilized "not only white men but also ideas about white manhood." For Tillman, the ideas that mattered were a set of "common, if implicit, understandings," derived from antebellum slave society, about "the relationship between race, gender, economic position, and social hierarchies—understandings that made white manhood the center around which all else revolved." If Tillman's "producerist" ideology, as Kantrowitz calls it, bears some resemblance to the republicanism that Hahn found among Georgia's yeomanry, it led to consequences that were a good bit uglier in South Carolina, where Tillman wielded it to undermine the Populist party and to endorse lynching and the repeal of the Fourteenth and Fifteenth Amendments.[55]

For Kantrowitz as for Dailey, the study of politics is a means to study, more broadly, the meaning of race in the wake of emancipation; in examining that subject, their books share several characteristics with other works discussed here. In contrast to an older literature that focused on what white southerners thought about African Americans, more recent historians focus at least as much on what white southerners thought about themselves—about what it meant, in other words, to be white, and more particularly, to be a white man. This approach has parallels, of course, to the growing scholarship on the his-

Women': Race, Gender and Sexual Violence during the Memphis Riot of 1866," in *Sex, Love, Race: Crossing Boundaries in North American History*, ed. Martha Hodes (New York: New York University Press, 1999), 267–293 (quotation at 268).

[54] Jane Dailey, *Before Jim Crow: The Politics of Race in Postemancipation Virginia* (Chapel Hill: University of North Carolina Press, 2000), 78.

[55] Stephen Kantrowitz, *Ben Tillman and the Reconstruction of White Supremacy* (Chapel Hill: University of North Carolina Press, 2000), 3, 4.

tory of whiteness, as does the related tendency to understand race as a matter of identity—a sense of self, of membership in a group defined in contrast or relation to other groups. In search of the meaning of whiteness, historians approach some of the familiar subjects of postbellum southern history with new goals in mind. Political history thus becomes a means less to examine policy and governance (when were segregation laws passed, and why?) than to explore the construction of white racial identity in political discourse. In similar fashion, historians are often less interested in instrumental questions about the causes and effects of lynching and mob violence than in interpreting them as symbolic performances of white manhood.

This scholarship on racial ideology and identity diverges in several striking ways from the literature both on the economic reconstruction of the postwar South and on segregation. Community studies have predominated among works on labor and the economy, emphasizing differences within the plantation South as well as between plantation and nonplantation areas. Likewise, historians who study the practice and law of segregation have often focused on individual cities and towns, or otherwise examined variations within the South and among white southerners: for example, by stressing differences in when and how extensively the region's older and newer cities adopted segregation, and by asking about the role that different groups of white southerners played in bringing it about. By comparison, few recent works on race take the form of community studies, nor do they tend to assign great explanatory importance to class differences within white society.

Thus, if recent historians certainly develop one of Woodward's key themes in *The Strange Career of Jim Crow*—about the changing and contingent nature of white southerners' racial views—they somewhat neglect another: that those views varied significantly among different groups in white society. A number of these historians, to be sure, seek to explore how white southerners of all classes participated in the making of racial identity, and to their credit, they avoid the spurious choice posed by some scholars who ask whether class "trumped" race, or vice versa. The question that might still receive more explicit attention in some works, nonetheless, is whether there existed a single racial ideology or identity that white southerners shared across class lines. Jane Dailey, for example, offers an intriguing analysis of how leading Readjusters and their opponents invoked the supposed relation between public and private spheres in political arguments about race. She does relatively little, however, to examine how those arguments were received by or affected white urban workers and small farmers in western Virginia, whom she identifies as key Readjuster constituencies.

What might be useful is more cross-fertilization between the extensive scholarship on class and labor relations in the postwar South and the growing literature on race. The few works that examine both in detail often provide a fuller sense of the divisions among white Southerners than do those focusing more exclusively on race. As Eric Arnesen makes clear in his study of the New Orleans waterfront, the racism of white dock workers did not prevent them from cooperating with their black counterparts against white employers.[56] In her comparative work, Rebecca Scott enriches the study of both labor relations and race by examining their intersection at the grassroots in Cuba and Louisiana. Alliances that drew together workers of various (and mixed) ancestries were more common in the former than the latter, where ex-slaves composed a much greater fraction of sugar plantation workers. But even in Louisiana, ferocious applications of violence—and not just rhetorical invocations of white supremacy—were necessary to suppress Republican activists and the Knights of Labor. Indeed, Scott argues, the Knights' 1887 strikes "did not simply draw upon a conflict of interests between those denominated black and those denominated white" but called forth a degree of "physical and rhetorical violence" from planters that helped "*define* groups in this way, radically simplifying complex social and racial categories."[57]

Exploring the limitations as well as the power of white supremacy, Scott and Arnesen avoid the pitfall of overstating its ability to unite white Southerners. That pitfall is by no means a new one, and posed a challenge even to as sure-footed a historian as Woodward, who wrote in *Strange Career* that the "magical formula of white supremacy" healed divisions in white society during the 1890s. If the word choice no doubt reflected Woodward's taste for irony, the claim was consistent with the broader argument of the book. It stood in contrast, however, to Woodward's more skeptical treatment in *Origins of the New South*, where he wrote that—appeals to white supremacy notwithstanding—the "real question was *which whites* should be supreme."[58] In the context of the race relations approach of *Strange Career*, in other words, the unifying power of white supremacy loomed far larger than in *Origins of the New South*, where Woodward wove it into a discussion of politics in which race was but one thread. The lesson perhaps is that accounts that start by focusing on the abstractions of white supremacy and whiteness can have a hard time finding their way back to the myriad differences among white southerners—even for historians who are well aware of them. In his occasional missteps as well as his many accomplishments, it would seem, Woodward has something to teach us yet.

[56] In similar fashion, labor organizing across the color line in the coalfields of post-Reconstruction Alabama is the subject of Daniel Letwin, *The Challenge of Interracial Unionism: Alabama Coal Miners, 1878–1921* (Chapel Hill: University of North Carolina Press, 1998), and Brian Kelly, *Race, Class, and Power in the Alabama Coalfields, 1908–1921* (Urbana: University of Illinois Press, 2001).

[57] Scott, "Fault Lines, Color Lines, and Party Lines," 80.

[58] Woodward, *Strange Career of Jim Crow*, 82; *Origins of the New South*, 328.

2

BLACK AGENCY AFTER SLAVERY

JOHN C. RODRIGUE

A mong the more significant developments in Reconstruction historiography during the past generation has been the ascendancy of the concept of black historical agency to the status of conventional wisdom. It is no longer new or original to see slaves and former slaves as historical agents who seized the initiative in destroying slavery and laying the foundations of the free black community, or to view the destruction of slavery as a revolutionary rendering of American society and ideals in which black people played a pivotal role. These seminal insights, first articulated by W. E. B. Du Bois and other black scholars early in the twentieth century, were largely although not entirely ignored by the historical profession before the 1960s.[1] They subsequently gained increasing currency until by the 1980s they came to serve as a veritable point of departure in the writing on black life after slavery. Revisionist works—from John Hope Franklin's *From Slavery to Freedom* (1947) to the publications of the Freedmen and Southern Society Project—championed the

I thank Scott P. Marler, Sylvia Frank Rodrigue, and Mart A. Stewart for assistance on this essay.

[1] W. E. B. Du Bois, *Black Reconstruction in America: An Essay toward a History of the Part Which Black Folk Played in the Attempt to Reconstruct Democracy in America, 1860–1880* (New York: Harcourt, Brace, 1935). Du Bois previewed some of the important findings of this work in earlier writings, especially in his article "Reconstruction and Its Benefits," *American Historical Review* 15 (July 1910): 781–799. Although, as Eric Foner has noted, the *American Historical Review* never reviewed *Black Reconstruction*, David Levering Lewis has shown that the historical profession did not completely ignore it. Many reviewers, in both scholarly journals and mainstream press, took the book's arguments seriously. Nonetheless, Du Bois's work had limited impact within the historical profession and none on white mainstream thinking on Reconstruction. Eric Foner, *Nothing but Freedom: Emancipation and Its Legacy* (Baton Rouge: Louisiana

principles of this previously overlooked scholarship and with it blazed a trail for later historians to follow.[2]

This essay will survey the recent literature on the origins and development of the free black community in the South after slavery.[3] As the previous essay reviewed studies of the structural transformation of the postbellum southern economy, this one will concentrate on interpretations of the daily, local efforts of former slaves to achieve economic independence. It will also address the creation of an autonomous black social and cultural life, which, as Eric Foner has shown, ranked among the most enduring accomplishments of Reconstruction, enabling African Americans to exercise a measure of personal and collective self-determination in their everyday lives long after 1877. In its interpretation of black economic, social, and cultural life during Reconstruction, Foner's *Reconstruction* was a watershed study. Not only did it synthesize revisionist scholarship since the 1950s but also it helped to spur a subsequent body of research on black life during Reconstruction that has started with assumptions—and has worked toward ends—different from those of previous revisionism.[4]

Agency, a concept that pervades the scholarship on black life during and after slavery, can be understood as the capacity to act on behalf of one's own interests and values. In essence, it involves the ability to remain independent, to some degree, of another's control and to exercise a measure of free will. While certain scholars have recently warned of a tendency to overstate the agency of slaves and freedpeople and to understate the formidable obstacles they confronted, it is worth noting, for the purposes of this essay, the distinction between the agency of slaves and that of free or freed people.[5] A slave's agency, however limited, represents a potential threat to the slave system, because enslavement,

State University Press, 1983); David Levering Lewis, *W. E. B. Du Bois: The Fight for Equality and the American Century, 1919–1963* (New York: Holt, 2000), chap. 10.

[2] John Hope Franklin, *From Slavery to Freedom: A History of American Negroes* (New York: Knopf, 1947); Ira Berlin et al., eds., *Freedom: A Documentary History of Emancipation, 1861–1867,* ser. 1, vol. 1, *The Destruction of Slavery* (Cambridge: Cambridge University Press, 1985); ser. 1, vol. 2, *The Wartime Genesis of Free Labor: The Upper South* (Cambridge: Cambridge University Press, 1993); ser. 1, vol. 3, *The Wartime Genesis of Free Labor: The Lower South* (Cambridge: Cambridge University Press, 1990); ser. 2, *The Black Military Experience* (Cambridge: Cambridge University Press, 1982).

[3] Consequently, this essay does not specifically examine the process of emancipation, nor does it review the "self-emancipation" debate, either of which would have contributed significantly to the essay's length and scope.

[4] Eric Foner, *Reconstruction: America's Unfinished Revolution, 1863–1877* (New York: Harper and Row, 1988).

[5] Peter Coclanis, for example, has identified a tendency to posit a degree of agency to slaves and freedpeople that "divinizes rather than humanizes" them. Would-be historical agents, he notes, "got crushed in the nineteenth century, crushed by overwhelming material, institutional, and ideological power that no subaltern formation anywhere in the world could even

by its essence, implies powerlessness or subordination to the will of another. A free person's agency, by contrast, does not necessarily threaten a social order predicated upon individual self-ownership. Nonetheless, to maintain that former slaves in the postbellum South exercised agency is to insist not only upon their essential humanity but also upon their ability to identify their own interests and to pursue their own agenda. It shows them to be neither manipulated dupes nor "faithful souls," neither hapless victims nor unwitting pawns, but historical actors in their own right who warrant serious scholarly study.

In large part because one of its main goals was to document the creation of an autonomous communal life, "pre-Foner" revisionism generally emphasized unity among former slaves. Although aware of conflict within the black community, it placed greater importance on African Americans' collective efforts to achieve autonomy. Revisionist scholarship since Foner, by contrast, has placed greater weight on differences and divisions among former slaves. Black people, it is now readily recognized, disagreed, sometimes vehemently, over goals as well as over tactics and methods. Even when it has not specifically emphasized conflict, "post-Foner" revisionism has demonstrated the diversity of black life by scrutinizing particular facets of it, which has also led at times to highlighting differences within the black community. Pre-Foner revisionism hardly lacked sophistication, but post-Foner revisionism—which has been able to assume black agency rather than having to prove it—has furnished a more textured understanding of the black struggle for autonomy. Because the point of departure for pre-Foner revisionists was that black people had been excluded from the story of Reconstruction, their task was to integrate blacks into it. For revisionist scholars since Foner, black agency has come to represent a new point of departure. Indeed, revisionists so successfully demonstrated black agency during Reconstruction that later scholars have almost been forced to seek out diversity and even conflict within the black community in order to have something new to say.

Although pre-Foner revisionism portrayed neither the southern black nor white communities as monolithic, the driving force behind Reconstruction tended to be racial conflict. Racial divisions did not simply trump class divisions in the postbellum South, nor does white racism alone explain the failure

---

begin to match." "Slavery, African-American Agency, and the World We Have Lost," *Georgia Historical Quarterly* 79 (Winter 1995): 873–884 (quotations at 880 and 882). Similarly, Walter Johnson suggests that scholars have collapsed the slaves' humanity, modern notions of selfhood, and slave resistance into the catchword "agency," which, he warns, better reflects the needs of the new social history of the 1960s and 1970s than it does the realities of the nineteenth-century South, and thus obfuscates more than it illuminates the conditions that slaves and former slaves confronted. "On Agency," *Journal of Social History* 37 (Fall 2003): 113–124. Barbara Fields also addresses agency in "Whiteness, Racism, and Identity," *International Labor and Working Class History* 60 (Fall 2001): 48–56.

of Reconstruction. But among pre-Foner revisionists, and for Foner, two critical elements to Reconstruction's failure were, first, how economic and political divisions among white southerners were eventually overcome and replaced by the color line and, second, how most northerners came to identify with white southerners after having supported, for a time, racial equality. Foner and his revisionist predecessors may have disagreed over how much of a role racial conflict played in ending Reconstruction, but most emphasized differences between white and black southerners rather than divisions within each group. Post-Foner scholarship, by contrast, has tended to highlight differences and divisions among black people, attributing as much importance to conflicts within the black community as to those between whites and blacks. Heightened interest in the black community's internal dynamics, moreover, has enabled scholars to document how certain segments of the black community cooperated with certain segments of an internally divided white community. Consequently, one challenge scholars face will be to fuse the pre-Foner emphasis on unity within the black community with the focus on black division and diversity that has tended to dominate recent historiography.[6]

If agency has saturated the writing on African-American history during and after slavery, scholars have also tended to conflate it with the issue of black centrality to the story of Reconstruction. Foner himself identifies one of his major themes in *Reconstruction* as "the centrality of the black experience." He further argues: "Rather than passive victims of the actions of others or simply a 'problem' confronting white society, blacks were active agents in the making of Reconstruction."[7] Critics of Foner who charged that he slighted the importance of white southerners to Reconstruction by emphasizing the black experience have perhaps overstated the case, since he devotes considerable attention to political and economic divisions among white southerners. Nonetheless, it is possible to argue that black people were active historical agents during Reconstruction while maintaining that the black experience, in all its diversity, was no more central to Reconstruction than was the southern white experience, in all *its* diversity. In other words, even if agency and centrality are sometimes used interchangeably, they are in fact two distinct ideas. It may no longer be pos-

[6]This interpretation admittedly runs the risk of conflating very different revisionist perspectives. A distinction can be made between the liberal-integrationist scholarship of the 1950s–1970s and Foner's neo–Du Boisian or other Marxian approaches. It is also possible to distinguish a proto–black separatist or black nationalist tendency within revisionism, as exemplified by Vincent Harding's *There Is a River: The Black Struggle for Freedom in America* (New York: Harcourt, Brace, Jovanovich, 1981). In dividing revisionist scholarship into pre- and post-Foner schools of thought, the analysis offered here accepts Foner's apologia of his work as synthesizing revisionist scholarship. Moreover, whatever disagreements individual scholars may have with Foner, the historical profession has generally come to see his *Reconstruction* as the definitive revisionist account.

[7]Foner, *Reconstruction*, xxiv.

sible to argue, as had previously been done, that the black experience merits less attention or seriousness than does the southern white experience, but black historical agency does not necessarily imply black centrality.

What black agency does imply, however, is responsibility. While a subsequent essay in this volume will consider the various explanations for the failure of Reconstruction as a political process, it is well to note here that scholars of black economic, social, and cultural life must also address how former slaves, as historical agents who exercised a measure of self-determination, contributed to Reconstruction's failure. The issue of black responsibility for this failure is distinct from, though related to, that of black unity and divisions. While black internal divisions might have contributed to the failure of Reconstruction, it is conceivable that a unified black community could also have done so by successfully pursuing goals that turned out, albeit only with the benefit of hindsight, to have been misguided. Without suggesting that white attitudes mattered little to the black struggle for autonomy, scholars who pursue this avenue of research face the dual challenges of documenting the "mistakes" that former slaves might have made without placing upon them the full burden of Reconstruction's demise, and of accounting for the very real difficulties that former slaves confronted without absolving them of all responsibility. In other words, historians must reconcile black agency with some measure of black responsibility for Reconstruction's failure.

The collapse of Reconstruction raises the issue of the significance of 1877, Reconstruction's traditional end date. Historians have debated its relevance both to the history of Reconstruction and to U.S. history generally, and valid arguments have been made both defending and questioning it. While 1877 still retains much legitimacy as the end of Reconstruction, it is probably less valid for the purposes of this essay. It is a truism that economic trends (broadly defined) do not conform to the periodization of traditional political history. But even more important, because the creation of an autonomous black social and cultural life was among the most significant of Reconstruction's long-term accomplishments, it is imperative that this essay consider developments after 1877.

Rural Economy

Black agency permeates examinations of the slave South's transition to free labor. The pre-Foner revisionist literature on this question devoted considerable attention to how the freedpeople's aspirations contributed to the development of various forms of tenancy and sharecropping in the cotton South, resulting in a sophisticated understanding of postbellum southern economic life at a macroeconomic level and producing a plethora of local and regional studies that explored the evolution of a new labor system and the reorganization of southern plantations. Despite disagreement among scholars on specific issues, the predominant view held that the former slaves' resistance to gang labor and to white control over their daily working lives were critical factors in the emergence of sharecropping, and that former slaves repudiated wage labor and aspired to landholding as a means to escape white control and provide an economic basis to freedom. Some scholars questioned whether freedpeople accepted the central tenets of northern capitalist society, but most agreed that black people desired property in order to gain access to the mainstream of American life. This early consensus on black economic aspirations has been replaced since Foner, who played an important role in this shift, by a divergence of views. Scholars disagree among themselves about what black people aspired to in the aftermath of slavery, and some emphasize differences among freedpeople on how to achieve economic independence. Still others stress diversity over internal conflict in examining the former slaves' economic aspirations, pointing to the various labor arrangements that prevailed throughout the South.

Recent works on the cotton South constitute something of an exception to the generalization that post-Foner writing has tended to emphasize conflict within the black community. Yet even here scholars have demonstrated the diversity of black economic life and aspirations. Julie Saville provides the most forceful account of a unified black community that refused to submit either to the authority of former masters or to "the discipline of an abstract market."[8] In both upcountry and lowcountry South Carolina (and on rice as well as cotton plantations), freedpeople linked conflict over land and labor to questions of family and kinship, community building, and political action. For Saville, mobilization spawned by the freedpeople's economic struggle enabled them to organize for collective self-defense. Joseph P. Reidy combines elements of both the pre- and post-Foner literature, positing unity among former slaves in their desire for economic independence while documenting the diverse strategies they undertook to achieve it. For Reidy, the freedpeople's striving for land marked less an acceptance of the tenets of American capitalist society than it did their subscribing to the nineteenth-century republican vision that saw property as the key to independence.[9] By contrast, Jonathan M. Bryant traces the intrusion of the world market into the rural South, a process that began before the Civil War. Although freedpeople failed to acquire landed property, they were not simply passive victims of white domination. Instead, they contributed to the triumph of the world market by, among other things, participating in a "nascent consumerism," attracted as they were to commodities that the world market made available.[10]

[8] Julie Saville, *The Work of Reconstruction: From Slave to Wage Laborer in South Carolina, 1860–1870* (Cambridge: Cambridge University Press, 1994), 2.

[9] Joseph P. Reidy, *From Slavery to Agrarian Capitalism in the Cotton Plantation South: Central Georgia, 1800–1880* (Chapel Hill: University of North Carolina Press, 1992).

[10] Jonathan M. Bryant, *How Curious a Land: Conflict and Change in Greene County, Georgia, 1850–1885* (Chapel Hill: University of North Carolina Press, 1996), 164.

Scholars investigating the transformation of labor in other crop regions have further documented the diversity of black economic aspirations while placing emphasis on different elements of those aspirations. My own examination of the cane sugar region of southern Louisiana argues that former slaves accommodated themselves to both wage labor and centralized plantation routine but also capitalized on the exigencies of sugar production and on a functioning regional labor market to exert considerable influence on wage rates and conditions of labor. Although labor arrangements on sugar plantations fostered cohesiveness within the work force, the freedpeople's desire for land remained a strong countervailing tendency in the sugar country.[11] Rebecca J. Scott finds a similar degree of unity among sugar plantation workers, a unity reinforced by black participation in local militias and by other forms of organized self-defense, but she places greater emphasis on black resistance to gang labor and on the freedpeople's hopes for landed property as a means to economic independence.[12]

Recent studies of the upper South's tobacco belt have likewise accentuated the differences between cotton and other crops while highlighting the heterogeneous quality of black economic life within a particular crop regime. Lynda J. Morgan explores the tensions among black Virginians that reflected their divergent antebellum and wartime economic activities within the tobacco region. Property, skill, or antebellum hiring experience, for Morgan, outweighed color or prewar legal status in the formation of class divisions within the black community.[13] Jeffrey R. Kerr-Ritchie documents considerable black landholding as well as a generational divide among Virginia's former slaves in their definition of freedom. The younger generation did not aspire to small property–holding, as had their parents or other elders, but instead abandoned the countryside altogether for the greater freedom and opportunities of urban life. For Kerr-Ritchie,

[11] John C. Rodrigue, *Reconstruction in the Cane Fields: From Slavery to Free Labor in Louisiana's Sugar Parishes, 1862–1880* (Baton Rouge: Louisiana State University Press, 2001).

[12] Rebecca J. Scott, "Defining the Boundaries of Freedom in the World of Cane: Cuba, Brazil, and Louisiana after Emancipation," *American Historical Review* 99 (February 1994): 70–102; "'Stubborn and Disposed to Stand Their Ground': Black Militia, Sugar Workers, and Dynamics of Collective Action in the Louisiana Sugar Bowl, 1863–1887," in *From Slavery to Emancipation in the Atlantic World*, ed. Sylvia R. Frey and Betty Wood (London: Frank Cass, 1999), 103–126, and "Fault Lines, Color Lines, and Party Lines: Race, Labor, and Collective Action in Louisiana and Cuba, 1862–1912," in Frederick Cooper, Thomas Holt, and Rebecca J. Scott, *Beyond Slavery: Explorations of Race, Labor, and Citizenship in Postemancipation Society* (Chapel Hill: University of North Carolina Press, 2000), 61–106. Scott elaborates upon these themes in her book, *Degrees of Freedom: Louisiana and Cuba after Slavery, 1862–1914* (Cambridge, Mass.: Harvard University Press, 2005), which appeared too late to be incorporated into this essay.

[13] Lynda J. Morgan, *Emancipation in Virginia's Tobacco Belt, 1850–1870* (Athens: University of Georgia Press, 1992).

"both landholding and exodus were the culmination of emancipation."[14] Nonetheless, both the older and younger generations were eventually compelled to
confront, though in different ways, the limitations of their aspirations.

While scholars have emphasized different aspects of black economic aspirations or have identified varying tendencies among freedpeople in the pursuit
of economic autonomy, an important recent trend has focused on what might
be labeled black economic "success"—the acquisition of property by former
slaves. These works have, of necessity, examined social and economic divisions
within the black community and the emergence of a black "elite," but they have
also demonstrated how the mass of ordinary black people pursued economic
independence through the acquisition of property. Scholars have ascribed different meanings to black property-holding: it could connote the former slaves'
acceptance of acquisitive individualism and bourgeois property rights, or it
could reflect a collectivist or communalist ethos among former slaves that was
rooted in the slave experience and offered a cultural critique of capitalist society.
Ira Berlin has hinted at these two contrasting tendencies.[15] If advocates of the
communalist tendency can be criticized for romanticizing black history, those
who emphasize acquisitive individualism are open to the charge of accentuat-
ing greed, ambition, opportunism, self-aggrandizement, and other such vices.
Between these two views, however, it is possible to identify a middle position that
likens the former slaves' attitudes on property to those of pre-capitalist small
producers or even protopeasants. Freedpeople, according to this view, envisioned a society characterized by male-headed households rooted in ownership
of productive property, but they eschewed notions of bourgeois acquisitiveness
and absolute property rights in favor of communally oriented strategies toward
racial uplift and advancement.

Loren Schweninger and Amy Dru Stanley have emphasized black acceptance of acquisitive or possessive individualism. For Schweninger, although
"[n]othing in their African heritage prepared them for the New World emphasis
on land ownership and economic individualism," black people nonetheless fully
embraced these defining features of American society. He implicitly sees a transition from earlier, presumably communalist, notions of property predicated
upon African Americans' "African heritage" to more distinctly Western, bourgeois conceptions of individualism and property.[16] Although her book is not

[14] Jeffrey R. Kerr-Ritchie, *Freedpeople in the Tobacco South: Virginia, 1860–1900* (Chapel Hill:
University of North Carolina Press, 1999), 209.

[15] Ira Berlin, *Generations of Captivity: A History of African-American Slaves* (Cambridge,
Mass.: Harvard University Press, 2003), 268–70.

[16] Loren Schweninger, *Black Property Owners in the South, 1790–1915* (Urbana: University
of Illinois Press, 1990), 236.

a study of black property-holding per se, Stanley maintains that most former slaves, male and female alike, subscribed to possessive individualism, though for different reasons. Most freedmen aspired to become property-holding heads of households to whose authority women would be subordinate, whereas many freedwomen employed possessive individualism as an argument against merely exchanging one form of subjugation for another.[17]

In contrast to the salience that Schweninger and Stanley accord to acquisitive or possessive individualism among former slaves, Robert C. Kenzer, Sharon Ann Holt, and John C. Willis each find, to varying degrees, some combination of individualism and communalism at work in the black community. Kenzer maintains that while black people generally subscribed to economic individualism, they also engaged in many collective economic enterprises. Family and kinship, education, and politics provided access to opportunity instead of enabling a black elite to set itself apart from propertyless, impoverished former slaves.[18] Holt likewise tends to highlight black acceptance of acquisitive individualism, and, like Kenzer, she identifies a communal quality to black economic progress. Through household production, North Carolina freed families amassed small amounts of surplus capital that they translated into land and other forms of property. Freedpeople may have internalized capitalist values through their "rural entrepreneurship," Holt argues, but they also displayed a communal ethos by using their modest resources to finance the building of churches and schools.[19] In his study of the Yazoo-Mississippi Delta, Willis finds widespread black property-holding during Reconstruction in an area that would later become one of the poorest in the nation. He describes the diverse strategies individual black people used to acquire land, and he documents black cooperative economic endeavors, in particular the independent colonies at Barefield and Mound Bayou. Like Kerr-Ritchie, Willis identifies a generational shift. Freedom's first generation enjoyed considerable opportunities to acquire land during the 1870s and 1880s, but new circumstances in the ensuing years combined to undermine black landholding and choke off opportunity for subsequent generations. By the early twentieth century, black residents of the Delta had been reduced to rural impoverishment, and the immediate postbellum decades became a "forgotten time."[20]

In *The Claims of Kinfolk* (2003), Dylan C. Penningroth systematically explores the larger cultural significance of black property-holding, and, in doing so, he

[17] Amy Dru Stanley, *From Bondage to Contract: Wage Labor, Marriage, and the Market in the Age of Slave Emancipation* (Cambridge: Cambridge University Press, 1998).

[18] Robert C. Kenzer, *Enterprising Southerners: Black Economic Success in North Carolina, 1865–1915* (Charlottesville: University Press of Virginia, 1997).

[19] Sharon Ann Holt, *Making Freedom Pay: North Carolina Freedpeople Working for Themselves, 1865–1900* (Athens: University of Georgia Press, 2000), xviii.

[20] John C. Willis, *Forgotten Time: The Yazoo-Mississippi Delta after the Civil War* (Charlottesville: University Press of Virginia, 2000).

attempts to shift the terms of debate not only about black property in particular but also about African-American history in general. Building upon the historiography on the "slaves' economy," Penningroth argues that slaves' and former slaves' claims to property were rooted in informal, evolving notions about access to economic resources, family, and community. Property, he posits, "was less an institution or a legal right than a social process." Confuting any linear progression from African communalism to Western acquisitive individualism, Penningroth maintains that property-holding among slaves and even freedpeople was based less upon individual bourgeois property rights than upon communally defined family and kinship ties that regulated claims to economic resources. According to Penningroth, "it was kin who defined access to resources, and it was through a language of kinship, not race, that people rationalized and understood their claims on one another. Kinship mattered, both because it helped 'make' property and helped people claim it, and because property—more precisely, people's interests in property and labor—helped 'make' kinship."[21]

Although Penningroth stresses a collectivist ethos over individualism among slaves and former slaves, he nonetheless eschews a "romanticize[d]" version of African-American history that posits an essential unity or egalitarian quality to the black community. Instead, kinship and property were as likely to divide black people as to lead to solidarity. Penningroth admits that focusing on the sources of dissension within the black community may come perilously close to "blaming black people for their own victimization," and he acknowledges "the power of white oppression." Nonetheless, he asserts that "[t]here is no reason to think that the black community in the 1800s was any more harmonious than the white community, or any more 'egalitarian' than it is today." Because property and kinship marked boundaries within the black community as much as race divided blacks and whites during the nineteenth century, Penningroth insists, any attempt to establish an essential unity among black southerners is flawed.[22] Penningroth may give short shrift to a shared African-American heritage rooted in systematic oppression. Yet in venturing to substitute the traditional emphasis on race relations with an approach that places intraracial relations, even conflict, at the center of African-American history, Penningroth suggests new avenues for research on black economic life and the black community in general after emancipation.

Whatever the disagreements among them, scholars since Foner who have written on black economic aspirations have established that, even assuming an

<hr />

[21] Dylan C. Penningroth, *The Claims of Kinfolk: African American Property and Community in the Nineteenth-Century South* (Chapel Hill: University of North Carolina Press, 2003), 189, 192.

[22] Penningroth, *Claims of Kinfolk*, 8 (first and fourth quotations), 188 (second quotation), and 189 (third quotation).

essential unity on the goal of economic independence, former slaves differed over how to achieve it. It no longer suffices to say that former slaves wanted land and that sharecropping resulted from the failure, for whatever reason, to obtain it. Moreover, while land was always central to black economic aspirations, other scholars have also recently demonstrated that African Americans in the nineteenth-century South possessed both knowledge and skills that enabled them to exploit their natural environment and thus functioned as vital resources for achieving economic autonomy. Mart A. Stewart's environmental history of coastal Georgia devotes little attention to the period of the Civil War and Reconstruction, but it suggests the possibilities available to scholars who focus on the landscape and on how former slaves interacted with it.[23] Such potential is also evident in J. William Harris's *Deep Souths* (2001), in Nicolas W. Proctor's study of hunting in the Old South (which has important implications for the postbellum South), and in Robert A. Outland's examination of the southern naval stores industry.[24] On the basis of these works, an argument can be made that exploring the myriad ways ex-slaves throughout the South used their knowledge and skills to achieve autonomy demonstrates as much agency as does the emphasis on the black community's political mobilization that has suffused the recent literature.

Family and Gender

Two critical and interrelated components of the former slaves' economic aspirations involved the reconstitution of black family life after slavery and the role and status of freedwomen within the black household. Scholars may agree or disagree with the criticism that Foner's *Reconstruction* ignored gender as an analytical category or slighted black women's particular experiences. Nonetheless, a demonstrable trend in Reconstruction historiography since Foner has been the elevation of gender to a rank equal to that of race and class, or at the very least a heightened sensitivity to the role that freedwomen played in constructing freedom. If one of the main accomplishments of pre-Foner revisionism was taking seriously black people's place in the story of Reconstruction, then a critical development since Foner has been a recognition of how emancipation forced a redefinition of relations not only between former masters and former slaves but

---

[23] Mart A. Stewart, *"What Nature Suffers to Groe": Life, Labor, and Landscape on the Georgia Coast, 1680–1920* (Athens: University of Georgia Press, 1996).

[24] J. William Harris, *Deep Souths: Delta, Piedmont, and Sea Island Society in the Age of Segregation* (Baltimore: Johns Hopkins University Press, 2001); Nicolas W. Proctor, *Bathed in Blood: Hunting and Mastery in the Old South* (Charlottesville: University Press of Virginia, 2002); and Robert B. Outland III, *Tapping the Pines: The Naval Stores Industry in the South* (Baton Rouge: Louisiana State University Press, 2004).

also between the various members of black families and households, in particular between black men and black women.

So pervasive has been the heightened attention to freedwomen's experiences or to gender that almost all the works noted previously deal with these issues, if to varying degrees. Some authors—in particular Bryant, Reidy, Scott, Willis, and me—document diversity within the black community by accounting for freedwomen's experiences but do not employ gender as an analytical category. Others, such as Saville and Holt, assign central importance to gender or utilize it as a mode of analysis but do not see it as a primary source of conflict within the black community. Included in this category is Elizabeth Regosin, who uses federal military pension records to show how slave families reconstituted themselves during the transition to freedom, and who emphasizes the cooperative strategies that black families employed to lay claim to pensions.[25] Similarly, Noralee Frankel shows how freedmen's and freedwomen's struggle for an autonomous family life led to a politicization of issues ordinarily thought to be "private," and she argues that black people's understandings of marriage and family defied definitions that white society tried to impose and instead reflected the black community's historical experiences.[26] Finally, not only do Leslie A. Schwalm and Mary J. Farmer employ gender as an analytical category but they also tend to see almost as much conflict between freedmen and freedwomen as between former (male and female) slaveholders and former (male and female) slaves.[27]

The increased attention to freedwomen's experiences and the "gendering" of Reconstruction have resulted in a significant shift from pre-Foner to post-Foner revisionism on black family life. Following the lead of Roger L. Ransom and Richard Sutch in One Kind of Freedom (1977), pre-Foner revisionists focused on the supposed withdrawal of black women and children from field labor after emancipation, and they debated whether it represented black emulation of the "dominant" white culture or reflected black people's experiences under slavery or even their "African" heritage.[28] But as Schwalm, Frankel, and others have

[25] Elizabeth Regosin, *Freedom's Promise: Ex-Slave Families and Citizenship in the Age of Emancipation* (Charlottesville: University Press of Virginia, 2002). See also Donald R. Shaffer, *After the Glory: The Struggles of Black Civil War Veterans* (Lawrence: University Press of Kansas, 2004).

[26] Noralee Frankel, *Freedom's Women: Black Women and Families in Civil War Era Mississippi* (Bloomington: Indiana University Press, 1999).

[27] Leslie A. Schwalm, *A Hard Fight for We: Women's Transition from Slavery to Freedom in South Carolina* (Urbana: University of Illinois Press, 1997); Mary J. Farmer, "'Because They Are Women': Gender and the Virginia Freedmen's Bureau's 'War on Dependency,'" in *The Freedmen's Bureau and Reconstruction: Reconsiderations*, ed. Paul A. Cimbala and Randall M. Miller (New York: Fordham University Press, 1999), 161–192.

[28] Roger L. Ransom and Richard Sutch, *One Kind of Freedom: The Economic Consequences of Emancipation* (Cambridge: Cambridge University Press, 1977).

noted, black women did not withdraw entirely from field labor, and even to the degree that they did, it was not, as many white contemporaries charged, to "play the lady." More important, instead of debating whether freedmen and freed-women emulated white society, post-Foner revisionists have instead explored how emancipation affected the internal dynamics of black families and house-holds. As Laura F. Edwards and Amy Dru Stanley have framed the question: did emancipation mean that black men would now enjoy the same authority over black women and other household dependents as white men enjoyed as heads of households in the mid-nineteenth-century United States?[29] In responding to this question, they and scholars such as Schwalm, Frankel, and Farmer have explored the conflict that resulted when black women resisted state-sponsored efforts to place black men in authority over them, or when black women com-plained to Freedmen's Bureau agents and other officials that their husbands or other male heads of households failed to fulfill their responsibility to provide the sustenance and protection that was an integral part of, and that justified, male authority over them.

These issues have been explored systematically in Nancy Bercaw's study of the reorganization of black and white households in the Yazoo-Mississippi Delta during and after the Civil War. Even before the war, slaves had envisioned an alternative to the prevailing view of the plantation household as the social expression of white patriarchal authority. Yet war and the abolition of slavery shattered the antebellum household as a social unit and led inevitably to a con-testing and reconfiguring of relations not only between former masters and for-mer slaves but also between white men and white women and between black men and black women. The collapse of the antebellum plantation household likewise resulted in the loss and subsequent redefinition of personal identity, which was itself inseparable from one's place within the household hierarchy, and, consequently, it also compelled all southerners, black and white, male and female, to reconceptualize their status within the political realm. Nonetheless, although the reorganization of households led to new contests over power and authority, and although those formerly defined as dependents within the house-hold could now claim greater rights, southerners did not embrace individualism as an ideology. Instead, they continued to frame their rights and identities in terms of the household: "Southerners, white and black, clung to the household because it was what they knew." Although essentially a local study, Bercaw's work suggests possibilities for further research by applying these issues and questions to other southern localities or to the South as a whole. Moreover, link-

---

[29] Laura F. Edwards, *Gendered Strife and Confusion: The Political Culture of Reconstruction* (Urbana: University of Illinois Press, 1997); Stanley, *From Bondage to Contract*, chap 5.

ing the reconstitution of black and white families and households to the reorganization of plantation labor also provides an opportunity to approach both topics with a fresh perspective.[30]

Urban Life

Not all former slaves were relegated to agricultural labor after emancipation. Among the most crucial of developments in black life that began during Reconstruction was the movement of freedpeople from countryside to urban areas. Pre-Foner revisionism on black urban life tended to be overshadowed by Howard N. Rabinowitz's classic *Race Relations in the Urban South, 1865–1890* (1978), which argued that de facto segregation began during Reconstruction and that black leaders generally accommodated themselves to it, recognizing that the alternative was not integration but complete exclusion.[31] Rabinowitz and other pre-Foner scholars were not unaware of intraracial tensions, but they generally focused on black-white conflict while presenting a unified black community. To the degree that they attended to intraracial conflict, it tended to be that between the antebellum free black elite and former slaves. Revisionist works since Foner have continued to address Rabinowitz to varying degrees, but they have also inquired into other sources of tension within the urban black community while uncovering instances of cooperation between segments of the black and white communities.

Several scholars document the complex divisions within the black urban community after emancipation. Bernard E. Powers Jr. focuses on the tensions between Charleston's antebellum free black elite and the newly emancipated former slaves, maintaining that even as emancipation eroded the legal barriers between the two groups it also "accelerated the rate of social differentiation" between them and made the free black elite more protective of its status.[32] Wilbert L. Jenkins concentrates on Charleston's former slave population and examines the divide between former urban slaves and the many rural freedpeople who migrated to the city. Urban slaves had occupied an elite position within the slave hierarchy, and because many of them possessed skills, had hired out, or had become literate, they had enjoyed a degree of personal autonomy unknown

---

[30] Nancy Bercaw, *Gendered Freedoms: Race, Rights, and the Politics of Household in the Delta, 1861–1875* (Gainesville: University Press of Florida, 2003), 189.

[31] Howard N. Rabinowitz, *Race Relations in the Urban South, 1865–1890* (New York: Oxford University Press, 1978).

[32] Bernard E. Powers Jr., *Black Charlestonians: A Social History, 1822–1885* (Fayetteville: University of Arkansas Press, 1994), 7.

to plantation slaves.[33] Michael W. Fitzgerald similarly explores divisions between Mobile's free and freed black population and the large number of former slaves who moved in from the countryside, and he shows how this urban-rural division manifested itself politically in Republican factional disputes during Radical Reconstruction.[34]

Even as they examine tensions within urban black communities, Powers, Jenkins, and Fitzgerald also document considerable interracial cooperation, as does Janette Thomas Greenwood's study of the black and white "better classes" in Charlotte. For Greenwood, the black better class emerged not from the antebellum free black elite but rather from a younger generation that came of age after the war. This new generation espoused racial uplift through education and property ownership and thus anticipated Booker T. Washington's racial accommodationism. Because Charlotte's new black elite formed alliances with white elites on particular issues, such as temperance, its efforts to convert the black community to its vision of racial progress "engendered severe class-based conflict that manifested itself in fiercely fought battles for control of the black community."[35] Caryn Cossé Bell is exceptional in the post-Foner literature with her emphasis on unity within the New Orleans black community. While Bell deals mostly with the antebellum period, her book also serves as an extended investigation into the ideological origins of New Orleans's black elite, or the "Afro-Creoles," during Reconstruction. Refuting the view that Afro-Creoles consciously distanced themselves from the slaves, Bell argues that they championed universal freedom and racial equality before the war and attempted to implement these ideals during Radical Reconstruction.[36]

A number of other scholars examine class divisions within the black community from the perspective of black urban or industrial workers. Eric Arnesen emphasizes racial and class solidarity among black dock workers in New Orleans while also documenting the alliances they formed with their white counterparts. Yet he also explores the evolution of hierarchies among black dock workers, the differences between rural and urban black workers, and the divisions between black dock workers and the city's black elite.[37] Tera W. Hunter's study of black female domestic workers in Atlanta places greater emphasis on

---

[33] Wilbert L. Jenkins, *Seizing the New Day: African Americans in Post–Civil War Charleston* (Bloomington: Indiana University Press, 1998).

[34] Michael W. Fitzgerald, *Urban Emancipation: Popular Politics in Reconstruction Mobile, 1860–1890* (Baton Rouge: Louisiana State University Press, 2002).

[35] Janette Thomas Greenwood, *Bittersweet Legacy: The Black and White "Better Classes" in Charlotte, 1850–1910* (Chapel Hill: University of North Carolina Press, 1994), 4.

[36] Caryn Cossé Bell, *Revolution, Romanticism, and the Afro-Creole Protest Tradition in Louisiana, 1718–1868* (Baton Rouge: Louisiana State University Press, 1997).

[37] Eric Arnesen, *Waterfront Workers of New Orleans: Race, Class, and Politics, 1863–1923* (New York: Oxford University Press, 1991).

white racism than on the possibilities for interracial working-class alliances. But central to her work is the struggle by black domestics to control not only their working lives but also their leisure time, and to resist the attempts by both white and black middle-class reformers to impose their own notions of respectability and morality upon black working-class women.[38] Mary Ellen Curtin similarly probes intraracial tensions in her examination of black convict labor in Alabama. Even on something it found as objectionable as convict lease, she insists, the black community did not speak with one voice. While some members of the black middle class and intellectual community condemned convict lease, others "remained defensive about black criminality," tempering their criticism of convict lease with calls for moral reform and condemning behavior associated with black working-class culture and urban life.[39]

Education and Religion

If labor and family life were essential to the black struggle for autonomy, education and religion were hardly less so. Indeed, scholars have identified the former slaves' unquenchable thirst for knowledge and their relentless efforts to organize churches as perhaps the strongest evidence of black agency during the transition from slavery to freedom. Although pre-Foner revisionists such as Jacqueline Jones, Ronald E. Butchart, and Robert C. Morris devoted considerable attention to black education, they tended to focus on white northerners who came South to teach freedpeople.[40] These works hardly treated black people as passive characters, demonstrating how the freedpeople's desire for independence and their resistance to the control of paternalistic reformers forced northerners to adjust their thinking and behavior. Nonetheless, they concerned themselves as much with the limits of northern reform ideals as they did with the freedpeople's own educational aspirations. Recent works on education have shifted the focus from northern reformers and their ideas to the freedpeople themselves and, in doing so, have identified sources of tension and conflict within the black community over education. Former slaves may have agreed on the importance of education, but the issues relating specifically to black education gave rise to a spirited

---

[38] Tera W. Hunter, *To 'Joy My Freedom: Southern Black Women's Lives and Labors after the Civil War* (Cambridge, Mass.: Harvard University Press, 1997).

[39] Mary Ellen Curtin, *Black Prisoners and Their World, Alabama, 1865–1900* (Charlottesville: University Press of Virginia, 2000), 9.

[40] Jacqueline Jones, *Soldiers of Light and Love: Northern Teachers and Georgia Blacks, 1865–1873* (Chapel Hill: University of North Carolina Press, 1980); Ronald E. Butchart, *Northern Schools, Southern Blacks, and Reconstruction: Freedmen's Education, 1862–1875* (Westport, Conn.: Greenwood Press, 1980); Robert C. Morris, *Reading, 'Riting, and Reconstruction: The Education of Freedmen in the South, 1861–1870* (Chicago: University of Chicago Press, 1981).

debate among them. This debate was part of and contributed to a larger discussion that took place within southern and American society, during and after Reconstruction, about the "proper" place of black people and thus about the goals of black education.

The famous late-nineteenth-century debate between W. E. B. Du Bois and Booker T. Washington over classical and industrial education had its origins in Reconstruction-era conflicts between—and among—former slaves, northern reformers, and white southerners over black education. As James D. Anderson and Heather Andrea Williams demonstrate, northern white reformers did not initiate black education in the South but instead tapped into a groundswell of instructional efforts that black people themselves had undertaken during, and even before, the war. For slaves and former slaves, gaining literacy was an inherently political act, a conscious and deliberate repudiation of their enslavement and an essential element of freedom. For Williams, "issues of power [were] ubiquitous in freedpeople's efforts to obtain education." According to Anderson, black southerners' embracing of the concept of universal public education as a fundamental right of citizenship helped pave the way for the establishment of statewide systems of public education during Reconstruction.[41]

The large majority of black people undoubtedly viewed education as an essential means of achieving racial equality and of gaining equal access to American society. However, Anderson's work and that of Robert Francis Engs on Samuel Chapman Armstrong and the Hampton Institute also demonstrate that some blacks, a number of northern reformers, and influential white southerners advocated, for very different reasons, an alternative philosophy that would come to be known as industrial education. "This new curriculum offered the possibility of adapting black education to the particular needs and interests of the South's dominant-class whites," notes Anderson, for whom the history of black education in the South during and after Reconstruction fits within a larger trend in which American public education, in addition to being the great social leveler, has also been inextricably linked to "the politics of oppression." Yet even if white southerners played an integral role in reshaping the black curriculum, Anderson also notes the irony that the principle of universal public education that most black people advocated during Reconstruction was ultimately undermined not by white southerners but by the Yankee reformer Samuel Chapman Armstrong and the former slave Booker T. Washington.[42]

[41] James D. Anderson, *The Education of Blacks in the South, 1860–1935* (Chapel Hill: University of North Carolina Press, 1988); Heather Andrea Williams, *Self-Taught: African American Education in Slavery and Freedom* (Chapel Hill: University of North Carolina Press, 2005), 4.

[42] Anderson, *Education of Blacks in the South*, 31 and 1; Robert Francis Engs, *Educating the Disfranchised and Disinherited: Samuel Chapman Armstrong and Hampton Institute, 1839–1893* (Knoxville: University of Tennessee Press, 1999).

Debate centered not only on secular education but also on denominational Sunday schools. As Sally G. McMillen demonstrates, many southerners envisioned the Sunday school as a springboard to regional uplift and as a means of improving individual lives while strengthening churches, denominations, and communities. Black Sunday schools in particular provided rudimentary literacy, and they fostered moral reform and anchored a vibrant black community life. Although most black Sunday school advocates agreed on these goals, they also faced debates on other issues—between proponents of a secular curriculum and those of the schools' evangelical mission; between those who wanted to address social and political issues at the Sunday schools and those who feared the possible repercussions of their politicization; and between poorly educated rural preachers and an urban black middle class that wanted to instill bourgeois respectability in children. Sunday schools were of crucial significance to the black community, especially once black access to public education was curtailed after Reconstruction. Yet the needs of the black community were so overwhelming, and the resources so meager, that the multiple goals and functions black people ascribed to the Sunday schools could not but produce disagreements.[43]

These debates over Sunday schools had their equivalents in black religious life after emancipation. Scholarship on the black religious experience has traditionally focused either on the formation of churches as an element of institution building within the black community or on the role of religion, in particular Christianity, as a component of the distinct cultural or spiritual life that African Americans created in the New World. Since the opportunities for slaves in the southern United States to form their own institutions were limited, works on institution building generally concentrated on free blacks, North or South, whereas those on the cultural and spiritual dimensions of black religion looked mostly at the slaves. The abolition of slavery enabled former slaves to create their own institutions, including churches, and this development was chronicled in pre-Foner revisionism on black religious life. Yet in documenting the creation of black churches, pre-Foner revisionists focused mainly on interactions between freedpeople and the northern missionaries who assisted them. Clarence E. Walker and Joe M. Richardson, for example, viewed freedpeople as historical agents, but the key question for each was how freedpeople responded to the proselytizing efforts of northern missionaries.[44] Of less concern were the internal dynamics of the former slaves' religious experiences. Moreover,

[43] Sally G. McMillen, *To Raise up the South: Sunday Schools in Black and White Churches, 1865–1915* (Baton Rouge: Louisiana State University Press, 2001).

[44] Clarence E. Walker, *A Rock in a Weary Land: The African Methodist Episcopal Church during the Civil War and Reconstruction* (Baton Rouge: Louisiana State University Press, 1982); Joe M. Richardson, *Christian Reconstruction: The American Missionary Association and Southern Blacks, 1861–1890* (Athens: University Press of Georgia, 1986).

although these works did not entirely ignore religious tensions among freed-people, they tended to downplay them in favor of unity within the free black community.

Revisionist works since Foner have devoted greater attention to the indigenous quality of black southern religious life after emancipation. In doing so, they have either highlighted conflicts among former slaves over various particular issues or they have emphasized different elements of the former slaves' religious experience, noting by implication that not all freedpeople agreed when it came to religion. Among post-Foner revisionists on black religious life, debates have emerged over two separate but interrelated questions. The first debate is between those who emphasize the black desire for autonomy in running churches, and who underscore the former slaves' distinct experiences while minimizing black-white relations in the emergence of black churches, and those who place greater emphasis on black-white relations, highlighting either white racism as an impetus to the creation of black churches or interracial interaction in their operation. The second debate is between those scholars who stress the black churches' involvement in social and political affairs and those who focus on spiritual matters. Some scholars deal with both questions, while others address only one of them. The interpretations they offer are not framed as absolutes—either autonomy or interaction, either political-social concerns or spiritual matters—but rather are couched in terms of relative emphasis. The differences are a matter of degree, not of kind.

Katharine L. Dvorak emphasizes the ex-slaves' desire for autonomy irrespective of white attitudes and actions. She refutes the notion that the segregation of southern churches during the 1860s merely emulated an earlier northern pattern of segregation, and she contests the view that religious segregation resulted from white southerners ejecting ex-slaves from the churches and thus foreshadowed the larger advent of Jim Crow. Instead, she notes, "the driving force in the segregation of the southern churches was the black Christians' surge toward self-separation acting on their own distinctive appropriation of Christianity."[45] For Dvorak, black southerners were not expelled from the churches but instead voluntarily seceded from them.

A number of other works attribute greater importance to black-white interactions in tracing the racial separation of the churches. These include Larry Eugene Rivers's and Canter Brown Jr.'s examination of the beginnings of the African Methodist Episcopal (AME) Church in Florida, Paul Harvey's study of southern Baptists between the end of the Civil War and the 1920s, and Daniel Stowell's exploration of the southern religious experience during Reconstruction. Rivers and Brown emphasize the desire for black autonomy, but they also

---

[45] Katharine L. Dvorak, *An African-American Exodus: The Segregation of the Southern Churches* (New York: Carlson, 1991), 2.

find evidence of interracial cooperation after the war, as some white Floridians assisted the AME Church even though they opposed its involvement in political affairs. Not until the 1890s, under circumstances much grimmer than those of Reconstruction, did Florida's AME Church face the challenge of survival with little or no white support.[46] Both Harvey and Stowell relate the familiar story of ex-slaves founding their own churches, yet they also maintain that separatism was tempered by the possibilities for black-white interaction, as black southerners, despite their desire for autonomy, recognized that they could not undertake the monumental task of church building without white assistance. For Harvey, black separatism occurred only after several failed efforts at biracial religious cooperation, as many Baptist leaders believed that the end of slavery might inaugurate new possibilities for race relations, and even then the practical realities of church building, as well as a common faith, necessitated a degree of racial interaction, as black and white Baptists found themselves undergoing similar experiences and parallel developments.[47] Stowell also explores divisions within the black community and the possibilities for interracial religious cooperation, but he concludes that even during Reconstruction, racial and sectional differences ultimately trumped similarities. "On the principal issues of religious reconstruction," he notes, "evangelicals did not forge bonds of gender, class, or denomination that transcended the cleavages of race and region."[48]

Several recent works, while hardly denying the spiritual component of the freedpeople's religious experience, emphasize instead the black churches' involvement in social and political affairs. In doing so, they address the internal strains and conflicts that black congregations and denominations inevitably faced as they concerned themselves with secular matters. Rivers and Brown ascribe crucial importance to the AME Church in the political mobilization of Florida's black community and the creation of the state's Republican Party. But combining religion and politics also had detrimental effects, as the party's bitter factional disputes infected the AME Church, which further contended with such issues as temperance, women's involvement in church affairs, rivalries among church leaders and between local church authorities and bishops, and regional conflicts within a geographically diverse state. William E. Montgomery similarly sees the church as the foundational cornerstone of the free black community after emancipation and at the same time uses the church as a window onto intraracial divisions and conflicts. These conflicts—both between

[46] Larry Eugene Rivers and Canter Brown Jr., *Laborers in the Vineyard of the Lord: The Beginnings of the AME Church in Florida, 1865–1895* (Gainesville: University Press of Florida, 2001).

[47] Paul Harvey, *Redeeming the South: Religious Cultures and Racial Identities among Southern Baptists, 1865–1925* (Chapel Hill: University of North Carolina Press, 1997).

[48] Daniel W. Stowell, *Rebuilding Zion: The Religious Reconstruction of the South, 1863–1877* (New York: Oxford University Press, 1998), 8.

and within the various denominations—resulted less from theological or litur-gical issues than from economic, political, and generational differences within the black community.[49]

The social-political approach to the black religious experience has received its strongest articulation from Reginald F. Hildebrand, who examines the debates among black Methodists—and by implication within the black community at large—"over different interpretations of the meaning of freedom." Arguing that no important theological or liturgical issues separated the various branches of Methodism, Hildebrand identifies three distinct modes of thought among Meth-odist preachers in defining freedom: an accommodationist "new paternalism"; an evangelical, proto–black nationalist or black separatist vein that he calls the "Gospel of Freedom"; and a radical "integrationist" strand that advocated dis-mantling the racial caste system. When former slaves made a religious affili-ation, Hildebrand insists, they were subscribing to one of these definitions of freedom. Downplaying both the theological component of black religious life and the importance of secular, political leaders to the former slaves, Hildebrand maintains that freedpeople looked to their ministers as much to articulate the meaning of freedom as to evangelize.[50]

Even those scholars who emphasize the black churches' involvement in secu-lar matters acknowledge that former slaves continued to draw spiritual suste-nance from Christianity after emancipation. Other scholars either stake out a middle ground in the secular-spiritual debate or focus more attention on the theological or liturgical issues that concerned former slaves. Stephen Ward Angell's study of AME bishop Henry McNeal Turner argues that Turner and the AME Church strove both to propagate the gospel and to foster an autonomous black community. Fulfilling this dual function engendered disputes—between northern and southern Methodists as well as among southern black Method-ists, and over both secular and spiritual issues—that Turner was frequently called upon to mediate.[51] Similarly, Dvorak devotes considerable attention to the theological content of black religion even as she documents the black churches' involvement in secular and political matters.

By contrast, Christopher H. Owen's study of Methodism in nineteenth-cen-tury Georgia acknowledges that black Methodists used religion to buttress the black community's political and economic aspirations, but he cautions against the tendency to emphasize the political implications of black religious experi-

[49] William E. Montgomery, *Under Their Own Vine and Fig Tree: The African-American Church in the South, 1865–1900* (Baton Rouge: Louisiana State University Press, 1993).

[50] Reginald F. Hildebrand, *The Times Were Strange and Stirring: Methodist Preachers and the Crisis of Emancipation* (Durham, N.C.: Duke University Press, 1995), xviii.

[51] Stephen Ward Angell, *Bishop Henry McNeal Turner and African-American Religion in the South* (Knoxville: University of Tennessee Press, 1992).

ence or to draw connections to an incipient black nationalism. Recognizing intraracial tensions over both the secular and the sacred, Owen nonetheless maintains that Methodism ultimately provided, more than anything else, doctrinal unity for its black adherents.[52] Likewise, Daniel Stowell recognizes the practical difficulties and the secular issues that former slaves confronted in creating their own churches, but he emphasizes the providential meaning they gave to the war and its outcome. Whereas white southerners saw religious Reconstruction in terms of restoration and white northerners saw it in terms of rejuvenation or purification, freedpeople viewed religious Reconstruction as an opportunity to create an entirely new religious experience. "Enabled for the first time to give expression to their own religious ideals," he notes, "they set to work establishing a new and separate religious life for themselves."[53]

Community

It is perhaps paradoxical that while a major trend in the historical writing on black economic, social, and cultural life since Foner's *Reconstruction* has been to explore relations among former slaves, resulting in a tendency to accentuate conflict and tension, recent works on the free black community as a whole have generally inclined toward emphasizing its essential unity. Ever since the concept of a distinct slave community first emerged in the historical literature during the 1960s, scholars have used "community" in two different but complementary ways: in a geographical sense, to describe slave life within a specific locality or region; and in a broader, cultural sense, to depict the shared historical experiences of all slaves. This approach has also applied to the post-emancipation period; thus, we can speak of a free black community within a particular geographical setting or as a larger, cultural entity that embraces, at some basic level, the diverse experiences of all ex-slaves. In either sense, and for both slaves and freedpeople, the idea of community presumes a fundamental harmony— even taking into account regional, ethnic, or demographic variations—in the history of people of African descent in the United States. For all the complexity, diversity, and conflict that scholars have documented among black people, and for all the connections that scholars have established between the experiences of African Americans and those of other peoples who have had to struggle for access to the American political and economic mainstream, African Americans share a unique experience—one rooted in enslavement and systematic racial

[52] Christopher H. Owen, *The Sacred Flame of Love: Methodism and Society in Nineteenth-Century Georgia* (Athens: University of Georgia Press, 1998).

[53] Stowell, *Rebuilding Zion*, 7.

subjugation—that no other indigenous or immigrant group in the United States has endured.[54]

Recent works that examine the free black community within a particular geographical setting—whether a single plantation, a locality, or a state—take into account internal tensions but emphasize interracial conflict and black solidarity. In her study of one Louisiana plantation over several generations, Laurie A. Wilkie shows how black people constructed multiple identities based upon gender, race, class, and ethnicity that were "expressed simultaneously in different areas of social life." She documents the web of institutions and networks that former slaves created after emancipation, centered around church, school, and workplace, as well as such customary practices as bartering, caring for the sick, and child-rearing, that helped forge a community. Moreover, in noting that "[t]he story of plantation life is one of cultural clashes, the perspective of the African Americans versus the perspectives of the European Americans," Wilkie not only gives priority to interracial over intraracial conflict but also recognizes multiple white perspectives while positing a unitary African-American perspective.[55] Patricia C. Click's history of the Freedmen's Colony at Roanoke Island during and after the Civil War likewise devotes considerable attention to conflicts between former slaves and the host of northern missionaries and federal officials who were attempting to assist them. Click relates a familiar story of conflicting hopes and aspirations, but she also shows that the black drive to create an autonomous economic and cultural life predated the arrival of missionaries and reformers. Indeed, northern missionaries did not engender but rather attempted to reshape—in accordance with their own ideals—the black community's desire for an autonomous economic and cultural life.[56] Examining the black community within one particular state (Maryland)

[54] Anthony E. Kaye has recently suggested that "neighborhood"—understood as a cluster of interconnected farms and plantations within a discrete geographical setting—better describes the mechanism by which slaves created a collective identity, and he notes that for the post-emancipation period the concept of neighborhood offers a way of combining the geographical and cultural meanings of community. After emancipation, not only did black people's geographical conception of neighborhood expand but, as freedom brought unprecedented opportunities for geographical and social mobility, former slaves also redefined neighborhood to reflect a collective identity that transcended particular localities. Kaye intriguingly proposes that fruitful results might be yielded by applying the concept of neighborhood to black political, economic, and social and cultural life during and after Reconstruction. "Neighbourhoods and Solidarity in the Natchez District of Mississippi: Rethinking the Antebellum Slave Community," *Slavery and Abolition* 23 (April 2002): 1–24.

[55] Laurie A. Wilkie, *Creating Freedom: Material Culture and African American Identity at Oakley Plantation, Louisiana, 1840–1950* (Baton Rouge: Louisiana State University Press, 2000), xv, xx.

[56] Patricia C. Click, *Time Full of Trial: The Roanoke Island Freedmen's Colony, 1862–1867* (Chapel Hill: University of North Carolina Press, 2001).

allows Richard Paul Fuke to explore in all its dimensions the former slaves' multifaceted campaign to achieve autonomy. By documenting the black experience in the realms of work, property, family, church, school, benevolent and fraternal societies, and legal and political rights, Fuke depicts a unified black community that faced challenges not only from white conservatives but also from white radicals unable to envision a genuinely meaningful black freedom, whose policies "contained inner limitations that undermined the very people they were intended to help."[57]

Steven Hahn's *A Nation under Our Feet* (2003), the most ambitious work that deals with the era of Reconstruction since Foner's *Reconstruction* and one of the most important works on African-American history to appear in the past two decades, takes the notion of a black cultural community to its logical conclusion by arguing that this community formed the wellspring of a separate black nation.[58] If Foner brought to a culmination nearly half a century of revisionist scholarship on Reconstruction, Hahn likewise brings to fruition an entire generation of historiography that has taken black historical agency as its point of departure. Hahn attends to the potential for conflict within the black community, but infinitely more important to his analysis is black people's common historical heritage. All the particular elements of what has come to be known as the free black community—land and labor, family and kinship, church and religion, schools and education, mutual aid and racial uplift, political power and legal rights, paramilitary organizations and armed self-defense—were part of the larger processes of political mobilization and development of a collective consciousness. For Hahn, the incipient black nation that was born of slavery and came of age during Reconstruction further matured with emigrationism and biracial politics during the late nineteenth century before reaching full bloom with the Great Migration and the emergence of Marcus Garvey in the twentieth century. Yet Hahn also attributes a dual meaning to "nation." Former slaves and their descendants not only created their own cultural nation but also played a central role in reconstituting the United States as a nation that, however briefly, was committed to the legal and political equality of all citizens and that would eventually have to fulfill this commitment.

Although Hahn employs black agency as his main underlying assumption, he reaches conclusions very much at odds with the historical literature of the past twenty years on black life after emancipation. To be sure, he relies upon the findings of the most recent scholarship, but his focus on black unity and collective self-determination is more characteristic of the pre-Foner literature than of

---

[57] Richard Paul Fuke, *Imperfect Equality: African Americans and the Confines of White Racial Attitudes in Post-Emancipation Maryland* (New York: Fordham University Press, 1991), xv–xvi.

[58] Steven Hahn, *A Nation under Our Feet: Black Political Struggles in the Rural South from Slavery to the Great Migration* (Cambridge, Mass.: Harvard University Press, 2003).

scholarship since Foner. Moreover, the entire tenor of the book—from its open-ing sentence to its concluding paragraph—has an almost heroic quality that is strikingly different from the approach taken in almost all of the works that have been considered in this essay. Hahn seems less intent on rebutting or refuting the more recent scholarship than he does on incorporating it into a larger perspec-tive that allows for internal diversity but ultimately emphasizes the centrality of slavery to the African-American experience. By "looking out from slavery," Hahn traces the origins of the African-American nation not to the Civil War and emancipation but to the antebellum period. For Hahn, slaves were politi-cal beings who, despite their ostensible powerlessness, had created an incipient political movement and had achieved an embryonic political consciousness that not only enabled them to resist their enslavement but also prepared them for the challenges of freedom. Despite the shifting political landscape and the con-stantly changing circumstances of the post–Civil War decades, everything that African Americans did had its origins in the slave experience, which "was not mere background or prologue; it was formative and foundational."[59] It seems safe to say that Hahn's work for years to come will frame the field of African-American history during the half century after emancipation, but the question remains exactly how. Just as some scholars wondered what more could be said about Reconstruction after Foner, it remains to be seen in what future directions scholars might take black agency as an analytical tool or the concept of a uni-fied black community in the nineteenth-century South following Hahn.

One possibility, which Hahn does not address, is for historians to consider more carefully than they have previously how the former slaves' efforts to con-struct an autonomous cultural life, while laying the necessary groundwork for future civil rights struggles, could possibly have undermined the fight for politi-cal and economic integration and thus contributed to Reconstruction's more immediate failure. Attributing responsibility to black people for the failure of Reconstruction is not to suggest the historiographical equivalent of "blaming the victim." Nor is it to propose that historians face the unattractive choice of either abandoning agency as an analytical approach or pushing it to the point where the only room left is to fault the freedpeople for their own predicament. But if slaves and former slaves are to be seen as historical agents, and if some measure of responsibility for one's destiny is implicit in agency, then devoting greater attention to the role African Americans may have played in Reconstruc-tion's demise would seem to afford one possibility for breaking new interpretive ground. At the very least, such an approach would provide a fresh perspective on the seemingly age-old questions of "why Reconstruction failed" and "what were Reconstruction's long-term accomplishments," questions that have domi-nated revisionist historiography. Ideally, such an approach might even challenge

[59] Hahn, Nation, 6.

scholars of Reconstruction and of the black experience in the postbellum South to pose entirely new questions about topics and issues that are still relevant to contemporary discussions of race and that continue to be endlessly fascinating in their own right.

In adopting such a strategy, scholars could follow one of two different paths. They could continue to explore—as revisionists since Foner have already done—how divisions and conflicts within the black community might have contributed to the undermining of Reconstruction. Alternatively, while positing an essential unity to the black community, they could speculate upon the unintended consequences of the goals former slaves pursued or the methods they used in pursuing them. This second path raises the troubling issue of passing judgment upon people in the past with the benefit of hindsight, something historians are generally loath to do. Historians' aversion to making such judgments, however, should not blind them to possible alternative historical outcomes. The essence of agency is that men and women make their own history, however limited the options available to them may be. In his classic *Roll, Jordan, Roll* (1974), Eugene D. Genovese provocatively argued that the slaves' rich cultural life provided psychological sustenance in the face of unspeakable oppression while also enabling the slaves to lay the foundations for a modern black nation that would later come to fruition. Yet even as it did these things, "the world the slaves made" also left its creators without the wherewithal to challenge fundamentally the slave system that oppressed them.[60] Notwithstanding the criticism leveled against Genovese, his thesis immeasurably advanced our understanding of slavery in general and of the slaves in particular. Genovese showed that if slaves in the U.S. South ultimately "failed," in however limited a sense, to overthrow slavery, their failure was not predetermined but resulted from distinct historical circumstances. Similarly, neither was the failure of Reconstruction—that is, the failure to integrate former slaves into the mainstream of American political and economic life—inevitable. Instead, it occurred for particular, historically specific reasons. Thus, if scholars of Reconstruction are not to abandon black historical agency as an analytical tool, they must at some point reconcile the self-determination implicit in agency with the consequent need to assess what responsibility these historical agents may bear for Reconstruction's failure.

[60] Eugene D. Genovese, *Roll, Jordan, Roll: The World the Slaves Made* (New York: Pantheon Books, 1974).

3

NORTH AND WEST
OF RECONSTRUCTION

Studies in Political Economy

HEATHER COX RICHARDSON

In 1898, Elizabeth Cady Stanton thought back over the events of Reconstruction and recalled how the emancipation of southern slaves had required a broad reworking of American government and citizenship. All inhabitants of the nation—men and women; black, white, Indian, and immigrant; North, South, and West—had to reconsider what it meant to be an American. "The reconstruction of the South," she wrote, "involved the reconsideration of the principles of our Government and the natural rights of man. The nation's heart was thrilled with prolonged debates in Congress and State legislatures, in the pulpits and public journals, and at every fireside on these vital questions."[1] The question of the nation's political economy was a critical one in the postwar years, for the nation had to work out a number of central problems in American society. The war had secured the triumph of free labor throughout the United States, but how that would actually play out in everyday life was unclear. It was inevitable that the establishment of free labor would require the involvement of the newly powerful government, but how and to what extent was also unclear. At the same time, the war had guaranteed that the Plains West would be settled by eastern Americans, but how free labor and the government would operate in the new region was, once again, unclear.

Political debates of the postwar years centered on these questions, and historians writing during the late nineteenth century, most of whom were politicians themselves, made these questions the heart of their analysis of Reconstruction. In his *Twenty Years of Congress* (1884–86), Republican senator James G. Blaine argued that the Republicans had used an increasingly strong national govern-

---

[1] Elizabeth Cady Stanton, *Eighty Years and More: Reminiscences, 1815–1897* (1898; reprint, Boston: Northeastern University Press, 1993), 241.

66

ment to defend the rights of African Americans to join the free labor economy; in *Three Decades of Federal Legislation, 1855–1885* (1885) Democratic representative Samuel Sullivan Cox of New York countered with accusations that Republicans had deliberately increased the power of the government and corrupted black voters to hand wealth and power to the very rich while crushing the average white worker. Southern senators led by Hilary Herbert weighed in on the debate in 1890 with their *Why the Solid South?* insisting that postwar southern Black Codes had simply mirrored northern apprenticeship laws and quite reasonably were designed to guarantee that men unprepared for the duties of citizenship were restrained from causing trouble to the community. Labor leader Terrence V. Powderly had his own version of this history; his *Thirty Years of Labor, 1859–1889* (1890) insisted that workers were excellent citizens, and had fought throughout the postwar years to return America to the ideal free labor state that had been corrupted by big business. To this debate over the relationship of government and citizens, Theodore Roosevelt and Frederick Jackson Turner added the argument that it was the West, not the East, that produced good citizens and an ideal American government. At the same time, woman suffragists like Elizabeth Cady Stanton insisted that the nation must include women as political actors.[2]

Considering the simmering anger in these histories as their authors tried to change contemporary politics, perhaps it was just as well that twentieth-century historians turned to other aspects of the postwar years. The Progressives focused on the misdeeds of governments and business and the heroism of those who opposed them, but by the second half of the twentieth century, historians were focusing on social history and the lives of workers and African Americans more often than they examined big business and government. Eric Foner's *Reconstruction* (1988) was the culmination of this mid-twentieth-century revisionism, firmly establishing the centrality of the black experience in the post–Civil War years and the importance of class struggle in Reconstruction.[3]

Reconstruction's treatment of the nation's political economy reflected twentieth-century historical work that emphasized the essential moderation of Reconstruction and the growing class struggles of the era. Foner traced the rapid postwar eclipse of those principled radical Republicans who were dedicated to free labor

---

[2] James G. Blaine, *Twenty Years of Congress: From Lincoln to Garfield*, 2 vols. (Norwich, Conn.: Henry Bill, 1884–86); Samuel Sullivan Cox, *Three Decades of Federal Legislation, 1855–1885*, 2 vols. (Providence, R.I.: J. A. and R. A. Reid, 1885); Hilary A. Herbert et al., *Why the Solid South? Or, Reconstruction and Its Results* (Baltimore: R. H. Woodward, 1890); Terrence V. Powderly, *Thirty Years of Labor, 1859–1889* (Philadelphia: T. V. Powderly, 1890); Theodore Roosevelt, *Hunting Trips of a Ranchman* (New York: Putnam's, 1885); Frederick Jackson Turner, *The Significance of the Frontier in American History* (Madison: State Historical Society of Wisconsin, 1894).

[3] Eric Foner, *Reconstruction: America's Unfinished Revolution, 1863–1877* (New York: Harper and Row, 1988).

and black rights. Professional politicians interested in patronage and the spoils of office came to dominate the Republican Party at the same time that Democrats desperate to regain control of offices and racial affairs downplayed their continuing insistence on white supremacy. The parties drifted toward a middle ground, with Republicans abandoning their black allies and Democrats using new language of good government to reach a common ground that permitted business to dominate the nation. After a brief postwar recession, industry boomed as railroad corporations operated in new national and international markets. With remarkable speed, the South and West came under the domination of eastern capitalists, whose efforts to "uplift" freedpeople and "civilize" the Indians reflected their own position at the hub of American economy and society.

Foner's *Reconstruction* covered familiar territory, but it also pointed the way to a new approach to the postwar years, one that reflected the concerns of Reconstruction-era historians. Two of the themes he highlighted—"the consolidation of a new class structure" and the "emergence of an activist national state"—were significant in the North and West as well as the South. The rise of an activist government "possessing vastly expanded authority and a new set of purposes, including an unprecedented commitment to the idea of a national citizenship whose equal rights belonged to all Americans regardless of race," meant that federal-state relations changed fundamentally and American citizenship was redefined. By 1877, he argued, this expansion of the government had been divorced from the interests of African Americans and harnessed to the interests of property owners. When "local authorities and middle-class citizens" could not maintain order during the Great Railroad Strike of that year, federal troops did. By 1877, Foner concluded, it was clear that "the Civil War era had tied the new industrial bourgeoisie to the Republican party and national state."[4]

Foner did not make his observations in either a historical or a historiographical vacuum. The Reagan Revolution brought with it intense scrutiny of the government and its relationship to American citizens, and scholars were not immune to this impulse. Political scientist Richard Bensel, in *Sectionalism and American Political Development* (1984), had reinvigorated studies of the American state by arguing that continuing economic conflict between geographic regions in the nation drove development of political parties and ideologies and the growth of the state.[5] Then, in 1991, western historian Richard White spoke directly to twentieth-century westerners who were decrying an activist government when he declared that "the American West, more than any other section of the United States, is a creation not so much of individual or local efforts, but of federal efforts." His book *It's Your Misfortune and None of My Own* pointed out that the federal government paved the way for settlers to pour West; it used

[4] Foner, *Reconstruction*, xxvi, 584, 587.
[5] Richard Franklin Bensel, *Sectionalism and American Political Development* (Madison: University of Wisconsin Press, 1984).

agents to explore the region, the army to conquer it, and federal bureaucrats to administer it. At the same time, as it developed and governed the West, the state took to itself more power and influence. The U.S. Army was largely a western institution, and federal bureaucracies like the Land Office, the Bureau of Indian Affairs, and so on, were western institutions. "In some basic ways the federal government created itself in the West," White wrote. "The West provided an arena for the expansion of federal powers that was initially available nowhere else in the country. By exercising power, the government increased its power."[6]

Since 1988, examinations of the relations between labor and capital, and between the state and citizens, have produced new understandings of the post–Civil War years. Because historians have come at these questions from a variety of different perspectives, though, it is hard to divide their work into discrete schools that address specific aspects of the question of northern political economy. Few studies of the relationship between labor and capital are not concerned with control of the state, for example; and few studies of state development avoid the question of who developed it. In addition, as White signaled, those new understandings are vastly enriched by those historians who have been studying the way these issues played out in the West. Western studies are critically important to our larger understanding of Reconstruction, and much work remains to be done as we learn from the West and tie its lessons into a national story. A broader perspective on the period will nurture the questions historians are currently asking. We are increasingly looking at the late nineteenth century as the period in which America constructed itself into a new nation after the bloody Civil War, deciding what America would stand for and who would be a welcome participant in that nation. In the years from 1865 to 1920, the American electorate expanded from its antebellum limit of white propertied men to include African Americans, immigrants, and women, even as voting restrictions controlled just which members of those groups would ultimately enjoy suffrage. What we now know as "Reconstruction" is being redefined as the Era of Citizenship, when Americans defined who would be citizens and what citizenship meant.

Individuals and the Government

At the heart of the question of the nation's political economy was the fight over who would control the state. Did the triumph of free labor during the war mean that America would develop a government that worked on behalf of wage laborers? Or did it mean that free labor's emphasis on the protection of prop-

---

[6] Richard White, *"It's Your Misfortune and None of My Own": A New History of the American West* (Norman: University of Oklahoma Press, 1991), 57–59.

erty would dominate government action in the postwar years? This question, of course, depended on who was doing the voting to elect representatives to the government, and different interests in society had strong ideas about just who qualified as a voter. Taking their cue from labor historians, late-twentieth-century students of these issues tended to focus on how they played out in struggles between organized industrial workers and their employers.

In 1967, labor historian David Montgomery set the historiographical stage for explorations of the struggle over who would control the post–Civil War state. His *Beyond Equality* (1967) met head-on the question of how the Republicans who fought to spread the idea of the dignity of labor came to abandon laborers in the immediate postwar years. Republicans recoiled from labor activism, he determined, and quickly abandoned their early rhetoric about the primacy of labor in American life. In the late twentieth century, a number of historians followed Montgomery and the similar conclusions in Foner's *Reconstruction* to look at how a dominant business or social elite turned against workers in the postwar years. While they came at the question from different perspectives, they tended to focus on eastern cities or areas of late-nineteenth-century labor struggles.[7]

Labor historians Grace Palladino and William E. Forbath fit this model, examining state repression of workers' movements. Palladino's *Another Civil War* (1990) found the state actively oppressing workers in the wartime Pennsylvania coal fields through the use of police, and federal and state troops, as a capitalist emphasis on private property overrode traditional notions of American republicanism.[8] Forbath's *Law and the Shaping of the American Labor Movement* (1991) revealed an even more repressive state. While Palladino showed government policy as an anchor to prevent worker agitation, Forbath argued that the state's pressure on labor activists had, in fact, changed the labor movement itself. Court interpretations of late-nineteenth-century law—the Sherman Anti-Trust Act, for example—benefited corporate employers and forced the American labor movement to ask for the freedom to negotiate contracts without government involvement. Indeed, he argued, the demands, tactics, and limits of the American labor movement itself were constructed in large part by the state's service to industrial capitalism.[9]

At the same time that Palladino and Forbath were examining the mechanics by which the state was harnessed to the services of industrial capitalists, schol-

---

[7] David Montgomery, *Beyond Equality: Labor and the Radical Republicans, 1862–1872* (New York: Knopf, 1967).

[8] Grace Palladino, *Another Civil War: Labor, Capital and the State in the Anthracite Regions of Pennsylvania, 1840–1868* (Urbana: University of Illinois Press, 1990). See also David Montgomery, *The Fall of the House of Labor: The Workplace, the State, and American Labor Activism, 1865–1925* (Cambridge: Cambridge University Press, 1987).

[9] William E. Forbath, *Law and the Shaping of the American Labor Movement* (Cambridge, Mass.: Harvard University Press, 1991).

ars studying the concept of "whiteness" in American history tried to explain the historic repression of African Americans. Led by Alexander Saxton and David Roediger, this historiographical school argued that racism determined the basic structures of American society and tried to find plausible explanations of the ways ideas about race served a ruling class. In *The Rise and Fall of the White Republic* (1990), Saxton argued that racist mid-nineteenth-century Republicans had harnessed the federal government to industrial capitalism before the Civil War. Then, as Americans moved west, racism became a large part of Republican legitimacy, sustaining the interests of "US ruling classes." Workers were complicit in the ideology that racism served, preventing the formation of a class consciousness that could overcome racial boundaries. "Wealth, privilege, power, tend to narrow the vision of ruling classes and their mercenary retainers," Saxton concluded.[10]

The following year, Roediger's *The Wages of Whiteness* (1991) went further, exploring whiteness as a creation of the working class itself, rather than as an ideology imposed upon it by elites seeking to divide the working classes. Grounding his study in Marxism and Freudian psychology, he argued that "whiteness was a way in which white workers responded to a fear of dependency on wage labor and to the necessities of capitalist work discipline." The way it happened was this: the heritage of the Revolution made men aspire to independence even as the new nation depended on slavery and wage labor. To distinguish themselves from slaves, white workers embraced the idea of free labor and denigrated black slaves as lazy, preindustrial "others." When emancipation challenged this construction, calling into question the "tendency to equate Blackness and servility," African Americans no longer provided a clear contrast to white workers. But there was not enough disruption in race positions to permit a complete rethinking of black/white relations. Seeing African Americans as lazy enabled whites to justify their own positions as steady wage laborers.[11]

The methodology of Saxton's and Roediger's rather impressionistic studies contrasted sharply both with that of Palladino and Forbath and with that of a number of urban histories digging at the question of how elites had come to take control of American society from workers after the Civil War. Quite close readings of eastern cities, primarily New York City and Chicago, yielded up insights on how politics and social connections had reinforced economic divisions to create a postwar world in which workers had less control of the state

---

[10] Alexander Saxton, *The Rise and Fall of the White Republic: Class Politics and Mass Culture in Nineteenth-Century America* (London: Verso, 1990), 387, 389.

[11] David Roediger, *The Wages of Whiteness: Race and the Making of the American Working Class* (London: Verso, 1991), 13, 174. For more on the historiography of whiteness, see Peter Kolchin, "Whiteness Studies: The New History of Race in America," *Journal of American History* 89 (June 2002): 154–173; and Eric Arnesen, "Up from Exclusion: Black and White Workers, Race, and the State of Labor History," *Reviews in American History* 26 (1998): 146–174.

than their employers did. Iver Bernstein and Sven Beckert tore into the history of postwar New York City; Robin Einhorn and Karen Sawislak investigated Chicago; and while their conclusions focused on different aspects of the question of elite domination of the state, those conclusions reinforced each other.[12]

It makes sense to begin with Bernstein's *The New York City Draft Riots* (1990), for not only was this book the first of the postwar urban studies to be published but also it tied the growth of the postwar elite into wartime changes in the balance of power between local and federal governments. Bernstein argued that the roots of the social and ethnic tensions of postwar New York City lay in the antebellum years and were exacerbated by the war, when New Yorkers began actively to debate who should control the city and the nation; whose interests the government should represent; and what, exactly, was "justice" in midcentury America. In 1863, a new federal conscription law forced this debate into the streets by pitting poor white draftees and local Democratic politicians against federal draft officers and supporters of a powerful national government, generally both African Americans and wealthy Republicans. Which group would manage to restore order would help to determine who would retain power in the postwar years. In the aftermath of the riots, Tammany Hall politicians managed to garner support by promising to broker between the different interest groups in the city, but in 1872, this rapprochement disintegrated when the end of sectional hostilities permitted the "better classes" of the city to work together to impose order on the increasingly assertive labor movement.[13]

Sven Beckert's *The Monied Metropolis* (2001) also began with the premise that elites had taken control of government in post–Civil War America, and set out to trace how they did so. Beckert asserted that, after the war, a powerful, self-conscious New York City bourgeoisie came to dictate the policies of the government in the interest of capital. While they had been divided before the war, capital-owning New Yorkers—"merchants, industrialists, bankers, real estate speculators, rentiers, and professionals," as Beckert termed them—overcame antebellum differences to form their own social networks and institutions as they came to articulate a vision of their own dominance in the economy, politics, and society of the nation. "Structurally dominant" by the end of the nineteenth century, Beckert asserted, bourgeois New Yorkers ran the country.[14]

Beckert's bourgeois elite did not spring spontaneously from capitalism, though. Rather, it was a direct product of the class collisions of the postwar years, as members of the New York City bourgeoisie self-consciously defined

[12] On postwar New York City, see also David Quigley, *Second Founding: New York City, Reconstruction, and the Making of American Democracy* (New York: Hill and Wang, 2003).

[13] Iver Bernstein, *The New York City Draft Riots: Their Significance for American Society and Politics in the Age of the Civil War* (New York: Oxford University Press, 1990).

[14] Sven Beckert, *The Monied Metropolis: New York City and the Consolidation of the American Bourgeoisie, 1850–1896* (Cambridge: Cambridge University Press, 2001).

themselves against the wage laborers they perceived as a threat to capitalist society. As they did so, they came to advocate certain kinds of political activity and economic regulation that would bolster their hegemony. To calm the ferocious economic competition that threatened to destroy them, they expanded the administrative capacity of the state. To protect their property from the working masses, they gave to the state the power to regulate society. In Beckert's view, the postwar New York City bourgeoisie ushered in the era of corporate capitalism that characterized the Progressive Era.

Bernstein and Beckert's investigations of the construction of a powerful elite that controlled government for its own good raised a number of questions. If it were true that a group of political elites and industrialists ultimately commandeered the government from a broader polity, how had they justified their coup? Careful studies of Chicago by Robin L. Einhorn and Karen Sawislak took on this question. Einhorn's *Property Rules* (1991) explored how Chicago city leaders could rationalize the prostration of the urban poor under the feet of late-nineteenth-century industrialists, who, for example, poured toxic waste into ghettos with impunity. Examining not so much the various divisions of society or the specifics of government power as the intellectual justification for elite control of society, Einhorn concluded that nineteenth-century Americans believed that those who owned property in the city literally owned the city, and that government owed to them—and only to them—protection and encouragement. Einhorn argued that what had previously been interpreted as "progressive" reforms benefiting the public in general rather than the elite were, in fact, an effective new way for elites to use public money for their own purposes. By the late nineteenth century, this system redistributed wealth upwardly, using public monies to fund public policy decisions that were made by a small number of elite players and powerful special interests. Ultimately, she suggested, the system developed at the municipal level mirrored that at the national level, firmly placing industrial elites in the control of American government.[15]

Sawislak's examination of responses to the Chicago fire of 1871 also sought to discover the thinking of different factions seeking to control urban government, but dug deeper than Einhorn had done into their interactions during a short, intense period to examine the process by which elites gained control of government. Sawislak's *Smouldering City* (1995) found various factions squaring off over relief efforts and urban reconstruction, just as factions had squared off during the New York City draft riots. Unlike Bernstein, though, Sawislak was concerned more with untangling the ways in which groups won and exercised power than with their identities. How, she asked, were "values such as justice, equality, or government by law" translated into "relations of power"? In the

---

[15] Robin L. Einhorn, *Property Rules: Political Economy in Chicago, 1833–1872* (Chicago: University of Chicago Press, 1991).

aftermath of the fire, Chicagoans had to determine how their community would handle charity, labor relations, morality, political authority, and state power. Different groups disagreed about these meanings, but it was ultimately native-born businessmen, Sawislak argued, who exercised the most influence in determining the way the city would address these questions. Their key to assuming control of the postwar city was their ability to claim that they spoke most clearly for the "public interest." The events in Chicago after the fire revealed the growing identification of the free market and liberal individualism with true democracy and urban order.[16]

Inevitably, studies based on the idea that a developing state came to be controlled by elite Americans invited contradiction. Was postwar America really dominated by capitalist elites who forced repressive wage labor on resisting workers? Some historians were not convinced. Coming from very different fields, both Lawrence B. Glickman and Alessandra Lorini presented an alternative version of the power of laborers and African Americans in the postwar state. Glickman's *A Living Wage* (1997) confronted the understanding that the post–Civil War years saw the unrelieved repression of workers at the hands of capitalists. Working from the new field of consumer history, Glickman straddled labor history, economic history, and cultural history to turn on its head the traditional argument of labor historians that workers' organizations in the late nineteenth century abandoned class identity to accept the inevitability of capitalist domination. Glickman argued that workers themselves helped to develop the idea that wages should be determined by human need, rather than productive value and market forces.

Glickman explored the identity of wage laborers as consumers who worked to shape the market for their own benefit. Wage labor allowed increased consumption in the late nineteenth and early twentieth centuries, he explained, and workers increasingly defined themselves as "proud citizen-workers earning living wages." Unlike previous generations, wage laborers by the end of the nineteenth century believed that working for "a living wage" was liberation, not slavery. They came to believe that a living wage should replace individual proprietorship as self-respecting wage earners both supported their families and enjoyed "the means and the leisure to participate in the civil life of the nation." In an era where the traditional hallmarks of citizenship—individual proprietorship and self-sufficiency—were unrealistic, Glickman's workers reconstructed their ideal of citizenship around the ideas of high wages and consumption.[17]

[16] Karen Sawislak, *Smouldering City: Chicagoans and the Great Fire, 1871–1874* (Chicago: University of Chicago Press, 1995).

[17] Lawrence B. Glickman, *A Living Wage: American Workers and the Making of Consumer Society* (Ithaca, N.Y.: Cornell University Press, 1997), 2, 3.

Alessandra Lorini also challenged the idea that elites had dominated the post-war era. Her *Rituals of Race* (1999) explored the quest of African Americans for inclusion in American ideals of liberty and equality—despite the limitations of traditional politics—through their use of public space. Working from a theoretical perspective, Lorini set out to examine "public culture, broadly defined, as a conflictual space in which gender, race, and class alliances are made and remade in the ongoing battle for the expansion of the boundaries of democracy." As African American rights were curtailed after the brief triumphs of early Reconstruction, she wrote, men and women created "autonomous spaces" in which to protest in favor of participatory democracy.[18] Lorini's work embraced the growing idea that everything is political, even events or actions that have traditionally been considered outside politics; her examination of public culture drew on parades, demonstrations, theater, association meetings, exhibitions, and so on. In these venues, she explained, those excluded from traditional politics worked for a broader democracy, challenging dominant groups in society.

Did capitalists control late-nineteenth-century America? Were nonelites excluded from participation in politics? Glickman and Lorini both show the need for a reexamination of the premise that elites dictated politics and the economy after the Civil War. Glickman's understanding of wage laborers as consumers in addition to their identity as employees and Lorini's astute observation that politics is about presence, pressure, and perception as well as the polls require an important reshuffling of our understanding of power relationships.

The complexities of the relationship between workers and capital after the Civil War and the implications of that relationship for the development of the state continue to be promising fields for exploration. How did workers themselves see their relationship with employers, especially those workers who did not identify with organized labor—strikebreakers, for example, or skilled workers? In addition to more general studies, it would be interesting to see major new biographies of Terrence V. Powderly and Samuel Gompers that examine not only the relative moderation that made their reputations suffer at the end of the twentieth century but also their interest in western workers as integral parts of the national labor question. What about industrialists themselves, and their supporters? Andrew Carnegie is certainly worth a reexamination, both a defender of labor organization and one of its chief opponents, both a champion of American individualism and a scathing critic of its corruption of the Philippines. What, too, of the Pinkertons, widely interpreted as pro-business thugs yet often made up of working-class men who defended their actions as promoting their own interests? How did someone like Charlie Siringo—individualist cowboy and Pinkerton spook—think about his life?

---

[18] Alessandra Lorini, *Rituals of Race: American Public Culture and the Search for Racial Equality* (Charlottesville: University of Virginia Press, 1999), xiv, xviii.

Another direction that offers interesting conclusions would be to take studies of class struggles out of urban areas. Were relationships different in rural areas than cities, as I suspect they were? What created the difference between city and country class relations? Throwing race and ethnicity into the mix would further complicate what we currently know. How did class pressures make or break alliances in multiethnic communities, both in cities and in rural areas like those in the postwar West?

These rather specific questions about laborers and their employers, though, should also give way to larger questions about the nation's political economy. It is time, I think, for us to turn back to examining institutional processes. How did money, debt, and assets move in postwar years? Who owned government bonds and banking capital; who could borrow money and at what cost? Financier Jay Cooke insisted that he had sold wartime treasury bonds widely throughout all social classes and to both men and women, but by the 1870s "bondholder" was an epithet for very wealthy men. The story of what happened to money after the war would tell us a great deal about how—or, perhaps, whether—industrial capitalists dominated government in the postwar North. Another subject that has been astonishingly neglected in studies of the post–Civil War era is the tariff. While the very mention of that word makes most historians cringe, it was one of the central issues of the nineteenth century, representing a host of different cultural divisions between different groups in society. Joanne Reitano's *The Tariff Question in the Gilded Age* (1994) began to unravel the cultural meaning of the tariff question much as Irwin Unger's *The Greenback Era* (1964) did for the money question in the postwar years, but there is room for more study.[19]

Among other things, an investigation into the tariff might explore how anti-tariff forces made much of women's role as consumers and encouraged women to oppose protariff politicians, an important investigation that would reassert the importance of women's struggles for inclusion in the postwar government. Historians have told us much about people like Elizabeth Cady Stanton and Susan B. Anthony, and about their radical National Woman Suffrage Association, which called for women's rights on the principle of absolute human equality. But we could learn from new studies of the American Woman Suffrage Association (AWSA), a group of postwar activists who based their calls for women's rights on women's identities as wives, mothers, and taxpayers, and who appealed to middle-class Americans far more than radical suffragists did. On this topic, a new scholarly biography of Julia Ward Howe, a leading spokesperson for the AWSA, would be most welcome.

[19] Joanne Reitano, *The Tariff Question in the Gilded Age: The Great Debate of 1888* (University Park, Pa.: Pennsylvania State University Press, 1994); Irwin Unger, *The Greenback Era: A Social and Political History of American Finance, 1865–1879* (Princeton: Princeton University Press, 1964).

The study of women's political agitation carries naturally into the late nineteenth century, when "municipal housekeepers"—usually women—softened the harsh edges of industrial capitalism. Anne Firor Scott's *Natural Allies* (1992) established that women's organizations were central actors in postwar America; Lori D. Ginzberg's *Women and the Work of Benevolence* (1990) traced the transformation of reform from a gender-based to a class-based movement, indicating that postwar middle-class suffragists would overlap with municipal reformers of the late nineteenth century. This connection offers room for study. While recent historians have tended to interpret late-nineteenth-century reform as an attempt at social control, there have been glimmerings that this view has weaknesses. Two notable biographies of postwar reformers—Kathryn Kish Sklar's *Florence Kelley and the Nation's Work* (1995) and Joan Waugh's *Unsentimental Reformer* (1997), a biography of Josephine Shaw Lowell—suggest that their subjects were more radical, or civic-minded, than previously thought. These new interpretations invite other scholars to jump into the water, exploring the relationship between women's social reforms of the late nineteenth century and the postwar expansion of ideas about who should or should not have a say in American government, ideas that could be progressive or retrogressive depending on the political crisis of the day.[20]

Returning foreign policy to a central place in the political economy of the postwar years would also yield important insights about relationships between individuals and the government, I think. In their recent study of violence in California, Clive Webb and William D. Carrigan have suggested that it was the demand of foreign governments for reparations when their citizens were lynched in the West that stopped lynching of people of Mexican descent in America. A similar argument could be made about the Chinese government's demand for reparations after the Rock Springs Massacre of 1885. To what extent was political violence influenced by foreign affairs?[21]

In short, it seems that turning the question of labor and capital into a larger question of the relationship of individuals to their government may offer fruitful ways of looking at postwar America. While struggles between wage labor-

[20] Anne Firor Scott, *Natural Allies: Women's Associations in American History* (Urbana: University of Illinois Press, 1992); Lori D. Ginzberg, *Women and the Work of Benevolence: Morality, Politics, and Class in the Nineteenth Century United States* (New Haven: Yale University Press, 1990); Kathryn Kish Sklar, *Florence Kelley and the Nation's Work: The Rise of Women's Political Culture, 1830–1900* (New Haven: Yale University Press, 1995); Joan Waugh, *Unsentimental Reformer: The Life of Josephine Shaw Lowell* (Cambridge, Mass.: Harvard University Press, 1997). For a recent overview of scholarship on women in the postwar North, see Nina Silber, "Northern Women during the Age of Emancipation," in *A Companion to the Civil War and Reconstruction*, ed. Lacy K. Ford (Madden, Mass.: Blackwell, 2005), 386–402.

[21] William D. Carrigan and Clive Webb, "The Lynching of Persons of Mexican Origin or Descent in the United States, 1848–1928," *Journal of Social History* 37 (Winter 2003): 411–438.

ers and capitalists were a central theme of the postwar years, they were not by any means the only ones. Men and women of different races and ethnicities, of different economic status, of different physical health, and of different ages all negotiated new relationships with the strengthening postwar government. They reacted to a variety of policies, from money and tariff issues to government acceptance of foreign demands for reparations payments after lynchings. What did they approve? What did they detest? Whose participation in government was welcome? Whose was abhorred? The more we know about these changing relationships, it seems, the more we will understand about how Americans came to expand or contract the boundaries of American citizenship.

The Postwar State

The conflict between different interests in the postwar years was couched at the time primarily as a fight over control of the growing power of government, and the question of how the state developed has returned to a central place in historiography. When Foner's *Reconstruction* came out, this field was dominated not by Reconstruction historians—who usually assumed that the need to protect African Americans prompted government action—but by scholars of the late nineteenth century exploring American liberalism and by political scientists. Scholars of liberalism looked back from the twentieth century, examining nineteenth-century state development to find the roots of America's peculiar liberalism in order to explain twentieth-century politics; political scientists examined structural state development over long periods of time. Neither group spoke directly to traditional Reconstruction historians, although the events they described often fell in the traditional period of Reconstruction. After Foner's *Reconstruction*, though, historians focusing on the post–Civil War North entered the conversation about the development of the American state and reclaimed it as their territory. Since the government developed in response to pressure, examinations of the construction of the postwar American state spoke directly to Reconstruction historians' question of who controlled postwar America.

Like historians of the struggle between labor and capital, scholars seeking to explain the creation of the modern state argued first about whether it was capital or labor that had sponsored its development, and thus whether an activist government was regressive or progressive. Martin J. Sklar and Richard Bensel saw businessmen at the heart of the late-nineteenth- and twentieth-century state, while Richard Schneirov argued that laborers had played a bigger role than Sklar and Bensel admitted. Elizabeth Sanders also entered the argument with a dramatic assertion that the ongoing debate was missing the point; *her* activist state was constructed by farmers.

Leading off the case for those who believed in the power of postwar industrialists, Sklar's *The Corporate Reconstruction of American Capitalism* (1988) focused on the period of trusts and antitrust agitation to argue that liberalism was a construction of the late 1890s and early twentieth century, when industrialization forced Americans to balance unrestrained competition and destructive monopoly. The "corporate liberal consensus" that emerged tied government and business together while restraining the excesses of corporate development.[22] At the same time that Sklar was searching for the nineteenth-century roots of the twentieth-century liberal state, political scientist Richard Bensel was continuing his own examination of the development of the American state from roots established in the antebellum years. While his focus was different than Sklar's, he, too, confirmed that postwar industrialists held the government in their own hands.

Bensel's *Yankee Leviathan* (1990) argued that a strong national state emerged in the middle of the nineteenth century, rather than at the end, but agreed that its development was driven by an eastern elite. In Bensel's formula, southern secession permitted northern Republicans to take control of the apparatus of the national government, and with this boon in their hands, they launched a program of national economic development that benefited their section. Binding financiers to the state, the government could not push Reconstruction measures that might weaken financiers' interests, and Reconstruction faltered.[23] Ten years later, Bensel's *The Political Economy of American Industrialization, 1877–1900* (2000) blamed the Republican Party for enabling businessmen to advance their interests at the expense of the mass of Americans. The nineteenth-century Republican Party brokered between industrialists and financiers on the one hand and the mass of voters on the other, using an economically nonessential tariff to solidify support by wooing producing constituencies and providing money to fund veterans' pensions.[24] In Bensel's view, the state became the crucial factor driving nineteenth-century American history, and it operated in the interest of industrialists.

Richard Schneirov was not convinced that northern industrialists had driven the construction of the American state. His *Labor and Urban Politics* (1998) spoke directly to Sklar, placing the creation of a liberal consensus at least ten years earlier than Sklar had done and finding it in the actions of labor in urban politics of the 1880s. Downplaying the role of industrialists in the creation of state activism, he argued that labor learned to work with reformers in the standard two-party system to create a "new liberalism" that rejected the

[22] Martin J. Sklar, *The Corporate Reconstruction of American Capitalism, 1890–1916: The Market, the Law, and Politics* (Cambridge: Cambridge University Press, 1988).

[23] Richard Franklin Bensel, *Yankee Leviathan: The Origins of Central State Authority in America, 1859–1877* (Cambridge: Cambridge University Press, 1990).

[24] Richard Franklin Bensel, *The Political Economy of American Industrialization, 1877–1900* (Cambridge: Cambridge University Press, 2000).

idea of self-regulating markets that caused social injustice and instead called for a modern regulatory state that would bring stability, fairness, and justice into market relations.[25]

Elizabeth Sanders's *Roots of Reform* (1999) also threw a monkey wrench into the consensus that industrialists had controlled the development of the state. Regulation of the economy and protection of citizens from the abuses of large-scale capitalism came not from industrialists themselves or from labor, she argued, but in response to the demands of farmers. Agrarian reformers instigated the expansion of the government and left the imprint of their agenda on the regulatory state of the twentieth century. Examining legislative programs and political policies, Sanders discovered that the drive of agrarians on the periphery of economic power to control "raging capitalism" pushed the government expansion of the late nineteenth century. Agrarians hoped to use the state to stop industrialization's concentration of wealth. Their aim was to reestablish free commerce and create a more widely prosperous society. Reaching out to industrial workers, she maintained, they created enough political pressure to force the creation of a regulatory state in the face of capitalist hostility. Farmers, not industrialists or laborers, were the driving force behind the development of the national government, Sanders asserted.[26]

Historians who examined the pressures of economic interests in society were not the only ones interested in the construction of the American state. Notably, scholars of gender weighed in early. Theda Skocpol's *Protecting Soldiers and Mothers* (1992) barely mentioned economics. Instead, her investigation of the creation of the American welfare system concluded that women were the critical factor in state development. Desperate to attract voters, late-nineteenth-century politicians endorsed a Civil War pension system that created a "kind of precocious social spending state," she argued, but efforts to launch a "paternalist" government failed in the face of fears of its corruption. In its place, a "maternalist" welfare state took shape in the early twentieth century, Skocpol maintained, as states restricted hours for working women, passed safety regulations for women, adopted pensions for mothers, and so on, to protect actual or potential mothers. Skocpol argued that middle-class American women induced this government action by organizing politically and agitating to project maternal

---

[25] Richard Schneirov, *Labor and Urban Politics: Class Conflict and the Origins of Modern Liberalism in Chicago, 1864–1897* (Urbana: University of Illinois Press, 1998). On "republican liberalism" that preceded corporate liberalism, see, for example, James L. Huston, *Securing the Fruits of Labor: The American Concept of Wealth Distribution, 1765–1900* (Baton Rouge: Louisiana State University Press, 1998). For a nuanced examination of changing ideas about liberalism in the early twentieth century, see Michael Willrich, *City of Courts: Socializing Justice in Progressive Era Chicago* (Cambridge: Cambridge University Press, 2003).

[26] Elizabeth Sanders, *Roots of Reform: Farmers, Workers, and the American State, 1877–1917* (Chicago: University of Chicago Press, 1999), 4.

values from their homes to the nation. This maternalism faltered in the 1920s as women disagreed on their program, but they had, briefly, managed to define the role of the state in welfare programs.[27]

Skocpol's suggestion that a strong state was created to protect women ran immediately into Stuart McConnell, and then five years later into Patrick J. Kelly and Rebecca Edwards, whose 1997 books advanced a very different vision from Skocpol's of government development in the post–Civil War years, returning to the idea that an activist state reinforced the power of traditional elites. McConnell's *Glorious Contentment* (1992) explored the creation of American state through the history of the post–Civil War veterans' movement. Following the war, veterans organized first as a political movement and then as a fraternal organization, McConnell explained. Most important, though, was the veterans' cultural construction of their service to the nation. By the 1890s, veterans' rhetoric rooted citizenship in the preservation of America, a model that was particularly attractive to white, middle-class northern men during the immigration and social upheavals of the late nineteenth century.[28]

Kelly's *Creating a National Home* (1997) responded directly to Skocpol, arguing that the roots of postwar welfare systems lay not in maternalism, but in changing ideas of citizenship after the Civil War, ideas that privileged men. What he called "martial citizenship" was limited to men who had fought for the nation: their dependents could only share their benefits, not receive them on their own. It was supported by the state, which used branches of the National Home for Disabled Volunteer Soldiers to become part of the culture and economy of the nation. The National Home system was a dramatic expansion of government's role in the lives of citizens, offering social welfare assistance to a restricted group of male citizen-soldiers and reinforcing the nation's traditional connection between citizenship and military service, thereby privileging men, not women.[29]

Edwards's *Angels in the Machinery* (1997) argued that state responsibilities increased as voters reacted to ideas about the proper relationship between men and women, ultimately reinforcing masculine authority. Entwined in the nineteenth-century political agendas of both men and women was the idea that

---

[27] Theda Skocpol, *Protecting Soldiers and Mothers: The Political Origins of Social Policy in the United States* (Cambridge, Mass.: Harvard University Press, 1992), 65–66. For an exploration of how pension programs permitted government oversight of wives and families, see Megan J. McClintock, "Civil War Pensions and the Reconstruction of Union Families," *Journal of American History* 83 (September 1996): 456–480.

[28] Stuart McConnell, *Glorious Contentment: The Grand Army of the Republic, 1865–1900* (Chapel Hill: University of North Carolina Press, 1992).

[29] Patrick J. Kelly, *Creating a National Home: Building the Veterans' Welfare State, 1860–1900* (Cambridge, Mass.: Harvard University Press, 1997), 198–199.

the family was the basic unit of American society, and that the state must preserve proper family relations at all costs, she explained. Economic dislocations of the late nineteenth century forced major parties to redefine "protection of the family" as an economic imperative rather than a cultural one. At the same time, more radical parties, including the Populists, called for increased political autonomy for women. But when Republicans and Democrats fell back on images of masculinity to hold their constituencies together, women's opportunities for political action outside of the rhetoric of home and motherhood were curtailed. Men recalled ideals of soldierhood and sexual honor to reassert their political authority. That same aggressive masculinity was behind increasing state activism, not only domestically but internationally in adventures like the Spanish-American War.[30]

Barbara Young Welke's *Recasting American Liberty* (2001) took a broader approach to state formation, finding the key to postwar government expansion not in a world divided between labor and capital or between men and women, but rather in the complicated interaction of ideas about liberty, gender, race, and government responsibility. Her central question was what "liberty" meant in the late nineteenth century, when manmade dangers like streetcars constantly threatened to cause both physical and psychological injury, while dramatic transformations in social organizations and in the Constitution meant that personal status was in flux. In a reflection of larger social concerns about powerful corporations, people turned against corporate railroads, blaming them for harm caused by their machines. Although both men and women were injured by railroads and streetcars, Welke argued, it was women who fundamentally shaped the legal recognition of an individual's right to physical safety, psychological protection from trauma, and social status. Government regulation of railroads to promote safety was designed to protect women. At the same time, though, this protection caused a loss of autonomy as individuals accepted limits to their independence that reached from the establishment of specific streetcar stops (rather than the right to step on the cars at will) to racial segregation. Welke argued that late-nineteenth-century Americans recognized the need for government power to protect the physical and emotional safety and status necessary to individual liberty, but that very state protection curtailed individual autonomy.[31]

While scholars of modern liberalism have examined how the modern state developed, historians of the Civil War and Reconstruction have come at the question of the construction of the postwar state very differently from those scholars with a later focus. Taking examinations of state expansion in a direction closer to that suggested by Foner, Gaines M. Foster and I argued that examining

[30] Rebecca Edwards, *Angels in the Machinery: Gender in American Party Politics from the Civil War to the Progressive Era* (New York: Oxford University Press, 1997).

[31] Barbara Young Welke, *Recasting American Liberty: Gender, Race, Law, and the Railroad Revolution, 1865–1920* (Cambridge, Mass.: Cambridge University Press, 2001.

postwar state development could uncover what nineteenth-century Americans believed was the proper relationship of the state to individuals, a critical question for Reconstruction.

My own *The Greatest Nation of the Earth* (1997) rooted the postwar state in the wartime legislation of the Republican Party and searched for the ideology that drove that state development. I argued that sweeping wartime legislation was a deliberate attempt on the part of Republicans to create an activist state that promoted economic development. Wartime Republicans intended to use the government actively to develop both the agricultural and business sectors of the economy, basing their activism on antebellum theories of political economy that were themselves outmoded by the dramatic changes of the war years. In the postwar era, the agricultural sector slumped, while laws initially designed to nurture a weak manufacturing sector became armor for an industrial juggernaut. Wartime Republicans had indeed harnessed the government to industry, but they had done so inadvertently.[32]

Five years later, *The Death of Reconstruction* (2001) continued to examine the development of the postwar state by exploring what it would not do. Following changing northern white attitudes toward African Americans, I concluded that racism and fear of labor radicalism worked together to make northerners who did not identify with a labor interest fear political domination by an underclass that would use government to redistribute wealth. Increasingly, upwardly mobile Americans feared government activism for special interests and came to embrace a rhetoric of individualism. Worried that the poor would vote for those politicians who promised to harness the government to their interests, upwardly mobile Americans acquiesced in the disfranchisement of southern African Americans even as they disfranchised workers in their own states, silencing their political voices. I argued that the labor and racial conflict of the Reconstruction years skewed government activism away from disadvantaged groups.[33]

Foster's *Moral Reconstruction* (2002) also examined the limits of the postwar state. Looking at the attempts of Christian moralists to use the newly powerful federal government to regulate behavior—efforts to add a Christian amendment to the Constitution, the temperance movement, the agitation for Sunday closings, and other popular postwar reforms—Foster argued that postwar activists were heartened by the federal government's assumption of powers during wartime and determined to use that power to reform America. Such attempts fell flat before the war, he explained, as white southerners recognized that government assumption of moral authority would quickly play into the hands of abolitionists, who saw slavery as the very worst sort of immorality. By the end of the

---

[32] Heather Cox Richardson, *The Greatest Nation of the Earth: Republican Economic Policies during the Civil War* (Cambridge, Mass.: Harvard University Press, 1997).

[33] Heather Cox Richardson, *The Death of Reconstruction: Race, Labor, and Politics in the Post–Civil War North, 1865–1901* (Cambridge, Mass.: Harvard University Press, 2001).

nineteenth century, though, when the politics of race had replaced the politics of slavery, white southerners swung behind the efforts of moral reformers to harness the government to their ends.

Ultimately, Foster concluded, reformers did get the federal government to play a greater role in regulating moral behavior than it had before the war, but they did not manage to force America to become a Christian state. Opponents of their agenda insisted on upholding America's tradition of personal liberty, states' rights, and moral suasion. They refused to change organic law to add a Christian amendment to the Constitution; they limited legislation to laws designed to protect individuals from exploitation by those people—like liquor dealers and pimps—who profited from vice. Americans insisted that theirs must remain a secular nation.[34]

The investigation of the construction of the American state has taken us in interesting new directions—most notably in looking at the influence of ideas about gender in state development—and offers continuing new discoveries. In contrast to studies of control of the state, these studies of state development tend to be national, compelling curiosity about how these developments played out on a smaller scale. What did individuals deeply involved in government development think they were doing? Biographies of major figures in this process—notably John Sherman and his key opponent, S. S. Cox—would enrich our understanding of government growth. Studies have also focused on the Republicans as the key architects of government development, and one is forced to wonder what the Democrats were up to while Republicans were expanding the government. A thorough study of the national Democratic Party after the Civil War would enhance our understanding of government growth considerably. A major biography of Wade Hampton is an obvious place to start, for his life covers both southern dislike of government activism and the later use of government against strikers, when, as a railroad commissioner, Hampton vehemently defended the use of the army to protect law and order. A call for a general history of the actions of both state and federal governments after the Civil War might sound terribly retrogressive, but, properly handled, such a work could speak volumes about the way nineteenth-century Americans viewed their nation.

The West

Questions of economic tensions in society and of state construction were, of course, questions that transcended region, an obvious observation that highlights just how unfortunate is the current divorce between eastern and western history. As numerous monographs have told us, the West replicated economic

[34] Gaines M. Foster, *Moral Reconstruction: Christian Lobbyists and the Federal Legislation of Morality, 1865–1920* (Chapel Hill: University of North Carolina Press, 2002).

patterns of the East, and was the most racially mixed area of the nation. As Richard White announced in *It's Your Misfortune and None of My Own*, nowhere did state development take place and matter more than in the West. Surely joining these two fields together offers enormously fertile ground for further study.

Western historians have long worked in the shadow of late nineteenth-century historians like Theodore Roosevelt and Frederick Jackson Turner who argued that, unlike the class-bound East, the West was a land of individualism and opportunity whose labor history was very different from that of the settled regions. Gunther Peck overturned this thesis in his *Reinventing Free Labor* (2000), and in the process identified how laborers, labor brokers, and politicians negotiated the idea of free labor when the work at hand involved massive numbers of unskilled workers in a sparsely settled area.[35] While setting out to interpret western labor history, Peck's work points toward a number of fruitful investigations for scholars of Reconstruction. What were the similarities and differences between eastern and western labor? When could they work together, when were they at odds? Some specific topics spring to mind. We desperately need a good history of the Coeur d'Alene uprisings in Idaho during the 1890s, as well as a study of how those opposed to the miners interpreted the strikes. What about the Coxeyites of the same decade, who are usually dismissed as a minor footnote to eastern monetary issues, but who played a dramatic political role in the West in 1894?

The question of how the state came to serve elites has also received attention by western historians, and their studies should be widely known by Reconstruction historians. In 2004, books by William D. Carrigan and Bonnie Lynn-Sherow examined racial conflict in the West, suggesting that the story of racial dominance is more complicated than eastern historians have generally acknowledged. Carrigan's study of multiethnic lynchings in Texas explored the many elements that created a culture that glorified violence and endorsed lynching.[36] Coming at race relations from an environmental perspective, Lynn-Sherow's *Red Earth* (2004) examined white, black, and Indian farmers in post–Civil War Oklahoma to see what factors led to white dominance of agricultural regions. Her conclusions suggested that that dominance came not from deliberate design, but rather from inadvertent systematic factors that consistently reduced the competitiveness of blacks and Indians in a free labor economy. Government activity in the West, for example, primarily army policing, was set up to keep Indians on their reservations and was designed for that one purpose. When it was necessary to protect Kiowa farmers from cattle thieves or from the cattlemen who grazed off their valuable pastures, the army organization was unable

---

[35] Gunther Peck, *Reinventing Free Labor: Padrones and Immigrant Workers in the North American West, 1880–1930* (New York: Cambridge University Press, 2000).

[36] William D. Carrigan, *The Making of a Lynching Culture: Violence and Vigilantism in Central Texas, 1836–1916* (Urbana: University of Illinois Press, 2004).

to make the transition from guarding Indians to protecting them. Making a connection between segregation patterns and economic success, she argued that small numbers of black farmers could not muster the community networks necessary to rebuild burned barns the way white farmers could. This sort of economic insurance often spelled the difference between success and failure in a period when drought, fire, and lost crops were more common than not. Lynn-Sherow's state worked for whites by default, rather than by deliberate design. What would studies of the East like those of Carrigan and Lynn-Sherow show? Would Roediger's "white republic" rest on a culture of violence and small-town social systems rather than racist plots?[37]

Lynn-Sherow's work follows notable studies of how Indians negotiated the pressures of government policy, case studies of how individuals related to government activism that offer much to Reconstruction historians not only for their central question but also because their methodology emphasizes environmental and cultural factors much more than eastern historians tend to. William T. Hagan's elegant little volume *Quanah Parker* (1993) traced how the most powerful Comanche of the nineteenth century jockeyed between tribe, army, and government, producing a complex portrait of Quanah's difficulties and opportunism that showed him as a representative of nineteenth-century humanity at large rather than as a symbol of his tribe. David Rich Lewis's *Neither Wolf nor Dog* (1994) took a different approach, tracing the Northern Ute, Hupa, and Tohono O'odham peoples' relationship to the U.S. government to conclude that the tribes fit government policies into their own agricultural practices whenever possible, undermining the government's misguided attempts to turn Indians into farmers on a free labor model. Frederick E. Hoxie, with *Parading through History* (1995), also emphasized the endurance of indigenous identity in the face of government and majority culture pressure, insisting that historians must take the Crow seriously as people who had a different vision of what America should be. These studies raise the questions not only of how other tribes interacted with the government but also of how those Indians who acculturated made the transition. New scholarly biographies of Charles Eastman and Sarah Winnemucca, to name only two individuals who left behind vast collections of material, could help us to reconstruct the negotiations individuals made with themselves, their communities, their states, and the U.S. government after the Civil War.[38]

[37] Bonnie Lynn-Sherow, *Red Earth: Race and Agriculture in Oklahoma Territory* (Lawrence: University Press of Kansas, 2004).

[38] William T. Hagan, *Quanah Parker: Comanche Chief* (Norman: University of Oklahoma Press, 1993); David Rich Lewis, *Neither Wolf nor Dog: American Indians, Environment, and Agrarian Change* (New York: Oxford University Press, 1994). Frederick E. Hoxie, *Parading through History: The Making of the Crow Nation in America, 1805–1935* (New York: Cambridge University Press, 1995).

Western historians have also begun to chase down government institutions in a useful way for Reconstruction historians to emulate. After Richard White insisted that the government cut its activist teeth in the West, Donald Worster investigated a crucial aspect of that activism. *A River Running West* (2001) examined John Wesley Powell's work as chief of the U.S. Geological Survey and as the head of the Smithsonian's Bureau of Ethnology. Tracing Powell's dangerous postwar exploration of the Colorado River and the Grand Canyon and his later involvement in debates over Indian assimilation, water rights, and irrigation, Worster argued that Powell was critical in tying the federal government to science. Worster's book should inspire a host of similar studies that focus on, for example, the actions of the Department of Agriculture, which touched most Americans at some point in their lives, and of government land surveyors, who were vital and vilified in the postwar West, and famous enough to be highlighted in Mark Twain's and Charles Dudley Warner's *The Gilded Age* (1873).[39]

While they have not been as completely neglected as the agricultural departments, there is still less interest in federal Indian policy than the subject warrants. Anchoring the field are Paul Francis Prucha, Frederick E. Hoxie, and William T. Hagan. Prucha's solid examinations of nineteenth-century army and Indian policies, most recently *American Indian Treaties* (1994); Frederick E. Hoxie's *A Final Promise* (1984) and his later work; and William T. Hagan's insightful books on Indian-white relations—most recently his *Theodore Roosevelt and Six Friends of the Indian* (1997)—have kept the field moving forward. There is plenty of room here for new scholars. What about a new biography of Carl Schurz that ties together his early Republicanism through his eventual work as the secretary of the Department of the Interior in charge of Indian affairs? Even more important, we need to know what made General Nelson A. Miles both a critic of Indian policy and one of its staunchest enforcers, bemoaning federal practices even as he rounded up Geronimo and moved against Sitting Bull in the years before he led the army against the Pullman strikers.

Further studies of the West will illuminate the development of the American state. It was in the West that the federal government first intervened in labor wars. How was the Coeur d'Alene uprising, which tore apart the mining regions, related to the Pullman strike (which, after all, put federal protection largely on western railroad lines)? For that matter, how was Wyoming's Johnson County war of 1892, which brought federal troops to the support of big ranchers in defiance of local government, related to eastern affairs? Was there a connection between the way the cattlemen handled Johnson County officials and the way Carnegie handled the men controlling the town of Homestead? Events like the Coeur d'Alene strikes and the Johnson County war happened in the West, but they were not limited to that region; rather they were crises that

[39] Donald Worster, *A River Running West: The Life of John Wesley Powell* (New York: Oxford University Press, 2001).

involved Americans across the nation and, eventually, affected the way the government operated. Richard White's forthcoming volume on the transcontinental railroad promises to be a model of the kind of study we need; his "Information, Markets, and Corruption" (2003) anticipated the book, examining how the national issue of corruption played out on the western railroad lines.[40]

Also affecting the whole nation was the way westerners thought about federal government activism. Elizabeth Sanders has given us some ideas about how westerners interpreted the federal government, but there is plenty of work left to be done. We need to take agrarian movements seriously again, examining their ideology as well as their political success. Thomas A. Wood's *Knights of the Plow: Oliver H. Kelley and the Origins of the Grange in Republican Ideology* (1991) and Gene Clanton's *Congressional Populism and the Crisis of the 1890s* (1998) have pointed in this direction, but we need to know much more. Both Woods and Clanton saw the agrarians as democratic heroes, but the strength of vicious racist Ben Tillman's candidacy for the 1896 Democratic presidential nomination, for one thing, invites a reconsideration both of the Populists and their opponents. So, too, does criminal Jesse James's enormous popularity in the agrarian West as an ex-Confederate antigovernment figure.[41] How did the agrarians get such power that they were able to launch quite effective attempts to direct both state and national governments? How did they inspire such popular enthusiasm? Why did they provoke such animosity from middle-class Americans?[42]

Although the West has much to say to us about the American government, western historians also invite us to question our enthusiasm for the idea that the development of the state was the critical element in postwar America. Environmental historian William Cronon, in *Nature's Metropolis* (1991), was skeptical about the dominant importance of the federal government in this era, carefully reasserting the critical importance of environmental history. Redefining the relationship of cities to the lands around them, *Nature's Metropolis* looked at the rise of Chicago, the lands that changed around it to feed its growing population, and the commodities that traveled over its railroads to conclude that the city and the country created each other. The central story of the nineteenth-century West was not of government activism, he argued, but of an expanding economy tying together city and country, East and West.[43] Cronon reminded us that there are forces in the world much more powerful than rich politicians and business-

[40] Richard White, "Information, Markets, and Corruption: Transcontinental Railroads in the Gilded Age," *Journal of American History* 90 (June 2003): 19–43.

[41] See T. J. Stiles, *Jesse James: Last Rebel of the Civil War* (New York: Knopf, 2002).

[42] Thomas A. Woods, *Knights of the Plow: Oliver H. Kelley and the Origins of the Grange in Republican Ideology* (Ames: Iowa State University Press, 1991); Gene Clanton, *Congressional Populists and the Crisis of the 1890s* (Lawrence: University Press of Kansas, 1998).

[43] William Cronon, *Nature's Metropolis: Chicago and the Great West* (New York: Norton, 1991).

men. What, he encourages us to wonder, would an environmental history of Reconstruction look like, and what would it tell us?

Elliott West's *Contested Plains* (1998) also challenged the supremacy of the importance of the government in postwar affairs, insisting that ideologies are the true motivating factors in western—and all human—development. Recognizing the importance of state intervention, West nonetheless identified the state as the instrument of a much more powerful force: the will of individuals. That will, he argued, was a product of human dreams about the potential for riches to be taken from the environment. On the Great Plains, West maintained, humans had envisioned new ways to live and new ways to garner power. Their subsequent actions affected both their physical and social environments.

West examined both changes in Plains Indian culture after the arrival of horses (imported by the Spanish) and changes in white culture after the discovery of gold in Colorado shortly before the Civil War. The great mobility provided by horses offered Plains tribes a route to power just as gold offered a similar promise to whites. In both promises, though, were hidden costs. Horses increased warfare among Plains tribes, increased Native American reliance on the bison, tied previously autonomous peoples into a trading system linked to a larger economy, stressed the buffalo herds, and threatened the grasslands on which large herds of horses and bison depended. The arrival of whites increased competition for increasingly pressured resources, and, in the end, whites turned violently against those Indians who tried to retain their hold on precious grasslands, water, timber, and buffalo. In his story, the interaction of environment and ideas determined the events of the nineteenth-century West. "In the middle of the nineteenth century, two cultures acted out two compelling visions in a land that could support only one," West concluded.[44] What would have happened, he wondered, if they had imagined a world in which they could coexist?

While West's investigation was limited to the Great Plains, his insistence on the importance of ideas in determining events and his focus on the interaction of different cultures as they sought to fulfill their dreams spoke directly to the question of the importance of the state in American life after the Civil War. Was it the state that lay at the heart of postwar history, or was it the ideologies of Americans that lay there? Individuals made decisions that affected events, and in the end, it was individuals who bore responsibility for those decisions and the events that followed. West's insistence on ideology had profound implications for postwar America. After all, the Reconstruction years were the ones in which the nation imagined itself into existence, he pointed out. After easterners confirmed the existence of the nation in a bloody war, they would need to figure out what that nation was. Reimagining the West as a land of promise would be vital

[44] Elliott West, *Contested Plains: Indians, Goldseekers, and the Rush to Colorado* (Lawrence: University of Kansas Press, 1998), 336.

to comprehending a new nation, West insisted. West's challenge to Reconstruction historians is legitimate, and should be engaged.

Almost two decades after the publication of Foner's *Reconstruction*, today's historians of the North during Reconstruction are in the enviable position of enjoying the opportunity to gather together insights on post–Civil War class consolidation, state development, and western history to reveal the larger patterns in late-nineteenth-century America that Foner suggested we might find. In the midst of the dramatic changes of the postwar years, Americans had to consider what their nation would become. What did it mean to be an American? Who was welcome in the nation? Who could participate in politics, the economy, society? If the emancipation of southern slaves had inaugurated a new era of human freedom in America, as many believed, what did that mean in a practical sense? Freedom for men to work? Freedom for men to vote? What about women? Or new immigrants? What rights did they have? What constitutes freedom, both in America and abroad? The answers to these questions were largely determined in the decades immediately after 1865, when questions of industrialization, citizenship, expansion, racism, gender, and government activism convulsed the nation. The process by which these questions were raised, and ultimately answered, is not purely academic, for America has come to be the world's leading power, exporting ideas and culture along with economic and political structures. The nation's choices will influence, if not determine, the future of the world.

Looked at from this perspective, Reconstruction is a process, not a time period. At what point was its work done? At what point was the country unified into a nation of freedom and equality? The editor of the *Chicago Tribune* claimed that the ratification of the Fifteenth Amendment to the Constitution ended Reconstruction in February 1870. Edward McPherson, the clerk of the House of Representatives, disagreed. He maintained that Reconstruction ended on July 15, 1870, when Congress readmitted Georgia to good standing within the Union.[45] White Southerners had yet another date for the end of Reconstruction. For them it was over on April 10, 1877, when President Rutherford B. Hayes removed the federal troops protecting the South Carolina state house, permitting Wade Hampton's "Redeemers" to take control of the state government. Elizabeth Cady Stanton was also preoccupied with the questions of freedom and equality; she might well have put the end of Reconstruction in 1920, when women won the right to vote. When—or if—the nation was reconstructed into a unified nation on principles of freedom and equality remains an open question.

---

[45] Edward McPherson, *Political History of the United States of America during the Period of Reconstruction* (Washington, D.C.: Solomons and Chapman, 1875).

4

RECONSTRUCTION POLITICS AND
THE POLITICS OF RECONSTRUCTION

MICHAEL W. FITZGERALD

The notion that historical scholarship reflects changing contemporary preoccupations and values is almost a truism. Nowhere has this been more evident than in the literature on southern Reconstruction, which has mirrored a changing national climate more than methodological innovations or wider historiographic trends. Reconstruction scholarship has been shaped by its utility in furthering one or another political agenda, or at least in expressing an evolving racial ethos. In particular, modern work has been conducted in the shadow of the civil rights movement—its stirring triumphs and unfinished legacy. For decades, the analogy with contemporary southern struggles animated scholarship. In recent years, as that parallel has become less compelling, interest in Reconstruction partisan contests has declined. This less politicized environment offers some compensations, and the time is perhaps opportune for taking stock.[1]

Revisionists and Post-Revisionists

If scholarship on Reconstruction has been present-minded, the stark previous evolution of the field explains why. Historians need little recounting of the racist enormities of the Dunning school of the early twentieth century, which used Reconstruction's presumed excesses to defend disfranchisement, Jim Crow, and even lynching. Those upholding the states' rights Democratic tradition drew such connections openly. William A. Dunning himself observed that southern

---

[1] For a discussion of the older literature at greater length, see Michael W. Fitzgerald, "Political Reconstruction, 1865–1877," in *A Companion to the American South*, ed. John B. Boles (Malden, Mass.: Blackwell, 2002), 84–302.

conditions remained "at the forefront of contemporaneous interest," adding that "the historian cannot but feel the influence of this fact." The abiding theme of the scholarship was that the federal imposition of black suffrage was folly.[2]

These trends represented the historiographic triumph of the largest stakeholders, for southern apologists long cared more about the memory of Reconstruction than any other powerful interest. Given the outright racism of the long-dominant interpretation, a seismic shift in scholarship was inevitable after World War II. Segregationists had "evoked the hobgoblins of reconstruction to advance their cause," Kenneth Stamp observed, so it was essential to debunk the "Tragic Legend of Reconstruction." This became the scholarly agenda for a generation and more. The parallels between the effort to protect southern freedpeople and events during the civil rights era were palpable. It was one of those rare moments when historians had something important to say and the educated public concurred.[3]

All of the interpretive strands of the previous scholarship came under withering assault, if sometimes in inconsistent ways. The volume edited by Leon Litwack and Kenneth M. Stampp, *Reconstruction* (1969), illustrates the themes. Reconstruction was not motivated by Radical vindictiveness or federal tyranny but by a reasonable concern for the former slaves. Black domination of the Reconstruction governments was wildly overstated. Southern taxation and corruption were exaggerated, while the Reconstruction-era expansion of schools and public facilities was long overdue. In sum, Reconstruction represented a laudable attempt to secure racial equality in the South through federal intervention.[4]

By the time the *Reconstruction* anthology appeared, a startling transformation had occurred. The authors proclaimed: "revisionism has won the day and bids fair to become the new orthodoxy." Clearly the heroic phase of the southern freedom struggle energized that sweeping reappraisal. The "Second Reconstruction" was fought over the same constitutional terrain—states' rights versus federal intervention—that had been in contention a century before. Drastic as the Reconstruction program appeared in contemporary context, it was basically a demand for equality before the law and for black political inclusion. For those sympathetic to the goals of Martin Luther King, integration and legal equality, the previous era posed few ideological challenges, certainly not of the sort that racial separatism would present to the white liberals who dominated

[2] William A. Dunning, *Reconstruction, Political and Economic, 1865–1877* (New York: Harper, 1907), I.

[3] Kenneth M. Stampp, *The Era of Reconstruction, 1865–1877* (New York: Knopf, 1965), vi.

[4] Leon Litwack and Kenneth M. Stampp, eds., *Reconstruction: An Anthology of Revisionist Writings* (Baton Rouge: Louisiana State University Press, 1969).

the historical profession. Reconstruction was the moment when African Americans most unequivocally sought inclusion in American society. This gave it a certain poignant appeal for scholars facing more complex demands for black empowerment.[5]

The revisionist heyday passed with the historical moment, and the changing political currents of the late 1960s encouraged reconsideration. Revisionists generally highlighted positive accomplishments, but Reconstruction, after all, was overthrown with devastating results. Simply inverting the moral evaluation of the participants could not long remain intellectually compelling. In the 1970s, a broad tendency emerged that became the most coherent of several candidates for a "postrevisionist" label. This viewpoint stressed the conservative implications of reform and took a jaundiced view of American institutions; it thus bore a resemblance to the New Left critique of American politics. Skepticism toward narrow legal equality as a goal reflected the reemergence of Marxist ideas in academe and also the contemporary rise of Black Power.

No single book encapsulated these arguments; it was more a theme running across many works. Scholars widely decried the lack of land redistribution, and the Freedmen's Bureau in particular came under scrutiny.[6] Because historians remained committed to egalitarian goals, the inclination was to suggest more thoroughgoing remedies—and the eventual dire outcome lent alternatives retrospective appeal. For example, Michael Les Benedict defended the rationale for Andrew Johnson's impeachment. He well articulated the emerging viewpoint, that Radical Reconstruction "was not very radical after all." In a sense, this interpretation parallels the revisionists, in that it stressed the essential moderation of the Reconstruction project. The difference is the moral evaluation, and the sense that stronger remedies were essential.[7] In this context, Republican leadership during Reconstruction could only look bleak. The final withdrawal of military protection appeared as a "blind pursuit of peace at any price" in William Gillette's phrase.[8]

[5] Litwack and Stampp, *Reconstruction*, viii.

[6] William S. McFeely, *Yankee Stepfather: General O. O. Howard and the Freedmen* (New Haven: Yale University Press, 1968); Donald G. Nieman, *To Set the Law in Motion: The Freedmen's Bureau and the Legal Rights of Blacks, 1865–1868* (Millwood, N.Y.: KTO Press, 1979).

[7] Michael Les Benedict, *The Impeachment and Trial of Andrew Johnson* (New York: Norton, 1973), "Preserving the Constitution: The Conservative Basis of Radical Reconstruction," *Journal of American History* 61 (June 1974): 65–90, and *A Compromise of Principle: Congressional Republicans and Reconstruction, 1863–1869* (New York: Norton, 1974), 13; Michael Perman, *Reunion without Compromise: The South and Reconstruction, 1865–1868* (Cambridge: Cambridge University Press, 1973).

[8] William Gillette, *Retreat from Reconstruction, 1869–1879* (Baton Rouge: Louisiana State University Press, 1979), 361.

Social History and Its Impact

The postrevisionist works on Reconstruction politics collectively enhanced our understanding, but they have worn less well as an overarching interpretation. As America moves politically ever to the right, stressing the limitations of Reconstruction change appears counterintuitive. A more enduring 1970s era influence on the direction of Reconstruction studies was what was once the "new social history." The point of the enterprise was recovering the historical agency of subordinate groups, and slavery's centrality in the literature made emancipation a pressing concern. The representative work was Leon Litwack's *Been in the Storm so Long* (1979). One emphasis was on the freedpeople's desire to put the practices of slavery behind them by sending children to school, withdrawing women from field work, and resisting overseers, gang labor, and other hated holdovers. The attention to freedpeople's social aspirations had direct implications for the study of Reconstruction politics.[9]

Social history nudged traditional narratives away from center stage, and political history will likely never regain the professional preeminence it once enjoyed. For scholars of Reconstruction politics, these trends posed challenges, but the interest in emancipation as a process also brought new energy. In particular, the new work highlighted the evolution of the labor regime. For political historians, the point is that military reconstruction coincided with the disruption of the centralized plantation system, particularly in cotton. My own *The Union League Movement in the Deep South* (1989) pursued this basic insight, examining the labor impact of the politicization of the freedpeople. Julie Saville's *The Work of Reconstruction* (1994) likewise socially situated the region's popular mobilization and the terrorist response. And, to anticipate, Eric Foner's work centers the era's whole political history in the conflict over the plantation system.[10]

The labor emphasis of Reconstruction studies has been augmented by the Freedmen and Southern Society Project. This ambitious documentary editing effort exercises an ongoing influence, because the relevant materials in the National Archives are so scattered that tracking evidence is invaluable. The project thus facilitates exploration of the social basis of popular politics.[11] The interpretations put forward by the editors of *Freedom* (1982–) have been influential,

[9] Leon Litwack, *Been in the Storm so Long: The Aftermath of Slavery* (New York: Knopf, 1979).

[10] Michael W. Fitzgerald, *The Union League Movement in the Deep South: Politics and Agricultural Change during Reconstruction* (Baton Rouge: Louisiana State University Press, 1989); Julie Saville, *The Work of Reconstruction: From Slave to Wage Laborer in South Carolina, 1860–1870* (Cambridge: Cambridge University Press, 1994); Eric Foner, *Reconstruction: America's Unfinished Revolution, 1863–1877* (New York: Harper and Row, 1988).

[11] Ira Berlin et al., eds., *Freedom: A Documentary History of Emancipation, 1861–1867* (Cambridge: Cambridge University Press, 1982–).

too. Ira Berlin contends that slaves' behavior pushed federal authorities toward freeing them. This formulation, sometimes labeled a "self-emancipation" viewpoint, highlights African American choices in ways relevant to Reconstruction politics. Subsequent scholars have pursued the wartime origins of black political consciousness. In addition to this direct interpretive influence, the project's former associates have been prolific, prominent among them Barbara Fields, Joseph Reidy, John Rodrigue, and Julie Saville. Each examines emancipation in a specific locale, and their work combines strong original research with attention to wider, even global, economic implications.[12]

The social basis of "scalawag" sentiment among whites has been explored too. For decades, the class-based dissent theme has been common in Civil War scholarship, though some recent correctives have appeared. Still, historians concur that anti-Confederate sentiments were strongest in the highland non-slaveholding enclaves. As a result, W. E. B. Du Bois's concept of Reconstruction as a biracial democratic coalition achieved a certain renewed vogue. In Armstead Robinson's formulation, "[e]conomic issues arose during Reconstruction in ways that divided the classes in white society more than racism united them." The groundbreaking contribution on upland whites was Steven Hahn's *Roots of Southern Populism* (1983). Hahn interpreted the self-sufficient "yeomanry" as resistant to full incorporation in the cash economy. Hahn's dual economy model socially situated scalawags within the tradition of upcountry political dissent.[13]

The Modern Syntheses: Perman and Foner

Since the revisionists overthrew the prevailing racist paradigm, a diversity of approaches has characterized Reconstruction studies. Synthesis has become correspondingly more complex, in part because social history is often local in focus. One hears complaints in many fields that the eclipse of political history has undermined a coherent narrative. However, two landmark 1980s works inte-

---

[12] Saville, *The Work of Reconstruction*; Barbara J. Fields, *Slavery and Freedom on the Middle Ground: Maryland during the Nineteenth Century* (New Haven: Yale University Press, 1985); Joseph P. Reidy, *From Slavery to Agrarian Capitalism in the Cotton Plantation South: Central Georgia, 1800–1880* (Chapel Hill: University of North Carolina Press, 1992); John C. Rodrigue, *Reconstruction in the Cane Fields: From Slavery to Free Labor in Louisiana's Sugar Parishes, 1862–1880* (Baton Rouge: Louisiana State University Press, 2001).

[13] Allen W. Trelease, "Who Were the Scalawags?" *Journal of Southern History* 29 (November 1963): 445–468; Armstead L. Robinson, "Beyond the Realm of Social Consensus: New Meanings of Reconstruction for American History," *Journal of American History*," 63 (September 1981): 287; Steven Hahn, *The Roots of Southern Populism: Yeoman Farmers and the Transformation of the Georgia Upcountry, 1850–1890* (New York: Oxford University Press, 1983).

grate the transformed modern understanding of southern Reconstruction and emancipation into a political narrative. Michael Perman's *Road to Redemption* (1984) and Eric Foner's *Reconstruction: America's Unfinished Revolution* (1988) remain the touchstones of contemporary study. Decades later, the interpretive differences between these two works still frame many of the debates.

Perman's *Road to Redemption* is straightforward political history but is unusual in focusing on the Redeemers. Perman sees Democrats as divided between those favoring rival "competitive" and "expressive" political strategies. Support for "conciliatory" policies "lay in the black belt," presumably among Whiggish planters who thought some appeal for freedmen's votes would be politically astute. Favoring Republican railroad subsidies, these conservatives accommodated to the Reconstruction regimes. On the other hand, former secessionists and agrarians emphasized the bedrock values of small government, states' rights, and white supremacy. This approach endorsed intimidation of black voters as necessary and legitimate.[14] On the Republican side, similar factional divisions unfolded in reverse. The "moderate" faction, mostly led by scalawags, downplayed civil rights to appeal to the white majority. These leaders emphasized economic development, but such priorities increasingly were challenged by a Radical opposition, led by "carpetbagger" federal office-holders and dependent on the black constituency.

Having conceptualized the issue in these terms, Perman depicts a straightforward evolution. President Grant's election in 1868, in which Klan atrocities figured prominently, sidelined Democratic extremists. Leadership passed in both parties to moderates, and a "politics of convergence" resulted. Moderate Republican governors promoted economic development, while Democrats sought tactical alliance with disaffected Republicans. These policies culminated with the presidential election of 1872, in which the Democrats endorsed the coalition candidacy of Horace Greeley. Crushing defeat undermined relative moderation, just as national depression sapped continued federal oversight in the South. Democratic fundamentalism now reemerged, in the form of White League campaigns of outright violence. It was under this leadership of racial extremists and agrarians that Redemption finally triumphed.

Perman's framework adeptly synthesizes individual state variations into a region-wide interpretation. Inevitably, though, the narrow focus on political history obscures certain realities. The framework normalizes Reconstruction politics, taking the emphasis off of its quasi-military character, as Perman perhaps tacitly concedes in a later essay.[15] He also contends that there was a contra-

---

[14] Michael Perman, *The Road to Redemption: Southern Politics, 1869–1879* (Chapel Hill: University of North Carolina Press, 1984), 66.

[15] Michael Perman, "Counter Reconstruction: The Role of Violence in Southern Redemption," in *The Facts of Reconstruction: Essays in Honor of John Hope Franklin*, ed. Eric Anderson and Alfred A. Moss Jr. (Baton Rouge: Louisiana State University Press, 1991), 121–140.

diction between moderate politics and Klan-style terrorism. That makes logical sense, but the actual behavior of the planters is less clear, frustrated by labor turmoil as they were. By starting his study in 1869, Perman lops off the previous year's quasi-insurrectionary presidential campaign. Conservative restraint was not much in evidence until Grant won and Reconstruction looked permanent. The book's narrative is most persuasive when it addresses how political tendencies evolved, as opposed to how real people behaved.

One could not make similar observations about Eric Foner's *Reconstruction: America's Unfinished Revolution*, for it fully integrates social history into the political narrative of the era—indeed, the interpenetration of these spheres constitutes the overarching interpretation. This feat of synthesis explains why it remains the outstanding contemporary work on Reconstruction. As his subtitle suggests, Foner distances himself from the postrevisionist emphases of the 1970s, observing that depicting the era as conservative "does not seem altogether persuasive." To take one important illustration, Foner agrees that land redistribution was an important aspiration for the freedpeople, but equality itself was perhaps even more fundamental. Foner's treatment of the Freedmen's Bureau also demonstrates his nuanced approach. The bureau inculcated northern conceptions of free labor, in a region shaped by slavery's coercive legacy; the bureau thus acted in some tension with the freedpeople's desires but considerably more with the planters'. Foner updates the favorable revisionist version of Reconstruction, but with central emphasis on the interrelationship of racial and class struggle. In keeping with this positive approach, he attends more to what Reconstruction temporarily achieved than its limitations.[16]

Foner centers the freedpeople's desires in his narrative, explicitly, and he contextualizes formal politics as paralleling the issue of labor control. In a previous comparative study of emancipation, *Nothing but Freedom* (1983), he found that former slaveholders everywhere used political power to preserve the plantation system. In the United States, however, Reconstruction uniquely vested freedmen with suffrage, which gave them the leverage to push for agricultural change. In *Reconstruction*, Foner expands on this insight. In terms of law enforcement, local officials, and labor legislation, the vote tangibly expanded freedom. In areas where freedmen numerically predominated, the effect on their lives was dramatic. The violent terrorist reaction was itself a measure of "how far change had progressed."[17]

Foner's emphasis on the labor struggle focuses attention on the planters, casting them as the major adversaries of black freedom. His treatment of the Ku Klux Klan exemplifies this theme. While terrorists admittedly mobilized a

[16] Foner, *Reconstruction*, xxiii.

[17] Foner, *Reconstruction*, 425; Foner, *Nothing but Freedom* (Baton Rouge: Louisiana State University Press, 1983).

cross-class constituency, elite motivation receives primary stress. The Klan was "a military force serving the interests of the Democratic party, the planter class, and all those who desired the restoration of white supremacy." Labor discipline appears as an important goal, and if "ordinary farmers and laborers" constituted the bulk of the Klan membership, so-called respectable citizens "chose the targets and often participated in the brutality." This emphasis likely overshadows certain issues. That small landowners might have their own motives for violence receives little attention, nor does the issue of petty theft, despite its universal prevalence in contemporary discourse.[18]

Foner's *Reconstruction* is a complex work, with a variety of interpretive threads. Not surprisingly for a scholar with extensive work on northern politics, he stresses the role of national economic developments in undermining southern Reconstruction. Like much of the modern literature, moreover, the book emphasizes the phenomenon of native white Republicanism, viewing it as growing out of class-based resistance to the slaveholders' rebellion. While the alliance with freedpeople was a "marriage of convenience," it also meant an "entirely unprecedented" commitment to protect civil rights.[19] This favorable attention to the Unionist yeomanry fades as most gradually abandoned the Republican cause. A broader lack of attention to the later phases of Reconstruction is apparent in Foner's book, in contrast to Perman's work. Only the last one hundred of over six hundred pages deal with the period after Grant's reelection in 1872, with interpretive emphasis on a decisive end to Reconstruction in 1877.

Foner concludes with an assessment of what Reconstruction meant for America. He does see the mobilization of the black community, the network of autonomous churches and social institutions, and public education as permanent changes. Furthermore, Radical Reconstruction foreclosed a more directly repressive labor regime. These gains notwithstanding, Foner offers a dispiriting verdict. Redemption was "a disaster" that "shifted the center of gravity of American politics to the right for generations to come."[20] The view of a revolution decisively turned back, however, may be too bleak. More recent scholars have contended that meaningful black political participation continued for decades. The Reconstruction amendments remained lodged in the Constitution, which made the issue of equality difficult to ignore entirely. Reconstruction also permanently secured African Americans the suffrage in most of the free states, which became vital with the Great Migration northward. Finally, the triumph of racial extremism did indeed cast a long shadow over the region, but it thereby

[18] Foner, *Reconstruction*, 425, 432.
[19] Foner, *Reconstruction*, 303.
[20] Foner, *Reconstruction*, 602, 604.

also set the stage for a self-immolating response to the renewed threat of federal intervention. If inclined toward optimism, one might view Reconstruction as an eventual triumph through disaster, with even the Dunning-style apologetics contributing to later transformation.

Between them, Foner and Perman's books illuminate complementary aspects of southern politics. However, one interpretive difference suggests that Foner's synthesis of political and social trends might flatten partisan complexities. Foner questions Perman's "politics of convergence" idea, believing that it existed primarily as Democratic rhetoric for northern consumption. The contention that moderates helped rein in the Klan by the early 1870s, Foner says, "cannot be sustained by the evidence." But Foner himself notes that in several overwhelmingly black regions, Klansmen never appeared, which suggests that some planters thought nightriding illadvised. If Perman's work is thin on how whites actually behaved, Foner's interpretation deemphasizes the differences among the plantation owners. Whiggish planters often distrusted former secessionist Democrats as extremists, hotheads who had repeatedly led the region to disaster. These convictions might logically have inhibited the resort to violence. Subsequent historians have been slow to engage this key issue, with Richard Zuczek's *State of Rebellion* (1996) being the exception. Zuczek emphasizes racist unity, contending that differences were only tactical: whites utilized terror whenever it seemed effective. Maybe so, but Stephen Kantrowitz's biography of Ben Tillman dramatizes the glaring Reconstruction disagreements over means among South Carolina's political elite. The broader interpretive issue is central enough to Reconstruction politics to merit further scrutiny, perhaps in a different venue from blood-soaked South Carolina.[21]

Since the two major works by Foner and Perman, few broad reworkings of the Reconstruction era as a whole have appeared. A recent historiographic essay on Reconstruction politics actually concluded with the mid-1980s, an indication of a certain maturity in the literature.[22] One possible explanation is that the creative energy liberated by the civil rights struggle has finally spent itself. Both revisionism and the rise of social history transformed the field, leaving the future agenda for political historians less clear. As the memories of the sixties recede, and as the analogy with the civil rights era becomes less compelling, scholarly interest in Reconstruction's racial politics will likely diminish, and public attention to the era will probably decline too. This prospect, disqui-

---

[21] Foner, *Reconstruction*, 434; Richard Zuczek, *State of Rebellion: Reconstruction in South Carolina* (Columbia: University of South Carolina Press, 1996); Stephen Kantrowitz, *Ben Tillman and the Reconstruction of White Supremacy* (Chapel Hill: University of North Carolina Press, 2000).

[22] Michael Perman, "The Politics of Reconstruction," in *A Companion to the Civil War and Reconstruction*, ed. Lacy K. Ford (Malden, Mass.: Blackwell, 2005), 323–341.

eting as it is, at least suggests a more intellectually challenging environment. One can see the impact on any number of topics previously thought marginal or simply out of vogue.

New Topics in Reconstruction Studies: Religion and Gender

The long-overlooked subject of institutional religion provides an excellent example of this wider tendency. Because militant sectionalism characterized Protestant churches during the Civil War era, Reconstruction politics had religious ramifications, but revisionists generally paid limited heed. The emergence of independent black denominations received most of the attention. Noteworthy is Clarence Walker's 1982 account, which offers an unromanticized look at the contentious African Methodists. Also insightful is Reginald Hildebrand's *The Times Were Strange and Stirring* (1995), which examines the ideological implications of Methodist rivalries.[23] Hildebrand describes a contest between the proto–black nationalism of the African Methodists, the anticaste radicalism of the white northern Methodists, and the old-style racial paternalism of the southern church. All won a black following, but the evident appeal of racial empowerment rhetoric has political implications. In the writing on religion, the hierarchically organized Methodists receive most of the attention. Other churches could use similar attention, though Paul Harvey's *Redeeming the South* (1997) does examine Baptist interracial contacts during the era. Overall, Daniel W. Stowell's *Rebuilding Zion* (1998) provides the best modern overview of the politics of religion. Stowell describes an ecclesiastical Reconstruction that mirrored political trends. He highlights southern whites who rejected sectionalism to reunite with a national church. Many of these religious scalawags, as he terms them, wound up as Republican partisans. None of this should surprise specialists, but it is useful to have Reconstruction struggles examined across the leading Protestant denominations.[24]

Edward J. Blum's *Reforging the White Republic* (2005) explores the influence of religion in less institutional terms. The focus is on how northern Protestant

---

[23] Clarence E. Walker, *A Rock in a Weary Land: The African Methodist Episcopal Zion Church during the Civil War and Reconstruction* (Baton Rouge: Louisiana State University Press, 1982).

[24] Reginald F. Hildebrand, *The Times Were Strange and Stirring: Methodist Preachers and the Crisis of Emancipation* (Durham, N.C.: Duke University Press, 1995); Daniel W. Stowell, *Rebuilding Zion: The Religious Reconstruction of the South, 1863–1877* (New York: Oxford University Press, 1998).

thought evolved in the postwar decades. Blum tells a tale of declension, of how reconciliation with southern whites meant abandoning commitments to equality for African Americans. Northern religion "played a critical role in reuniting northern and southern whites," so that by the turn of the century "white ethnic nationalism" prevailed. The interpretation and tone echo the work of David Blight on Civil War memory, but with a specifically religious focus. Though effective as an interpretation of where Protestants were headed, Blum's interpretation may be less sure-handed on the Reconstruction decade itself. For example, Henry Ward Beecher's postwar embrace of reconciliation left him out of step with religious sentiment; he is not a representative figure after the war. The very figures Blum cites to show diminishing financial commitment to the freedpeople could be interpreted differently, as demonstrating how many people continued giving money. One could argue that Protestant churchgoers remained far more supportive of Reconstruction, and for longer, than most other northerners. Blum's focus on the longer term trend may obscure that aspect, and his discussion of Reconstruction politics slights the constraints under which policy-makers operated. It seems odd to emphasize President Grant's pardons of Klansmen, given that contemporaries perceived his overall policies as aggressive antiterrorist intervention.[25]

Gender, of course, is far more central than religion in contemporary Reconstruction scholarship. The development of women's history is the crucial cause, though the decreasing urgency of the revisionist project likely contributed as well. Because constitutional debates bore directly on women's suffrage, feminist scholars gravitated first toward that traditional political topic. Ellen DuBois's *Feminism and Suffrage* (1978) stressed the expedient abandonment of women's suffrage by postwar abolitionists. DuBois explains the single-issue suffrage movement as resulting from this betrayal, an insight that has been widely accepted. Still, subsequent scholars have perhaps been more interested in reformers less single-minded than the feminist icons Susan B. Anthony or Elizabeth Cady Stanton. Lyde Cullen Sizer's work on women writers sees them as pursuing a muted gender-empowerment strategy, through intervention in the political issues of the war and emancipation. Rebecca Edwards's *Angels in the Machinery* (1997) explores how gender issues fared in mainstream politics. She not surprisingly finds the Republicans committed to Victorian values, contending that they were consistently more supportive of women's social activism and political involvement than their Democratic opponents.[26]

[25] Edward J. Blum, *Reforging the White Republic: Race, Religion, and American Nationalism, 1865–1898* (Baton Rouge: Louisiana State University Press, 2005), 3, 107, 108. See also Edward J. Blum and W. Scott Poole, eds., *Vale of Tears: New Essays on Religion and Reconstruction* (Macon, Ga.: Mercer University Press, 2005).

[26] Ellen DuBois, *Feminism and Suffrage: The Emergence of an Independent Women's Movement in America, 1848–1869* (Ithaca, N.Y.: Cornell University Press, 1978); Lyde Cullen Sizer,

Given the priorities of modern scholarship, freedwomen have been the obvious focus for gender analysis. Emancipation allowed the ex-slaves to reconfigure their lives with family needs in mind. This is an important insight, but what is less clear is where the formal political process fits in, given that women didn't enjoy the vote. Elsa Barkley Brown's work on black women and politics provides one answer. Before the war, gender exclusion had not characterized the forms of community participation available to slaves, but Reconstruction privileged male political involvement. Freedwomen were only somewhat inclined to respect Victorian gender constraints, given the urgency of public issues. Brown argues that female involvement marked Reconstruction politics, and many subsequent scholars have found that freedwomen intervened in moments of crisis. On the other hand, Julie Saville instead contends that suffrage and self-defense efforts primarily empowered men. Other works are under way to substantiate that position as well, among them Susan O'Donovan's forthcoming study of emancipation in southwestern Georgia. The issue remains unresolved, as does how it intersects with the larger evolution of postwar gender relationships.[27]

White women in the South have received less attention, perhaps reflecting the field's racially egalitarian emphasis. As Jane Censer observes in *The Reconstruction of White Southern Womanhood* (2003), for no period have elite females been "so little studied." While Victorian expectations sidelined them from political life, these women shared the regressive social views of their men. Censer describes a racially motivated effort by upper-class women to limit reliance on free domestics. Censer's interpretation suggests elite women's irrelevance to formal politics, in stark contrast with the freedwomen's role as described by Barkley Brown. As for gender issues among the nonelite, the engaging topic of then-transgressive sexual behavior has received sustained attention. Victoria Bynum's *The Free State of Jones* (2002) examines the legendary Unionist Newt Knight, tracing how his black and white descendents contested his public memory. Martha Hodes's *White Women, Black Men* (1997) explores the politics of sexuality. She demonstrates through court proceedings hardening attitudes toward interracial sex after emancipation. During slavery, disrespect of poorer white women encouraged quiet tolerance of interracial liaisons, but after eman-

---

The Political Work of Northern Women Writers and the Civil War, 1850–1872 (Chapel Hill: University of North Carolina Press, 2000); Rebecca Edwards, *Angels in the Machinery: Gender in American Party Politics from the Civil War to the Progressive Era* (New York: Oxford University Press, 1997).

[27] Elsa Barkley Brown, "Race, Identity and Political Activism: The Shifting Contours of the African American Public Sphere," in *The Black Public Sphere: A Public Culture Book*, ed. Black Public Sphere Collective (Chicago: University of Chicago Press, 1995), 111–150; Julie Saville, "Rites and Power: Reflections on Slavery, Freedom, and Political Ritual," *Slavery and Abolition* 20 (January 1999): 81–102; Susan E. O'Donovan, *Slavery's Legacies: Becoming Free in the Cotton South* (Cambridge, Mass.: Harvard University Press, forthcoming).

cipation the stress on female purity intensified, with violent public implications. Diane Miller Sommerville's provocative article and recent book on antebellum rape trials suggest the same thing.[28]

For Reconstruction scholars, these works suggest the need to broaden the definition of politics. In emerging fields of study, such as women's history, fresh insights are continually mainstreamed into the political narrative. Where this is conceptually easiest, as with the suffrage struggle, formerly neglected topics move easily into textbooks and classroom lectures. After Stephanie McCurry's pathbreaking book on antebellum South Carolina, there has been a tendency to bring women into the political account indirectly, through the concept of the household. The premise is that even though women were excluded from power, policy-makers necessarily took account of gender, especially in the slave South, where social order represented such an overriding concern. Peter W. Bardaglio, in his study *Reconstructing the Household* (1995), traced the Reconstruction legislatures' reworking of statutory law. Republicans sought to institutionalize equality, so they granted black men all the legal control over their households that white men enjoyed. Under the doctrine of coverture, this conveyed expansive power, and as Laura Edwards observed in *Gendered Strife and Confusion* (1997), the redefinition was turned to racially repressive uses after Redemption. The Republicans expanded male privilege on egalitarian principle: this is a major if unsettling insight into Reconstruction politics. Edwards depicts this as a conceptual flaw, but other interpretations are possible. Radicals seldom prosper by spelling out the ultimate implications of their reforms; nor does embracing revolutionary gender changes seem a promising tactic before an all-male electorate. One could as easily treat Republican policies as a measure of the lawmakers' pragmatism as of their devotion to regressive Victorian expectations.[29]

[28] Jane Turner Censer, *The Reconstruction of White Southern Womanhood, 1865–1895* (Baton Rouge: Louisiana State University Press, 2003), 1; Victoria E. Bynum, *The Free State of Jones: Mississippi's Longest Civil War* (Chapel Hill: University of North Carolina Press, 2001), and also see Bynum, *Unruly Women: The Politics of Social and Sexual Control in the Old South* (Chapel Hill: University of North Carolina Press, 1992); Martha Hodes, *White Women, Black Men: Illicit Sex in the Nineteenth-Century South* (New Haven: Yale University Press, 1997); Diane Miller Sommerville, "The Rape Myth in the Old South Reconsidered," *Journal of Southern History* 61 (August 1995): 481–518, and *Rape and Race in the Nineteenth-Century South* (Chapel Hill: University of North Carolina Press, 2004).

[29] Stephanie McCurry, *Masters of Small Worlds: Yeoman Households, Gender Relations, and the Political Culture of the Antebellum South Carolina Low Country* (New York: Oxford University Press, 1995); Peter W. Bardaglio, *Reconstructing the Household: Families, Sex and the Law in the Nineteenth-Century South* (Chapel Hill: University of North Carolina Press, 1995); Laura F. Edwards, *Gendered Strife and Confusion: The Political Culture of Reconstruction* (Urbana: University of Illinois Press, 1997).

The household concept has also been utilized in examining the conservative opposition. The most important such work is that of Stephen Kantrowitz, who reconceptualizes partisan politics through a biography of the agrarian tribune Ben Tillman. Kantrowitz gives Tillman's well-known career a gender dimension and situates it more explicitly in Reconstruction terrorism. Tillman defended the independence of his male agrarian following, imperiled as it was by outside economic forces and dependent on subordination of black workers. Physical protection of dependent households became an empowering white male responsibility. As a minority surrounded by those they assumed to be resentful racial inferiors—now dangerously liberated—white men wanted their own women and children under close control. Southern historians have seldom articulated the issue this way, but the grim logic is evident: racial oppression and the subjugation of women reinforced each other.[30]

Contemporary interest in gender, and specifically the emerging concept of the household, are pervasive trends. The sparse treatment of such issues in Foner's 1988 book, noted in reviews at the time, stands out now more starkly. One byproduct is that Redemption as an endpoint seems less natural. For instance, Barbara Welke's study of gender and race in public transportation, *Recasting American Liberty* (2001), spans the postwar decades. For Welke, women travelers' needs redefined liability law, forcing greater corporate responsibility for the safety of customers by the Progressive Era—and contributing to the codification of legal segregation as well. Jane Dailey's analysis of post-Redemption insurgent politics and its gender limitations likewise extends the Reconstruction process. Virginia's "Readjusters" demonstrated that interracial coalition politics could succeed well into the 1880s. White dissidents tried to separate issues of social equality from fair treatment in the civil sphere, but this expedient insulation proved unstable. Dailey emphasizes that racial justice long remained central to black politics, touching upon white sexual sensitivities in explosive ways. An anthology highlighting the gender politics of the 1898 riot in Wilmington, North Carolina, also extends the time frame of Reconstruction-style struggles. Redemption clearly makes more sense as a dividing line on race and politics narrowly defined than for the gender-related issues currently under study.[31]

[30] Stephen Kantrowitz, *Ben Tillman and the Reconstruction of White Supremacy* (Chapel Hill: University of North Carolina Press, 2000); Anne Sarah Rubin, *A Shattered Nation: The Rise and Fall of the Confederacy, 1861–1868* (Chapel Hill: University of North Carolina Press, 2005).

[31] Barbara Young Welke, *Recasting American Liberty: Gender, Race, Law, and the Railroad Revolution, 1865–1920* (Cambridge: Cambridge University Press, 2001); Jane Dailey, *Before Jim Crow: The Politics of Race in Postemancipation Virginia* (Chapel Hill: University of North Carolina Press, 2000); David S. Cecelski and Timothy Tyson, eds., *Democracy Betrayed: The Wilmington Race Riot of 1898 and Its Legacy* (Chapel Hill: University of North Carolina Press, 1998).

These changes notwithstanding, the gender scholarship does not generally challenge the long-prevalent favorable depiction of Reconstruction. If some are critical of the Republican regimes, the Redeemers come off worse, on gender issues nearly as much as race. Nor is this scholarship focused on the political issues that animated the revisionist critiques of the Dunning school. However, other contemporary currents impinge on the basics of the now-entrenched revisionist viewpoint on politics. As the civil rights parallel becomes less salient, more political space opens to reconsider the modern narrative. Traditional political historians have reasserted themselves in recent decades, suggesting that issues of Reconstruction governance have been neglected. Given the changing climate, historians can more readily address subjects that are less consistent with the revisionist project of rehabilitating Reconstruction. The moment is thus opportune for a reassessment of what it was able to achieve in practice and what it could not.

Revisionism Reexamined

Second thoughts about the revisionist consensus are not altogether new; what one might term pragmatic strains of revisionism long existed. The choice of protagonists in southern Republican factional struggles furnishes one example. Most revisionists tacitly approved of the Radical "carpetbagger" faction because of its inclination toward civil rights. Some, however, expressed misgivings about the implications of the Radical carpetbaggers' factional predominance. Several revisionist state studies, often by southerners, depicted native Republicans as plausible leaders. The idea was that only those rooted in the community had the requisite legitimacy to neutralize white hostility. For example, William C. Harris's *Day of the Carpetbagger* (1979) defended the conciliatory policies of Mississippi's Whiggish governor James Alcorn. These works usefully highlighted the practical issue of how Republicans might have sustained an electoral majority.[32]

The favorable interest in scalawags has grown lately. Hyman S. Rubin's forthcoming study of South Carolina's tiny cohort emphasizes dissident origins and diverse class backgrounds. He views them as pushed by circumstances toward a democratic reform agenda. Though Margaret Storey's *Loyalty and Loss* (2004) similarly emphasizes the Unionist origins of postwar white Republicans, she

---

[32] Elizabeth Studley Nathans, *Losing the Peace: Georgia Republicans and Reconstruction, 1865–1871* (Baton Rouge: Louisiana State University Press, 1968); Sarah W. Wiggins, *The Scalawag in Alabama Politics, 1865–1881* (University, Ala.: University of Alabama Press,1977); William C. Harris, *The Day of the Carpetbagger: Republican Reconstruction in Mississippi* (Baton Rouge: Louisiana State University Press, 1979).

challenges the impoverished mountaineer image. Drawing on the underutilized Southern Claims Commission records, she describes a cross-class subculture solidified by common persecution. One arresting finding is the cooperation between dissident Unionist planters and the slaves, a collaboration that prefigured the later Republican coalition. In *The Scalawags* (2003), James Alex Baggett also articulates a favorable view. His ambitious collective biography demonstrates that prominent scalawags were nearly as prosperous and welleducated as their Redeemer counterparts. They mostly had Whig backgrounds and opposed secession overwhelmingly. One sees a logical unfolding of Unionist beliefs, which rather absolves these leaders of the traditional taint of opportunism. The account suggests, however, how little their commitments had to do with racial equality. Treatment of this issue is problematic for sympathetic studies of the scalawags. These works often deemphasize such topics, rather than engaging fully with how native whites addressed black concerns.[33]

Since the 1980s, a skeptical reappraisal of the Reconstruction leadership has become more common. Lawrence N. Powell's article "The Politics of Livelihood" (1982) was the first modern examination of Republican factionalism. Powell's previous book on northern migrants, who generally lost large sums in postwar planting, provides the social underpinning for his study. Yankee newcomers, and Republican politicians more broadly, were so proscribed by white society that they depended financially on government patronage and public office. This contributed to the infighting that characterized the party's predominantly white leadership. Many of the internal battles thus boiled down to "naked struggles for spoils between the ins and the outs." Powell's reexamination of the social basis for the older negative stereotypes represents a striking departure.[34]

The revisionists were partisan toward the Republicans, but the literature on politics is becoming more heterodox. Following Perman's lead, historians have engaged more readily with what conservative whites were thinking. For example, Anne Sarah Rubin's *A Shattered Nation* (2005) emphasized the emotional loyalty to the Confederate legacy that united most of the white population; she carefully assesses the role of racial supremacy without allowing it to overshadow everything else. Along these lines, studies of Reconstruction governance have explored what besides racism motivated white opponents. J. Mills Thornton's important 1982 article examined the impact of Reconstruction financial policy.

---

[33] Hyman S. Rubin III, *South Carolina Scalawags* (Columbia: University of South Carolina Press, 2006); Margaret M. Storey, *Loyalty and Loss: Alabama's Unionists in the Civil War and Reconstruction* (Baton Rouge: Louisiana State University Press, 2004); James Alex Baggett, *The Scalawags: Southern Dissenters in the Civil War and Reconstruction* (Baton Rouge: Louisiana State University Press, 2003).

[34] Lawrence N. Powell, "The Politics of Livelihood: Carpetbaggers in the Deep South," in *Region, Race and Reconstruction: Essays in Honor of C. Vann Woodward*, ed. J. Morgan Kousser and James M. McPherson (New York: Oxford University Press, 1982), 315–347 (quotation at 333).

Revisionists generally minimized the impact of changes in tax policy, but Thornton demonstrated that state and local governments increased property levies dramatically. Thus the Republicans' fiscal policies "drove" small landowners "into the arms of the Redeemers." Thornton downplays racism in this process, perhaps too much, but his account demonstrates that Republicans offered poorer whites little. Richard H. Abbott's posthumously published study of Republican newspapers illustrates this theme vividly. *For Free Press and Equal Rights* (2004) demonstrates that class arguments appeared opportunistically, especially at election times, but the party made little headway among whites with a coherent antielite economic appeal. Given what the Republicans stood for nationally, perhaps this was not a realistic option, but the issue needs exploration.[35]

Mark W. Summers best exemplifies a more skeptical tone toward the Republicans in his various studies of political corruption. His *Railroads, Reconstruction, and the Gospel of Prosperity* (1984) explored the southern railroad subsidy program. His was the first examination of the topic since the Dunning school, an "astonishing" gap, as Summers notes. He understands the rationale for the aid program but finds it shot through with malfeasance. On the basis of their performance, "the Republican leaders deserved to lose power," personally "bitter" though this conclusion is for Summers. As with other criticisms of Republican rule, few of these observations would surprise specialists, but such issues long saw little open discussion. Summers's subsequent work *The Era of Good Stealings* (1993) takes a similarly disillusioned look at how the corruption issue undermined support for an active federal role. The Republicans clearly figure as the protagonists of modern writing, but this bleak account of the Grant administration might make one question why. Summers's latest nuts-and-bolts study, *Party Games* (2004), also detracts from the Republicans' moral luster.[36]

The implications of such ideas for Reconstruction politics are substantial, if indistinct. In keeping with the corpus of revisionist scholarship, Foner's *Reconstruction* can be read as an endorsement of the era's constitutional changes, especially an expanded national government that could protect citizens' civil rights. Foner knows Republican rule facilitated corruption and corporate power, but these appear as secondary issues relative to racial justice. However, Summers's work, as well as an essay by Benedict, "Reform Republicans and the Retreat from Reconstruction" (1991), suggests that another ethical reading of the Grant era

[35] J. Mills Thornton III, "Fiscal Policy and the Failure of Radical Reconstruction in the Lower South" in Kousser and McPherson, *Region, Race and Reconstruction*, 349–394 (quotation at 350); Richard H. Abbott, *For Free Press and Equal Rights: Republican Newspapers in the Reconstruction South* (Athens: University of Georgia Press, 2004).

[36] Mark W. Summers, *Railroads, Reconstruction, and the Gospel of Prosperity: Aid under the Radical Republicans, 1865–1877* (Princeton: Princeton University Press, 1984), ix, 295, *The Era of Good Stealings* (New York: Oxford University Press, 1993), and *Party Games: Getting, Keeping and Using Power in Gilded Age Politics* (Chapel Hill: University of North Carolina Press, 2004).

might be plausible. In his study of education policy *Religion, Race, and Reconstruction* (1998), Ward M. McAfee is so appalled by Republican exploitation of anti-Catholicism as to downplay their other claims on sympathy. Though that response is extreme, over time the scholarly consensus may well become less partisan, especially with respect to the liberal Republican challenge to Grant's reelection. Andrew L. Slap's dissertation, "Transforming Politics" (2002), argues for a more favorable evaluation, emphasizing the reform movement's origins among a cadre of idealistic and racially enlightened journalists. On the other hand, the era's mainstream Democrats were so steeped in white supremacy and violence that historians probably will never find them attractive. That is, unless society shifts much farther to the right, or, conversely, America achieves such interracial amity as to render Reconstruction's ugly race relations less relevant. The likelier prospect is for reevaluation of Republican rule as the moral urgency of defending Reconstruction lessens. Of course, postrevisionists of the 1970s often took a critical view of Reconstruction, but the new writing abandons the assumption that more radical measures would have worked better. More common now is the grim suspicion that nothing would have yielded a decent outcome. As Perman recently concluded, the political issues were so intractable that Reconstruction now looks more like an unfolding tragedy than failure.[37]

The practical constraints posed by northern opinion are Heather Cox Richardson's point in *The Death of Reconstruction* (2001). She examines the national press, finding that concern with restive laborers determined responses to southern events. The freedpeople became a proxy for discomfort with the industrial working class, and blacks won approval on the basis of their resemblance to the ideal of hard-working, independent laborers. It was a tenuous lease on sympathy, and Richardson suggests that the freedpeople's class interests were not that consistent with those of prosperous northerners. To illustrate, Richardson emphasizes press treatment of the scandal-ridden South Carolina government, which was depicted as a fright-mask of proletarian misrule and corruption. The implication is that nothing could have sustained support for civil rights enforcement indefinitely, given northerners' competing priorities. Here, too, postrevisionists had emphasized the limits of northern sympathy, but Richardson is less condemnatory and explicitly downplays racism as a factor.[38]

A tone of practical-minded reconsideration is evident with respect to national policy-makers. The Freedmen's Bureau, for example, remains a focus of atten-

---

[37] Michael Les Benedict, "Reform Republicans and the Retreat from Reconstruction," in Anderson and Moss, *The Facts of Reconstruction*, 53–77; Andrew L. Slap, "Transforming Politics: The Liberal Republican Movement and the End of Civil War Era Political Culture" (Ph.D. diss., Pennsylvania State University, 2002); Ward M. McAfee, *Religion, Race, and Reconstruction: The Public School in the Politics of the 1870s* (Albany: State University of New York Press, 1998).

[38] Heather Cox Richardson, *The Death of Reconstruction: Race, Labor, and Politics in the Post–Civil War North, 1865–1901* (Cambridge, Mass.: Harvard University Press, 2001).

tion, but scholars are now less inclined to find fault on grounds of paternalism. For instance, LaWanda Cox presented a moving biographic sketch of an obscure agent who threw himself into his work, caught up by the importance of what he was doing. The most carefully researched of the newer works is Paul A. Cimbala's study of Georgia, *Under the Guardianship of the Nation* (1997). Cimbala offers a sympathetic portrait of Davis Tillson, long regarded as one of the more conservative bureau state heads, on the grounds that his apolitical profile enabled him to mediate with the planters. Cimbala's work, like most of the recent scholarship, is indistinct on what the bureau was actually able to accomplish. The prevailing emphasis is that the bureau men were well-intentioned, probably achieving what was realistically possible. An anthology on the bureau, edited by Cimbala and Randall Miller, takes a similar position. A striking dissent is *Women's Radical Reconstruction* (2003), by Carol Faulkner, which critiques in gender terms the humanitarian limitations of the bureau and its allied aid organizations. The male-dominated body sought to discourage dependency and to appear before the public as tough-minded, so that it downplayed the desperate need that female teachers and missionaries saw so vividly.[39]

The realistic—or politically resigned—emphasis in the newer Reconstruction literature is evident with respect to presidential leadership. Criticisms of Abraham Lincoln's racial policies grow more muted. Michael Vorenberg's examination of the Thirteenth Amendment stresses Lincoln's positive leadership. William C. Harris's sympathetic *Lincoln's Last Months* (2004) likewise defends Lincoln's moderate Reconstruction policies, with the implication that Andrew Johnson was following existing precedents. Despite this, historians' distaste for Johnson's leadership only intensifies, both on the grounds of his racism and his political rigidity. Still, one wonders if recent developments will prompt rethinking of the Nixon-era scholarship favorable to Johnson's impeachment.[40]

[39] LaWanda Cox, "The Perception of Injustice and Race Policy: James F. McGogy and the Freedmen's Bureau in Alabama," in *Freedom, Racism, and Reconstruction: Collected Writings of LaWanda Cox*, ed. Donald G. Nieman (Athens: University of Georgia Press, 1997), 172–243; Paul A. Cimbala, *Under the Guardianship of the Nation: The Freedmen's Bureau and the Reconstruction of Georgia, 1865–1870* (Athens: University of Georgia Press, 1997); Paul A. Cimbala and Randall M. Miller, eds., *The Freedmen's Bureau and Reconstruction: Reconsiderations* (New York: Fordham University Press, 1999); Carol Faulkner, *Women's Radical Reconstruction: The Freedmen's Aid Movement* (Philadelphia: University of Pennsylvania Press, 2004). See also Barry Crouch, *The Freedmen's Bureau and Black Texans* (Austin: University of Texas Press, 1992); Katherine Masur, "Reconstructing the Nation's Capital: The Politics of Race and Citizenship in the District of Columbia, 1862–1878" (Ph.D. dissertation, University of Michigan, 2001). In reference to Cimbala's work, one should also acknowledge his role in making Fordham University Press an important venue for strong monographs in Reconstruction.

[40] Michael Vorenberg, *Final Freedom: The Civil War, the Abolition of Slavery, and the Thirteenth Amendment* (New York: Cambridge University Press, 2001); William C. Harris, *Lincoln's Last Months* (Cambridge, Mass.: Harvard University Press, 2004).

As for Ulysses S. Grant, opinions of his southern policies have grown more favorable. In several works, Brooks D. Simpson emphasizes Grant's evolving commitment to racial justice. In *The Reconstruction Presidents* (1998), he notes that Grant faced strong political constraints on military intervention in the South. Nothing practical could be done when white majorities freely voted out Republicans. In the black majority states, the showdowns came after the depression of 1873 undermined Grant's power. Perhaps, Simpson concludes, Reconstruction's failure "simply wasn't his fault." Simpson similarly finds that Rutherford B. Hayes had few options but to withdraw federal protection from the last Reconstruction regimes. The state of northern opinion, and the possibility of a bloodbath, made the decision all but inevitable. Recent biographies of Hayes by Ari Hoogenboom and by Hans Trefousse concur. All depict President Hayes as crediting Redeemers' guarantees of free suffrage and legal protection. When this proved mistaken, he repeatedly vetoed congressional attempts to repeal election laws. Subsequent Republican electoral victories demonstrated northern public support.[41]

The recent writing mitigates the censorious view of Redemption as a culminating, decisive betrayal. It now looks more like a signpost on a winding downhill road. The current emphasis is that northern Republicans maintained some interest in civil rights. Robert R. Dykstra's quantitative study *Bright Radical Star* (1993) demonstrates Iowa's intensifying electoral support for equal rights. The bloody shirt energized Republican voters for a generation, precisely because southern events long troubled them. And in *The Trial of Democracy* (1997), Xi Wang argues that the federal government's lingering commitment had real-world implications. Contested elections before Congress and periodic Republican enforcement of election laws constrained the Redeemers. Only when Democratic control of the federal government resulted in repeal in 1894 could southern whites eliminate black voting safely. Brooks Simpson, however, offers a qualification in a recent article: northern voters responded better to antisouthern symbolism than actual federal intervention, for they had little stomach for another serious Reconstruction attempt.[42]

[41] Brooks D. Simpson, *Let Us Have Peace: Ulysses S. Grant and the Politics of War and Reconstruction, 1861–1868* (Chapel Hill: University of North Carolina Press, 1991), and *The Reconstruction Presidents* (Lawrence: University Press of Kansas, 1998), 299; Ari Hoogenboom, *Rutherford B. Hayes, Warrior and President* (Lawrence: University Press of Kansas, 1995); Hans L. Trefousse, *Rutherford B. Hayes* (New York: Times Books, 2002).

[42] Robert R. Dykstra, *Bright Radical Star: Black Freedom and White Supremacy on the Hawkeye Frontier* (Cambridge, Mass.: Harvard University Press, 1993); Xi Wang, *The Trial of Democracy: Black Suffrage and Northern Republicans* (Athens: University of Georgia Press, 1997); Brooks D. Simpson, "Reforging of a Republican Majority," in *The Birth of the Grand Old Party: The Republicans' First Generation*, ed. Robert F. Engs and Randall Miller (Philadelphia: University of Pennsylvania Press, 2002), 148–170.

Recent legal scholarship follows much the same trajectory. Lou Falkner Williams's study of Ku Klux Klan trials illustrates the practical limits facing even courts inclined to prosecute terrorists. Due process hamstrung effectiveness in confronting massive violence. Michael A. Ross has demonstrated how conservatives used the state courts to tie the Republican government of Louisiana in knots. Legal scholars have also reexamined the widely decried Supreme Court decisions of the era. Rather than depict the *Slaughterhouse* decision as surrender, Ross viewed it as preserving core civil rights protections in the face of a national retreat from Reconstruction. His recent biography of Justice Samuel Miller likewise emphasizes his subject's continuing commitment to equal rights. Wholesale surrender by the federal courts only came later, when they gave up the effort to enforce the Constitution. Scholars still agree with the revisionists on the eventual depressing outcome, *Plessy v. Ferguson*, but differ on the route taken to arrive there.[43]

African Americans' Choices and Reconstruction

The previous examples suggest what might be termed the ethical recalibration of Reconstruction studies. The trend probably represents a benign updating of the revisionist literature, rather than a resurrection of long-discredited views. However, the movement away from an exclusive stress on race has a problematic feature: it deemphasizes African Americans' political behavior when their views most counted. To take one example, Summers's study of railroads looks at almost every angle but black politicians' role. Nor does he examine how black voters responded to the railroad issue, though they decided scores of local bond referenda. Finding black perspectives on these issues can be difficult, but more is involved. Historians have been slow to engage with such matters, perhaps for fear of reflecting poorly on black leadership. The result is that scholars unconsciously sanitize black politics through omission. For example, a 1995 biography of Robert Smalls presents strong evidence that the congressman took bribes but refrains from saying so clearly; the book actually ends with a celebratory conclusion.[44]

[43] Lou Falkner Williams, *The Great South Carolina Ku Klux Klan Trials, 1871–1872* (Athens: University of Georgia Press, 1996); Michael A. Ross, "Obstructing Reconstruction: John Archibald Campbell and the Legal Campaign Against Louisiana's Republican Government," *Civil War History* 49 (September 2003): 235–253, "Justice Miller's Reconstruction: The *Slaughter-House Cases*, Health Codes, and Civil Rights in New Orleans, 1861–1873," *Journal of Southern History* 64 (November 1998): 649–676, and *Justice of Shattered Dreams: Samuel Freeman Miller and the Supreme Court during the Civil War Era* (Baton Rouge: Louisiana State University Press, 2003).

[44] Edward A. Miller, *Gullah Statesman: Robert Smalls from Slavery to Congress, 1839–1915* (Columbia: University of South Carolina Press, 1995), 245–250. For one of the few studies

Decades ago, Thomas Holt's pathbreaking *Black over White* (1977) raised the issue of the influence of caste and class divisions within the African-American leadership. Few then pursued the issue, but in recent years, a more skeptical tone toward individual black leaders has become evident. John David Smith's study of the conservative gadfly William Hannibal Thomas, *Black Judas* (2000), is expansive on his varied moral lapses. The most forthright foray into this terrain is Tunde Adeleke's *Without Regard to Race* (2003), a reassessment of the emblematic black nationalist Martin Delany. Because the literature on African-American history privileges critiques of American society, Delany's conservative Reconstruction views long received little attention. Delany was "appropriated by the militant and radical generation of the 1960s as their ideological mentor and guru," in Adeleke's tart phrase.[45] Adeleke's depiction of the postwar Delany as integrationist may be oversimplified, but his account does highlight how patronage concerns drove activists' ideological choices. Adeleke's explicit criticisms of the African-American literature are analogous to the pragmatic strain now evident in Reconstruction scholarship.

The prevailing tendency on African-American politics has long been for an upbeat emphasis, understandably in view of the racist biases of the older literature. But if one is trying to understand black political agency, a candid modern reexamination is necessary, and on a wider range of public issues than civil rights. One suspects that African-American leaders will come off at least as well as their white Republican counterparts, and far better than their blood-splattered opponents, but the research remains to be done. The time may be opportune, moreover, for more complex studies of African-American motivation. In *The Claims of Kinfolk* (2003), Dylan C. Penningroth observes that prevailing assumptions of racial unity can "romanticize the experience of black people." His study of de facto property ownership by slaves, drawing on black testimony before the Southern Claims Commission, offers insights into class divisions after emancipation. For Penningroth, one cannot conclude that the slave community was "any more harmonious than the white community, or any more 'egalitarian' than it is today."[46]

Local politics allows fresh examination of African-American choices, along with the still crucial question of what Republicans in power actually accom-

---

from the era emphasizing corruption, see Euline W. Brock, "Thomas W. Cardozo, Fallible Black Reconstruction Leader," *Journal of Southern History* 47 (May 1981): 183–206.

[45] Thomas Holt, *Black over White: Negro Political Leadership in South Carolina during Reconstruction* (Urbana: University of Illinois Press, 1977); John David Smith, *Black Judas: William Hannibal Thomas and the American Negro* (Athens: University of Georgia Press, 2000); Tunde Adeleke, *Without Regard to Race: The Other Martin Robinson Delany* (Jackson: University Press of Mississippi, 2003), xxiv.

[46] Dylan C. Penningroth, *The Claims of Kinfolk: African American Property and Community in the Nineteenth-Century South* (Chapel Hill: University of North Carolina Press, 2003), 8.

plished. Christopher Waldrep's *Roots of Disorder* (1998) explores the politics of law enforcement around Vicksburg. He finds, strikingly enough, that African Americans eagerly availed themselves of the legal process even under the harsh Black Codes. Congressional Reconstruction vastly expanded legal participation, as the black majority increasingly used the courts against whites and even one another. Black participation on juries was substantial and notably evenhanded; those selected were disproportionately literate and had property, and they routinely convicted black defendants. Jurors were, however, unreceptive to charges of malfeasance against Republican office-holders, which suggests how partisan loyalty could overshadow other civic goals. Another local study, my *Urban Emancipation* (2002), examines different aspects of political behavior. In Mobile, rival groups of black activists, with contrasting class backgrounds, seized upon Republican factional divisions for individual and collective advantage. The underlying social cleavage was between longtime residents and the destitute rural freedpeople surging into the city. The implication is that factionalism emanated from within the African-American community, as well as from the Republican leadership. Such struggles among activists have not been much examined in the literature, but they had civil rights implications. If one is looking for African-American agency, the grubby mechanics of patronage politics are an important vehicle.[47]

Steven Hahn's *A Nation under Our Feet* (2003) presents the most ideologically forthright recent reinterpretation of black politics. In his brief introduction, Hahn observes that on this topic, "most of the relevant scholarship has been governed by a liberal integrationist framework." This highlighted certain aspects, like "inclusion and assimilation" and the "pursuit of individual rights." Hahn instead emphasizes collective empowerment, seeing a rural tradition of popular black nationalism stretching from before emancipation to Garveyism. He agrees with Foner and others that the struggle over the plantation system was the core political issue. But he returns to the postrevisionist stress on land reform, and the Union Leagues appear prominently as an agrarian movement. For Hahn, Reconstruction was something of a dead end, and the trappings of law and elections muffled the true "paramilitary politics" of class struggle under way. Blacks supported the Republicans avidly, but the prospects for social revolution at the ballot box were "virtually nonexistent," and even most black officeholders "appeared to pursue relatively moderate objectives." Like most of the recent literature, Hahn does not see a sharp break in 1877. Black voters kept trying to utilize their suffrage, and if Hahn's previous work on the white yeomanry

[47] Christopher Waldrep, *Roots of Disorder: Race and Criminal Justice in the American South, 1817–1880* (Urbana: University of Illinois Press, 1998); Michael W. Fitzgerald, *Urban Emancipation: Popular Politics in Reconstruction Mobile, 1860–1890* (Baton Rouge: Louisiana State University Press, 2002).

offered too optimistic an assessment of interracial insurgent politics, this book corrects it. Insurgent white offers of alliance were so weak or halfhearted that the straight-out Democrats often seemed a better bet. The prospects for influence were limited, and disfranchisement eventually eliminated them altogether. These developments strengthened the grassroots emigrationism, emanating from the rural poor, that culminated in the Great Migration.[48]

Hahn's book is the most ambitious rethinking of emancipation since Foner. The black nationalist strains of Reconstruction politics have long gone without systematic exploration, precisely for the ideological reasons Hahn describes. At this writing, it is unclear how this book will influence the wider Reconstruction literature, in part because Hahn engages that topic only glancingly. But the political tone, at least, is different from previous writing. Rather than viewing Reconstruction as an interracial movement for social change, Hahn emphasizes a tradition of race-based communal resistance. In contrast to the upbeat revisionists, Hahn's book suggests a different analogy between emancipation and the civil rights movement: in both, white participation and northern opinion remained tangential to the remorseless black liberation struggle. This would be quite a different implication from the story others have seen in the Reconstruction era.

Where does this, finally, leave the study of political Reconstruction? A reconsideration of the era is under way, much of it in a pragmatic direction, but Hahn's work would suggest that its ultimate meaning is again up for grabs. In assessing where this field should go, several recent positive trends seem likely to continue. One important emphasis has been on reevaluating what Reconstruction meant in practice. Racial issues naturally have received predominant emphasis since the revisionists, but much more was going on in Reconstruction governance. For instance, Elizabeth Lee Thompson's *The Reconstruction of Southern Debtors* (2004) is the first modern examination of bankruptcy laws, which congressional Republicans rewrote in ways surprisingly favorable to plantation owners.[49] Political patronage, railroad promotion, state militias, or even public education—all these topics bear upon the wider struggle for racial justice, and all could use reevaluation by energetic graduate students. We still need to separate fact from fiction on corrupt practices and other issues the Dunning school emphasized so invidiously. Scholars also need to explore continuities of black participation extending into later decades. The inadequacy of traditional political periodization is similarly highlighted by the themes of gender scholarship. And perhaps most important, exploration of the social origins of black political behavior should illuminate all these other issues.

---

[48] Steven Hahn, *A Nation under Our Feet: Black Political Struggles in the Rural South from Slavery to the Great Migration* (Cambridge, Mass.: Harvard University Press, 2003), 6, 237.

[49] Elizabeth Lee Thompson, *The Reconstruction of Southern Debtors: Bankruptcy after the Civil War* (Athens: University of Georgia Press, 2004).

Reconstruction Politics
and Contemporary America

Since the time of Dunning, changes in the political and racial climate have driven reinterpretation in this field, and they are certain to do so in future. Controversies over the display of the Confederate flag have encouraged scholars to think about the uses of public memory. David W. Blight's magisterial study of the racist appropriation of the Civil War's legacy, *Race and Reunion* (2001), reemphasizes the point.[50] Reconstruction has not been much emphasized in this body of work, perhaps because the political and racial implications were overt in the literature all along. Historians have been uncomfortably aware of the gulf between the revisionist scholarship and what substantial segments of the public wanted—or were willing—to hear. As Mark Grimsley observed, for most Americans, Reconstruction is "shrouded by a fog of tragic era mythology, on the one hand, and densely argued academic studies, on the other."[51] No one would disagree who has encountered undergraduate notions of the subject, or spent much time conversing with genealogists at southern archives.

The current trends might help narrow this gap, with a less partisan scholarly viewpoint toward Radical Reconstruction facilitating public outreach. America's recent difficulties in the Middle East might also encourage reflection upon earlier military sponsorship of social change. The term "Reconstruction" now elicits an unfamiliar crop of titles in database searches, which itself suggests a transformed relevance for contemporary America. Comparisons along these lines have appeared in the press, and Edward L. Ayers reflected on the tendency of these efforts to go sour in a recent essay.[52] Moreover, in domestic politics, there is another factor potentially at work. The contemporary surge of southern whites toward the Republicans has reversed the traditional partisan polarity. Conservative southerners no longer identify automatically with the states' rights Democratic tradition. In the long run, this might allow a more thoughtful public engagement with serious scholarship, at least with respect to Reconstruction. That would seem logical, though as yet southern Republicans show little sign of embracing their party's egalitarian origins as a usable past.

This essay has generally applauded the recent reconsideration of the field, on the premise that overstating the chances for dramatic transformation of race relations in that era helps us little now. If the realities of biracial governance, or the choices made by the black community, now get more notice, that might

[50] David W. Blight, *Race and Reunion: The Civil War in American History* (Cambridge, Mass.: Harvard University Press, 2001).

[51] Mark Grimsley, review of *A Year in the South*, by Stephen V. Ash, *Journal of American History* 91 (June 2004): 248–249.

[52] Edward L. Ayers, "Exporting Reconstruction," in *What Caused the Civil War? Reflections on the South and Southern History* (New York: Norton, 2005), 145–166.

encourage wholesome reflection on avoiding a future backlash. Still, it might be appropriate to end on a cautionary note, calling attention to the multiple constituencies for historians' work. The danger is that in moving beyond the revisionist emphases, historians lend unwitting credence to the racist misunderstandings that have been so destructive in the past. It would, therefore, be well to bear in mind how innovations might sound to those with different social agendas. Academics may find that somebody out there is paying attention, possibly in disquieting ways.

5

THE PAST AS A FOREIGN COUNTRY

Reconstruction, Inside and Out

MARK M. SMITH

Many historians of Reconstruction have assumed an air of studied indifference toward foreign affairs. This essay attempts to prick their interest in the topic. It reviews what little work there is on the subject, surveys the modest contributions to the field made by diplomatic historians, and points to examples of recent work that suggest how and why we might begin to appreciate the importance of foreign affairs for our understanding of Reconstruction and how that appreciation itself might shape our intellectual understanding of the relationship between the ostensibly stable and discrete categories of "domestic" and "foreign."

Any reasonable, full, and nuanced understanding of Reconstruction must include an awareness of events that took place outside of the United States. In this sense, my essay is a call for inclusion. But more than that, I argue that slighting the importance of events beyond the United States and downplaying Americans' awareness of the foreign during Reconstruction blinds us to the depth, meaning, and subtleties of what Reconstruction at home actually meant. Reconstruction as a domestic episode, in short, is best understood by appreciating foreign developments and initiatives.

Most historians of nineteenth-century America say little about foreign affairs between 1865 and 1877. In some respects, the silence is curious. While it is certainly the case that diplomatic history has fallen on hard times—thus, perhaps, helping to account for the dearth of work by diplomatic historians on Reconstruction—it is also true that even during diplomatic history's heyday,

Thanks to my fellow contributors as well as to David Prior, Jay Richardson, and Scott Marler for helpful suggestions and leads. I'm especially indebted to Tom Brown, Ken Clements, and Mitchell Snay for characteristically helpful comments and recommendations.

Reconstruction remained virtually untouched by its practitioners. Very recent work by Jay Sexton notwithstanding, diplomatic historians have remained steadfastly uninterested in foreign relations in the "Civil War era." And while Reconstruction specialists have produced significant studies on comparative history, such work does not show us how foreign matters affected attitudes and events at home or how domestic matters shaped foreign policy. Indeed, the field's impressive ventures into comparative history might well have diverted historians' attention from diplomatic history and the importance of foreign affairs during Reconstruction. Whatever the reason, one thing is clear: In the sweep of writing on nineteenth-century American foreign policy generally, the silence on the Reconstruction period is marked—an anechoic chamber of historical study sandwiched between noisy analyses. For the 1850s, we have good studies on southern expansion and designs abroad; on the Civil War, lots of work on foreign affairs; and, beginning in the 1880s, a veritable cacophony of studies on the origins of American imperialism. The years in between barely squeak.[1]

What, specifically, do we gain by incorporating the foreign into Reconstruction narratives? I should first note that including the foreign will be a significant (though hardly unattractive) undertaking, one requiring extended research in unfamiliar repositories, often in "foreign" places, sometimes wrestling with sources written in a different tongue. I believe, though, that such an investment yields at least six healthy dividends. First (and as limited research already

---

[1] Then there are the few studies that tend to be of American opinion of specific foreign events that, for all analytic purposes, just happened to occur during Reconstruction. While there are some suggestive essays and works that try to integrate the foreign into the domestic, they tend to focus on a specific event, a particular country, and are usually weighted in favor of the Civil War, not Reconstruction. See, for example, John Gazley, *American Opinion of German Unification, 1848–1871* (New York: Columbia University Press, 1926), and the very thoughtful study by Thomas David Schoonover, *Dollars over Dominion: The Triumph of Liberalism in Mexican-United States Relations, 1861–1867* (Baton Rouge: Louisiana State University Press, 1978). Obvious landmark comparative studies of Reconstruction include Eric Foner, *Nothing but Freedom: Emancipation and Its Legacy* (Baton Rouge: Louisiana State University Press, 1983), and Steven Hahn, "Class and State in Postemancipation Societies: Southern Planters in Comparative Perspective," *American Historical Review* 95 (February 1990): 75–98. Note, too, Norbert Finzsch and Jürgen Martschukat, eds., *Different Restorations: Reconstruction and "Wiederaufbau" in Germany and the United States: 1865, 1945 and 1989* (Oxford: Berghahn Books, 1996). For a "global" emphasis, see Matthew Pratt Guterl, "After Slavery: Asian Labor, the American South, and the Age of Emancipation," *Journal of World History* 14 (June 2003): 209–241. On the years surrounding Reconstruction, the literature is extensive, but for the 1850s, see, for example, Robert E. May, *The Southern Dream of a Caribbean Empire, 1854–1861* (Baton Rouge: Louisiana State University Press, 1973); for the war, Frank L. Owsley, *King Cotton Diplomacy: Foreign Relations of the Confederate States of America*, 2nd ed., rev. Harriet Chappell Owsley (Chicago: Uni-

suggests), such an inclusion will certainly give us a deeper appreciation of the prevailing—and sometimes competing—racial ideologies among Americans during Reconstruction, ideologies that were sometimes applied to foreign, racialized "others," as well as to southern freedpeople, and sometimes suspended, depending on the event and context and particular audience. Americans did not simply project onto foreign policy a set of domestically developed ideas; rather, experiences abroad were also important for people interested in Reconstruction. Second, and related: inclusion will not only illustrate the well-known argument among diplomatic historians that foreign policy was designed to bolster American commercial might but will also suggest both the importance of an early, pre-1890s imperial conceit—one often ignored by foreign policy specialists—of "civilizing savages" abroad and the limits of that ideology. Third—and perhaps most obviously—foreign matters tell us a good deal about divided Republican commitments to the Reconstruction project. The little work that has been done on foreign policy during Reconstruction certainly points in this direction. Fourth, including foreign affairs in narratives of Reconstruction helps historians approach a fidelity to the past. After all, Americans developed a growing sense of their interconnectedness with the world during Reconstruction, courtesy of the massive increase in the movement of information, people, and goods following the Civil War. Americans' embrace of the notion of their exceptionalism made sense only in a comparative framework. Fifth, an understanding of foreign policy during Reconstruc-

versity of Chicago Press, 1959); R. J. M. Blackett, *Divided Hearts: Britain and the American Civil War* (Baton Rouge: Louisiana State University Press, 2001); James A. Rawley, "The American Civil War and the Atlantic Community," *Georgia Review* 21 (1967): 185–194. On the post-1877 literature, see the works referred to herein. For a general call on the importance of studying the domestic context and background to foreign affairs, see Robert J. McMahon, "The Study of American Foreign Relations: National History or International History?" in *Explaining the History of American Foreign Relations*, ed. Michael J. Hogan and Thomas G. Paterson (Cambridge: Cambridge University Press, 1991), 11–23. Let me be the first to note my own silence on the matter. Neither *Mastered by the Clock: Time, Slavery, and Freedom in the American South* (Chapel Hill: University of North Carolina Press, 1997) nor *Listening to Nineteenth-Century America* (Chapel Hill: University of North Carolina Press, 2001)—both of which have chapters on Reconstruction—say much about the importance, meaning, or relevance of foreign affairs. For Jay Sexton's recent, thoughtful comments on U.S. foreign policy during the Civil War era, see his "Toward a Synthesis of Foreign Relations in the Civil War Era, 1848–1877," *American Nineteenth Century History* 5 (Fall 2004): 50–73. Sexton certainly sees the need to examine foreign relations during Reconstruction, although his broader temporal reference sometimes leads him to overlook the specific ways in which domestic and foreign affairs related during the Reconstruction period. Moreover, Sexton is often unaware of some of the key recent works discussed in this essay that have, in fact, made a healthy start toward the integration of considerations of foreign affairs in the 1865–77 period.

tion also broadens and enriches our understanding of changing conceptions of class, democracy, and nationhood.[2]

Lastly, an awareness of foreign affairs, broadly conceived, has the ironic effect of at once deepening our understanding of Reconstruction in the South and North but also redirecting our attention toward the often overlooked West, principally because certain foreign policy initiatives in the Pacific and some events in Europe spoke precisely to ostensibly "domestic" policies (which were also simultaneously "foreign" in some respects) regarding Native Americans. This inclusion and reorientation is a valuable dividend. Not only does it include a significant group that is hardly ever mentioned in Reconstruction histories (Native Americans) but it shows with powerful clarity both the intellectual and historical unhelpfulness of maintaining a strict division between events that historians (but not contemporaries) tend to consider exclusively "foreign" or wholly "domestic."

What follows is far from an effort to summarize every conceivably relevant work on the topic. Rather, the essay tries to identify and explore the implications of a selected set of suggestive works that will help us not only include foreign affairs in studies of Reconstruction but might well refine our understanding of the meaning of home and abroad, domestic and foreign.

Foreign Land, Virgin Soil: Diplomatic and Reconstruction Historiographies

Pity the poor teacher who wishes to include even the most rudimentary history of foreign affairs in a course on Reconstruction. Who to read for an understanding of the French presence in Mexico, to understand why they withdrew in 1867? How best to comprehend the devilish intricacies of the so-called Alabama Claims immediately after the war, their importance to the Canadian situation (the Dominion of Canada was formed in 1867), the Oregon question, and their relevance to evolving Anglo-American relations into the 1870s? Quickly, questions proliferate: What was the Johnson-Clarendon convention of 1869? How best to characterize Hamilton Fish's tenure as secretary of state, 1869–77? Was

---

[2] Numbers suggest the importance of relating foreign to domestic in the period. In 1850 there were 254 daily newspapers in the United States; by 1870, there were 574, with a gross annual circulation of 426 million copies. In 1873 alone, 460,000 foreigners entered the United States, bringing with them a consciousness of the abroad even as they made America "home." See Philip M. Katz, *From Appomattox to Montmartre: Americans and the Paris Commune* (Cambridge, Mass.: Harvard University Press, 1998), 62–63, 74–75; Mark W. Summers, *The Press Gang: Newspapers and Politics, 1865–1878* (Chapel Hill: University of North Carolina Press, 1994); Charles S. Campbell, *Transformation of American Foreign Relations 1865–1900* (New York: Harper and Row, 1976), 2.

American interest in the Caribbean and a Central American isthmian canal related solely to Secretary of State William Henry Seward's expansionist tendencies? What happened as a result of Seward's 1866 cruise (ostensibly "for his health") to the Danish West Indies, Santo Domingo, Haiti, and Cuba? And just what were Americans doing in Hawaii in the immediate postwar period? To what extent did growing economic and strategic ties between the United States and Hawaii in the 1870s make eventual annexation "a natural consequence"? Why on earth did Russia decide to sell Alaska (Russian-America), why did Seward want it, and why did the deal almost come undone? The questions could go on, of course, but our teacher would find few answers from historians of Reconstruction.[3]

This is not to say that foreign affairs are never mentioned by these historians. Most often the matter crops up in biographies. Indeed, the little work that has been done on foreign policy during Reconstruction relies quite heavily on such biographical work. Eric Foner's discussion, Charles S. Campbell's work, and the brief survey by Walter LaFeber all use Nathan I. Huggins's biography of Frederick Douglass, Allan Nevins's 1936 study of Hamilton Fish, David Donald's exquisite work on Charles Sumner, biographies of William Henry Seward by Ernest Paolino and Glyndon G. Van Deusen, and William S. McFeely's *Grant* (1981) for basic, factual information.[4] But as helpful as these biographical studies are, they are limited insofar as their subjects' interests in foreign affairs naturally yield a partial picture of the period and tend to stress very particular perspectives and thinking.

[3] On these events, see Campbell, *Transformation of American Foreign Relations*, 2–77 (quotations on 17, 72). For the nitty-gritty of many of these events, the best sources remain some very old essays. See, for example, William A. Dunning, "Paying for Alaska: Some Unfamiliar Incidents in the Process," *Political Science Quarterly* 27 (1912): 385–398; Thomas A. Bailey, "Why the United States Purchased Alaska," *Pacific Historical Review* 3 (1934): 39–49; Tyler Dennett, "Seward's Far Eastern Policy," *American Historical Review* 28 (1922): 45–62; Theodore C. Smith, "Expansion after the Civil War, 1865–71," *Political Science Quarterly* 16 (1901): 412–436; Donald M. Dozer, "Anti-Expansionism during the Johnson Administration," *Pacific Historical Review* 12 (1943): 253–275; Joe P. Smith, *The Republican Expansionists of the Early Reconstruction Era* (Chicago: University of Chicago Libraries, 1933). On Canadian-U.S. relations, see Donald F. Warner, *The Idea of Continental Union: Agitation for the Annexation of Canada to the United States, 1849–1893* (Lexington: University of Kentucky Press, 1960). For the Danish West Indies, see Charles Callan Tansil, *The Purchase of the Danish West Indies* (Baltimore: Johns Hopkins University Press, 1932), 1–179 especially.

[4] Nathan I. Huggins, *Slave and Citizen: The Life of Frederick Douglass* (Boston: Little, Brown, 1980); Allan Nevins, *Hamilton Fish: The Inner History of the Grant Administration* (New York: Dodd, Mead, 1936); David Donald, *Charles Sumner and the Rights of Man* (New York: Knopf, 1970); Ernest N. Paolino, *The Foundations of the American Empire: William Henry Seward and U.S. Foreign Policy* (Ithaca, N.Y.: Cornell University Press, 1973); Glyndon G. Van Deusen, *William Henry Seward* (New York: Oxford University Press, 1967); William S. McFeely, *Grant: A Biography* (New York: Norton, 1981). For the influence of these biographies, see Eric Foner, *Reconstruc-*

Beyond biographies, few works pay any sustained attention to foreign developments. Certainly, as Mark W. Summers's innovative work on journalism and Reconstruction shows, Americans were keenly interested in foreign matters. Their awareness was kept alive by a press determined to use both domestic and foreign affairs to help shape public opinion, especially concerning the Alaska purchase and the wrangling over Santo Domingo. Similarly, James Roark's study *Masters without Slaves* (1977) takes us far beyond the South's borders during Reconstruction by detailing postbellum planters' ventures to Mexico and Brazil. And yet, as stimulating as these books are, they are plainly not efforts to systematically investigate foreign relations during Reconstruction. In Roark's case, the foreign context is used principally to elucidate southern planters' domestic concerns, and there is not much by way of reference to foreign policy and the interplay between home and abroad; in Summers's work, foreign affairs are mentioned briefly, serving as nifty sidebars to illustrate the political activities and machinations of the domestic press.[5]

Where else might our teacher turn? Most obviously, she or he could appeal to a rich body of work covering the late nineteenth century written by diplomatic historians. Certainly, there are a few (though surprisingly few) works that deal with the Reconstruction period, but our teacher will be hard pressed to find any piece of diplomatic history that shows how Reconstruction at home influenced foreign policy or, for that matter, how foreign affairs impacted Reconstruction. Just as historians of Reconstruction tend to segregate domestic and foreign, so diplomatic historians—on the rare occasions that they broach Reconstruction's diplomatic initiatives—do very little, if anything, to contextualize the foreign. One reason for this inattention is probably because historians of Reconstruction rarely seem to have conversations with the ever-dwindling number of specialists in the field of diplomatic history. Moreover, many diplomatic historians seem, understandably, preoccupied with their own questions and historiographical disputes.[6]

---

tion: *America's Unfinished Revolution, 1863–1877* (New York: Harper and Row, 1988), 494–495; Campbell, *Transformation of American Foreign Policy*, 1–77; and Walter LaFeber, *The Cambridge History of American Foreign Relations*, vol. 2, *The American Search for Opportunity, 1865–1913* (Cambridge: Cambridge University Press, 1993), esp. 1–26, 60–67. See also Joseph A. Fry, *Dixie Looks Abroad: The South and Foreign Relations 1789–1973* (Baton Rouge: Louisiana State University Press, 2002), 2 n. 2. Other helpful biographies include William M. Armstrong, *E. L. Godkin and American Foreign Policy, 1865–1900* (New York: Bookman, 1957). On the limitations of biography for understanding Reconstruction, see David Donald, *The Politics of Reconstruction 1863–1867* (Baton Rouge: Louisiana State University Press, 1965), xii.

[5] Summers, *The Press Gang*, 110–112, 115–116, 126, 172–174, 181–182, 241–243; James L. Roark, *Masters without Slaves: Southern Planters in the Civil War and Reconstruction* (New York: Norton, 1977).

[6] Brief discussions of foreign relations during Reconstruction are to be found in a few old survey texts, some of which are quite helpful for understanding some (though by no means all)

Recent work by Eric T. L. Love notwithstanding, diplomatic historians still debate the nature and cause of U.S. imperialist expansion, which many date as beginning in the late nineteenth century. Their analyses sometimes touch on matters pertinent to Reconstruction, but more often than not the arguments are framed within a very particular historiography with its own stakes and genealogies. Even in work purporting to cover the period 1865–1900, most of the attention is directed toward the 1890s. Questions concerning the meaning and significance of the Spanish-American War overwhelm other diplomatic events and foreign policy initiatives of, say, the 1870s.[7]

So, choice is limited, and our teacher would probably have to rely on three main diplomatic works just to get a decent sense of events and chronology. Certainly she or he would find much of benefit in Charles S. Campbell's 1976 study *The Transformation of American Foreign Relations, 1865–1900*. In addition to detailing the main diplomatic events of the period, Campbell also offers an argument, namely, that the 1870s and 1880s were frustrating years for expansionists, whose desires were often thwarted by the lingering but potent strands of an American anticolonial tradition. Campbell also explains why imperialism emerged at century's end, and part of his explanation is rooted in an awareness of the importance of events at home in initiating and cementing the change: the role of foreign and colonial markets in absorbing excess American industrial capacity, the activities of missionaries, the demands of the navy, the attraction of social Darwinism, and the raw force of racism. Yet Campbell's awareness of the interrelationship between domestic changes and foreign affairs is limited principally to the 1880s and 1890s. In Campbell's formulation, the absence of rugged and obvious imperialist expansion (à la 1898) means that there is little of real interest going on in American foreign policy beyond a general malaise in the 1870s. Campbell connects home and abroad during Reconstruction only by

of the specific diplomatic events of the period. But these surveys say precious little about the relationship between domestic policy and foreign affairs during Reconstruction. See Alexander DeConde, *A History of American Foreign Policy* (New York: Scribner's, 1963), 263–291; Samuel Flagg Bemis, *A Diplomatic History of the United States* (1936; reprint, New York: Holt, Rinehart, and Winston, 1965), 340–431; Thomas A. Bailey, *A Diplomatic History of the American People* (1940; reprint, Englewood Cliffs, N.J.: Prentice-Hall, 1980), 360–390.

[7] Good examples of books that focus on the developments of the 1890s even while claiming to begin analysis in 1865 or the early 1870s include John A. S. Grenville and George Berkley Young, *Politics, Strategy, and American Diplomacy: Studies in Foreign Policy, 1873–1917* (New Haven: Yale University Press, 1966); Milton Plesur, *America's Outward Thrust: Approaches to Foreign Affairs* (DeKalb: Northern Illinois University Press, 1971). For the economic argument (but, again, with heavy emphasis on the period after 1877), see Walter LaFeber, *The New Empire: An Interpretation of American Expansion, 1860–1898* (Ithaca, N.Y.: Cornell University Press, 1963). A good deal of very helpful, recent work stressing the interdependence between what happened at home and American foreign policy focuses on the late nineteenth century, after the conventional 1877 end of Reconstruction. See, for example, Matthew Frye Jacobson, *Barbarian*

way of fleeting reference to the wrangles during the Johnson administration—the arguments over impeachment were so fraught that foreign policy seemed mired, sluggish, and a cause of "postwar frustrations."[8]

Whatever the specific shortcomings of Campbell's work, it is arguably, if depressingly, the best diplomatic book covering Reconstruction. I don't mean to suggest that the period has not been treated ably by other diplomatic historians. Robert L. Beisner's *From the Old Diplomacy to the New, 1865–1900* (1975)—a short survey of the literature—offers solid detail and links domestic events to the evolution of a new, more coordinated foreign policy in the 1890s. But Beisner's emphasis is less on the "old" and more on the rise of the "new" diplomacy, and since he bookends the "old," unsystematic diplomacy between 1865 and 1889, Reconstruction per se occupies relatively little of his intelligent discussion. Similarly, Walter LaFeber's fine Cambridge history covers some of the main diplomatic developments during Reconstruction. Like Beisner, LaFeber discusses William Henry Seward's imperial-economic strategy in China (Seward signed a treaty in 1868 with the Chinese to provide needed labor in the West), the acquisition of Alaska in 1867 (itself made with an eye toward possible annexation of British Columbia), adventures in Central America, gaining a foothold in Hawaii, tentative ventures into Southeast Asia, the nettlesome problem of the Alabama Claims, and, of course, the debacle over Santo Domingo. For Seward, argues LaFeber, Reconstruction was a noisy aside, a misguided project interfering with the business of American expansion. Seward told liberal friends in 1866: "the North has nothing to do with the negroes. I have no more concern for them than I have for Hottentots. . . . They are not of our race. . . . The North must get over this notion of interference with the affairs of the South." Seward's views were clear, and Horace Greeley's were equally so—while he rejected expansion into Hawaii, he believed Canada's

Virtues: The United States Encounters Foreign Peoples at Home and Abroad, 1876–1917 (New York: Hill and Wang, 2000); H. W. Brands, "The Idea of the National Interest," *Diplomatic History* 23 (Spring 1999): 239–261; Robert Dallek, "National Mood and American Foreign Policy," *Diplomatic History* 34 (Fall 1982): 339–361; and Edward P. Crapol, "Coming to Terms with Empire: The Historiography of Late-Nineteenth-Century American Foreign Relations," *Diplomatic History* 16 (Fall 1992): 573–597. More specialized diplomatic histories are of little help. Judging by titles, Joseph A. Fry, *Dixie Looks Abroad: The South and Foreign Relations 1789–1973*—especially his chapter "Confronting the Reality of Dependence, 1865–1912"—looks promising. For our teacher, it would prove disappointing: *Dixie Looks Abroad* has its blind spots when it comes to Reconstruction. Neither is Tennant S. McWilliams's important study *The New South Faces the World: Foreign Affairs and the Southern Sense of Self, 1877–1950* (Baton Rouge: Louisiana State University Press, 1988) of use in this regard: for reasons that remain unclear, it begins its analysis in 1877. The exception is Eric T. L. Love's recent study of Santo Domingo, an important chapter in his *Race over Empire: Racism and U.S. Imperialism, 1865–1900* (Chapel Hill: University of North Carolina Press, 2004).

[8] Campbell, *Transformation of American Foreign Relations*, 8, 11, 21.

white population was better suited to incorporation. Helpful though LaFeber's survey is—all twenty or so pages of it—it is less detailed than either Beisner's or Campbell's, emphasizes the economic aspects of Reconstruction's foreign initiatives, and does not do much by way of braiding events at home with developments abroad in any detailed, sustained fashion.[9]

Reconstruction on Foreign Affairs

The publication in 1988 of Eric Foner's synthesis *Reconstruction* represented something of an unacknowledged turning point in the historiography of foreign affairs during Reconstruction. It is a book that would be immensely helpful to our bedraggled teacher. With the exception of two hugely neglected, if narrowly focused and poorly documented, essays published in 1966 (one by W. L. Morton, "Canada and Reconstruction, 1863–79," the other by Harry Bernstein, "South America Looks at North American Reconstruction"), Foner's five or so pages on foreign matters are the only pages in which a modern historian of Reconstruction inquires seriously into the broad significance, relevance, and meaning of foreign affairs to the period.[10]

Judging by book reviews, most historians missed the importance—or even the presence—of Foner's discussion of foreign policy, preferring instead to talk about Foner's main theme: the centrality of the black experience to Reconstruction. Most reviewers seemed stunned by the book, perhaps overwhelmed by its scope. "What is left to be done?" asked a dazed Michael Perman. In short, "Where now?" was the prevailing byline following the book's publication. Almost no one commented on the inclusion of foreign policy in the book. Indeed, the only review to mention Foner's handling and inclusion of foreign affairs was dismissive. Toward the end of his review of Foner's book, David Donald remarked: "Foreign relations are passed over lightly." Donald was right but unduly tart. After all, of all the main synthetic works on Reconstruction, only Foner's pays any real attention to foreign policy and how it affected Reconstruction. The ordinarily thorough William Dunning did offer a chapter entitled "A Critical Period in Foreign Affairs" in which he presented farsighted commentary on the relationship between Grant's designs for Santo Domingo and troubles within the Republican Party (arriving at conclusions not unlike Foner's). But Dunning's treat-

[9] Robert L. Beisner, *From the Old Diplomacy to the New, 1865–1900*, 2nd ed. (Arlington Heights, Ill.: Harlan Davidson, 1986; orig. 1975); LaFeber, *Cambridge History of American Foreign Relations*, 10–11, 1–20.

[10] Bernstein's and Morton's essays are in *New Frontiers of the American Reconstruction*, ed. Harold M. Hyman (Urbana, Ill.: University of Illinois Press, 1966), 87–104, 105–124, respectively.

ment is brief, temporally constructed (he examines only the 1865–73 period), and, besides his commentary on Grant, does almost nothing to connect domestic and foreign. W. E. B. Du Bois's magnificent *Black Reconstruction* was, curiously enough for a leftist, even less attentive to foreign matters than Dunning and remained virtually silent on the matter. And E. Merton Coulter's otherwise solid, even imaginative, volume is quiet, too.[11]

Foner's attention to the interrelationship of foreign and domestic policy, while relatively modest, should prove helpful for anyone who wants to think about writing a history of Reconstruction that includes the impact of foreign policy initiatives on domestic economic and social programs, north and south. As Foner shows, there were important developments in U.S. foreign policy during Reconstruction, developments that foreshadowed America's aggressive look outward during the 1880s and 1890s, developments indicative of the core values of the architects of Reconstruction. Reconstruction didn't end prematurely because of foreign policy interests, but these interests did temper the Republican Party's commitment to fulfilling the promise of Reconstruction.

By Foner's account, most foreign policy initiatives during Reconstruction, especially under Seward, were really efforts by Republicans to cement the move toward a nation-state. Republican thinking on foreign relations was very much shaped by the two overriding concerns of Reconstruction: race and economic development. Matters of foreign affairs, while not foremost in most minds, were nonetheless present. Congressman Hernando D. Money of Mississippi, for example, argued in 1876 that the United States must acquire Hawaii to complement "the march of empire" and to enable Americans to continue to enjoy "Asiatic commerce." Foner's brief but perceptive remarks show that foreign policy initiatives were an important source of friction within the Republican Party. Grant wanted to acquire Santo Domingo "partly in the belief that Afri-

---

[11] Michael Perman, "Eric Foner's *Reconstruction*: A Finished Revolution," *Reviews in American History* 17 (March 1989): 78; Peter Kolchin, review, *Georgia Historical Quarterly* 72 (Winter 1988): 753; David Donald, "The Black Side of the Story," *New Republic*, August 1, 1988, 44; see also C. Vann Woodward, "Unfinished Business," *New York Review of Books*, May 12, 1988, 22. William A. Dunning, *Reconstruction, Political and Economic* (New York: Harper, 1907), 151–173. His most helpful insights are on 164–165; E. Merton Coulter, *The South during Reconstruction, 1865–1877* (Baton Rouge: Louisiana State University Press, 1947). Foner's discussion of foreign affairs takes place principally on pages 492–496 of *Reconstruction*. See also Henry Steele Commager and Richard B. Morris, editors' introduction to Foner, *Reconstruction*, xvii. I note with interest that another book in the New American Nation series, also under the guidance of Commager and Morris—Campbell's *Transformation of American Foreign Relations, 1865–1900*—at least attends to diplomatic history during Reconstruction. For his part, David Donald offered some tantalizing but underdeveloped remarks on the importance of diplomatic developments during Reconstruction, particularly on the ways foreign policy reveals the ambivalence of postwar nationalism. See David Herbert Donald, *Liberty and Union* (Boston: Little, Brown, 1978), 219–223.

can Americans might want to leave for the new possession, partly in the hope of helping his friends acquire a prized naval base." Charles Sumner opposed its annexation, while black leaders, including Frederick Douglass—who served as secretary of a commission that visited the Dominican Republic in 1871—and Senator Hiram Revels and Congressman Joseph Rainey hoped that annexation would help ease the plight of impoverished Dominicans. Annexation failed, but its importance lies in showing that black and white leaders were actively engaged in affairs outside of domestic policy and that foreign affairs fissured the Republican Party.[12]

As refreshing and innovative as Foner's discussion is, however, there is a limit to what even the best historians can do in half a dozen or so pages. Yes, Foner integrates foreign affairs into the period, but he does so for very specific purposes. In short, Foner—rightly and effectively—uses foreign initiatives (with emphasis on the Dominican Republic) to stress the growing conservatism of the Grant administration and the growing split between liberal-minded reformers and those who would eventually abandon Reconstruction. Essentially, Foner uses the debate over Dominican annexation to reveal with special clarity emerging splits within the Republican Party and a growing indifference to the plight of freedpeople. For Foner "nothing revealed more starkly the President's lack of concern for reformers' sensibilities than his effort to annex the Dominican Republic."[13] But this leaves many empirical questions hanging and raises more theoretical ones than it answers. Empirically, we might ask about the other initiatives noted by Campbell, Beisner, and LaFeber but not analyzed by Foner. How did Alaska, China, and events in Europe speak, if at all, to Reconstruction? Conceptually, Foner tends to leave us with the impression that foreign policy during Reconstruction is relevant only insofar as it tells us about the unraveling of domestic events and the end of Reconstruction. But might a closer consideration of foreign matters broaden our scope of "foreign" affairs, help us better understand developments within the United States, encourage us to look beyond the North/South binary, and even lead us to reconsider the meaning that contemporaries attached to the terms "foreign" and "domestic"?

Hawaii Within

In her recent study *The Anarchy of Empire* (2002), Amy Kaplan calls for a dedicated exploration of the interrelationship between domestic and foreign in U.S. history. Arguing that "domestic and foreign spaces are closer than we think,"

---

[12] LaFeber, *Cambridge History of American Foreign Relations*, 25, 67; Foner, *Reconstruction*, 492–494.

[13] Foner, *Reconstruction*, 494.

Kaplan tries to "challenge the traditional understanding of imperialism as a one-way imposition of power in distant colonies." Critically, Kaplan "explore[s] how international struggles for domination abroad profoundly shape representations of American national identity at home, and how, in turn, cultural phenomena we think of as domestic or particularly national are forged in a crucible of foreign relations." Domestic concerns—the "idea of the nation as home"—are woven into foreign policy and affairs.[14]

Kaplan's argument is no mere abstraction. Even in dry legal deliberations we see the ambiguity and slipperiness of place and designation, foreign and domestic. Puerto Rico, for example—which Spain ceded to the United States as a result of the 1898 Spanish-American War—was not, in the words of Justice Edward Douglas White, "a foreign country, since it was subject to the sovereignty of and was owned by the United States." That much said, "it was foreign to the United States in a domestic sense, because the island had not been incorporated into the United States, but was merely appurtenant thereto as a possession." Kaplan rightly asks "What does it mean to be 'foreign' in the 'domestic sense'?" and she uses the question as the basis for an argument that should be helpful to historians of Reconstruction. If she is right that "domestic metaphors of national identity are intimately intertwined with renderings of the foreign and the alien, and that the notions of the domestic and the foreign mutually constitute one another," we are under no small obligation to broaden our empirical and analytical radar to include the "foreign." Moreover, failure to do so will appreciably stunt our understanding of the domestic.[15]

Kaplan shows how late-nineteenth-century U.S. foreign policy designated others—such as Puerto Ricans—"foreign to the United States in a domestic sense." They were "rendered racially other through familiar and recognizable stereotypes of nonwhite citizens at home, who were seen as foreign within the nation." These "others" at home included Native Americans (already domestic dependent nations, courtesy of the 1831 *Cherokee Nation v. the State of Georgia*), freedpeople, and immigrants. Kaplan argues that "the racialized analogies that empire deployed at home and abroad created dissonance as well as resonance, as they mutually defined and destabilized one another." The anarchy of empire resided in this interplay: anarchy abroad was used to justify American imperialism, even as outward expansion led to closer self-scrutiny. Kaplan explains: "If the fantasy of American imperialism aspires to a borderless world where it finds its own reflection everywhere, then the fruition of this dream shatters the

<hr/>

[14] Amy Kaplan, *The Anarchy of Empire in the Making of U.S. Culture* (Cambridge, Mass.: Harvard University Press, 2002), 1. For an earlier work that makes a similar (if more limited) argument, see Schoonover, *Dollars over Dominion*, 212–250. Note, too, Sexton, "Toward a Synthesis of Foreign Relations in the Civil War Era," 58–59.

[15] Kaplan, *The Anarchy of Empire*, 2, 3, 4.

coherence of national identity, as the boundaries that distinguish it from the outside world promise to collapse."[16]

Kaplan's chronology is broad, ranging from the evolution of domestic ideology and its influence on foreign relations in the antebellum period to developments in the twentieth century. In the middle of her discussion is a topic that speaks directly to historians of Reconstruction: Hawaii, long before its formal annexation—and the assumed beginnings of American imperialism—in 1898. Kaplan uses Mark Twain's writings on Hawaiian colonization just after the Civil War to illustrate the close connection between slavery, emancipation, and U.S. imperial expansion. Although Twain is known for his opposition to annexation of the Philippines, it was his first trip abroad—to Hawaii for six months in 1866—that influenced him most and, in Kaplan's estimation, "Americanized" him.[17]

Kaplan's discussion is full of examples of the foreign becoming the domestic, the domestic the foreign. In his lectures to American audiences about native Hawaiians, Twain rendered them "as both exotic and familiar in their unspoken resemblance to stereotypes of black slaves [sic] at home." Twain's Hawaiians were remarkably similar to Americans' freedpeople: "rich, dark brown, and kind of black and tan" with the old association of heat and indolence making an expected appearance: "The tropical sun and easy going ways inherited from their ancestors have made them rather idle." In a suggestive section, "Hawaii and the Reconstruction of the Old South," Kaplan argues that the last leg of Twain's Pacific journey was more than just a physical venture westward, for it also "took Twain homeward into the American South to explore the meaning of slavery and freedom." Parallels, comparisons, and analogies abounded: emerging sugar plantations in Hawaii echoed Louisiana's; "remnants of imperial violence that would not stay buried in the Hawaiian landscape" favored comparison to continued violence in the postbellum South; the sights and sounds of Hawaii—including native music and "dark-skinned savages"—at once made Hawaii different but also "brings Hawaii closer to home."[18]

Twain also understood economics through the domestic/foreign lens. Both southern and Hawaiian planters (mostly displaced New Englanders and Unionists) faced similar problems: how to make laborers work on plantations. Vagrancy laws were used to keep labor in check in both locations, not least because southern and Hawaiian planters shared the assumption that nonwhite

[16] Kaplan, *The Anarchy of Empire*, 10, 16.

[17] Kaplan, *The Anarchy of Empire*, 19, 52, 55.

[18] Kaplan, *The Anarchy of Empire*, 59, 74–78. Note, too, the similarities between Twain's depiction of the Hawaiian hula-hula—full of sensory extravagance, sexual meaning, "dismal" howls, and "distressing noises" (73) and white America's sensory stereotypes of freedpeople in the 1870s as documented in Smith, *Listening to Nineteenth-Century America*, ch. 10.

workers were incorrigibly idle. According to Kaplan, "Twain found Hawaii and America closer than he imagined geographically, on a map of international struggle that linked emancipation and imperialism in creating a coercive system of nonwhite free labor."[19]

So, too, with politics. At the same time that southern Democrats caricatured black and tan interracial legislatures, "Twain reported on Hawaii's interracial legislature with fascination and repulsion," describing their deliberations in ways that would not have been alien to a southern planter. For Twain, Hawaiian interracial governance was silly, incompetent, corrupt, run by a group incapable of honest self-government. Fears of nonwhites presiding over whites circulated in large eddies, swirling from deep within the postbellum South, stretching out across an ocean, and meeting their reflection mid-Pacific.[20]

Home and abroad, domestic and foreign, Hawaii and Virginia, were all related. Twain's notes for a novel on the Sandwich Islands twice mention Samuel Armstrong—a man who was active in Reconstruction with family influence in Hawaii and in Virginia. Samuel Armstrong's missionary father helped establish a system of education stressing the value of manual labor that was to prepare native Hawaiians for plantation work. Samuel, who was born in Hawaii, worked with his father until 1860, when he went to Williams College. He later enlisted in the Union army, led a black regiment, worked for the Freedmen's Bureau, and then founded Hampton Institute in Virginia. In Samuel Armstrong, Hawaii and Virginia braided, and his early experiences training native Hawaiians for manual labor had a significant impact on how he—and many others—came to understand the nature of freedpeople's labor. Armstrong lumped Indians, Africans, and Polynesians together as people lacking self-discipline, a group needing direction. He said of the "negro" and the "Polynesian": "Of both it is true that not mere ignorance, but deficiency of character is the chief difficulty, and to build up character is the true objective of education . . . conditioned very largely on a routine of industrious habit." His conclusion summed up the worldview of Hawaiian and southern planters (and, increasingly, northern conservatives): "Morality and industry go together. Especially in weak tropical races, idleness like ignorance breeds vice."[21]

Of course, as Eric T. L. Love's recent study shows, we must exercise care when trying to understand the relative importance of racism in shaping foreign

[19] Kaplan, *The Anarchy of Empire*, 78–80, quotation on 79.

[20] Kaplan, *The Anarchy of Empire*, 82–83.

[21] Kaplan, *The Anarchy of Empire*, 88–89. On Armstrong's influence among northerners, see Heather Cox Richardson, *The Death of Reconstruction: Race, Labor, and Politics in the Post–Civil War North, 1865–1901* (Cambridge, Mass.: Harvard University Press, 2001), 193, 208, 229. On northern attitudes, also see Sven Beckert, *The Monied Metropolis: New York City and the Consolidation of the American Bourgeoisie, 1850–1896* (New York: Cambridge University Press, 2001), especially 273–292.

policy. For Love, historians have too frequently and too incautiously explained late-nineteenth-century U.S. foreign policy in terms of race and racism alone. "Race was an imperfect crusading ideology," writes Love, "far too volatile a thing, politically, for the imperialists to place at the center of their furiously contested campaign." As with most studies of postbellum foreign policy, the majority of Love's book focuses on events of the 1880s and 1890s, U.S. dealings with Hawaii and the Philippines especially. But he offers a chapter on Santo Domingo that shows just how helpful and revisionist a tightly honed examination of the interplay between "domestic" and "foreign" during Reconstruction might be. Careful attention to the exploits of American adventures and capitalists already in Santo Domingo prior to Grant's presidency—men such as William Cazneau and Joseph Fabens—allows Love to explain the often pragmatic, political, and economic concerns governing relationships among American businessmen abroad, America diplomats in both Washington, D.C. (notably Hamilton Fish), and Santo Domingo (particularly General Orville Babcock), and Dominican politicians. For some, such as Fish, race was an important factor in the annexation debate; for others, such as Cazneau, Fabens, and Babcock, personal economic imperatives framed their understanding of the issue; and still others, like Grant, understood annexation as an issue at once intimately connected to domestic questions regarding sectional reconciliation and party politics. For Love, Santo Domingo cannot be understood independently of what was happening at home, how domestic concerns fed and shaped individuals' attitudes toward annexation, and how events in Santo Domingo—events often subject to manipulation and interpretation by interested Americans on the island nation—served in turn to alter domestic impressions of annexation. Love's rich, textured analysis not only tempers the heavy emphasis on racism alone as the guiding light of postbellum U.S. foreign policy but also helpfully explains that foreign and domestic affairs were constituted and framed dialectically by an evolving set of interpenetrating economic and political and not just racial concerns.[22]

Finding West in East: Korea

While hesitating to situate itself within the historiography of Reconstruction, recent work by diplomatic historian Gordon Chang on the United States–Korea war of 1871 nevertheless points to the close connections linking "home" and "abroad" during Reconstruction. On one level, Chang is concerned simply to recount the story—known to "only a small minority of American diplomatic historians" and never mentioned in accounts of Reconstruction by specialists—

---

[22] Love, *Race over Empire*, quotation on xviii. The discussion of Santo Domingo is on 27–72.

and to offer a more reliable factual account of what turned out to be a bloody and diplomatically significant encounter. But Chang's work also reveals more than one foreign policy during Reconstruction and suggests how American perceptions of Koreans influenced impressions of African Americans in the South and Native Americans in the West.[23]

The American public was well aware of the 1871 conflict. In Chang's telling, it was "one of the largest, if not the largest, and bloodiest uses of military forces overseas by the United States in the fifty years between the Mexican-American War of 1846–1848 and the Spanish-American War of 1898." Americans killed at least 250 Korean soldiers. "It was also the first time that American ground forces actually seized, held, and raised the American flag over territory in Asia."[24]

Chang's treatment deepens our understanding of Reconstruction and foreign affairs in the 1870s. For example, American expeditionary leaders found their behavior toward the Koreans shaped by notions about race and the oriental character, ideas that were remarkably similar to those many white Americans held about African Americans and Native Americans. The 1871 United States–Korea war also challenges the traditional interpretation of U.S. foreign policy, especially with regard to East Asia. Conventionally, U.S. policy in the region and attendant ventures into China and Japan have been explained as largely commercial imperatives. Chang finds this emphasis misleading. He sees American intervention in Korea as having less to do with trade and more to do with "American assumptions about races and civilization" and efforts to convert the "heathen" and civilize the savage.[25]

Expedition leaders and American officials generally confessed to knowing "very little" about the Koreans, and established racial stereotypes shaped their

[23] Gordon H. Chang, "Whose 'Barbarism'? Whose 'Treachery'? Race and Civilization in the Unknown United States–Korea War of 1871," *Journal of American History* 89 (March 2003): 1331–1365, quotation on 1332.

[24] Chang, "Whose 'Barbarism,'" 1333–1334.

[25] Chang, "Whose 'Barbarism,'" 1332, 1334. On American expansion and ideas of race generally, also see Paul A. Kramer, "Empires, Exceptions, and Anglo-Saxons: Race and Rule between the British and United States Empires, 1880–1910," *Journal of American History* 88 (March 2002): 1315–1353; Gerald Horne, "Race from Power: U.S. Foreign Policy and the General Crisis of 'White Supremacy,'" *Diplomatic History* 23 (Summer 1999): 437–461; Rubin Francis Weston, *Racism in U.S. Imperialism: The Influence of Racial Assumptions on American Foreign Policy, 1893–1946* (Columbia: University of South Carolina Press, 1972); and Alexander DeConde, *Ethnicity, Race, and American Foreign Policy: A History* (Boston: Northeastern University Press, 1992), 45–49 especially. For the conventional foreign policy interpretation, see William Appleman Williams, *The Tragedy of American Diplomacy*, rev. ed. (New York: Dell, 1962; orig. 1959); LaFeber, *Cambridge History of American Foreign Relations*; and Michael H. Hunt, *The Making of a Special Relationship: The United States and China to 1914* (New York: Columbia University Press, 1983).

actions and dealings. They thought Asians morally deficient, "mendacious, backward, and simply barbaric," as Chang expresses it. Frederick Low—expedition leader, newly appointed minister to China, and former governor of California—believed the "oriental character" to be distinguished by "cunning and sophistry" and thought the only way to deal with such people was to hit hard and decisively. What Low recommended in communicating with the Asian character many a southern planter and northern lessee said of southern freedpeople: do not let insults and bad behavior go unpunished because "[s]uch lenity" will only increase their "hostility." Similarly, Admiral John Rodgers, commander of the expedition's forces, considered Asians immature and physically repugnant. Dishonest, childish, in need of instruction, at times cunning but largely stolid, weak: such stereotypes affected the emerging debate in California concerning Chinese immigration and echoed racial stereotypes applied to southern blacks in precisely the same period. The similarity shouldn't be surprising: Rodgers and his men had fought "Seminoles in Florida, Mexicans during the 1846 war, and Confederates during the Civil War" and so were perfectly fluent in the idiom of race.[26]

While these racial stereotypes, as Chang suggests, go some way to explaining how and why American expeditionary leaders behaved as they did in 1871, the specificity of some of the images, how very closely they approximated widespread representations of African Americans in the same period, suggests that the nature of white American racial prejudice was much deeper and applied far more broadly to all sorts of "others" than a focus on the South during Reconstruction alone would suggest. Of course, the implication of this is very worrying indeed, namely, that postbellum racism was so extensive, so applicable to all nonwhites that to see or expect any genuine move toward racial equality in the 1870s is fanciful. Racism was so universal that all others—not just African Americans—were vilified and tainted, the application and migration of stereotypes between and among groups serving to lump all nonwhites into a group singularly inferior and simultaneously internal and external.[27]

For example, Low's experience in Korea deepened his hostility toward Asians at home. In 1876, Low served as an expert witness before a congressional committee on Chinese immigration. He urged restricting immigration, arguing that racial differences between whites and Asians were too extreme for harmony to reign. Like "negros," said Low, Asians were "incapable" of amalgamation with the "Anglo-Saxon race." In Low's mind, very quickly, blacks had become Asians,

[26] Chang, "Whose 'Barbarism,'" 1336, 1337, 1338, 1339. On domestic stereotypes of the Chinese, see Stuart Creighton Miller, *The Unwelcome Immigrant: The American Image of the Chinese, 1785–1882* (Berkeley: University of California Press, 1969).

[27] See also Matthew Frye Jacobson, *Whiteness of a Different Color: European Immigrants and the Alchemy of Race* (Cambridge, Mass.: Harvard University Press, 1998), esp. 157–158.

Asians had become blacks, and both had become other—separate, inassimilable, different: foreigners at home.[28]

Finding Reconstruction in Paris

Philip M. Katz's *From Appomattox to Montmartre* (1998) reminds us, first and foremost, that many Americans experienced Reconstruction indirectly, even in their physical absence. On the eve of the Franco-Prussian War in 1870, roughly five thousand Americans lived in Paris, many of them keenly involved in French society and politics. A cross-section of the U.S. middle class, they "brought with them to France all the same ideological preconceptions."[29]

Katz shows that Americans abroad tended to try to make sense of events—in his study, the events leading up to and including the Paris Commune—through the lens of Reconstruction. As he argues: "a common and compelling way to explain what happened in France was to offer analogies between the Commune and the American Civil War, including Reconstruction." Americans abroad also used their experiences to try to make better sense of what they had experienced at home. Indeed, "even when the Civil War was being used to make sense of the Commune, the Commune itself was being incorporated into the ongoing debate about the meaning of the Civil War."[30]

While American opinion was certainly aware of the Franco-Prussian War, it was very much split over which side to support. But once the Third French Republic had replaced Napoleon III's Second Empire, many Americans—both at home and in Paris—applauded the establishment of the Republic. On September 7, 1870, the United States became the first foreign power to recognize the Third Republic.[31]

Far more interesting for understanding the importance of foreign affairs and events and their relationship to contemporary understanding of Reconstruction, though, are instances of criticism, not support. Some Americans in Paris—including those who were solid Republicans back home—deemed French republicanism entirely too proletarian, gaudy, and raucous. They found French workers' apparent disregard for private property especially worrying. In this respect, Americans abroad said in the early 1870s what conservatives (Democrats and Republicans) would articulate after 1873 in the United States (and what elite southerners had been arguing all along): that revolutions had

---

[28] Chang, "Whose 'Barbarism,'" 1359–1360.

[29] Katz, *From Appomattox to Montmartre*, 26, 58.

[30] Katz, *From Appomattox to Montmartre*, 86.

[31] Katz, *From Appomattox to Montmartre*, 33–35.

to be conservative if they were to be helpful and that transfers of power to non-elites threatened the stability of the nation-state. Both southerners and northerners who lived in Paris expressed these fears, and after 1873, troubled American elites eagerly turned to the example of the Paris Commune to express their deep concerns about the possibility of the emergence of an American Commune.[32] Southern observers of the Commune in particular "brought the memory of historical misfortunes at home to their analysis" and used their experience to recreate an idealized past and invent an antebellum southern tradition. While in Paris, southerners argued that the Communards "are worse than the 'niggers,'" not least because, so the fantasy went, "negroes were faithful to their masters."[33]

But so, too, with northerners who repudiated the new French republic because of their own "growing doubts about the inherent desirability of popular government." As Katz explains, during the 1850s and the Civil War, these doubts had remained submerged, clouded, and muted by the question of slavery. Reconstruction clarified fundamental questions about citizenship, democracy, and politics. Increasingly, northern elites retreated from their earlier egalitarian claims about the desirability of universal suffrage. "In fact," argues Katz, echoing John Sproat's important work, "a mistrust of popular government in all its forms had been spreading for years among the genteel elite of the late nineteenth century." Many of these doubters—"Best Men"—had been enthusiastic antislavery Republicans; now their distrust was evidenced in their rejection of women's suffrage, the emerging liberal Republican movement, their fear of the working classes (especially during the Great Strike of 1877 but also, more generally, following the labor unrests after the 1873 Panic), and their surrender to southern postbellum independence. "The same mistrust tempered enthusiasm for the French Republic," argues Katz, elaborating: "in the midst of Reconstruction the French Republic and later the Commune became useful ways to focus and excuse the ideological shift away from popular government."[34]

The parallels were striking, especially when it came to evaluating who was capable of self-government. The increasingly violent events in Paris profiled developments within the United States so that political and economic agitation—ranging from the activities of southern freedpeople to women's suffrage supporters to the influx of immigrants—assumed a sinister aspect, one that elites of all political persuasions increasingly came to see as a threat to political order and individual liberty. Not everyone accepted the legitimacy of these

---

[32] Katz, *From Appomattox to Montmartre*, 37, 38, 161; Foner, *Reconstruction*, chap. 10; Richardson, *Death of Reconstruction*; Smith, *Listening to Nineteenth-Century America*, chap. 10.

[33] Katz, *From Appomattox to Montmartre*, 45, 46–47.

[34] Katz, *From Appomattox to Montmartre*, 92, 173–175; John G. Sproat, *"The Best Men": Liberal Reformers in the Gilded Age* (New York: Oxford University Press, 1968).

analogies, of course, and comparisons proved fluid and politically flexible—the Commune was used by defenders of states' rights as well as supporters of Reconstruction—but many serious people looked increasingly to the 1871 events in Paris, shuddered at what they saw, and braced themselves for a similar unraveling of order in the United States. Democrats and Republicans used "the Commune as a metaphor for illegitimate force," an example of ignorance co-opting democracy, an illustration of the world turned upside down, of corruption run riot in their discussions over the meaning and desirability of Reconstruction at home. Awareness of the Commune was important, for, as Katz ventures, it "provided Americans with a handy critique of democracy at home, which they might have been reluctant to offer without a foreign catalyst." In short, "whenever the Commune was likened to America, it became more plausible that soon the United States would be like Paris—a frightening thought, if the Commune signified disorder."[35]

Domestic Foreigners: Native Americans

All of this, of course, brings us to Native Americans. Or, put another way: by domesticating the Paris Commune in order to express fears about domestic instability and order, Americans came to compare the Reds of Paris with the Reds of the Southwest and Great Plains. Indians were at once both domestic and foreign, both in but not of the United States. By comparing Paris Communards with Native Americans, Americans achieved several things, and the analogy suggests why we need to incorporate the foreign if we are to fully understand the domestic.[36]

There is no doubt that the Communards were compared to particular Native American tribes. Analogies ran the gamut: both French Communards and Apaches were violent, destructive, blood-thirsty, barbarous; the French and the Arapaho and the Darien Indians of Panama embraced "communal chiefs and system of government" and rejected private property. To many, the comparison was natural: both the Indian and the Communard were on the warpath in the early 1870s, and both were imagined as foreign and barbaric in an effort to keep the "other" at bay—thus preserving notions of American distinctiveness—while also reminding American leaders that "others" were often nearer the American heartland than was sometimes supposed. On one level, distancing such foes made Americans feel safer; on another, deploying domestic analogies also invited insecurity, which in turn helped justify warring against Native

---

[35] Katz, *From Appomattox to Montmartre*, 96, 102, 119, 123.
[36] Katz, *From Appomattox to Montmartre*, 131.

Americans. In effect, then, the foreign became the domestic just as the domestic became the foreign.[37]

By examining the ways foreigners (Parisian Communards) stood in for and helped profile domestic worries (Native Americans), Katz furthers the point raised by Kaplan about what, exactly, constituted foreign and domestic during Reconstruction. But more needs to be made of these insights. After all, the work by Katz, Chang, and Kaplan tends to leave us with the false impression that while white racism was indeed rampant during the period, with foreign events serving to lump racialized "others"—African Americans, Asians, Native Americans—into one undifferentiated group, those groups who were "othered" apparently shared the common status of victim and didn't harbor their own racism. All of these topics—the place of Native Americans during Reconstruction, the definition of "foreign" and "domestic," and the racism of "othered" groups—have recently been explored by Claudio Saunt, who, ironically enough, seems unaware of the work by Chang, Kaplan, and Katz.[38]

Saunt explores the meaning of freedom for African Americans by reading the often unrelated fields of Native American and Reconstruction history.[39] Foremost, Saunt shows that the "story of ex-slaves and native peoples in Indian Territory complicates both Native American and Reconstruction historiography" by arguing that the "case of the Five Tribes suggests that freedom was at its most problematic in Indian Territory, where so-called natural rights had to be imposed by a colonial power" and that Native American leaders ended up employing "a language that resembled the rhetoric of states' rights." He also helpfully reminds us that between 10 and 30 percent of the populations of the Five Tribes (the Choctaws, Chickasaws, Creeks, Cherokees, and Seminoles—themselves hardly a united group) was made up of enslaved African Americans in 1860.[40]

[37] Katz, *From Appomattox to Montmartre*, 132, 90.

[38] Claudio Saunt, "The Paradox of Freedom: Tribal Sovereignty and Emancipation during the Reconstruction of Indian Territory," *Journal of Southern History* 70 (January 2004): 63–94.

[39] On the relative absence of detailed work on Native Americans during Reconstruction, see Saunt, "Paradox of Freedom," 65–66. Also see chaps. 6 and 7 of Saunt, *Black, White, and Indian: Race and the Unmaking of an American Family* (New York: Oxford University Press, 2005). Older work includes M. Thomas Bailey, *Reconstruction in Indian Territory: A Story of Avarice, Discrimination, and Opportunism* (Port Washington, N.Y.: Kennikat Press, 1972); Annie Heloise Abel, *The American Indian under Reconstruction* (Cleveland: Arthur H. Clark, 1925); and W. McKee Evans, *To Die Game: The Story of the Lowry Band, Indian Guerillas of Reconstruction* (Baton Rouge: Louisiana State University Press, 1971). For suggestive remarks on Indians and segregation during Reconstruction, see Malinda Maynor, "Native American Identity in the Segregated South: The Indians of Robeson County, North Carolina, 1872–1956" (Ph.D. diss., University of North Carolina at Chapel Hill, 2005), 2–3.

[40] Saunt, "Paradox of Freedom," 94, 64–65.

Embedded in Saunt's stimulating analysis is the basic understanding that his story is, above all, a story of American imperialism, of competing and connected definitions of "foreign" and "domestic," a story that suggests we should think very hard about a continued partitioning of home and abroad in historical writing on the period. In a revealing footnote, Saunt writes:

> In American history the age of imperialism traditionally begins in 1898 with the Spanish-American War. Yet this periodization overlooks the continuity between the U.S. colonization of Indian country and of the Philippines and Puerto Rico. At the turn of the nineteenth century, politicians and journalists frequently drew explicit connections among Indians, Filipinos, and Puerto Ricans and looked to the history of U.S.-Indian relations for lessons on how to govern their overseas colonies.

Plainly, for Saunt, at the intersection of debates over the freedom of Indian-owned black slaves, natural rights, the authority of the U.S. government, and Indian sovereignty stands the question of imperialism. It is an issue that has escaped our attention, Saunt suggests, because historians of foreign affairs train our eyes toward century's end. Implicit here is a helpful caution: while any effort to expand the temporal scope of Reconstruction to include the years after 1877 is useful, it should not be at the expense of ignoring critical developments in foreign relations before 1877, lest we repeat diplomatic history's unhelpful end-of-century focus.[41]

Saunt's work helps us see that the definition of who was and was not foreign or "other" was slippery and contingent. "In some ways," he argues, "Indian planters were as southern as their white counterparts." Many believed in the desirability of racial hierarchy, endorsed scientific racism, and bridled at federal efforts to assert the supremacy of the nation-state by imposing on the Five Tribes civil and political rights for blacks at war's end. Native Americans rightly saw such efforts as anticipating "a time when the Five Tribes would be folded into the United States." In this way, Saunt reveals how many Native American former slaveholders viewed African Americans as foreign to their culture and unworthy of equality; how some Native Americans viewed the United States as a foreign government intent on imposing its authority on Indian Territory and sovereignty; and how the U.S. Reconstruction governments considered the incorporation of largely "foreign" Indian nations into the United States essential to the "domestic" project of the American nation-state. Whatever Saunt's

[41] Saunt, "Paradox of Freedom," 66 n. 9. Saunt relies on the discussion offered in Walter L. Williams, "United States Indian Policy and the Debate over Philippine Annexation: Implications for the Origins of American Imperialism," *Journal of American History* 66 (March 1980): 810–831.

specific conclusions, his work shows, quite clearly, that notions of domestic and foreign, of external and internal, were far more complicated and varied than a traditional view of U.S. foreign policy in the period suggests.[42]

Recent works, then, offer hope. They speak precisely to calls to internationalize U.S. history and help rescue a topic that has remained something of an intellectual backwater. But much remains to be done, and, in terms of research, dozens of areas cry out for either further, more detailed consideration or initial investigation. In both instances, insights concerning the interrelationship between domestic and foreign affairs will deepen understanding. For example, monographs dedicated to exploring the underexamined Dominican annexation and on the poorly understood projects for African colonization during Reconstruction would be helpful. We might also consider in more detail how foreigners viewed and evaluated Reconstruction, and we would be well advised to examine more closely events in, and the meaning of, the borderlands, north and south, to Reconstruction as both a period and a project. Early (and neglected) work by Harry Bernstein entitled "South America Looks at North American Reconstruction" (1966) and Thomas Schoonover's later analysis of Mexico and the United States from 1865 to 1867 should prove useful building blocks here. Building on work by Richard Franklin Bensel and, more recently, Jay Sexton, such an emphasis might also lead us to think more deeply about how, for example, the international finance community viewed Republican fiscal policy and how their impressions affected foreign investment during Reconstruction. Mitchell Snay's recent work exploring the connections between Fenianism and "other political and ideological struggles during Reconstruction" opens up a profitable avenue of inquiry because it suggests not only the centrality of the idea of democracy to Reconstruction—one often framed by Fenians in terms of nationalism and self-determination—but also the extent to which the Fenian movement in the United States built on, and helped promote, an impressive awareness of foreign events and parallels.[43]

[42] Saunt, "Paradox of Freedom," 71, 75, quotations 69, 72.

[43] Thomas Bender, ed., *Rethinking American History in a Global Age* (Berkeley: University of California Press, 2002); Bernstein, "South America Looks at North American Reconstruction," in Hyman, *New Frontiers of the American Reconstruction*; Schoonover, *Dollars over Dominion*, chap. 8. On Canada, the Northwest, and the importance of the border during Reconstruction, see Beth LaDow, *The Medicine Line: Life and Death on a North American Borderland* (New York: Routledge, 2001), esp. 7–18, 43–58. Also useful in this context is Morton, "Canada and Reconstruction," in Hyman, *New Frontiers of the American Reconstruction*. On finance, see Richard Franklin Bensel, *Yankee Leviathan: The Origins of Central State Authority in America, 1859–1877* (New York: Cambridge University Press, 1990); Jay Sexton, *Debtor Diplomacy: Finance and American Foreign Relations in the Civil War Era, 1837–1873* (Oxford: Oxford University Press, 2005). On the Fenians, see Mitchell Snay, "The Imagined Republic: The Fenians, Irish American Nationalism, and the Political Culture of Reconstruction," *Proceedings of the American Antiquarian Society* 112, pt. 2 (2004): 291–313.

Fundamentally, though, we still need to know a lot more about basic events. Amy Kaplan's book, for example, is an important one, certainly relevant to historians of Reconstruction. But it is an unapologetically suggestive work, more concerned with theory than evidence, and since it is a book about how to better understand U.S. foreign policy, neither is it strictly concerned with refining our understanding of Reconstruction. Basic questions remain: how aware were southern planters, northern capitalists, freedpeople, the public generally of the developments in Hawaii or, for that matter, Korea? Did people include observations on Hawaii and the Paris Commune in their letters and diaries? If so, what did they say about such events? Did they consider them "foreign" or was the appreciation of "foreign" more complicated and contingent, as the aforementioned work suggests? In short, if we are to fulfill the promise of recent efforts to look abroad to understand home and to comprehend the domestic by examining the foreign, we need rather more empirical research.

A telling irony in all of this is that the main advances made in the study of foreign affairs during Reconstruction are courtesy of nonspecialists: diplomatic historians (Chang and, to some extent, Love and Sexton), an intellectual historian (Katz), and a student of literature (Kaplan). It is time for mainstream historians of Reconstruction to apply their knowledge to foreign affairs during Reconstruction. Doing so will not only expand our knowledge of a variety of domestic and foreign matters but will also heighten our appreciation of the interplay between home and abroad, self and other, in a period that very much shaped the trajectory of foreign policy in the late nineteenth century. Should the revised narrative be successful, diplomatic historians might well take the Reconstruction period more seriously than they have, not least because their full understanding of late-nineteenth-century developments will necessarily have to include earlier developments. Moreover, a systematic and dedicated consideration of foreign policy during Reconstruction might have the additional dividend of recovering the complexity of the past for the American public, reminding them that our growing awareness of the braided nature of "domestic" and "foreign," courtesy of the recent acceleration in the global circulation of goods, people, and information, has a deeper genealogy than they might appreciate. But before historians of Reconstruction can educate historians of diplomacy, they must educate themselves.

6

RECONSTRUCTION AS A CONSTITUTIONAL CRISIS

MICHAEL VORENBERG

The one-handed historian of Reconstruction is as elusive as the one-handed economist asked for by President Harry S. Truman, who had heard one too many assessments of the nation's financial condition that begin with "on one hand . . . but on the other." When asked to describe Reconstruction as a success or failure, we historians, like Truman's economists, tend to follow our list of the impressive achievements of the period with caveats and disclaimers. Slavery was abolished, but, on the other hand, African Americans did not fare as well as some had hoped. The economic system became more modern, more industrialized, but, on the other hand, workers were slow to reap any benefits from industrialization. The nation became stronger, but, on the other hand, it was weakened by persistent corruption, sectionalism, and factionalism.

Even with one hand tied behind the back, however, the historian can offer one undisputable result of Reconstruction: a new United States Constitution. Between 1865 and 1870, three constitutional amendments were adopted, securing the most far-reaching personal rights ever written into the nation's charter. Attached to each of these measures was powerful congressional enforcement legislation. The federal court system, which the victors in the Civil War had once regarded as a mere tool of the "Slave Power," came to be regarded as a coequal branch of government. Naysayers at the start of the Civil War who had bewailed the inadequacy of the Constitution and predicted its demise now sang a different tune. Listen to the 1875 paean of the normally staid Theophilus Parsons, a leading legal theorist of the nineteenth century:

> Over us all the Constitution bends like a universal sky, holding us all within its embrace, but lifted up too high for any one to reach it with a sacrilegious hand. Like the sky, it . . . surrounds us at every step and at every moment, and

yet so soft, so yielding and invisible, that we do not think of it . . . and yet it may, when there is need, put forth its strength,—and who can stand against the might of the unfettered wind.[1]

The Constitution, it would seem, was tested by the Civil War and strengthened by Reconstruction.

Or was it? Did Reconstruction change Americans' relation to the Constitution in any significant way? Historians have tended to accept that the Civil War was a crucial period of change for the Constitution. Arthur Bestor went so far as to title his landmark article of 1964 "The American Civil War as a Constitutional Crisis."[2] Was Reconstruction also a constitutional crisis, a watershed moment in constitutional development? The question is crucial, not only for the history of Reconstruction but for current constitutional interpretation. If the constitutional developments of Reconstruction were incidental only, then constitutional interpreters today need not give these developments—even the Reconstruction amendments—any special attention. But if Reconstruction was a dramatic period of constitutional change, then interpreters need to understand the nature of that change and be willing to act as radically as their forebears. Not to do so is to commit an unjust act of willful forgetting. Such a "desire to forget" characterizes the current Supreme Court's view of Reconstruction, argues Norman W. Spaulding, who claims that the Court seems to wish that the legal questions raised during Reconstruction would "just hurry up and disappear."[3]

With so much at stake, it would seem natural that the Reconstruction-era Constitution would be a favorite subject of historians. But the dominant trend in Reconstruction history has not been the discovery of the Constitution but rather its disappearance. For Reconstruction history to thrive, it must again take up the subject of the Constitution, though in ways that keep pace with larger trends in legal and constitutional history.

The Mysterious Disappearance of the Constitutional History of Reconstruction

In early histories of Reconstruction, the Constitution took center stage. Leading historians of Reconstruction in the early twentieth century, from William A. Dunning and John Burgess to W. E. B. Du Bois, highlighted constitutional

[1] Theophilus Parsons, *The Political, Personal, and Property Rights of a Citizen of the United States* (Hartford: S. S. Scranton, 1875), 4–5.

[2] Arthur Bestor, "The American Civil War as a Constitutional Crisis," *American Historical Review* 69 (January 1964): 327–353.

[3] Norman W. Spaulding, "Constitution as Countermonument: Federalism, Reconstruction, and the Problem of Collective Memory," *Columbia Law Review* 103 (December 2003): 2001.

improvement as a leading benefit resulting from Reconstruction.[4] Even critics of constitutional developments of the era, most famous among them James G. Randall, put constitutional history at the center of the story of the Civil War and Reconstruction.[5] These histories wisely set the time parameters of Reconstruction to include the Civil War. As more than a few historians have noted, Reconstruction began not with Appomattox in 1865 but with Fort Sumter in 1861. And, for the purposes of this essay, the first shot again will mark the beginning of Reconstruction, though the more traditional date of 1877 will be the endpoint.

Although these early studies defined the temporal bounds of Reconstruction broadly, they suffered from a thin archival base and an even narrower definition of what made up the Constitution. For these scholars, the Constitution consisted mainly of the document itself, a few famous tracts by constitutional scholars, and the published opinions of the Supreme Court and a few leading law-makers, including presidents, attorneys general, and congressmen.

By midcentury, historians were broadening the scope of their sources and questions. They moved fearlessly into the archives, especially as the personal papers of jurists and congressmen became available. More important, they redefined "constitutional" as including the large set of relationships between the nation's government and its people, and they heeded the call of Bestor's "Constitutional Crisis" article, which argued that constitutional questions encompassed a "torrent of ideas and interests and anxieties" beyond legislative actions and court decisions.[6]

Pioneering the new constitutional history of Reconstruction was Harold M. Hyman, who already had published his seminal works on loyalty oaths prior to Bestor's article but then, in 1973, published the most comprehensive study to date of the Reconstruction Constitution: *A More Perfect Union*.[7] Unlike previous scholars, who had taken on faith the notion that a nearly perfect Constitution had grown more perfect during Reconstruction, and that the Constitution had saved Reconstruction from spinning the nation into utter turmoil,

---

[4] W. A. Dunning, *Constitution of the United States in Civil War and Reconstruction, 1860–1867* (New York: J. F. Pearson, 1885); John Burgess, *Reconstruction and the Constitution, 1866–1876* (New York: Scribner's, 1902); W. E. B. Dubois, "Reconstruction and Its Benefits," *American Historical Review* 15 (1910): 781–799.

[5] James G. Randall, *The Confiscation of Property during the Civil War* (Indianapolis: Bobbs-Merrill, 1913), and Randall, *Constitutional Problems under Lincoln* (New York: Appleton, 1926).

[6] Bestor, "The American Civil War as a Constitutional Crisis," 352.

[7] Harold M. Hyman, *A More Perfect Union: The Impact of the Civil War and Reconstruction on the Constitution* (New York: Knopf, 1973). For Hyman's earlier work on loyalty oaths, see Harold M. Hyman, *The Era of the Oath: Northern Loyalty Tests during the Civil War and Reconstruction* (Philadelphia: University of Pennsylvania Press, 1954); and Hyman, *To Try Men's Souls: Loyalty Tests in American History* (Berkeley: University of California Press, 1959).

Hyman emphasized the improvised quality with which law-makers took steps that altered the Constitution in unforeseeable, if short-lived, ways. Moreover, he questioned the triumphalist narrative of his predecessors, pointing out that while many architects of the new Constitution of the Reconstruction era, especially the more radical Republicans, had intended to create a new nation firmly committed to liberty and equality for all, preexisting norms of constitutional practice and theory "failed to translate into reality the substance of the Republicans' vision of equality for Americans before states' laws as a characteristic of national citizenship."[8]

Hyman's two leading students, Phillip S. Paludan and Michael Les Benedict, carried his ideas even further, shedding light on the precise way that impulses toward egalitarian constitutionalism lost their traction in the face of more traditional, formalistic modes of constitutional practice and theory. Paludan concentrated on the first generation of postwar constitutional scholars—Francis Lieber, Joel Parker, and Thomas M. Cooley, among others—to show the essentially conservative bent of the minds behind the new constitutional law. Limited by older ideas of federalism, by racism in new forms, and by laissez-faire attitudes toward federal power, these thinkers felt bound by the Constitution, not unleashed by it. "We have done all that we could," they said. And, in Paludan's assessment, "they were right, tragically right."[9]

Benedict blamed the failure to realize complete constitutional egalitarianism on the day-to-day developments in partisan politics, which forced "a compromise of principle"—a phrase he used for the title of a remarkable monograph that combined the best of the new constitutional history with the best of the "new" political history. ("New" is a difficult word to track, especially in political history; at that time, "new" referred to careful quantitative analysis of political data.) Through a close examination of policy creation and partisan politics at the state and national levels, Benedict revealed that not all so-called Radical Republicans were radical in their attitudes toward race and the Constitution, and that constitutional change was always channeled through the distinctive terrain of American party politics.[10]

Concurrent with the work of Hyman and his students came equally impressive volumes from Herman Belz, who went even further than Benedict in positing a conservative basis to Radical Reconstruction. Radicals were distinguished by their political style, not their constitutional ideas, Belz argued. In fact, ele-

[8] Hyman, *A More Perfect Union*, 553.

[9] Phillip S. Paludan, *A Covenant with Death: The Constitution, Law, and Equality in the Civil War Era* (Urbana: University of Illinois Press, 1975), 282.

[10] Michael Les Benedict, *A Compromise of Principle: Congressional Republicans and Reconstruction, 1863–1869* (New York: Norton, 1974), and "Preserving the Constitution: The Conservative Basis of 'Radical Reconstruction,'" *Journal of American History* 61 (June 1974): 65–90.

ments of the Radical program were more conservative than those of some of their more conservative rivals.[11]

If the arguments of Benedict and Belz seemed pointed, if not barbed, compared to those of Hyman and an earlier generation of constitutional historians, it may have been because they were often aimed at a specific group of law professors who were new to the field of Reconstruction history and seemed at times in thrall to the Radical Republicans of the 1860s and 1870s. In the midst of national debates over civil liberties and civil rights beginning in the 1950s, it was natural that the issues being debated in and between history departments would also grab the attention of historically minded scholars in the law schools. In 1951, the legal scholar Jacobus tenBroek wrote a book that gleaned from Reconstruction-era congressional debates a justification for a progressive program of equal rights. That volume, *Equal under Law*, gained even greater notice as the *Brown v. Board of Education* case made its way to the Supreme Court.[12]

Suddenly, it seemed, historians could be useful. Advocates for both sides of the *Brown* case solicited the help of historians of Reconstruction, including John Hope Franklin and C. Vann Woodward, to bolster their arguments. Meanwhile, other legal scholars followed the lead of tenBroek and did their own research into Reconstruction-era documents. Arthur Kinoy joined tenBroek on the left side of the issue, arguing that the architects of civil rights law during Reconstruction possessed an egalitarianism that should guide modern lawmakers and jurists.[13] Charles Fairman journeyed through the same historical documents but landed to the right of tenBroek and Kinoy. His major study of 1971, which appeared in the much-esteemed work *History of the Supreme Court of the United States*, dug much more deeply into the archives and lower federal court cases than did the work of his academic rivals, whom he accused of reading selectively and ignoring the way Reconstruction-era law-makers were focused far more on immediate political matters than on larger moral questions. Moreover, argued Fairman, the moral universe in which Reconstruction-era law-makers operated was fundamentally different from, and thus irrelevant to, modern constitutional matters.[14]

For more than a decade after Arthur Bestor's 1964 article on "Constitutional Crisis," historians had answered with penetrating studies that examined the

[11] Herman Belz, *Reconstructing the Union: Theory and Policy During the Civil War* (Ithaca, N.Y.: Cornell University Press, 1969); *Emancipation and Equal Rights: Politics and Constitutionalism during the War* (New York: Norton, 1978); *A New Birth of Freedom: The Republican Party and Freedmen's Rights, 1861 to 1866* (Westport, Conn.: Greenwood Press, 1976).

[12] Jacobus tenBroek, *Equal under Law* (Berkeley: University of California Press, 1951).

[13] Arthur Kinoy, "The Constitutional Right of Negro Freedom," *Rutgers Law Review* 21 (1967): 387–441.

[14] Charles Fairman, *Reconstruction and Reunion, 1864–1888*, pt. 1, vol. 6 of *History of the Supreme Court of the United States* (New York: Macmillan, 1971).

most important constitutional matters using new bodies of evidence and new angles of inquiry. And then, suddenly, constitutional history, not only of the Reconstruction era but of all periods of American history, was declared dead. That seemed to be the message delivered by the American Society for Legal History when it considered making "Is Constitutional History Dead?" the theme of its 1980 annual meeting.[15] Courses on constitutional history began disappearing from college catalogues, and, in the words of one scholar in 1981, evidence suggested "a serious erosion of concern with constitutional law and history in the training of both undergraduate and graduate students."[16]

Who had killed off constitutional history? For scholars of the Reconstruction era, some of the leading suspects were constitutional historians themselves, who by the end of the 1970s had arrived at a stalemate on the question of whether law-makers one hundred years earlier had been essentially liberal or conservative, or whether they were driven more by morality or expediency.[17] With stalemate came staleness. Students of Reconstruction understandably assumed that all of the most interesting questions concerning constitutional development in the period had been asked and answered. Such beliefs were undoubtedly reinforced by the publication in 1982 of *Equal Justice under Law*, a volume coauthored by Hyman and William M. Wiecek, which covered constitutional history from 1835 to 1875. The chapters on Reconstruction, most of which were authored by Hyman, offered new research as well as a synthesis of Hyman's own work with the new scholarship of the 1970s, producing seemingly definitive, if carefully hedged, answers to the crucial questions that had dominated the field in the twentieth century.[18]

Although constitutional historians might have contributed to the demise of the constitutional history of Reconstruction, the prime suspects were practitioners of the "new legal history." (As with political history, what was labeled "new" in legal history beginning in the 1960s might seem outdated today.) In many ways the stepchild of the legal realism movement of the early twentieth century, the "new legal history" was concerned less with the origins and designs of governmental policies than with what J. Willard Hurst, one of the pioneers of the new practice, called "the social functions of law."[19] For the new legal historians, law was neither an inherently important, isolated institution nor an accurate indicator, as Bestor had once suggested, of popular attitudes. Rather,

[15] Harry N. Scheiber, "American Constitutional History and the New Legal History: Complementary Themes in Two Modes," *Journal of American History* 68 (September 1981): 337.

[16] Scheiber, "American Constitutional History and the New Legal History," 339.

[17] Michael Les Benedict, "Equality and Expediency in the Reconstruction Era: A Review Essay," *Civil War History* 23 (December 1977): 322–335.

[18] Harold M. Hyman and William M. Wiecek, *Equal Justice under Law: Constitutional Development, 1835–1875* (New York: Harper and Row, 1982).

[19] Cited in Scheiber, "American Constitutional History and the New Legal History," 340.

law was a lens into the way power—not simply abstract, *governmental* power but *economic* power—structured society. One of the implicit assumptions of the new legal history was that long-term, less readily detectable phenomena, such as the concentration of economic power into a narrow segment of society, had a greater impact on law than did manifest events such as the Civil War. In addition, the lens of the new legal historians was wider than that of their predecessors: they spent as much time, if not more, examining private law instead of public law.

With the rise of the new legal history, the old subject of the impact of the Civil War and Reconstruction on the law, which tended to involve short-lived phenomena and the eclipsing of private law by public constitutional debates, garnered less and less interest. The Civil War and Reconstruction played no part in the work of Hurst or of Morton J. Horwitz and Lawrence M. Friedman, the best known practitioners of the new legal history. Friedman's inattention was as much the result of organizational structure as interpretation. His magisterial *History of American Law*, the first edition of which was published in 1973, was organized thematically rather than chronologically, so a sustained focus on the single period of Reconstruction would have been inappropriate. To the extent that he *was* interested in public law during Reconstruction, Friedman attended more to state rather than federal constitutional change, and he regarded the best-known legal developments of the period as more nominal than substantive, especially when it came to achieving legal equality among the races.[20]

The absence of the Civil War and Reconstruction is more pronounced in the work of Horwitz. The first volume of his *The Transformation of American Law* ended in 1860; the second began in 1870. One might have assumed that there was no transformation of American law during the Civil War and Reconstruction were it not for one tantalizing statement in Horwitz's second volume that "the trauma of the Civil War" may have helped trigger the longing for a strong, neutral state that characterized the "classical legal thought" of the late nineteenth century. Horwitz gave more attention to public law in his second volume than his first, but because his emphasis remained on private law, Reconstruction, unsurprisingly, did not occupy a central place in his work.[21]

More recently, the historian Howard Schweber has written *The Creation of American Common Law, 1850–1880: Technology, Politics, and the Construction of Citizenship* (2004), a book that follows the lead of Horwitz and other legal historians in paying special attention to property law. With a subtitle that includes the

[20] Lawrence M. Friedman, *A History of American Law*, 2nd ed. (New York: Simon and Schuster, 1985); see esp. 346–347, 504–510.

[21] Morton J. Horwitz, *The Transformation of American Law, 1780–1860* (Cambridge, Mass: Harvard University Press, 1977), and *The Transformation of American Law, 1870–1960: The Crisis of Legal Orthodoxy* (New York: Oxford University Press, 1992), 20.

words "politics" and "citizenship" and a temporal focus on the middle decades of the nineteenth century, Schweber's book seemed a likely candidate to fill the gap between Horwitz's two volumes and to deal with some of the high politics and constitutionalism that Horwitz tended to ignore. Instead, while Schweber's study offered an important examination of the way technological developments, especially those involving railroads and heavy industry, forced judges at the state level to reconceptualize the nature of property, it was as neglectful of Reconstruction-era constitutionalism as Horwitz's work had been. The U.S. Constitution, the Civil War, Reconstruction—none of these subjects was mentioned in Schweber's book.[22] Whether written by Horwitz or historians who have followed his lead, the new legal history continued to slight constitutional history, just as constitutional scholars tended to neglect legal history. The historiographical segregation was much as Harold Hyman in 1976 had predicted it would be:

> the more that constitutionalists attended to a few great law cases, the greater the tendency for constitutional history to separate from legal history, and for the legal history of the Civil War and Reconstruction to remain unstudied. Constitutional history suffered as it lost sight of legal history, and *vice versa*.[23]

The trend away from the close study of the Reconstruction-era constitutionalism and toward the examination of subjects of special interest to younger legal historians was embodied in the trajectory of the work of William M. Wiecek. After coauthoring *Equal Justice under Law* with Hyman, Wiecek seemed to lose interest in Reconstruction and joined the ever-growing cadre of legal historians fascinated by the "classical legal thought" of the late nineteenth and early twentieth centuries. His volume *The Lost World of Classical Legal Thought: Law and Ideology in America, 1886–1937* (1998) offered the most thorough analysis of that subject, and it went further than any of the new legal history in connecting the turmoil of the sectional conflict to the emergence of a new style of legal reasoning after Reconstruction. Acknowledging that "the Civil War was a trauma for the bench and bar," Wiecek contended that "fear of disorder and social disintegration constituted the matrix of legal classicism in its triumphant phase from 1873 to 1905. Anxiety drove lawyers to articulate a comprehensive vision of law—legal classicism—in a determined, even desperate, attempt to preserve social order, individual liberty, and republican government."[24] Finally, here was

[22] Howard Schweber, *The Creation of American Common Law, 1850–1880: Technology, Politics, and the Construction of Citizenship* (Cambridge: Cambridge University Press, 2004).

[23] Harold M. Hyman, "The Misery of Historians: Legal History and the Civil War," *Law Library Journal* 69 (1976): 332.

[24] William M. Wiecek, *The Lost World of Classical Legal Thought: Law and Ideology in America, 1886–1937* (New York: Oxford University Press, 1998), 79.

a practitioner of the "new legal history" who was willing to grapple with Reconstruction. But, then again, the book was not primarily about Reconstruction. Only about a fifth of it dealt with that era. As the subtitle suggested, the bulk of the volume examined a later period.

At least Wiecek attended to Reconstruction, however briefly. Most legal historians continued to ignore it altogether, yielding the study of Reconstruction-era constitutional developments to political scientists and others trained in constitutional theory rather than history. The result was a body of work engaged mostly in normative questions—how the history of the Reconstruction-era Constitution might shape current constitutional adjudication—rather than in the legal history of Reconstruction as a worthy subject in its own right.[25] Practitioners of this present-minded scholarship adopted new methodologies and theories of their own, disregarding what was going on in the new legal history. Moreover, for sources they relied on the classic texts of Supreme Court opinions and congressional debates, thus assuring that the new legal historians would pay as little attention to them as they were paying to the new legal historians. The constitutional history of Reconstruction faded from sight, eclipsed on one side by constitutional theory and on the other by the new legal history.

Sticking out from the Shadows:
New Light on Constitutional History

The eclipse was only partial, however. In 1981, Harry N. Scheiber, a legal historian much in the mode of Hurst, suggested that historians might reconsider the primacy that they now gave to legal over constitutional history. After all, he argued, the two subfields were but "complementary themes in two modes." Then, six years later, on the bicentennial of the Constitution, he proclaimed that all was now well, for "there is an abundance of new historical scholarship on legal and constitutional themes."[26] Scheiber was right, but only to a degree. "Abundance" might have characterized the outpouring of works on legal history, but it overstated the lesser flow of scholarship on constitutional history, especially constitutional history of the Reconstruction era.

To be sure, a few historians revisited old arguments about Reconstruction constitutionalism. On civil rights, Herman Belz held his line on the essentially

[25] On the differences in these methodologies, see Michael Les Benedict, "Constitutional History and Constitutional Theory: Reflections on Ackerman, Reconstruction, and the Transformation of the American Constitution," *Yale Law Journal* 108 (July 1999): 2011–2038; see esp. 2017–2027.

[26] Scheiber, "American Constitutional History and the New Legal History," and "Introduction: The Bicentennial and the Rediscovery of Constitutional History," *Journal of American History* 74 (December 1987): 667.

conservative nature of Reconstruction-era egalitarianism—and was joined there by the legal scholar Earl M. Maltz—but a new generation of constitutional scholars, including Robert J. Kaczorowski, David A. J. Richards, and Akhil Reed Amar, revived the old arguments of Kinoy and tenBroek with new sophistication and a greater depth of historical research.[27] On civil liberties, Mark E. Neely exploded old myths put forward by critics of Abraham Lincoln and the Union, critics not only from Lincoln's time but from the earliest twentieth century. In one book, Neely dug into the actual cases of thousands of Union prisoners to debunk the notion that Lincoln and his underlings whimsically imprisoned political enemies. In another, he exposed the many civil liberties violations of the Jefferson Davis administration, putting to rest the neo-Confederate myth that civil liberties were better protected in the South than in the North during the Civil War.[28]

Like much constitutional history, regardless of when it has been written, the newer work was tinged with a concern for contemporary issues in American society, especially civil liberties and civil rights. Constitutional history, perhaps more than any other subfield of American history, has had a prescriptive dimension. Either constitutional historians themselves have been interested in shaping constitutional interpretation, or, if they had no such agenda, they knew that others who did would be reading their work closely. Constitutional historians now, as in the past, carry a burden, one that some would gladly relinquish, of describing not only who "we the people" were but who they are and should be. As they have kept their eyes on the present, constitutional historians have been especially vulnerable to the error of flattening out distinctions between different eras.

In recent years, however, constitutional scholars have been careful to take more of a contextualist than a normative approach to history, to see laws not as end products of lawmakers' careful deliberations about future policy but rather as contingent results of complex, unpredictable political processes

<hr />

[27] Herman Belz, "Equality and the Fourteenth Amendment: The Original Understanding," in *Abraham Lincoln, Constitutionalism, and Equal Rights in the Civil War Era* (New York: Fordham University Press, 1998), 170–186; Earl M. Maltz, *Civil Rights, the Constitution, and Congress, 1863–1869* (Lawrence: University of Kansas Press, 1990); Robert J. Kaczorowski, "To Begin the Nation Anew: Congress, Citizenship, and Civil Rights after the Civil War," *American Historical Review* 92 (February 1987): 45–68, and *The Politics of Judicial Interpretation: The Federal Courts, Department of Justice and Civil Rights, 1866–1876* (New York: Oceana, 1985); David A. J. Richards, *Conscience and the Constitution: History, Theory, and Law of the Reconstruction Amendments* (Princeton: Princeton University Press, 1993); Akhil Reed Amar, *The Bill of Rights: Creation and Reconstruction* (New Haven: Yale University Press, 1998), esp. 137–214.

[28] Mark E. Neely Jr., *The Fate of Liberty: Abraham Lincoln and Civil Liberties* (New York: Oxford University Press, 1991), and *Southern Rights: Political Prisoners and the Myth of Confederate Constitutionalism* (Charlottesville: University Press of Virginia, 1999).

involving office-holders, low-level politicos, and ordinary Americans. Works of this sort include Alexander Tsesis's and Michael Vorenberg's books on the Thirteenth Amendment, William E. Nelson's and James E. Bond's on the Fourteenth Amendment, and the studies by Xi Wang, Alexander Keyssar, and Robert Goldman on the Fifteenth Amendment and voting rights in general.[29] Despite all of these authors' efforts to provide as complete a context as possible for the political climate in which Reconstruction laws emerged, and to stay neutral on the question of whether Reconstruction represented a time of advancement or retreat for rights, their personal opinions leaked through. Most of the authors upheld the old idea that Reconstruction represented a watershed period for American rights but that the transformation was constrained, if not at times retarded, by old commitments to legal formalism, racism, and antistatism. Newer constitutional history thus echoed Eric Foner's *Reconstruction* (1988), a seminal work, but one that played lightly on constitutional issues in comparison to social ones.[30] A notable exception to this trend was Keyssar's *The Right to Vote* (2000), which, through close examination of state laws and constitutions, demonstrated that "the dominant trend of the era was toward a narrowing of the franchise: in many states, the years between 1855 and World War I constituted something of a slow Thermidor, a piecemeal rolling back of gains achieved in earlier decades."[31]

Keyssar's emphasis on *state* constitutional development suggests at least one way that constitutional historians can still bring fresh material to old debates. As recent books on the Jacksonian era have demonstrated, the evolution of state constitutions tells us much about developments in political culture. Every state study of Reconstruction by necessity includes an examination of that state's constitutional changes, but the book has yet to be written that attempts to make sense of constitutional change in all of the states during the period. To be sure, scholarship on Reconstruction-era constitutions in different states exists, but it

---

[29] Alexander Tsesis, *The Thirteenth Amendment and American Freedom: A Legal History* (New York: New York University Press, 2004); Michael Vorenberg, *Final Freedom: The Civil War, the Abolition of Slavery, and the Thirteenth Amendment* (Cambridge: Cambridge University Press, 2001); William E. Nelson, *The Fourteenth Amendment: From Political Principle to Judicial Doctrine* (Cambridge, Mass.: Harvard University Press, 1988); James E. Bond, *No Easy Walk to Freedom: Reconstruction and the Ratification of the Fourteenth Amendment* (Westport, Conn.: Praeger, 1997); Xi Wang, *The Trial of Democracy: Black Suffrage and Northern Republicans, 1860–1910* (Athens: University of Georgia Press, 1997); Alexander Keyssar, *The Right to Vote: The Contested History of Democracy in the United States* (New York: Basic Books, 2000); Robert Goldman, *Reconstruction and Black Suffrage: Losing the Vote in Reese and Cruikshank* (Lawrence: University Press of Kansas, 2001).

[30] Eric Foner, *Reconstruction: America's Unfinished Revolution, 1863–1877* (New York: Harper and Row, 1988).

[31] Keyssar, *The Right to Vote*, 80.

focuses almost exclusively on the South, despite the fact that constitutional revision was almost as frequent in the North in the 1860s and 1870s. Historians tend to agree that, by the 1880s, state constitutions throughout the Union tended to act as bulwarks for traditional elites against radical democratic impulses, but, with only a few significant exceptions, they have given too little attention to the experiments in constitution-making during Reconstruction that gave way to the conservative constitutions of the Gilded Age. Were Reconstruction-era state constitutions more or less reactionary than the ones that followed, and did they develop independently of or in conjunction with one another?[32]

The study of state constitutions during Reconstruction offers constitutional historians one way to stick their heads out from the shadows cast by the new legal history; judicial biography offers another. Readers' appetite for biographies of Supreme Court justices, and authors' willingness to write them, have not diminished in the face of the new legal history. A few of these biographies—John Niven's study of Salmon P. Chase, for example—offer unprecedented detail about the lives of their subjects without explaining much about constitutional change during Reconstruction.[33] Others, such as the brief studies of Chase by Harold M. Hyman and of Stephen J. Field by Charles W. McCurdy, use biography to stress the continuity between antebellum and Reconstruction constitutionalism. For Hyman, Chase's opinions as chief justice in *In Re Turner* and *Texas v. White* displayed the natural, almost predictable egalitarianism of the antislavery lawyer that Chase had become long before the Civil War.[34] For McCurdy, Field was ever the Jacksonian Democrat, sniffing for corporate monsters (such as a state-sanctioned slaughterhouse) that could be slain only with the enhanced power of the federal judiciary.[35]

Far more common among judicial biographies dealing with the Reconstruction period is the theme of the Civil War as a transforming experience that forced a more modern view of constitutionalism upon jurists. Thus John Marshall Harlan, in the hands of his biographer Linda Przybyszewski, became far more pro-

---

[32] Laura J. Scalia, *America's Jeffersonian Experiment: Remaking State Constitutions, 1820–1850* (DeKalb: Northern Illinois University Press, 1999); Gerald D. Leonard, *The Invention of Party Politics: Federalism, Popular Sovereignty, and Constitutional Development in Jacksonian Illinois* (Chapel Hill: University of North Carolina Press, 2002). On state constitutions in general, see G. Alan Tarr, *Understanding State Constitutions* (Princeton: Princeton University Press, 1998).

[33] John Niven, *Salmon P. Chase: A Biography* (New York: Oxford University Press, 1995).

[34] Harold M. Hyman, *The Reconstruction Justice of Salmon P. Chase: In* Re Turner *and* Texas v. White (Lawrence: University Press of Kansas, 1997).

[35] Charles W. McCurdy, "Justice Field and the Jurisprudence of Government-Business Relations: Some Parameters of Laissez Faire Constitutionalism, 1863–1897," *Journal of American History* 61 (1975): 970–1005, and "Stephen J. Field and the American Judicial Tradition," in *The Fields and the Law*, ed. Philip J. Bergan, Owen M. Fiss, and Charles W. McCurdy (San Francisco: U.S. District Court for the Northern District of California Historical Society, 1986), 5–19.

gressive in his racial views as a result of his wartime experience as a Kentucky Unionist.[36] And Samuel F. Miller, as described by Michael A. Ross, learned from the war about the benefits that increased governmental power can bring to public health and safety.[37] Oliver Wendell Holmes Jr. was still a young man during the Civil War and Reconstruction, but his experience during that period, more than the wartime experience of any other jurist, has received careful examination by historians. Whereas Charles Royster and Louis Menand attempted to connect the chaos of war felt by Holmes to his later advocacy of lived experience over abstract principles as the correct basis of judicial reasoning, G. Edward White was dubious of that connection. Instead, he emphasized the romantic attachment to unquestioning devotion that Holmes developed during the war as the source of his later belief in the need for people's faith in the authority of the Supreme Court.[38] Despite the steady stream of judicial biographies dealing with the Civil War and Reconstruction produced by historians, an odd lacuna remains. Why do we still not have a respectable biography of Joseph P. Bradley, the railroad lawyer turned Supreme Court justice, the primary architect of substantive due process in his dissent in *Slaughter-House*, and the assailant of Reconstruction racial egalitarianism in the *Civil Rights Cases?*[39]

Sometimes judicial biographies are imbedded in studies of single legal cases, which are in themselves potentially effective means of conveying the nature of constitutional change during Reconstruction. The recent study *The Slaughter-house Cases* (2003) by Ronald M. Labbé and Jonathan Lurie, for example, reconciles some of the apparent conflicts in Bradley's jurisprudence, and it even finds wisdom in the reasoning of Miller, who is usually regarded as the villain of *Slaughter-House*. The book demonstrates how a microhistory of a single case or perhaps a few related cases (such as Hyman's book on *In Re Turner* and *Texas v. White*) can do much to reveal broad patterns of legal development. Surpris-

[36] Linda Przybyszewski, *The Republic According to John Marshall Harlan* (Chapel Hill: University of North Carolina Press, 1999).

[37] Michael A. Ross, *Justice of Shattered Dreams: Samuel Freeman Miller and the Supreme Court during the Civil War Era* (Baton Rouge: Louisiana State University Press, 2003), and "Justice Miller's Reconstruction: The *Slaughter-House Cases*, Health Codes, and Civil Rights in New Orleans, 1861–1873," *Journal of Southern History* 64 (November 1998): 649–676.

[38] Charles W. Royster, *The Destructive War: William Tecumseh Sherman, Stonewall Jackson, and the Americans* (New York: Knopf, 1991), 280–284; Louis Menand, *The Metaphysical Club: A Story of Ideas in America* (New York: Farrar, Straus and Giroux, 2001), 23–69; G. Edward White, *Justice Oliver Wendell Holmes: Law and the Inner Self* (New York: Oxford University Press, 1993), 49–86.

[39] Dennis H. Pope, "Personality and Judicial Performance: A Psychobiography of Justice Joseph P. Bradley" (Ph.D. diss., Rutgers University, 1988), tells us much about Bradley's character but little about Reconstruction-era constitutionalism. A small but rich collection of Bradley's personal papers in the New Jersey Historical Society in Newark awaits the future biographer of the justice.

ingly, few such studies exist for Reconstruction. Constitutional scholars such as Frank J. Scaturro provide excellent detail on the judicial ideas behind the Supreme Court's retreat from Reconstruction, but they tend to give little attention to the political and social contexts surrounding those decisions. The story of the judicial retreat from Reconstruction begs for a storyteller as skilled as Richard Kluger, whose *Simple Justice* rendered a textured history of the 1954 *Brown v. Board of Education* decision. The tale of the Court's assault on Reconstruction is more disheartening than the story of the Court's role in the modern civil rights movement, but it is nonetheless a story that must be told—and in a way that fleshes out the social, cultural, economic, and political strands behind the jurisprudence.[40]

Valuable microhistories also remain to be written of legal cases that may not have been significant in the history of constitutional development but nonetheless offer insight into the legal culture or popular constitutionalism of the day. Michael Grossberg's *A Judgment for Solomon*, though an examination of an antebellum case, offers a model of what can be done for a Reconstruction-era case. The d'Hauteville case, the subject of Grossberg's book, had little effect on legal *thought* but was highly illustrative of legal *experience*, specifically the way that courts perpetuated cultural attitudes toward patriarchy. Elizabeth Alexander's study of the Myra Gaines inheritance case is another fine example of legal microhistory. Like Grossberg's study, it uses one case to illustrate the interconnection between legal culture and gender norms. Unlike Grossberg, Alexander had an opportunity to engage directly with Reconstruction—the Gaines case, which began in the 1830s, was not fully resolved until the 1890s—but she follows others who have studied the case by not making the impact of Reconstruction on the life of the law a dimension of the study. It would be interesting to explore, for example, whether there was a link between on one hand the courts' repeated efforts to protect the property of the Gaines estate against government confiscation and on the other the anticonfiscatory, antiregulatory thrust of Reconstruction-era jurisprudence. Other cases besides that of Myra Gaines offer opportunities for microhistories that connect Reconstruction to legal culture and popular constitutionalism in general. In 1871, for example, the case of Laura Fair, a San Francisco woman accused of murdering her lover, garnered national attention, in part because women were excluded from the jury. Did a heightened rights consciousness brought on by Reconstruction account in any

---

[40] Ronald M. Labbé and Jonathan Lurie, *The Slaughterhouse Cases: Regulation, Reconstruction, and the Fourteenth Amendment* (Lawrence: University Press of Kansas, 2003); Hyman, *The Reconstruction Justice of Salmon P. Chase: In Re Turner and Texas v. White*; Frank J. Scaturro, *The Supreme Court's Retreat from Reconstruction: A Distortion of Constitutional Jurisprudence* (Westport, Conn.: Greenwood Press, 2000); Richard Kluger, *Simple Justice: The History of Brown v. Board of Education and Black America's Struggle for Equality* (New York: Knopf, 1976).

way for the public outrage? Answers to this and similar questions are elusive, as no sustained examination of the case or of others like it yet exists.[41]

Rather than dissecting a single case or set of cases, a successful scholar in the future might fruitfully explore the relationship between law and society in one Reconstruction-era community. Christopher Waldrep's *Roots of Disorder* (1998), which focuses on race relations in Warren County, Mississippi, from the antebellum period through Reconstruction, is a model of how to trace the effect of national constitutional developments on a local population. Waldrep reveals with unprecedented texture the way whites adopted new local laws and enforcement methods intended to preserve the racial order in the community without violating new national policies, only to find African Americans adeptly using these new laws to further their interests in unforeseen ways.[42] An even more ambitious study would seek to contrast the legal impact of Reconstruction in a southern *and* a northern community. A hint of the riches to be reaped from such an approach can be seen in Christine Doyle Dee's dissertation on Scioto County, Ohio, and Madison County, Alabama. Dee's work focuses mainly on the war years and only briefly on postwar Reconstruction, but it goes a long way toward highlighting how the legal effects of Reconstruction were experienced similarly in the North and South. Members of northern communities no less than those in southern ones felt caught in new strands of legal authority created by the war, but they managed to adapt to, if not manipulate, the web.[43]

Although some of the most interesting work in Reconstruction-era southern legal history has been concerned with local matters, much is still left to be done in the study of the legal significance of the Confederacy's national government. As for the Confederate constitution, for example, scholars only recently have begun to take the document seriously rather than regarding it is a flawed deviation from the U.S. Constitution. Marshall L. DeRosa's study claimed that the

[41] Michael Grossberg, *A Judgment for Solomon: The d'Hauteville Case and Legal Experience in Antebellum America* (Cambridge: Cambridge University Press, 1996); Elizabeth Urban Alexander, *Notorious Woman: The Celebrated Case of Myra Clark Gaines* (Baton Rouge: Louisiana State University Press, 2001). On the Gaines case, see also Carl B. Swisher, *History of the Supreme Court of the United States*, vol. 5, *The Taney Period, 1836–64* (New York: Macmillan, 1974), 756–772; Nolan B. Harmon Jr., *The Famous Case of Myra Clark Gaines* (Baton Rouge: Louisiana State University Press, 1946). For preliminary information on the Laura Fair case, see Ann Jones, *Women Who Kill* (New York: Holt, Rinehart, and Winston, 1980), 281–301; Bryant Morey French, *Mark Twain and the Gilded Age* (Dallas: Southern Methodist University Press, 1965), 96–116; and Kenneth Church Lamott, *Who Killed Mr. Crittenden?* (New York: McKay, 1963).

[42] Christopher Waldrep, *Roots of Disorder: Race and Criminal Justice in the American South, 1817–1880* (Urbana: University of Illinois Press, 1998), and "Substituting Law for the Lash: Emancipation and Legal Formalism in a Mississippi County Court," *Journal of American History* 82 (March 1996): 1425–1451.

[43] Christine Doyle Dee, "Land Worth Fighting For: Scioto County, Ohio and Madison County, Alabama during the American Civil War" (Ph.D. diss., Harvard University, 2002).

Confederate constitution represented the most visible fulfillment of attitudes toward limited government that had flourished nationally during the antebellum period.[44] Donald Nieman argued in a similar vein. Far from being a regressive document, Nieman observed, the Confederate constitution embodied the more progressive strains of republican thought inherited from the Revolutionary era, including measures restraining the spoils system, political parties, and legislative discretion. "Many of the Confederate Constitution's innovations," Nieman wrote, "were strikingly similar in both spirit and practice to [state] constitutional changes in the North before and after the Civil War."[45] Constitutional scholars like David P. Currie remained skeptical, however. In Currie's view, the Confederate constitution was a strange "looking-glass variant" of the U.S. Constitution and deserved to fail.[46] The disagreement about the nature of the Confederate constitution suggests that the topic is far from exhausted. For example, no one has systematically examined efforts to amend the Confederate constitution during the war and compared such proposals to similar ones in the Union.

The Confederate court system has been even more neglected than the Confederate constitution. The only monograph on the subject, William M. Robinson's *Justice in Grey* (1941), is more than sixty years old. It depicted a Confederate court system lacking effectiveness or innovation, a portrayal undermined by *Southern Rights* (1999), Mark E. Neely's study of the dogged pursuit of dissenters by Confederate legal officials. Some of Robinson's flaws can be excused by the fact that he did not have as much access as legal historians have today to the actual Confederate case materials, which, since the publication of his work, have been organized and deposited in local branches of the National Archives (though the bulk of them were long ago destroyed). Neely's work only scratched the surface of these sources. In contrast, Daniel W. Hamilton mined them expertly in his recent dissertation comparing sequestration in the Confederacy with confiscation in the Union. The Confederacy, it turns out, was at least as aggressive as the Union in using lower federal courts to raise revenue, and it could be as disrespectful of individual property rights as it was of civil liberties. Hamilton's conclusions find support in the close examination by Mark A. Weitz of the most important piracy and sequestration cases to come before Confederate courts. But many questions about the Confederate legal system still remain. How did Confederate courts operate from day to day? Did the absence of a Con-

[44] Marshall L. DeRosa, *The Confederate Constitution of 1861: An Inquiry into American Constitutionalism* (Columbia: University of Missouri Press, 1991).

[45] Donald Nieman, "Republicanism, the Confederate Constitution, and the American Constitutional Tradition," in *An Uncertain Tradition: Constitutionalism and the History of the South*, ed. Kermit L. Hall and James W. Ely (Athens: University of Georgia Press, 1989), 219.

[46] David P. Currie, "Through the Looking-Glass: The Confederate Constitution in Congress, 1861–1865," *Virginia Law Review* 90 (September 2004): 1257–1399, quotation at 1399.

federate supreme court have any actual impact? (The constitution called for a supreme court, but one was never organized.) Did southern state judges change their thinking or style when they became *national* judges? And most important: what effect, if any, did the Confederate legal system have on Reconstruction? For example, one might argue that if Union authorities during Reconstruction had been more aware of the nature of the Confederate court system, they might have had fewer reservations about imposing a more powerful national court system on the South.[47]

Comparative works like those of Hamilton and Dee speak to the need for more study contrasting the northern and southern experience of constitutional change during Reconstruction, but such scholarship also exposes the glaring absence of scholarship comparing postwar constitutionalism in the United States with post-war constitutionalism in other countries. In the late 1960s, Harold Hyman edited two essay collections that called for this kind of comparative work.[48] The books never came, though. In the past two decades, pathbreaking comparative studies in the field of Reconstruction *have* appeared, but they focus less on law and the Constitution than on the experience of emancipation in the United States and other one-time slave societies of the Western Hemisphere.[49] Fruitful paths into the forests of comparative history remain open to scholars interested in constitutionalism in postwar societies, a subject relevant not only to American Reconstruction but to nation-building in today's post–Cold War world.

A Newer Constitutional History
in Light of the New Legal History

If the constitutional history of Reconstruction is to have a healthy future, it must do more than simply poke its head out from the limelight of the new legal history; it must integrate itself with that new legal history. Historians must meld the methods of the new legal history with the sources of the newer con-

---

[47] William M. Robinson Jr., *Justice in Grey: A History of the Judicial System of the Confederate States of America* (Cambridge, Mass.: Harvard University Press, 1941); Neely, *Southern Rights*; Daniel W. Hamilton, "The Limits of Sovereignty: Legislative Property Confiscation in the Union and the Confederacy" (Ph.D. diss., Harvard University, 2003); and Mark A. Weitz, *The Confederacy on Trial: The Piracy and Sequestration Cases of 1861* (Lawrence: University Press of Kansas, 2005). See also Michael Paul Douglas, "To Secure True and Loyal Southerners: Alien Enemies, Sequestration, and Confederate Identity" (M.A. thesis, Ohio State University, 2004).

[48] Harold M. Hyman, ed., *New Frontiers of the American Reconstruction* (Urbana: University of Illinois Press, 1966); Hyman, ed., *Heard Round the World: The Impact of the American Civil War Abroad* (New York: Knopf, 1968).

[49] One exception to this trend was the brief attention given to political institutions in the comparative work of Eric Foner, *Nothing but Freedom: Emancipation and Its Legacy* (Baton Rouge: Louisiana State University Press, 1983), 39–73.

stitutional history to create a history of both institutions and social relations that fulfills not only Arthur Bestor's forty-year-old vision of the promise of constitutional history but more recent calls for an integration of social, political, and institutional history. Such integration is probably the most important challenge facing a Reconstruction historian, especially one interested in the Constitution.[50]

Adapting the constitutional history of Reconstruction to modern currents of legal history will not be easy. Witness the recent exchange between Hendrik Hartog, a leading practitioner of the new legal history, and David Hollinger, an advocate of more traditional forms of intellectual history. With excitement Hartog proclaimed: "there are so many more people doing legal history now than then [the 1970s], and they are doing it in so many different ways." To which Hollinger responded: "Constitutional history is not accorded the importance it once was. Is this a problem? Yes. Constitutional history deals with events that not only happen on site, but constitute the site to begin with."[51] Is there any hope for integrating these supposedly complementary modes of history, especially when it comes to the history of Reconstruction?

Yes. But potential studies seeking to meld the goals of constitutional history with the methods of the new legal history face a daunting challenge: they must at once examine the social consequences of legal and political institutions while also analyzing the transformation of those institutions themselves. A single study of Reconstruction that takes this kind of an integrative approach and seeks to be comprehensive does not yet exist, and such a book, daunting as it would be to write, is perhaps what the field of Reconstruction most needs. Until that grand work is written, historians interested in the integration of constitutional and social history must satisfy themselves with narrower topics that offer the possibility of such methodological multitasking on a smaller scale.

Take, for example, the subject of the transformation of the legal profession beginning in the 1870s, which has been largely ignored by Reconstruction historians but has received some attention from legal historians. One of these historians, Maxwell Bloomfield, provided intriguing studies of two Reconstruction-era attorneys in his 1976 study of the legal profession in the century following the Declaration of Independence. The first, William Pitt Ballinger, was a white attorney with a large private practice in the antebellum South who turned to the

---

[50] On the integration of social, political, and institutional history, see Meg Jacobs and Julian E. Zelizer, "The Democratic Experiment: New Directions in Political History," in *The Democratic Experiment: New Directions in American Political History*, ed. Meg Jacobs, William J. Novak, and Julian E. Zelizer (Princeton: Princeton University Press, 2003), 1–19; and William W. Freehling, *The Reintegration of American History: Slavery and the Civil War* (New York: Oxford University Press, 1994), 253–274.

[51] Hendrik Hartog and David A. Hollinger, "Interchange: The Practice of History," *Journal of American History* 90 (September 2003): 580.

public sector during the war, acting as a receiving agent for goods and debts confiscated by the Confederacy under the Sequestration Act. After the war, he had only moderate success in brokering presidential pardons for fellow southerners but then became fabulously wealthy as a corporate attorney. During the same period, the African-American lawyer John Mercer Langston promoted legal education for the freedpeople and ultimately served as the head of the Howard University Law School. Although Langston eventually left Howard amid scandal and infighting, his work had a powerful impact on public law: a majority of the practicing attorneys he had helped to train, all of whom were African-American, worked for government departments or as civil rights attorneys. Bloomfield's close study of a handful of lawyers led him to the tentative suggestion that "the new-style bar leader of the late nineteenth century was more policy-oriented than his antebellum counterpart, since his managerial role forced him to confront major public issues that threatened his client's welfare."[52]

Unfortunately, in the thirty years since the publication of Bloomfield's volume, legal historians have not delved more deeply into the connection between Reconstruction and the changes in the legal profession. They need to take up this connection in a more systematic way than was done in Bloomfield's suggestive essays. To be sure, historians acknowledge a difference between antebellum legal education, with its emphasis on memorization and practical training, and postbellum legal education, with its emphasis on the case method and academic study of formal principles, but they have chosen not to explore the possibility that events of Reconstruction played the crucial role in this development. Legal historians tend to identify the key transformation in the history of legal education not as the outbreak of war, not as Union victory in war, and not as postwar Reconstruction. Rather, they see the turning point in an event that stands outside the story of Reconstruction: Christopher C. Langdell's arrival as dean of Harvard Law School in 1870.

Langdell's pedagogical innovations, especially the use of the case method, did indeed have a major impact on law and the Constitution, for they accelerated the growth of formalism in legal training at a time when formalism was taking root in legal thought in general. But is there no way to connect this development in legal education with Reconstruction? Did the experience of war and reunion tilt Langdell and his allies toward formalism in legal education? In other

---

[52] Maxwell Bloomfield, *American Lawyers in a Changing Society, 1776–1876* (Cambridge, Mass.: Harvard University Press, 1976), 347. Another work beside Bloomfield's that suggests the crucial connection between Reconstruction and the development of African-American professional culture in the law is James Lowell Underwood and W. Lewis Burke, Jr., eds., *At Freedom's Door: African American Founding Fathers and Lawyers in Reconstruction South Carolina* (Columbia: University of South Carolina Press, 2000), which examines African-American students at the University of South Carolina School of Law and African-American members of the state bar during Reconstruction.

words, did the sectional conflict have on the formalists the opposite effect it had on Oliver Wendell Holmes Jr., whose rejection of formalism, rooted in the Civil War, has already been closely studied by historians? Studies of Langdell and his contemporaries and the way they reshaped the legal profession will continue to pour forth. Perhaps some of them will go so far as to argue that the key changes in the legal profession occurred not simply *during* Reconstruction but *because of* Reconstruction.[53] Whatever specific argument future historians of the legal profession make, they need to assess the effect of the sectional conflict on the profession with the same vigor they already have brought to bear on the impact of the American Revolution on lawyering.[54]

Another favorite topic of recent legal historians, the cultural study of law, usually involving literary analysis of legal texts, also suggests a promising avenue of inquiry for historians interested in a broader approach to the Reconstruction-era Constitution. Adapting the sources and methods of the literary critic might allow for, among other things, a reconsideration of popular constitutionalism during the Reconstruction era. It has been nearly twenty years since Michael Kammen published his study of the Constitution in American culture.[55] Since then, historians have yielded this subject to English departments. Literary critics have proven to be far more intrepid than historians in revealing the informal ways that, during Reconstruction, the idea of a higher-order rule of law guided the pens and connected the minds of Americans as disparate as Thaddeus Stevens and Herman Melville.[56] Already the legal scholar Pamela Brandwein has used similar methods to reveal how the writings of postwar Supreme Court justices and constitutional scholars reworked the meanings of

[53] The most recent study of post-Revolutionary American legal education, William P. LaPiana, *Logic and Experience: The Origin of Modern American Legal Education* (New York: Oxford University Press, 1994), skips from the antebellum era to the Langdell era with no mention of the Civil War and Reconstruction. On the possibilities for future research on Langdell, see Bruce A. Kimball, "The Langdell Problem: Historicizing the Century of Historiography, 1906–2000s," *Law and History Review* 22 (Summer 2004): 277–337.

[54] For the effect of the Revolution on the legal profession, see the early chapters of Bloomfield, *American Lawyers in a Changing Society*, and Robert A. Ferguson, *Law and Letters in American Culture* (Cambridge, Mass.: Harvard University Press, 1984).

[55] Michael Kammen, *A Machine That Would Go of Itself: The Constitution in American Culture* (New York: Knopf, 1986).

[56] Deak Nabers, "'Victory of LAW': Melville and Reconstruction," *American Literature* 75 (2003): 1–30; Kathleen Diffley, *Where My Heart Is Turning Ever: Civil War Stories and Constitutional Reform, 1861–1876* (Athens: University of Georgia Press, 1992); William E. Moddelmog, *Reconstituting Authority: American Fiction in the Province of Law, 1880–1920* (Iowa City: University of Iowa Press, 2001); Brook Thomas, *American Literary Realism and the Failed Promise of Contract* (Berkeley: University of California Press, 1997); Priscilla Wald, *Constituting Americans: Cultural Anxiety and Narrative Form* (Durham, N.C.: Duke University Press, 1995).

Reconstruction. But Brandwein's focus is mainly on the twentieth century, not the nineteenth. Research topics abound for the constitutional historian whose primary interest is in Reconstruction and who is willing to venture into the province of literary criticism.[57]

The greatest progress in integrating recent interests of legal historians with the traditional concerns of constitutional history has been in work examining those once regarded as marginal to the political order—women, minorities, and poor laborers, for example—and revealing them as constitutive of that order. In conjoining the voices of the dispossessed with those of the powerful elite, these historians have begun to answer the call of scholars such as Eric Hobsbawm, Robert Cover, James Scott, and Nancy Fraser, who have urged us to broaden our conception of the political and constitutional, a step first requiring us to jettison old notions about clear boundaries between private and public power.[58] One argument along these lines—though inspired more by Hegel than by these recent scholars—suggests that slaves were the true authors of the Thirteenth Amendment and that, by implication, their descendants are the best interpreters of the measure.[59]

Perhaps the most impressive historical writing seeking to redraw the borders of legal and constitutional history—at least for the Reconstruction period—has been focused on gender. Amy Dru Stanley's study of contract as a means of connecting the private institution of marriage to the more public institution of labor is exemplary. Like practitioners of the new legal history, Stanley relies on obscure tracts and state-level cases and statutes—especially those relating to divorce—but, like more traditional constitutional historians, she examines as well congressional debates and Supreme Court opinions.[60] While Stanley uses the device of contract to connect the private to the public, Laura F. Edwards invokes political culture to similar ends, though she, like Stanley, is largely concerned with marriage law. "With the abolition of slavery," Edwards explains, "marriage acquired even greater importance in structuring southern society

[57] Pamela Brandwein, *Reconstructing Reconstruction: The Supreme Court and the Production of Historical Truth* (Durham, N.C.: Duke University Press, 1999).

[58] E. J. Hobsbawm, *Primitive Rebels: Studies in Archaic Forms of Social Movement in the Nineteenth and Twentieth Centuries* (New York: Norton, 1965); Robert M. Cover, "The Supreme Court, 1982 Term: Foreword: Nomos and Narrative," *Harvard Law Review* 97 (November 1983): 4–68; Nancy Fraser, *Unruly Practices: Power, Discourse, and Gender in Contemporary Social Theory* (Minneapolis: University of Minnesota Press, 1989); James C. Scott, *Domination and the Arts of Resistance: Hidden Transcripts* (New Haven, Conn.: Yale University Press, 1990).

[59] Guyora Binder, "Did the Slaves Author the Thirteenth Amendment? An Essay in Redemptive History," *Yale Journal of Law and Humanities* 5 (Summer 1993): 471–505; and Richards, *Conscience and the Constitution*, 257.

[60] Amy Dru Stanley, *From Bondage to Contract: Wage Labor, Marriage, and the Market in the Age of Slave Emancipation* (Cambridge: Cambridge University Press, 1998).

because it became the only institution that legally constituted households."[61] Focusing on a small section of North Carolina, Edwards uses local legal records as well as public speeches to link reactionary reconstructions of marriage at the level of the household to similar, conservative rhetorical strategies at the level of party politics. Although the themes and scopes of their studies are different, both Edwards and Stanley offer models of how the new legal history might be employed to create an even newer constitutional history of Reconstruction.

Along with the topic of gender relations, labor law offers historians an opportunity to merge legal and constitutional history. The quest for the ideal free labor system is one of the central themes of Reconstruction, yet surprisingly little scholarship exists that connects the pronouncements of policy-makers about free labor to the actions of low-level courts seeking to discipline labor in the field. Stanley's book is an important exception, and so is James D. Schmidt's *Free to Work*. Schmidt's lens widens and narrows, moving between congressional debates in the center of the postwar nation and the workings of the Freedmen's Bureau courts at the periphery. The result is an enlightening portrait of law-makers at all levels taking the principles of northern antebellum labor law, which concerned such matters as partial contract, the right to quit, and vagrancy, and attempting to import them, with mixed success, into the postwar South. By focusing on labor law rather than labor movements, Schmidt's work takes us in an interesting new direction, away from David Montgomery's older study of the relationship between Reconstruction and labor. But we still await a thorough study of the relationship between labor law and state-building during Reconstruction, a work that might be modeled on excellent studies of this relationship during the post-Reconstruction period by William E. Forbath and James Gray Pope.[62]

State-building in general, a subject that has received much attention in recent years, almost by necessity must engage the topic of constitutional and legal change because of the new legal foundation on which the bureaucracies of the postwar state rested, not to mention the legal and constitutional conflicts that the bureaucracies triggered. Political scientists such as Stephen

<hr />

[61] Laura F. Edwards, *Gendered Strife and Confusion: The Political Culture of Reconstruction* (Urbana: University of Illinois Press, 1997), 28.

[62] James D. Schmidt, *Free to Work: Labor Law, Emancipation, and Reconstruction, 1815–1880* (Athens: University of Georgia Press, 1998); David Montgomery, *Beyond Equality: Labor and the Radical Republicans, 1862–1872* (New York: Knopf, 1967), and *Citizen Worker: The Experience of Workers in the United States with Democracy and the Free Market during the Nineteenth Century* (New York: Cambridge University Press, 1993); William E. Forbath, *Law and the Shaping of the American Labor Movement* (Cambridge, Mass.: Harvard University Press, 1991), and "Caste, Class, and Equal Citizenship," in *Moral Problems in American Life: New Perspectives on Cultural History*, ed. Karen Halttunen and Lewis Perry (Ithaca, N.Y.: Cornell University Press, 1998), 167–200; James Gray Pope, "Labor's Constitution of Freedom," *Yale Law Journal* 106 (January 1997): 941–1031.

Skowronek, Theda Skocpol, and Richard Franklin Bensel took the lead over historians in positing Reconstruction as the crucial moment in the making of an American administrative state.[63] Of these works, Bensel's was the richest in historical research and the most attentive to developments during *wartime* Reconstruction.

To be sure, legal and constitutional historians examined some Reconstruction-era bureaucracies before political scientists took a special interest in the period. But these older histories, which looked at such institutions as the U.S. Army during Reconstruction, the Freedmen's Bureau, and the judicial and civil service systems in the Union and Confederacy, were understandably not as engaged as they might have been with the themes that later came to direct research on state-building: the relative strength of the American state in the late nineteenth century, the social imperatives of political and legal institutions, and the autonomous nature of modern bureaucracies.[64] Intellectual historians have long been interested in the question of whether the war and Reconstruction made institutions more or less palatable to one-time individualists, but their work has been more on the individualists than on the institutions; they seem little interested in how institutions operated, how they took on lives of their own, and how they shaped and were shaped by the legal structures of Reconstruction. Meanwhile, social historians have made excellent use of the voluminous records of such institutions as the U.S. Southern Claims Commission and the U.S. Pension Office but rarely have they expressed interest in these institutions *as* institutions.[65]

[63] Theda Skocpol, *Protecting Soldiers and Mothers: The Political Origins of Social Policy in the United States* (Cambridge, Mass.: Harvard University Press, 1992); Richard Franklin Bensel, *Yankee Leviathan: The Origins of Central State Authority in America, 1859–1877* (New York: Cambridge University Press, 1990); and Stephen Skowronek, *Building a New American State: The Expansion of National Administrative Capacities, 1877–1920* (New York: Cambridge University Press, 1982).

[64] James E. Sefton, *The United States Army and Reconstruction, 1865–1877* (Baton Rouge: Louisiana State University Press, 1967); Donald G. Nieman, *To Set the Law in Motion: The Freedmen's Bureau and the Legal Rights of Blacks, 1865–1868* (Millwood, N.Y.: KTO Press, 1979); Kaczorowski, *The Politics of Judicial Interpretation*; Stanley I. Kutler, *Judicial Power and Reconstruction Politics* (Chicago: University of Chicago Press, 1968); Ari Hoogenboom, *Outlawing the Spoils: A History of the Civil Service Reform Movement, 1865–1883* (Urbana: University of Illinois Press, 1961); Paul P. Van Riper and Harry N. Scheiber, "The Confederate Civil Service," *Journal of Southern History* 25 (November 1959): 465–469.

[65] See, for example, Elizabeth Regosin, *Freedom's Promise: Ex-Slave Families and Citizenship in the Age of Emancipation* (Charlottesville: University Press of Virginia, 2002), which draws on records of the U.S. Pension Office; and Dylan C. Penningroth, *The Claims of Kinfolk: African American Property and Community in the Nineteenth-Century South* (Chapel Hill: University of North Carolina Press, 2003), esp. 131–186, which makes use of the U.S. Southern Claims Commission. Susanna Michele Lee, "Claiming the Union: Stories of Loyalty from the Post–Civil War South" (Ph.D. diss., University of Virginia, 2005), also examines records of the Claims Commission. None of these works, however, provides an institutional history of the bureaucracy examined.

If potential researchers are less than titillated at the prospect of studying a Reconstruction-era bureaucracy, they should consider that such a project may offer a way of integrating social and institutional history. Historians of Reconstruction interested in taking up the challenge would do well to revisit some of the subjects of older constitutional histories, such as the establishment and operation of law-making or policy-making bureaucracies. Already historians have begun to produce some important work along these lines. Mark Russell Wilson's dissertation on the U.S. Quartermaster General's Office, for example, analyzes the relationship between government and private enterprise from the low level of the procurement agents to the high level of War Department policy-makers. Kyle S. Sinisi takes a similar approach in his recent book on state-level claims commissions, revealing how claims agencies worked in practice to reinforce popular faith in federalism while providing economic relief.[66]

Instead of focusing on only one government entity, a potential researcher might examine regulation across various law-making bodies as a way of understanding the intellectual and cultural norms of the nation. Excellent work of this sort exists for the early nineteenth century, such as William J. Novak's *The People's Welfare* (1996), and for the late nineteenth and early twentieth centuries, such as Ross Evans Paulson's *Liberty, Equality, and Justice* (1997), which examines business regulation in general, and Barbara Young Welke's *Recasting American Liberty* (2001), which focuses on the railroad industry. To the latter group we might add Sarah Barringer Gordon's *The Mormon Question* (2002), Gaines M. Foster's *Moral Reconstruction* (2002), and Philip Hamburger's *Separation of Church and State* (2002), all of which highlight the increasing willingness of state and federal lawmakers after the mid–nineteenth century to prescribe and enforce rules of moral behavior. But the Reconstruction period is slighted in most of these books. It is an epilogue in *The People's Welfare* and a prologue in most of the others. And although all of these historians, especially Novak and Welke, offer models of how to look beneath regulations ostensibly aimed only at the economy to reveal elite efforts to impose broader cultural order, none of them is primarily interested in assessing the role of Reconstruction in shaping this regulation. Historians might do well to ask whether the new state governments and federal agencies of Reconstruction believed that the sectional crisis,

---

[66]Mark Russell Wilson, "The Business of Civil War" (Ph.D. diss., University of Chicago, 2002); Kyle S. Sinisi, *Sacred Debts: State Civil War Claims and American Federalism, 1861–1880* (New York: Fordham University Press, 2003). Frank W. Klingberg, *The Southern Claims Commission* (Berkeley: University of California Press, 1955), is another important study of a bureaucracy, but it was written too early to be informed by recent work on institutional history. On the trend away from individualism and toward institutionalism, see George M. Frederickson, *The Inner Civil War: Northern Intellectuals and the Crisis of the Union* (New York: Harper and Row, 1965).

more than any other factor, had given them the mandate, if not the duty, to use their increased power to reorder society using new regulations.[67]

Another way to study state-building is to use a comparative approach. Already a number of works comparing the Union and Confederacy have been mentioned, but none of these takes an institutional approach. Richard Bensel, by contrast, interrogates the administrative capacities of the Union and the Confederacy, arriving at the surprising argument that the Confederacy was a more advanced nation-state than the Union.[68]

Equally fruitful comparisons might be made of postwar institutional life in the United States and other countries. How did Reconstruction agencies such as the Pension Office, for example, compare to similar institutions in other nations transformed by war, and what does the comparison tell us about the effects of the Civil War on American institutional life? An essay collection of 1997, *On the Road to Total War: The American Civil War and the German Wars of Unification, 1861–1871*, was tantalizing in its implicit promise of a comparative approach. Unfortunately, each essay focused exclusively on the United States, the Confederacy, or Germany, and the only truly comparative analyses appeared in the introduction and conclusion, provocative pieces hinting at the wealth of research possibilities lying along the path of comparative institutional history. Perhaps future historians will pick up the trail.[69]

A quite different means of understanding state-building in the Reconstruction era lies in the realm of material culture. What was the physical evidence

---

[67] On antebellum economic regulation, see William J. Novak, *The People's Welfare: Law and Regulation in Nineteenth-Century America* (Chapel Hill: University of North Carolina Press, 1996), though also see Austin Allen, "The Political Economy of Blackness: Citizenship, Corporations, and Race in *Dred Scott*," *Civil War History* 50 (September 2004): 229–260. On postwar economic regulation, see Barbara Young Welke, *Recasting American Liberty: Gender, Race, Law, and the Railroad Revolution, 1865–1920* (Cambridge: Cambridge University Press, 2001), and Ross Evans Paulson, *Liberty, Equality, and Justice: Civil Rights, Women's Rights, and the Regulation of Business, 1865–1932* (Durham, N.C.: Duke University Press, 1997). On morals regulation, see Gaines M. Foster, *Moral Reconstruction: Christian Lobbyists and the Federal Legislation of Morality, 1865–1920* (Chapel Hill: University of North Carolina Press, 2002); Sarah Barringer Gordon, *The Mormon Question: Polygamy and Constitutional Conflict in Nineteenth-Century America* (Chapel Hill: University of North Carolina Press, 2002); and Philip Hamburger, *Separation of Church and State* (Cambridge, Mass.: Harvard University Press, 2002).

[68] Bensel, *Yankee Leviathan*, 94–237.

[69] A. Stig Förster and Jörg Nagler, introduction, and Roger Chickering, "The American Civil War and the German Wars of Unification: Some Parting Shots," in *On the Road to Total War: The American Civil War and the German Wars of Unification, 1861–1871*, ed. Förster and Nagler (Cambridge: Cambridge University Press, 1997), 1–28, 683–692. For a model work outside of United States history comparing postwar state-building, especially as it related to veterans, see Deborah Cohen, *The War Come Home: Disabled Veterans in Britain and German, 1914–1939* (Berkeley: University of California Press, 2001).

of state-building in the Reconstruction era, and what does this evidence tell us about legal and constitutional culture in the period? Wayne K. Durrill's study of the changing appearances of courthouses in a North Carolina county, for example, suggests that these buildings during Reconstruction increasingly became standardized across geographical borders. That is, architects would purposefully ignore local designs and instead model buildings on courthouses in states as far away as New York and Pennsylvania. In this way, the space where law was administered, and not simply the law itself, had a nationalizing influence.[70] In contrast, as Jennifer Ossman argues in a recent dissertation, the State, War and Navy Building in Washington, D.C. (now known as the Old Executive Office Building), constructed in the 1870s and 1880s, failed to fulfill its planners' hopes of kindling a new national style of baroque elegance over classical simplicity. Instead of becoming an emblem of a more grandiose, powerful administrative state, the structure came to symbolize the corruption and decadence of the Grant administration.[71] Once historians open their minds to the material culture of the law as a fruitful sphere of study, all sorts of possibilities present themselves: How did the garb of judges and attorneys change in the Reconstruction era, and did it become standardized across state boundaries? Were cheap copies of the Constitution more readily available after the Civil War than before? What efforts were made to standardize the arrangement of physical space in the Freedmen's Bureau courts? Historians need to pay attention to the sights, sounds, and feel of legal change during Reconstruction, not simply to the new laws and the people who made them.

One final topic—nationalism—is worth mentioning, in part because it has received enormous attention in the last two decades, but especially because it may offer the most fruitful means of understanding the relationship between individuals and institutions during Reconstruction while combining the methods of constitutional history and the new legal history. Historians of nationalism and the corollary subject of citizenship have not given Reconstruction its due. Too often historians of nationalism and citizenship focus only on segments of the population. Recent books by Linda K. Kerber, Candace Bredbenner, Jeanie Attie, and Nancy Isenberg, for example, have built on older work by Ellen C. DuBois, among others, to awaken interest in the history of women's distinctive role in shaping the meaning of nationhood and citizenship, but they tend to neglect Reconstruction or larger trends in nationalism and citizenship specific

---

[70] Wayne K. Durrill, "A Tale of Two Courthouses: Civic Space, Political Power, and Capitalist Development in a New South Community, 1843–1940," *Journal of Social History* 35 (2002): 659–681.

[71] Jennifer Laurie Ossman, "Reconstructing a National Image: The State, War and Navy Building and the Politics of Federal Design, 1866–1890" (Ph.D. diss, University of Virginia, 1996).

to that period.[72] Other historical works are neglectful in a different way: they take the teleological approach of examining only the making and adjudication of the Fourteenth Amendment, which set the terms of reunion and citizenship into the Constitution.[73] Although many political scientists, including Michael Schudson and Rogers M. Smith, have written sweeping histories of citizenship, only one historian, James H. Kettner, has done so.[74] But Kettner's study, *The Development of American Citizenship* (1978), now twenty-five years old, stalls at the Civil War, adding a short epilogue on the principle of birthright citizenship enshrined in the Fourteenth Amendment.

In the late 1980s and 1990s, a burst of theoretical works on nationalism and citizenship by such luminaries as Hobsbawm, Liah Greenfeld, and, perhaps most famously, Benedict Anderson, helped trigger a resurgence of interest in these subjects among historians.[75] Informed by such ideas as invented traditions (Hobsbawm) and imagined communities (Anderson), historians have begun to give closer attention to Reconstruction as a period when Americans began consciously and systematically to fashion clear, if competing, definitions of citizenship. Robert Bonner and Brian Dirck, for example, have explored the extent to which the Union and the Confederacy were imagined communities, while Anne Sarah Rubin has made the persuasive argument that the Confeder-

[72] Jeanie Attie, *Patriotic Toil: Northern Women and the American Civil War* (Ithaca, N.Y.: Cornell University Press, 1998); Nancy Isenberg, *Sex and Citizenship in Antebellum America* (Chapel Hill: University of North Carolina Press, 1998); Linda K. Kerber, *No Constitutional Right to be Ladies: Women and the Obligations of Citizenship* (New York: Hill and Wang, 1998); Candace Lewis Bredbenner, *A Nationality of Her Own: Women, Marriage, and the Law of Citizenship* (Berkeley: University of California Press, 1998); Nancy F. Cott, *Public Vows: A History of Marriage and the Nation* (Cambridge, Mass.: Harvard University Press, 2000); Ellen C. DuBois, *Feminism and Suffrage: The Emergence of an Independent Women's Movement in America, 1848–1869* (Ithaca, N.Y.: Cornell University Press, 1978).

[73] For an introduction to competing historical views of the Fourteenth Amendment, see Earl M. Maltz, *The Fourteenth Amendment and the Law of the Constitution* (Durham, N.C.: Carolina Academic Press, 2003).

[74] Michael Schudson, *The Good Citizen: A History of American Civic Life* (New York: Free Press, 1998); Rogers M. Smith, *Civic Ideals: Conflicting Visions of Citizenship in U.S. History* (New Haven: Yale University Press, 1997); James H. Kettner, *The Development of American Citizenship, 1608–1870* (Chapel Hill: University of North Carolina Press, 1978). Although Schudson and Smith are most often cited on the subject of nationalism and citizenship, two other works by political scientists are at least as provocative on those subjects: Anthony W. Marx, *Faith in Nation: Exclusionary Origins of Nationalism* (New York: Oxford University Press, 2003); and Judith Shklar, *American Citizenship: The Quest for Inclusion* (Cambridge, Mass.: Harvard University Press, 1991).

[75] Eric J. Hobsbawm, *Nations and Nationalism since 1780: Programme, Myth, Reality*, 2nd ed. (New York: Cambridge University Press, 1992); Liah Greenfeld, *Nationalism: Five Roads to Modernity* (Cambridge, Mass.: Harvard University Press, 1992); Benedict Anderson, *Imagined Communities: Reflections on the Origin and Spread of Nationalism*, rev. ed. (London: Verso, 1991).

acy was more important as a construct of postwar southern nationalism than as a wartime political entity.[76] The nature and legitimacy of nationalism will continue to be hotly debated. In the United States, no less than in other nations, waves of patriotic and religious fervor will keep alive the question of who "we the people" are.

From the perspective of legal and constitutional history, however, current work on nationalism during Reconstruction is insufficient. Too much of the scholarship dwells on abstract notions of citizenship and not enough on how real institutions and laws touched real lives, forcing people to define for themselves and legal authorities their national identities.

Consider the institution of the Union naval blockade, which frequently forced ordinary sailors whose ideas of citizenship were only embryonic to claim a distinct national affiliation. Blockading warships regularly captured commercial ships suspected of trading with the Confederacy, seized the goods, and deposed or even imprisoned the sailors. Although historians have written much about the impact of these actions on the Constitution—the legality of the seizures was ultimately tested and upheld in the *Prize Cases*—they have had little to say about their effect on the sailors who were detained.

All of these sailors were asked a set of questions, or "standing interrogatories," the first of which asked them to specify their citizenship and allegiance. Had they not been stopped by the blockade, these sailors might never have had to identify for themselves and their interrogators their citizenship and allegiance, or whether these two terms, *citizenship* and *allegiance*, meant the same thing. But because of the war and the institutions it spawned, men like Charles J. Praisted, the second mate on the *A. J. View*, were forced to assert a national identity. Deposed by a New York City federal prize commissioner on February 19, 1862, Praisted revealed his confusion about citizenship in the face of an institutional demand for clarity. "I was born in the City of New York," he began. "I now live at New Orleans and have lived there 15 years. I am a resident of Louisiana. I am a Citizen of the United States. I owe my allegiance to the State of Louisiana, and she is one of the Confederate States."[77] Could someone be a citizen of the United States but owe allegiance elsewhere? William Blakeney, the master of Praisted's ship, thought so. He also had been born in New York state—Batavia, not New York City—and had lived in New Orleans for about fifteen years. "In the present

[76] Robert E. Bonner, "Americans Apart: Nationality in the Slaveholding South" (Ph.D. diss., Yale University, 1998), pt. 2; Brian R. Dirck, *Lincoln and Davis: Imagining America, 1809–1865* (Lawrence: University Press of Kansas, 2001); Anne S. Rubin, *A Shattered Nation: The Rise and Fall of the Confederacy, 1861–1868* (Chapel Hill: University of North Carolina Press, 2005).

[77] "Deposition of Charles J. Praisted," in *U.S. v. A. J. View*, box 11, file A17-85, R.G. 21, entry 106, U.S. District Court, Southern District of N.Y., "Prize Case Files—Civil War," National Archives Northeast Regional Research Center, New York City.

condition of public affairs in the Country," he confessed, "I do not know where my allegiance is due. I am a citizen of the United States, or I was a citizen of the United States before the difficulties in the Country, but all my interests are in the South."[78] Blakeney and Praisted may seem confused to us, but that is our problem, not theirs. We tend to regard citizenship and allegiance as synonymous. Were Blakeney and Praisted any less logical in thinking of citizenship merely as an incident of birth and allegiance as the crucial choice of national affiliation? The notion of an imagined community would have made no sense to them, for they were members of multiple communities—some created by incident, some created by choice, and all potentially in conflict with one another. Furthermore, they were simply not in the habit of imagining communities. Rather, it took an institution created by war to force them to identify their communities. If they imagined communities, it was only at gunpoint.

If white men like Blakeney and Praisted were confused about their citizenship status, imagine how freeborn African Americans on these ships must have felt. Having lived as free people, if not as legal citizens, for years, they, like all African Americans, had been declared noncitizens by Chief Justice Roger B. Taney's infamous opinion in the *Dred Scott* decision of 1857. But the Republicans who had denounced that decision now held power in the Union, so were freeborn African Americans citizens once again? Samuel Robinson, who had been born in New York City, gave not a thought to the *Dred Scott* decision when, in June 1861, he told the prize commissioner that he was a "citizen of New York and owe[d] allegiance to the United States of America."[79] Like the white sailors on the *A. J. View*, Robinson regarded citizenship merely as a descriptive term relating to one's birthplace, whereas allegiance was an ascriptive term of affiliation. Other African Americans invested citizenship with greater meaning. James Edwin Simpson testified that he "owe[d] allegiance to the government of the United States of America" but was not "a citizen of the United States because I am a coloured man, but I was born and bred there."[80] The testimony of Charles Hall, an African American from the same ship as Simpson, was most revealing: "I owe allegiance to the Northern Country. I belong to the United States. . . . I must be a citizen of the United States of America if I am a citizen at all."[81] The first part of the statement suggested an imagined community: he "belonged" to the nation of the United States and owed allegiance to it (much as his forebears

---

[78] "Deposition of William Blakeney," in *U.S. v. A. J. View*.

[79] "Deposition of Samuel Robinson," in *U.S. v. Crenshaw*, box 5, file A16-415, R.G. 21, entry 106, U.S. District Court, Southern District of N.Y., "Prize Case Files—Civil War," National Archives Northeast Regional Research Center, New York City.

[80] "Deposition of James Edwin Simpson," in *U.S. v. Tropic Wind*, box 4, file A16-384, R.G. 21, entry 106, U.S. District Court, Southern District of N.Y., "Prize Case Files—Civil War," National Archives Northeast Regional Research Center, New York City.

[81] "Deposition of Charles Hall," in *U.S. v. Tropic Wind*.

might have belonged to a slaveowner and owed allegiance to him). But the second part showed the tenuous nature of the bonds of the community: belonging to a nation was not the same as being a citizen. Hall doubted whether he was a citizen at all. If he was one, it was only by default—he could claim no other nation as his own.

Sailors like Hall were not the only ones puzzled by their status. Even the U.S. attorney general, Edward Bates, called upon to define the citizenship status of a freeborn African American who had captured a Confederate ship and piloted it to Union waters, eventually declared that the sailor was a U.S. citizen, but only after venting his frustration that "eighty years of practical enjoyment of citizenship, under the Constitution, have not sufficed to teach us either the exact meaning of the word, or the constituent elements of the thing we prize so highly."[82]

The meanings of citizenship and nationality contained in the prize case depositions, much like similar sentiments found in testimonies to pension bureaus and claims commissions, cannot simply be dismissed as the muddled notions of people with little education and no legal training. First, the testimonies are legitimate expressions of popular constitutionalism—a view of the Constitution from the bottom. They help us to appreciate why, for example, Americans might have been slow to adopt a shared sense of nationalism even after Union victory in 1865 and a common definition of citizenship even after the adoption of the Fourteenth Amendment in 1868. Further, they are reflections of the power of institutions to shape constitutional thought—a view of the Constitution from above. Without institutions such as prize courts, claims commissions, and pension bureaus, all products of state-building during the Civil War and Reconstruction, a significant group of Americans might not have been forced to confront for themselves the ambiguity of their national identity.

Using the tools of the new legal history and keeping an eye on the Constitution, an enterprising historian might use the subject of nationalism to explore the connective tissue between the state and society during Reconstruction. Indeed, the nature of nationalism in the Reconstruction era is one of the implicit or explicit subjects accessed by most of the promising avenues of research identified here, including comparative history, bureaucratic growth and regulation, and the material culture of state-building. But, regardless of how one approaches the subjects of nationalism and citizenship, it is important to remember that these were not well-grasped entities that can be mapped by us today, though often that seems to be an assumption of modern political scientists. Rather, they were embryonic ideas at best, and the task of future historians will be to analyze the contingent circumstances that forced latent, ill-defined concepts of nationhood and citizenship to crystallize so quickly during and because of Reconstruction.

[82] Edward Bates, "Citizenship," *Opinions of the Attorney General* 10, November 29, 1862, 382–383.

The revival of interest in nationalism and citizenship bodes well for the history of Reconstruction-era constitutional history. No respectable study of nationalism can fail to struggle with the close relationship between the new nation and the new Constitution forged by Reconstruction. Even Albion W. Tourgée, who delivered one of the most pessimistic assessments of Reconstruction in his well-known novel *A Fool's Errand*, conceded that the reconstructed Constitution was a great achievement of Reconstruction—indeed, perhaps the only achievement. At the end of the novel, when Tourgée's "fool," Comfort Servosse, returns North after his failed venture as an agent of Reconstruction to the South, he visits his old mentor Enos Martin. Servosse tries to argue that something was achieved by Reconstruction. Then, point after point, he yields to Martin's argument that nothing was in fact accomplished. But Servosse holds his ground on the Constitution: "Reconstruction was a great step in advance, in that it formulated a confession of error. It gave us a construction of 'we the people' in the preamble of our Federal Constitution which gave the lie to that which had formerly prevailed." "And is this all that has been gained by all these years of toil and struggle and blood?" asks Martin. "Is it not enough, my friend?" reproaches Servosse. "Is not almost a century of falsehood and hypocrisy cheaply atoned by a decade of chastisement? The confession of error is the hardest part of repentance, whether in a man or in a nation."[83] Constitutional change was the ever-present reminder of nationalism's protean character, its deep flaws and bright promise. In the future, as in the past, the study of constitutional development in the Reconstruction era will help us better to understand who "we the people" were—and are.

[83] Albion W. Tourgée, *A Fool's Errand*, ed. John Hope Franklin (Cambridge, Mass: Harvard University Press, 1961), 378.

7

RECONSTRUCTIONS IN INTELLECTUAL AND CULTURAL LIFE

LESLIE BUTLER

It cannot be repeated too often, that this war was a war of ideas, and that, until one idea or the other has secured a settled triumph, there can be no real peace between the parties to the war.
—Charles Eliot Norton, "American Political Ideas" (1865)

All that is left the South is the "war of ideas." She has thrown down the sword to take up the weapons of argument, not indeed under any banner of fanaticism, or to enforce a dogma, but simply to make the honourable conquest of reason and justice.
—Edward Pollard, *The Lost Cause: The Standard Southern History of the War of the Confederates* (1866)

The great concussion which has taken place in the American mind, must have loosened the foundations of all prejudice, and secured a fair hearing for impartial reason on all subjects, such as it might not otherwise have had for many generations.
—John Stuart Mill, letter to E. L. Godkin (1865)

Charles Eliot Norton, descendant of Puritan divines and wartime editor of the *North American Review*, and Edward Pollard, advocate of the African slave trade and wartime editor of the Richmond *Examiner*, agreed on very little. Yet both perceived, as did the British liberal political philosopher John Stuart Mill, that ideas were at the heart of the American Civil War.[1] Norton envi-

---

[1] Norton's article quoted in the epigraph is in *North American Review* 101 (October 1865), 564; Pollard's book was published by E. B. Treat (New York), 750; Mill's letter of May 24 is

sioned an epic battle between two systems of thought, Pollard understood ideas as weapons with which to win the peace, and Mill diagnosed a mental jolt so forceful it would make the American mind newly receptive to reasoned inquiry.

Recent scholarship has taken up and extended all three of these viewpoints, establishing that the massive upheaval of the 1860s did mobilize and transform American thought. The Civil War and its aftermath elicited reconstructions in intellectual terms no less than in social, political, or economic ones. No matter how one defines "Reconstruction"—as the reentry of the former Confederate states into the Union, as the adjustment to the emancipation of some four million slaves, or as the integration of the national economy under a newly powerful centralized state—the process of moving from Civil War to a civil peace required mental adaptation. All major wars undoubtedly result in periods of cultural and intellectual activity. Participants struggle to define the conflict, give purpose to the loss of life, reconcile initial aspirations with postwar realities, and vie for the meaning of the peace.[2] But the stakes were especially high during Reconstruction, a revolutionary moment when America's first principles seemed up for grabs.

Difficulties that attend a discussion of the intellectual and cultural history of Reconstruction are best acknowledged upfront. In most basic terms, how narrowly should the intellectual historian define Reconstruction? Should the term refer to a moment in time (1863–77) or to those processes set in motion during the war, such as emancipation, the enactment of race-neutral citizenship and suffrage, and the readmittance of all the Confederate states? Or does an intellectual history of Reconstruction need to address those larger (though far more amorphous) postwar transformations that are not time-delimited, region-delimited, or even event-delimited, exploring the impact that industrialization, incorporation, state-building, cultural consolidation, social reorganization, or general "modernization" had on American thought? In this essay, I have opted for the broadest definition possible, largely because many intellectual and cultural historians have not focused specifically on the "classic" period of Reconstruction or the constitutional, political, or economic processes of Reconstruction. Included here is work that falls in the general time period, addresses emancipation and national reorganization, or concerns itself with the legacy and impact

printed in *The Collected Works of John Stuart Mill: The Later Letters, 1849–1872* (Toronto: University of Toronto Press, 1972), 16:1055–1056.

[2] Some exemplary studies that investigate the impact of wars on thought and culture include Paul Fussell, *The Great War and Modern Memory* (New York: Oxford University Press, 1975); Lynn Hunt, *Politics, Culture, and Class in the French Revolution* (Berkeley: University of California Press, 1984); Robert Westbrook, "Fighting for the American Family," in *The Power of Culture: Critical Essays in American History*, ed. Richard W. Fox and T. J. Jackson Lears (Chicago: University of Chicago, 1993); and Wilfred M. McClay, *The Masterless: Self and Society in Modern America* (Chapel Hill: University of North Carolina Press, 1994).

of the Civil War and its aftermath. I have tried to make clear when historians attribute causal force directly to the sectional conflict, when they simply consider it a convenient moment in time, or when they do not treat it explicitly at all but its importance may be inferred.

It is perhaps a peculiarity of intellectual and cultural history that one might read a book about the 1870s that does not even mention Reconstruction.[3] This is understandable, given that some of the most important modern developments emerged in this decade, from the rise of Darwinian evolution and the authority of science, corporate capitalism, and the modern university to the challenges of socialism, feminism, and countless other "isms." These momentous trends have often preoccupied the attentions of intellectual historians interested in topics like the erosion of religious faith, the organization and specialization of knowledge, the meaning of the self in a modern, bureaucratized world, and the series of challenges to liberal democracy. These developments occurred at the same time as the Civil War and Reconstruction, a simultaneity suggested by the shared birth date of Abraham Lincoln and Charles Darwin or by the fact that John Brown launched his failed raid on Harpers Ferry within months of the publication of both Darwin's *On the Origin of the Species* and Marx's *Contribution to a Critique of Political Economy*.

The result is that the second half of the nineteenth century clearly stands out as a moment of major intellectual transformation, but for reasons other than the American challenge of postwar Reconstruction. Many scholars, beginning with Vernon Parrington in his *Main Currents in American Thought* (1927–30) and Merle Curti in his *The Growth of American Thought* (1943), have convincingly argued that the war and its aftermath hastened and intensified forces already in motion. These influential early works were less interested in the intellectual legacies of the war itself than in American thinkers' response to industrial capitalism and modern science. The Civil War and Reconstruction, then, were important because, in destroying slavery, they removed a crucial barrier to national capitalist expansion, thereby accelerating, in Parrington's words, the demise of antebellum "romantic optimism" and the rise of late-nineteenth-century "mechanistic pessimism."[4]

One need also keep in mind that the major developments of the era occurred across the Atlantic world, not just within the United States. Historians who pur-

[3] One, admittedly limited, example of Reconstruction's absence from the radar screen of intellectual historians can be found in the fact there is no entry on "Reconstruction" in the encyclopedic *Companion to American Thought* (Cambridge: Blackwell, 1995), edited by two leading intellectual historians, Richard W. Fox and James T. Kloppenberg. While there is a lengthy entry on the Civil War, written by Edward Ayers, it focuses on the changing interpretations of the war in American thought rather than on the war's impact on thought.

[4] Vernon L. Parrington, *Main Currents in American Thought* (New York: Harcourt Brace, 1927–30); Merle Curti, *The Growth of American Thought* (New York: Harper and Row, 1943).

sue connections across national boundaries tend to be even less attentive than otherwise to the specific dynamics of Reconstruction. A monograph on the conflict between religion and science, or the rise of "agnosticism" (after the coining of that term in 1869) might not address Reconstruction at all. That being said, recent developments in American intellectual history have driven more and more historians to connect their treatment of ideas to the varied processes of postwar Reconstruction.

Inside and Outside *The Inner Civil War*

In 1965, George Fredrickson went beyond Parrington and Curti, each of whom had recognized, but not fully explained, the gulf in American intellectual history demarcated by the crisis of the Civil War. In *The Inner Civil War*, Frederickson connected the dots and attributed causal force to the war and its aftermath, doing more than any other book to craft a narrative of war-induced intellectual transformation. Though limited to northern intellectuals and written almost forty years ago, this book provided the dominant interpretation that continues to influence scholarship today.[5]

In a sweeping and strongly thesis-driven interpretation, Fredrickson argued that the "collective trauma" of the war "had consequences for the history of ideas which were comparable to its well-known political and economic effects."[6] In particular, the crisis of war led northern intellectuals to abandon the idealism of the antebellum years for a more hardheaded realism thereafter. Fredrickson divided the dominant intellectual styles before and after the war into a series of dichotomies: the radical, antiinstitutional, and individualist tendencies of the antebellum era gave way to the conservative, authoritarian, and bureaucratic inclinations of the postbellum era. The massive death and destruction

---

[5] Fredrickson's book has been most influential among historians, but in literary terms, Edmund Wilson's *Patriotic Gore: Studies in the Literature of the American Civil War* (New York: Oxford University Press, 1962), Daniel Aaron, *The Unwritten War: American Writers and the Civil War* (New York: Knopf, 1973), and Lewis Simpson, *Mind and the American Civil War: A Meditation on Lost Causes* (Baton Rouge: Louisiana State University Press, 1989), are all indispensable to a full reckoning with the cultural and intellectual impact of the Civil War and Reconstruction.

[6] George M. Fredrickson, *The Inner Civil War: Northern Intellectuals and the Crisis of the Union* (1965; reprint, Urbana: University of Illinois Press, 1993), xv. In the preface to the 1993 edition, Fredrickson acknowledges that "the book may somewhat overemphasize the war experience itself as a cause of this transformation." He finds instead "a kind of elective affinity" between the modernizing trends of an industrial capitalist order and "the modes of thought directly inspired by the opportunities and necessities of the conflict" (ix). In short, the war was not the sole causal force in intellectual transformation, but it was a decisive and accelerating one.

caused by the war led to "a process of natural selection," Fredrickson suggested, whereby "pity or compassion" gave way to "impersonal efficiency" as the preferred response to suffering. Fredrickson fleshed out these abstractions with some telling details and anecdotes, written in admirably clear prose. The radical humanitarianism of antislavery gave way to the bureaucratic professionalization of poor relief. Emerson the "transparent eyeball," the iconoclastic poet of nature and the self, became Emerson the visitor to West Point and advocate of a taste-setting National Academy of Literature and Art. And then there was Dorothea Dix vexing the busy professionals at the Sanitary Commission as she mourned the suffering of a sun-stricken cow.

Fredrickson's work was at once bold and flawed, brilliant and frustrating. Admittedly influenced by Allan Nevins's conception of "the organized war," Fredrickson generalized from one clear strain of the war effort to describe the entire culture. More recent work has revealed that *The Inner Civil War* significantly overstated both the antiinstitutionalism of the antebellum years and the demise of idealism in the postwar years. Scholars like John Higham, Thomas Bender, and Lori Ginzburg have found consolidating and bureaucratizing trends well under way by the 1850s, while James McPherson, Anne Rose, and others have chronicled the persistence of idealism and humanitarianism in the years after the war.[7] The portraits of specific individuals—and especially their awkward division into stark, either/or groups of conservatives and humanitarians, or abolitionists and elitists—at times verge on the brink of caricature.[8] Fredrickson's almost exclusive reliance on published writings could not sustain the sort of biographical claims he ventured. These were simply problems of using too broad a brush to capture nuanced detail, of sacrificing some complexity in the interest of writing the grand narrative.

Other limitations of *The Inner Civil War* result from it being a work of the 1960s. It is interesting that a critique of the turn to tough-minded realism should be written in such a tough-minded manner. Fredrickson's tone revealed

[7] For antebellum years, John Higham, "From Boundlessness to Consolidation," in *Hanging Together: Unity and Diversity in American Culture* (New Haven: Yale University Press, 2001), 149–166; Thomas Bender, *New York Intellect: A History of Intellectual Life in New York City, from 1750 to the Beginnings of Our Own Time* (New York: Random House, 1987); Lori D. Ginzburg, *Women and the Work of Benevolence: Morality, Politics, and Class in the Nineteenth-Century United States* (New Haven: Yale University Press, 1990). See also Anne Rose, *Transcendentalism as a Social Movement, 1830–1850* (New Haven: Yale University Press, 1981); Len Gougeon, *Virtue's Hero: Emerson, Antislavery, and Reform* (Athens: University of Georgia Press, 1990). On postbellum years, see James M. McPherson, *The Abolitionist Legacy: From Reconstruction to the NAACP* (Princeton: Princeton University Press, 1975); Anne Rose, *Victorian America and the Civil War* (New York: Cambridge University Press, 1992).

[8] For example, Fredrickson divides those who mourned Robert Gould Shaw into either abolitionists or elitists, as if one could not be both at the same time. For a more nuanced account, see the collected essays in Martin H. Blatt, Thomas J. Brown, and Donald Yacovone, eds., *Hope*

a kind of Niebuhrian realism that bordered on cynicism. If Reinhold Niebuhr loomed as a silent influence, Nathaniel Hawthorne hovered as a model for the appropriate intellectual stance toward the war. Fredrickson opened the book with an invocation of Hawthorne's "detached and critical view of the Union cause" and his ironic "calling into question all exalted hopes and pretensions." Like many other historians writing at the time, Fredrickson exhibited a similar detachment, irony, and coolness toward his subject.[9] While few historians would deny the salutary effects of such a critical stance, Fredrickson's ironic detachment can at times appear jarring to a postrevisionist generation of readers. He equated denying the legitimacy of secession with the betrayal of the Declaration of Independence and its revolutionary legacy, glimpsing in Unionism little more than a lurking divine right theory of the state. Even emancipation offered no liberatory moment, only further instancing of a conservative, institutional turn on the part of northern reformers. He ignored, or refused to take seriously, how the northern intellectuals he examined, along with President Lincoln and Fredrick Douglass, made a virtual fetish of the Declaration (its equality principle, not its independence principle, which they forcefully denied applied to 1861), and how they saw emancipation as finally narrowing the gap between American practice and American principle. Written on the eve of a veritable revolution in our understanding of the Civil War and Reconstruction, Fredrickson's interpretations can seem at times quite dated.

So why does *The Inner Civil War* remain the standard citation? The answer has as much to do with changes in the subfield of intellectual history as with the book itself. *The Inner Civil War* appeared at what can be seen in retrospect as the beginning of the end of the intellectual history that had been dominant since the 1940s. The 1960s undermined the legitimacy of studying elites in general and intellectual history in particular. So at least part of the explanation for the persistence of *The Inner Civil War* as the standard citation lies in the fact it has not had many rivals, at least until quite recently.[10] The rise of

---

and Glory: Essays on the Legacy of the Fifty-Fourth Massachusetts Regiment (Amherst: University of Massachusetts Press, 2001). Another topic Fredrickson discusses, the seemingly incongruous relationship between humanitarian idealism and violence, has also received further treatment in, for example, John Stauffer, *The Black Hearts of Men: Radical Abolitionists and the Transformation of Race* (Cambridge, Mass.: Harvard University Press, 2001). For fully nuanced and revised individual portraits, see especially James Turner, *The Liberal Education of Charles Eliot Norton* (Baltimore: Johns Hopkins University Press, 1999); Thomas J. Brown, *Dorothea Dix, New England Reformer* (Cambridge, Mass.: Harvard University Press, 1998); Gougeon, *Virtue's Hero*; Joan Waugh, *Unsentimental Reformer: The Life of Josephine Shaw Lowell* (Cambridge, Mass.: Harvard University Press, 1997); Dean Grodzins, *American Heretic: Theodore Parker and Transcendentalism* (Chapel Hill: University of North Carolina Press, 2002).

[9] Fredrickson, *Inner Civil War*, 2.

[10] Mia Bay has made a similar point about Fredrickson's second book, *The Black Image in the White Mind*, in "Remembering Racism," *Reviews in American History* 27 (1999): 646–656.

the "new social history," with its related desire to write history "from the bottom up" and its emphasis on quantitative methods, made the more top-down, qualitative approaches of intellectual historians instantly unfashionable and even politically suspect. Further, the discovery of diversity and contestation throughout the American past led to the breakdown of the "consensus" school, which had implicitly undergirded much of the American studies–based work in cultural and intellectual history. Suddenly it became highly problematic to imagine or discuss a unitary "American mind" that was best revealed in the writings of the well-known figures who made up an "American tradition."[11]

But if the late 1960s and 1970s marked the low point of intellectual history and the ascendancy of social history, things soon began to change for intellectual historians and, in some ways, thanks to the work of social historians. Labor historians like Herbert Gutman and E. P. Thompson became interested in examining the worldviews, or "mentalités," of their working-class subjects. Other historians grew interested in unpacking "ideologies" (Geertzian and Gramscian variants), "discourses," and "languages" and began to borrow the tools of the intellectual historian. Historians of political thought like Quentin Skinner and J. G. A. Pocock soon found themselves asking new questions about the interactions among ideas, politics, and social action, as did the American historians Bernard Bailyn, Gordon Wood, Eric Foner, and David Brion Davis.[12] The attention to systems of meaning only became more intense in the 1990s, as many subfields followed the philosopher Richard Rorty's invocation of a "linguistic turn," which in the hands of historians heightened the importance of rigorously contextualizing language and meaning. Interested especially in understanding how race, class, and gender have been constructed in different historical moments, the new "cultural history" burst onto the scene, attracting the

[11] Intellectual historians' sense of their field at bay can be seen in the defensive tone struck in John Higham and Paul Conkin, eds., *New Directions in American Intellectual History* (Baltimore: Johns Hopkins University Press, 1979). For a thorough examination of the long history of intellectual history see Donald R. Kelley, *The Descent of Ideas: The History of Intellectual History* (Aldershot, England: Ashgate, 2002).

[12] See, for example, J. G. A. Pocock, *The Machiavellian Moment: Florentine Political Thought and the Atlantic Republican Tradition* (Princeton: Princeton University Press, 1974); Quentin Skinner, *The Foundations of Modern Political Thought* (New York: Cambridge University Press, 1978). Some classic works in the history of American ideology include Bernard Bailyn, *The Ideological Origins of the American Revolution* (Cambridge, Mass.: Harvard University Press, 1967); Gordon S. Wood, *The Creation of the American Republic* (Chapel Hill: University of North Carolina Press, 1969); Eric Foner, *Free Soil, Free Labor, Free Men: The Ideology of the Republican Party before the Civil War* (New York: Oxford University Press, 1970); David Brion Davis, *The Problem of Slavery in the Age of Revolution* (Ithaca, N.Y.: Cornell University Press, 1973).

attention of social and intellectual historians alike. Thanks to all these developments, as Thomas Bender has recently argued, where once intellectual history faced disappearance, it now faces appropriation by every field.[13]

Some scholars have found in cultural history—with its attention to the larger contexts of meaning that can both empower and limit ordinary Americans as well as elites—a chance to reunite social and intellectual history. In this view, a cultural approach to ideas and thought may be less an innovation than a return to the very best of the tradition, without its overconfident (or naïve) assumption of consensus and a unitary American mind. One strain of the field, the "externalist" school associated with Merle Curti and, later, John Higham, had always studied elite as well as popular expressions in its attempt to reveal the broad "spirit" of the age. For example, Curti's chapter on the Civil War examines with equal seriousness the reading material of average soldiers and the nationalist theories of Francis Lieber.[14] More recently, the subfield known as "the history of the book" offers one instance where social and intellectual histories seem to have been happily merged. Exemplary work in this field has combined close readings of texts with research into how those texts were produced, distributed, and read by (often) ordinary readers.[15]

Cultural history—especially the more theoretically driven "cultural studies"—and intellectual history are not indistinguishable, nor do they always exist in harmony. Some cultural historians continue to express disdain for studying formal thought or "elite" expressions, preferring dime novels to declarations and advertisements to arguments. Many intellectual historians, on the other hand, fear the incursion into their scholarly turf of an invasive cultural history and question the methodological rigor of some of its more amorphous productions. But these internecine squabbles aside, nearly all intellectual historians would agree that the rise of cultural history has been a benefit to intellectual history. Not only has it pushed intellectual historians to consider a wider range of voices and a greater variety of sources in their analyses, opening up new

[13] Thomas Bender, "Intellectual and Cultural History," in *New Directions in American History*, ed. Eric Foner (Philadelphia: Temple University Press, 1997), 181–202.

[14] Curti, *Growth of American Thought*, 454–480. Kelley, *The Descent of Ideas*, has stressed that nearly all developments in intellectual and cultural history have venerable historical antecedents and are less novel than their practitioners often claim.

[15] For example, Jonathan Rose's recent study of reading among the British working class has expanded the demographic base of intellectual history and, in so doing, has further exposed as false the assumption that so-called elite or canonical texts held no meaning for ordinary people. Rose, *The Intellectual Life of the British Working Class* (New Haven: Yale University Press, 2001). For an incisive historiographical discussion of the history of the book, see Joan Shelley Rubin, "What Is the History of the History of Books?" *Journal of American History* 90 (September 2003): 555–575.

ways to contextualize ideas and trace their dissemination, but it has also helped shift historical focus onto questions of meaning and interpretation, where the intellectual historian has much to contribute.[16]

The shifting tones of Fredrickson's two prefaces demonstrate some of the changes in intellectual history over the past forty years. Writing in 1993 in the preface to the reprint edition, he found himself "slightly embarrassed" by the "rather glib assertion" in the 1965 preface that "the few who have a genuine interest in ideas and a powerful urge to find meaning in their experience are able to tell us more about a crisis of values, with its inevitable confusion and ambivalence, than the many who avoid difficult issues and are content to speak in outdated clichés." Embedded in this 1965 assertion are several assumptions that reveal some of the ways the field has changed. Intellectual and cultural historians no longer assume that the ordinary, less reflective folk tend to evade "difficult issues" or, for that matter, that intellectual elites necessarily address them. As to whether or not the "many"—or even the "few"—speak in "outdated clichés," those clichés might now be considered highly revealing of shared cultural values and hidden attitudes. Some historians today might doubt that the expressions of the intellectually inclined few are necessarily more revealing than those of the many, but even they would probably agree at least that the expressions of those idea-oriented few hold more cultural authority and therefore deserve considerable scholarly attention. Most intellectual historians, however, would still insist on the primacy of those dedicated to ideas but would take such an assertion less for granted than they would have forty years ago.

But as Fredrickson also pointed out in the revised preface, in many ways *The Inner Civil War* was ahead of its time. Fredrickson included the thought and work of several women in his narrative, an increasing feature of recent cultural and intellectual history. He attended to noncanonical as well as canonical voices, demonstrating the cultural importance of such figures as Henry Bellows, Horace Bushnell, and Josephine Shaw Lowell, even though they were not "considered significant contributors to American thought" in the 1960s. Further, Fredrickson's emphasis on what might be called "the social role of intellectuals" pointed the way toward a new social history approach to ideas and intellectuals

---

[16] For important debates over the relationships among intellectual history, cultural history, and cultural studies, see especially John Toews, "Intellectual History after the Linguistic Turn: The Autonomy of Meaning and the Irreducibility of Experience, *American Historical Review* 92 (October 1987): 879–907; the interchange between David Harlan and David Hollinger in the *American Historical Review* 94 (June 1989): 581–562; and the symposium "Intellectual History in the Age of Cultural Studies," *Intellectual History Newsletter* 18 (1996): 3–69. Paula Fass has recently offered a powerful critique of the "new cultural history" from the perspective of a social historian in "Cultural History/Social History: Some Reflections on a Continuing Dialogue" *Journal of Social History* 37 (Fall 2003): 38–46.

that has opened fresh avenues of inquiry to intellectual and cultural historians. Finally, as the remainder of this essay will show, even where Fredrickson's research and interpretation have been considerably modified, intellectual and cultural historians have in many ways continued to grapple with the questions and issues framed by him in the 1960s.

Intellectuals and the Sites
of Intellectual and Cultural Life

The history of American thought has often remained, as was the case for Frederickson, the history of distinct thinkers. Biographical studies by James Kloppenberg, Wilfred McClay, Louis Menand, and others have shown, as David Brion Davis once put it, "how cultural tensions and contradictions may be internalized, struggled with, and resolved within actual individuals."[17] Closest to Fredrickson's concerns is Menand's *The Metaphysical Club* (2001), a study of Oliver Wendell Holmes, William James, Charles Sanders Peirce, and John Dewey. As in *The Inner Civil War*, the searing experience of war helped nudge Menand's set of intellectually inclined northerners away from romantic idealism and toward science and institutions, best embodied in the young Oliver Wendell Holmes, who went off to war a twenty-year-old abolitionist and Emersonian and returned a twenty-four-year-old skeptic of "causes" and grand ideas. To Menand, the war did more than transform ideas; it helped give rise to a new "idea about ideas." His four protagonists came to believe that "ideas are not 'out there' waiting to be discovered, but are tools—like forks and knives and microchips—that people devise to cope with the world in which they find themselves." Such a belief represented the birth of American pragmatism, the intellectual movement away from orthodoxy and toward uncertainty and experimentation in many fields of inquiry. In other words, though Menand's narrative charts how a prominent group of northeastern thinkers moved from romanticism to realism, *The Metaphysical Club* does much more than retell Fredrickson's story. Where Fredrickson found a "conservative" and authoritarian intellectual turn, Menand argues

---

[17] David Brion Davis, "Some Recent Directions in Cultural History," *American Historical Review* 73 (February 1968): 705, quoted in one of the classic biographical studies of intellectual and cultural history, Daniel Walker Howe, *The Political Culture of the American Whigs* (Chicago: University of Chicago Press, 1979), 4. Group biographies have been a particularly rich venue for uncovering and exploring the various discursive communities in which intellectuals have participated (with varying degrees of consciousness). For some of the methodological underpinnings of the study of discourse in intellectual history, see David A. Hollinger, "Historians and the Discourse of Intellectuals," in *In the American Province: Studies in the History and Historiography of Ideas* (Bloomington: Indiana University Press, 1985), 130–151.

that the war's ultimate impact culminated in the tolerance and pluralism of pragmatism, an account that works best in the careers of William James and John Dewey.[18]

Biographies of single individuals grappling directly with Reconstruction represent another approach. Two studies of Henry Adams focus particularly on the intellectual and cultural contours of his postwar career. Brooks Simpson, well known as a political historian and biographer of Ulysses S. Grant, turns to intellectual history to explore the intellectual currents that underlay Adams's postbellum reform ambitions—particularly his wartime reading of Tocqueville and John Stuart Mill while in London with his father, the minister to England—and to detail his failure to attain the "influence" he so clearly sought on his move to Washington in 1868. Beginning with Adams's intellectual denigration of the South (where southerners had no "mind" but only "temperament"), Michael O'Brien offers a deep history of Adams's attitudes toward and relationships with the South and its people—relatives, friends, servants, historical actors, and fictional characters alike. O'Brien argues that Adams was both attracted to and repulsed by "the South," which was always more an imaginative "counterpoint" to the "social damage of pell-mell American industrialization" that Adams increasingly found in the postwar, modern North than a real place inhabited by actual thinking and acting people.[19]

Though one perhaps less readily associates Charles Eliot Norton with Reconstruction, James Turner's careful biography demonstrates how exhaustive archival work can bring to life a figure often reduced to caricature in more general studies, including (and perhaps especially) *The Inner Civil War*. In Turner's hands, Norton emerges as a three-dimensional, complex thinker at the center of nearly every postwar intellectual trend and on whom the war and its aftermath had a profound intellectual impact. The war revealed to Norton the centrality and indis-

[18] Louis Menand, *The Metaphysical Club: A Story of Ideas in America* (New York: Farrar, Straus, and Giroux, 2001) xi. Menand draws not just from Fredrickson here but from that rich body of scholarship on Oliver Wendell Holmes Jr., beginning with Edmund Wilson, that sees his "realism" as a product of the war. See Wilson, *Patriotic Gore*; Morton White, *Social Thought in America: The Revolt against Formalism* (Boston: Beacon Press, 1957); and David E. Shi, *Facing Facts: Realism in American Thought and Culture* (New York: Oxford University Press, 1995).

[19] Simpson, *The Political Education of Henry Adams* (Columbia: University of South Carolina, 1996); Michael O'Brien, *Henry Adams and the Southern Question* (Athens: University of Georgia Press, 2005), 124. See also Garry Wills, *Henry Adams and the Making of America* (Boston: Houghton Mifflin, 2005); Leslie Butler, "'Investigating the Great American Mystery': Theory and Style in Henry Adams's Political Reform Moment," in William Merrill Decker and Earl S. Harbert, eds., *Henry Adams and the Need to Know* (Charlottesville: University of Virginia Press, 2005). On other uses of the South as a fictive "counterpoint" to the postbellum North, see C. Vann Woodward, "A Southern Critique for the Gilded Age: Melville, Adams, and James," in *The Burden of Southern History* (1960; reprint, Baton Rouge: Louisiana State University Press, 1968), 109–140.

pensability of liberty in every realm of experience, and Turner intriguingly presents Norton's falling away from the Unitarian faith of his Harvard divine father as something of a personal reconstruction occurring amid the larger national process. Like many of his friends and allies in the North (as well as across the Atlantic), Norton looked to the postwar period with great hope for a national rebirth in both politics and culture, a hope that would be dimmed, though never fully dashed, with each succeeding decade of the late nineteenth century.[20]

Southern intellectuals have not garnered as much scholarly attention as northern intellectuals. Historians may have been more drawn to the northern victors, who had a greater impact on national life, or they may have concluded that the elaboration of the Lost Cause myth overwhelmed all other aspects of intellectual life in this period.[21] In general, historians of southern thought seem to have followed Michael O'Brien in concluding that the half century "between Appomattox and the Southern Renaissance is the most uninviting of Southern moments, drab, impoverished, obscure, unprescient."[22] The studies we do have largely emphasize the regional nature of intellectual life and the contours of what Edward Pollard called a "war of ideas" against Yankee dominance. Jack Maddex's short but compelling *The Reconstruction of Edward A. Pollard* (1974) has made Pollard not just a southern apologist, though, but a thinker whose transformation from advocate of proslavery southern nationalism to proponent of white supremacist conservative Unionism sheds light on the larger dynamics of intellectual accommodation and resistance.[23] Fred Hobson's *Tell about the South* (1983), a study of southern writers from 1850 to 1970, has provided a

---

[20] Turner, *The Liberal Education of Charles Eliot Norton*, 211–214; 200–207. See also Leslie Butler, *Cultivating American Democracy: Victorian Men of Letters and Transatlantic Liberal Reform, 1840–1900* (Chapel Hill: University of North Carolina Press, forthcoming), chap. 3.

[21] On histories of the Lost Cause, see especially Charles Reagan Wilson, *Baptized in Blood: The Religion of the Lost Cause* (Athens: University of Georgia Press, 1980); Gaines Foster, *Ghosts of the Confederacy: Defeat, the Lost Cause, and the Emergence of the New South, 1865 to 1913* (New York: Oxford University Press, 1987); and, more recently, David Blight, *Race and Reunion: The Civil War in American Memory* (Cambridge, Mass.: Harvard University Press, 2001), and Thomas Brown's essay, chapter 8 here.

[22] Michael O'Brien, "The Middle Years: Edwin Mims," in *Rethinking the South: Essays in Intellectual History* (Athens: University of Georgia Press, 1988), 131. O'Brien and others have invigorated antebellum southern intellectual history, as can be seen in his own *Conjectures of Order: Intellectual Life in the American South, 1820–1860* (Chapel Hill: University of North Carolina Press, 2004); Drew Faust, *A Sacred Circle: The Dilemma of the Intellectual in the Old South, 1840–1860* (Baltimore: Johns Hopkins Press, 1977); and Eugene Genovese, *The Slaveholder's Dilemma: Freedom and Progress in Southern Conservative Thought, 1820–1860* (Columbia: University of South Carolina Press, 1992). Further evidence of the absence, or marginalization, of postbellum southern intellectuals is that almost none are included, even in capsule form, in *Companion to American Thought*.

[23] Jack P. Maddex, *The Reconstruction of Edward A. Pollard: A Rebel's Conversion to Postbellum Unionism* (Chapel Hill: University of North Carolina Press, 1974). See also Jonathan M.

counterpart in his examination of Pollard's fellow unreconstructed publicists, briefly sketching writers like Alfred Taylor Bledsoe and the minister Robert Lewis Dabney while also presenting the skeptical fiction writer George Washington Cable.[24]

More recently, Charles J. Holden's *In the Great Maelstrom* (2002) has produced a study of four figures writing between the antebellum years and World War II in an effort to demonstrate the persistence of southern conservatism. These men's devotion to white supremacy was matched by a no less fervent attachment to elite rule, and Holden argues that while their specific positions shifted in response to new developments, they clung to a conservative core that proved remarkably resilient.[25] In *Blood and Irony* (2004), Sarah Gardner has provided an account of how white women novelists reckoned with Confederate defeat, in a book that moves from Augusta Jane Evans during the war to Margaret Mitchell in the 1930s. Gardner's chronological approach allows her to demonstrate how "postbellum politics and culture shaped narratives of the war as much as did the events of the conflict itself." Writers in the midst of Reconstruction shared a sense of confusion and uncertainty, not about the end of the Confederacy but about the future of the South, that gave their writing an urgency and immediacy not seen in later contributions that became reconciled to the concept of defeat.[26] While these studies contribute new perspectives to postwar intellectual history, it is curious that no work of equal ambition to *The Inner Civil War* has emerged for southern thinkers, though such a study would not only be valuable in its own right but also might allow for an intellectual history that could compare the impact of the war on northern and southern intellectuals, as Edmund Wilson and Daniel Aaron have done for literary figures.

Wiener, "Coming to Terms with Capitalism: The Postwar Thought of George Fitzhugh," *Virginia Magazine of History and Biography* 87 (1979): 438–447; Neal C. Gillespie, *The Collapse of Orthodoxy: The Intellectual Ordeal of George Frederick Holmes* (Charlottesville: University of Virginia Press, 1972), which situates the University of Virginia professor less in regional frameworks than in European debates over religion, faith, science, and history.

[24] Hobson, *Tell about the South: The Southern Rage to Explain* (Baton Rouge: Louisiana State University Press, 1983), pt. 2, chap. 1. See also the several discussions of southern writers in Wilson, *Patriotic Gore*; Aaron, *The Unwritten War*; Wayne Mixon, *Southern Writers and the New South Movement, 1865–1913* (Chapel Hill: University of North Carolina Press, 1980); and the collected Civil War writings of the eminent German-trained southern classicist in Ward W. Briggs Jr. ed., *Soldier and Scholar: Basil Lanneau Gildersleeve and the Civil War* (Charlottesville: University Press of Virginia, 1998).

[25] Charles J. Holden, *In the Great Maelstrom: Conservatives in Post–Civil War South Carolina* (Columbia: University of South Carolina Press, 2002). The southern conservative tradition has also been delineated in Richard B. Weaver, *The Southern Tradition at Bay: A History of Postbellum Thought* (Washington, D.C.: Regnery Gateway, 1968).

[26] Sarah E. Gardner, *Blood and Irony: Southern White Women's Narratives of the Civil War, 1861–1937* (Chapel Hill: University of North Carolina Press, 2004), 7.

But intellectuals are not the whole story. Just as Fredrickson charted the move of humanitarian idealists into bureaucratic institutions after the war, so historians have devoted great energy in recent years to understanding the development of the institutions and sites of cultural and intellectual life. The university, the professionalizing organizations of social science, and the literary marketplace have all received particular attention.

Higher education received an enormous boost during the Civil War and its aftermath, a point Merle Curti established long ago. The federal government, through the Morrill Land Grant Act, gave tremendous aid to states establishing colleges devoted to scientific studies in engineering and agriculture. New war-built fortunes poured dollars into planning such new colleges as Cornell University, the Massachusetts Institute of Technology, and Swarthmore College and expanding older ones. This university expansion drew new kinds of students into its orb, especially women, who suddenly had an array of their own colleges to choose from, including Bryn Mawr, Vassar, Smith, and Wellesley. Some African Americans in the South also had the opportunity of a college education for the first time, in vocational and, less frequently, liberal arts settings, which helped to develop an important professional class long before the debates of W. E. B. Du Bois and Booker T. Washington over black education.[27]

Recent work on the "age of the university" has considerably modified the older narrative of the classical college's demise in the wake of a postwar interest in modern science and professionalization. Formerly stark dichotomies between old and new, classical and modern, sacred and secular have been challenged by Louise Stevenson's account of earlier university reformers, as well as by George Marsden, Julie Reuben, Jon Roberts, and James Turner, each of whom has shown that the late-century reformers initially believed the new "science" could accommodate an enduring emphasis on religion or, at the very least, on morality and the unity of knowledge. Caroline Winterer has shown that the "classics" did not simply disappear from the modern research university, and that classicists

---

[27] Curti, *The Growth of American Thought*, 464–469. Scholarship on the university is vast; some important contributions include: Laurence R. Veysey, *The Emergence of the American University* (Chicago: University of Chicago Press, 1965); Helen Horowitz, *Alma Mater: Design and Experience in the Women's Colleges from their Nineteenth-Century Beginnings to the 1930s* (New York: Knopf, 1984); Barbara M. Solomon, *In the Company of Educated Women: A History of Women and Higher Education in America* (New Haven: Yale University Press, 1985); James D. Anderson, *The Education of Blacks in the South, 1860–1935* (Chapel Hill: University of North Carolina Press, 1988). Glenda Gilmore notes the relative advancement of black college women over white college women in the postwar years in *Gender and Jim Crow: Women and the Politics of White Supremacy in North Carolina, 1896–1920* (Chapel Hill: University of North Carolina Press, 1996), 31–36. While the population attending college in the postbellum years grew more diverse, it did not actually expand, at least as a percentage of total population, according to figures cited in Caroline Winterer, *The Culture of Classicism: Ancient Greece and Rome in American Intellectual Life, 1780–1910* (Baltimore: Johns Hopkins University Press, 2002), 101.

revealed themselves to be innovators as well as traditionalists.[28] Innovations in white southern higher education have also received some much-needed attention. Dan Frost's *Thinking Confederates* (2000) has argued that the Confederacy's desperate attempts to industrialize during the war shaped the outlook of those many military leaders who followed Robert E. Lee into college classrooms after the war. These men did not simply take up the fight for southern tradition but pioneered "progressivist" efforts to combine their faith in the Lost Cause with "scientific" approaches to every subject from engineering to history. White southern educational life lagged behind its nationalizing, northern counterpart because constituencies of these leaders rejected their call to embrace new methods.[29]

Related to the development of universities, and indeed underpinning their postwar expansion, was the emergence of social science as a new source of cultural authority.[30] Slowly, and with some variability, over the last decades of the nineteenth century, religious or moral understandings of society gave way to scientific ones. Fredrickson's notice of the founding of the American Social Science Association (ASSA) in 1865 has been more fully elaborated in Thomas Haskell's *The Emergence of Professional Social Science* (1977), in which the organization helped middle-class reformers confront their own crisis of authority. An increasing awareness of "interdependence" in society led a younger generation to pursue social science in a more academic and professionalized manner, so that by end of the century, social science had become the special preserve of the universities, not of the public-spirited men of letters who had first formed the ASSA.[31] Dorothy Ross's *The Origins of American Social Science* (1991) has also told how the postwar period was pivotal in the story of professional social science,

[28] Louise Stevenson, *Scholarly Means to Evangelical Ends: The New Haven Scholars and the Transformation of Higher Learning in America, 1830–1890* (Baltimore: Johns Hopkins Press, 1986); George Marsden, *The Soul of the American University: From Protestant Establishment to Established Nonbelief* (New York: Oxford University Press, 1994); Julie A. Reuben, *The Making of a Modern University: Intellectual Transformation and the Marginalization of Morality* (Chicago: University of Chicago Press, 1996); Jon H. Roberts and James Turner, *The Sacred and the Secular University* (Princeton: Princeton University Press, 2000); Winterer, *The Culture of Classicism*, chaps. 4 and 5.

[29] Dan Frost, *Thinking Confederates: Academia and the Idea of Progress in the New South* (Knoxville: University of Tennessee Press, 2000).

[30] Social scientists drew increasingly from the natural sciences to bolster their authority. For connections between Darwinian evolution and social science, see Mike Hawkins, *Social Darwinism in European and American Thought, 1860–1945: Nature as Model and Nature as Threat* (Cambridge: Cambridge University Press, 1997), which offers some revisions to Robert Bannister, *Social Darwinism: Science and Myth in Anglo-American Social Thought* (Philadelphia: Temple University Press, 1979), which in turn had set out to revise the classic work by Richard Hofstadter, *Social Darwinism in America* (Philadelphia: University of Pennsylvania Press, 1945). See also Cynthia Russett, *Darwin in America: The Intellectual Response, 1865–1912* (San Francisco: Freeman, 1976).

[31] Thomas L. Haskell, *The Emergence of Professional Social Science: the American Social Science Association and the Nineteenth-Century Crisis of Authority* (Urbana: University of Illinois Press, 1977). On the development of the discipline of economics, see Mary O. Furner, *Advocacy*

though, like Haskell, she does not invoke the Civil War as a causal force. For her, it was the crisis of intense industrialization that forced social scientists to reconsider their view of an America exempt from Old World problems. Her book has located the founding of several new academic disciplines in this sense of crisis, as the first generations of professional social scientists tried to subject the seeming chaos around them to the orderly control of natural laws. In his *Positivist Republic: August Comte and the Reconstruction of American Liberalism* (1995), Gillis Harp makes a spirited case for the significance of Comtean positivism to the development of American progressivism in the same arenas.[32]

While universities modernized and professionalized, it should also be noted that the postbellum period saw the flowering of the nonutilitarian conception of "culture" (as in "liberal culture" or "Western culture") as an antidote to materialism in all its forms. In Caroline Winterer's book, classicists and their allies are shown responding to their displacement at the center of the college curriculum by articulating a broad view of the classics, and by extension the "humanities," as crucial to character formation and the cultivation of civic virtue. James Turner has also explored this nonutilitarian aspect of education through the career of Charles Eliot Norton, who, through his fostering of literary and archaeological societies both at home and abroad and his humanistic instruction in the Harvard classroom and the pages of middle-class periodicals, helped to "invent western civilization" as a repository of secular morality and humane ideals.[33]

If "culture" weathered the utilitarian storm of science, scholars have also made clear that religion did not simply disappear. James Moore's *The Post-Darwinian Controversies* (1979) and Jon Roberts's *Darwinism and the Divine in America* (1988) have demonstrated how liberal Protestants adapted evolution into their Christian apologetics, replacing Darwin's notion of nonlinear and random change with a more comforting understanding of providential progress.[34] If liberal Protestants could accommodate the British naturalist Darwin, they

and Objectivity: A Crisis in the Professionalization of American Social Science 1865–1905 (Lexington: University of Kentucky Press, 1975).

[32] Dorothy Ross, *The Origins of American Social Science* (New York: Cambridge University Press, 1991); Gillis Harp, *Positivist Republic: August Comte and the Reconstruction of American Liberalism* (University Park: Pennsylvania State University, 1995).

[33] Winterer, *The Culture of Classicism*. Turner credits Norton with the "invention of western civilization" in *The Liberal Education of Charles Eliot Norton*, 384–388. On the connection between postwar social and economic change and the development of "high culture," see also Alan Trachtenberg, *The Incorporation of America: Culture and Society in the Gilded Age* (New York: Hill and Wang, 1982), chap. 5, and Lawrence Levine, *Highbrow/Lowbrow: The Emergence of Cultural Hierarchy in America* (Cambridge, Mass.: Harvard University Press, 1988).

[34] James Moore, *The Post-Darwinian Controversies: A Study of the Protestant Struggle to Come to Terms with Darwin in Great Britain and America, 1870–1900* (New York: Cambridge University Press, 1979); Jon H. Roberts, *Darwinism and the Divine in America: Protestant Intellectuals and Organic Evolution, 1859–1900* (Madison: University of Wisconsin Press, 1988).

less easily wrestled with the French positivist Auguste Comte who, according to Charles Cashdollar's *The Transformation of American Theology* (1989), actually presented a more serious threat than Darwin. Comte's three-stage model of historical development, which moved from the "theological" through the "metaphysical" and on to the scientific or "positive" stage, and his restriction of human knowledge to strictly observable phenomena directly challenged religious belief and authority. Still, according to Cashdollar, some liberal Protestant intellectuals made their peace with Comtean positivism, especially by finding common ground in social ethics.[35]

Recent work on the late-nineteenth-century "loss of faith" has deemphasized the notion of an all-out struggle between religion and science by probing the connections and parallels between them. Paul Jerome Croce, in *Religion and Science in the Era of William James* (1995), argues that religion and science, for all their obvious epistemological and methodological differences, shared a fundamental absence of certainty. For James Turner in *Without God, without Creed* (1984), the scientific orientation of liberal Protestants unintentionally contributed to the ultimate erosion of religious authority. Bernard Lightman has pursued a related, if inverse, argument in his persuasive *The Origins of Agnosticism* (1987), where he shows a lingering reliance on faith among British Victorian scientific agnostics. The Civil War plays no explicit role in these specific studies, but the impact on religious faith of an enormous cataclysm like the Civil War seems ripe for analysis.[36]

The war years transformed mass media no less than the universities. The heightened desire for war news encouraged the expansion and technological advancement of all kinds of print media, from Loyal Publication Society pamphlets to the founding of new periodicals like the New York *Nation*. As many scholars have demonstrated, an explosion of print media created a new literary marketplace in which a whole generation of authors could now support themselves financially by publishing their work in a series of national monthlies. Mark Twain, William Dean Howells, and Henry James all published their novels serially in *Harper's*, the *Atlantic Monthly*, and the *Century* magazine. The postwar national literary establishment (based in New York City) was open as well to the series of newly marketed "regional" or "local color" writers of whom

---

[35] Charles D. Cashdollar, *The Transformation of Theology, 1830–1890: Positivism and Protestant Thought in Britain and America* (Princeton: Princeton University Press, 1989).

[36] Paul Jerome Croce, *Religion and Science in the Era of William James: The Eclipse of Certainty* (Chapel Hill: University of North Carolina Press, 1995); James Turner, *Without God, without Creed: The Origins of Unbelief in America* (Baltimore: Johns Hopkins University Press, 1984); and Bernard Lightman, *The Origins of Agnosticism: Victorian Unbelief and the Limits of Knowledge* (Baltimore: Johns Hopkins Press, 1987).

George Washington Cable, Sarah Orne Jewett, and Bret Harte are just the best-known examples.[37]

Recent work on the literary marketplace has also enhanced our understanding of how this burgeoning print culture produced varied meanings of the war itself. Alice Fahs's *The Imagined Civil War* (2001) has provided a new overview of northern and southern popular wartime literature that emerged in such genres as poetry, adventure stories, and humor. Together with Kathleen Diffley and Lyde Cullen Sizer, Fahs has effectively countered the judgments of Edmund Wilson and Daniel Aaron that the war did not elicit much in the way of a literary response. If the Civil War did "get into the books," it do so through a range of voices (particularly female ones) and concerns (the changing status of African Americans) that earlier accounts had largely neglected.[38]

Diffley, Sizer, and Fahs have provided a partial corrective to the prevailing emphasis on professionalization and organization in postbellum culture. Both find a strikingly personal dimension to popular literature of the era—one that even dramatized the "liberatory potential of war for individuals"—that suggests that individualism and idealism did not simply disappear under the assault of the "organized" war. There was, according to Sizer, a "gender gap" in American understandings of the war and its legacy; female writers like Louisa May Alcott, Fanny Fern, Elizabeth Stuart Phelps, and Frances Ellen Watkins Harper registered their commitment to an earlier model of moral reform and gestured toward a cross-class, cross-race female solidarity that other scholars suggested had withered in the postwar decades.[39] Popular literary interest in war-related issues tended to wane in tandem with interest in Reconstruction in the late 1870s;

[37] On the postwar literary marketplace, see especially Richard Brodhead, "Literature and Culture," in *Columbia Literary History of the United States*, ed. Emory Elliott (New York: Columbia University Press, 1988); Susan Coultrap-McQuinn, *Doing Literary Business: American Women Writers in the Nineteenth Century* (Chapel Hill: University of North Carolina Press, 1990); Richard Brodhead, *Cultures of Letters: Scenes of Reading and Writing in Nineteenth-Century America* (Chicago: University of Chicago Press, 1993). Michael O'Brien has succinctly described the connection between postwar nationalism and "the idea of regionalism" in *Henry Adams and the Southern Tradition*, 73–74.

[38] Alice Fahs, *The Imagined Civil War: Popular Literature of the North and South, 1861–1865* (Chapel Hill: University of North Carolina Press, 2001); Kathleen Diffley, *Where My Heart Is Turning Ever: Civil War Stories and Constitutional Reform, 1861–1876* (Athens: University of Georgia Press, 1992); Lyde Cullen Sizer, *The Political Work of Northern Women Writers and the Civil War, 1850–1872* (Chapel Hill: University of North Carolina Press, 2000). While Aaron largely focused on canonical male writers, Wilson did include a range of women writers, including southern diarists like Kate Stone, Sarah Morgan, and Mary Chesnut, as well as the northerner Charlotte Forten.

[39] Quotation in Fahs, *Imagined Civil War*, 13. For arguments about the elitism and racism of the postwar woman's movement, see Ginzburg, *Women and the Work of Benevolence*, and Louise Newman, *White Women's Rights: The Racial Origins of Feminism in the United States* (New York: Oxford University Press, 1999).

when attention to the conflict reemerged in the late 1880s and 1890s, Fahs and Sizer both agree, women and African Americans would be largely excluded from what became a national fascination with the "Battles and Leaders of the Civil War." That this later heavily gendered and racialized narrative was not always dominant tells us much about the expansive ways in which readers and writers reckoned with the war and its legacy in the first decades after Appomattox.

Consolidation

A major theme of Reconstruction, established by Fredrickson and elaborated elsewhere, has been the way Americans experienced consolidation on a variety of levels: the establishment of massive military force, the national integration of the economy, the expanded reach of the postwar state, and the centralization of a national culture. Centripetal forces clearly affected the cultural and intellectual institutions discussed earlier, from the efforts of universities to nationalize their student bodies (and faculties) to the acceleration of a centralized literary marketplace based in New York City. In addition to these private institutions, the federal government—*the* major force, of course, of wartime and postwar centralization—played an increasingly important role in the organization of knowledge. In a trend that was distinct from but overlapped considerably with the development of the social sciences and the related rise of the expert, the postwar government accumulated information through various new bureaus and agencies and disseminated it in museums and national exhibitions. In *A Laboratory for Anthropology* (2000), Don L. Fowler examines the way an image of the Southwest was "constructed" primarily by government-funded army officers, geologists, ethnologists, and anthropologists who interpreted the region and its people for "Anglo" audiences back East. Though the Civil War and Reconstruction play little to no role in Fowler's analysis, the connections between war service and postwar government work are highly suggestive and merit further analysis. To take just two examples: the anthropologist John Wesley Powell and the sociologist Lester Frank Ward both went from service in the Union army to employment by the federal government in, respectively, the Bureau of Ethnology and the Geological Survey.[40]

---

[40]Though it reads more like an encyclopedia than a scholarly monograph, Don L. Fowler, *A Laboratory for Anthropology: Science and Romanticism in the American Southwest, 1846–1930* (Albuquerque: University of New Mexico Press, 2000), especially chaps. 5–13, contains a wealth of information. Elliott West includes a nice discussion of the role the U.S. government played in the "scientific" collection of Indian bones in "Reconstructing Race," *Western Historical Quarterly* 34 (2003): 7–26. The historical geographer Matthew G. Hannah uses Foucault's concept of "governmentality" and the career of the Union veteran Francis A. Walker, the director of the U.S. Census Bureau and the commissioner of Indian affairs, to discuss the modernization

While consolidation established new structures of intellectual activity, it also challenged earlier American understandings of selfhood and autonomy. Parrington, Curti, and Fredrickson each saw the Civil War as marking the end of the radical individualism of the antebellum years, when boundlessness, to use John Higham's terms (though not his periodization), gave way to consolidation. The nature and implications of this transition have been taken up most systematically by Wilfred McClay, who has explored the tension, first noted by Tocqueville, between individualism and community, or autonomy and conformity. Like *The Inner Civil War*, McClay's *The Masterless* (1994) set out to "illustrate how dramatic a reversal the Civil War wrought in projective social ideals," in particular how it thrust Americans toward national coalescence. The book evocatively opens with the Grand Review of the victorious Union army at war's end, using this set piece to explore the new national embrace of solidarity and unity, which would be memorably captured some twenty years later in Edward Bellamy's utopian-collectivist dream. Yet, according to McClay, Americans' longing for connection and community was nonetheless balanced by a countervailing attachment to autonomy, as could be seen in the ambivalence and tension evident in the group of intellectuals he has submitted to searching scrutiny.[41]

Jeffrey Sklansky's provocative *The Soul's Economy* (2002) has similarly attended to the fate of the "sovereign self" over the course of the long nineteenth century. In Sklansky's view, the decline of a political economy model of selfhood, premised on the autonomy and self-possession that presumably came from the ownership of property, gave way to a social psychology model of the "social self," premised on the psychic freedom that gained meaning only when one recognized the interdependence of self and society. The expansion of industrial capitalism, and not the Civil War and its aftermath, drives Sklansky's narrative, and he marshals an eclectic group of antebellum and postbellum intellectuals, from transcendentalists to proslavery ideologues to pioneers of the "new psychology," to explain this gradual but crucial change in social thought. The latter, including especially William James and John Dewey, offered critiques of society and urged greater inclusion in self-government but at the

and expansion of the postwar state, *Governmentality and the Mastery of Territory in Nineteenth-Century America* (Cambridge: Cambridge University Press, 2000). On exhibitions and world's fairs, see Robert Rydell, *All the World's a Fair: Visions of Empire at American International Expositions, 1876–1916* (Chicago: University of Chicago Press, 1984). For a slightly later period, the 1890s, Paul Kramer probes the connections between anthropology and the American imperial venture in the Philippines in his superb dissertation "The Pragmatic Empire: U.S. Anthropology and Colonial Politics in the Occupied Philippines, 1898–1916" (Ph.D. diss., Princeton University, 1998).

[41] Higham located the movement for consolidation before the Civil War, in the 1850s, in "From Boundlessness to Consolidation." McClay, *The Masterless*, argues for the significance of "wars in shaping the history of ideas" and examines the impact on intellectual life not just of the Civil War but of both world wars as well, 7.

same time "tended to set aside older questions about the structure of political and economic power." The end result, Sklansky contends, calling to mind Warren Sussman's older description of the shift from "character" to "personality," was the development of an understanding of selfhood based on consumption rather than production, on participation in a market society rather than ownership within it.[42]

Earlier scholars might have considered this development a triumph, heralding a more democratic, communitarian way of thinking that allowed American intellectuals and reformers finally to overcome the debilitating obsession with individual liberty. But for Sklansky what might have been lost is at least as important. The old political economic, self-owning individual provided a language of conflict with which to critique unequal material relations that the new social self lacked. If the radical and egalitarian promise of the sovereign self was never even remotely achieved in practice, Sklansky asserts nonetheless that "twentieth-century notions of interdependence and social selfhood represented something less than an unambiguous advance upon outdated ideals." The paradoxes and ambivalences surrounding American ideas about individualism and community that McClay has explored continue to abound.[43]

Racial Thought

While *The Inner Civil War* only intermittently addressed issues of emancipation and race, George Fredrickson produced in his second book, *The Black Image in the White Mind, 1817–1914* (1971), the standard survey of nineteenth-century white supremacist thought.[44] A similar shift of focus has occurred among practitioners of intellectual history more generally in recent decades; studies concerned with postwar national consolidation have increasingly come to share the stage

[42] Jeffrey Sklansky, *The Soul's Economy: Market Society and Selfhood in American Thought, 1820–1920* (Chapel Hill: University of North Carolina, 2002), quotation at 9.

[43] Sklansky, *The Soul's Economy*, 4. Many scholars have seen the move away from the political economy model of individual liberty as a crucial step on the road to the welfare state. See, for example, Sidney Fine, *Laissez Faire and the General-Welfare State: A Conflict in American Thought, 1865–1901* (Ann Arbor: University of Michigan Press, 1956); James T. Kloppenberg, *Uncertain Victory: Social Democracy and Progressivism in European and American Thought, 1870–1920* (New York: Oxford University Press, 1986); Robert Westbrook, *John Dewey and American Democracy* (Ithaca, N.Y.: Cornell University Press, 1991). James Livingston offers a related but different perspective in his *Pragmatism and the Political Economy of Cultural Revolution, 1850–1940* (Chapel Hill: University of North Carolina Press, 1994), where he sees a greater potential for the development of the postmodern self in the move to a consumer-based democracy, away from one of small producers.

[44] George Fredrickson, *The Black Image in the White Mind: The Debate on African-American History and Destiny, 1817–1914* (New York: Oxford University Press, 1971).

with accounts of what the emancipation of four million slaves meant for the development of American thought. In the resulting body of work, black minds have come to receive the serious attention once reserved for white ones, while historians' abiding interest in racism has been accompanied by still wider considerations of post-emancipation challenges to the emerging hegemony of free labor and social relations based on contract.

The racism of white Americans has continued to be a primary theme for intellectual historians, as it was for Fredrickson. His explanation of northern "racial romanticism" remains influential, as does his discussion of a more scientifically based racism, rooted specifically in evolutionary thinking about stages of civilization and stronger and weaker races. What he noted about the shortcomings of northern antislavery intellectuals similarly finds many echoes in a series of individual biographies. The latest study of Emerson, written by Lawrence Buell, notes, in terms that could well apply to a much wider range of figures, that the transcendentalist's "dream of black emancipation had a disconcerting way of metamorphosing into a dream of white emancipation."[45]

In some respects, the dire picture Fredrickson painted of the last third of the nineteenth century becomes even more dreary in accounts that go beyond individual thinkers to consider structures of intellectual authority. The increasing disillusionment whites expressed about black capabilities tended to be disassociated from the legacy of slavery—or of the dehumanization of the slave environment—and began to be taken increasingly as evidence of a natural, biological difference that either could not be overcome over time or should not be interfered with. Nancy Leys Stepan and Sander Gilman have found that white assumptions of racial inequality were so pervasive that there was virtually no contestation of scientific racism from within the mainstream of the scientific community between 1870 and 1920. In a period when science "acquired its modern, epistemological, institutional, and cultural forms," it became increasingly difficult to contest the claims of science: "The outcome was a narrowing of the cultural space within which, and the cultural forms by which, the claims of biological determinism could be effectively challenged." Stepan and Gilman argue that the recourse to rights, justice, or morality—strategies Frederick Douglass successfully employed in contesting the claims of ethnology in 1860—became increasingly less legitimate in the face of an emerging scientific authority that dismissed all nonscientific work as mere sentiment.[46]

Stepan and Gilman find a glimmer of hope in the activities of black and Jewish scientists themselves, who provided by century's end a critical stance toward racism that effectively rebutted its claims. Mia Bay has painted a rather differ-

---

[45] Lawrence Buell, *Emerson* (Cambridge, Mass.: Harvard University Press, 2003), 269.

[46] Nancy Leys Stepan and Sander L. Gilman, "Appropriating the Idioms of Science: The Rejection of Scientific Racism," in *The Bounds of Race: Perspectives of Hegemony and Resistance*, ed. Dominick La Capra (Ithaca, N.Y.: Cornell University Press, 1991), 73–103, quotations at 98.

ent picture in *The White Image in the Black Mind*, a work that moves between the formal ethnology first nurtured within free black communities and the "folk" thought characteristic of the southern plantation world. Neither of these broad groups discarded racial differences altogether, even if the levels of universalism and environmentalism were far more prevalent than among whites at the time. The antebellum ethnology of men like James McCune Smith carved out a place for African Americans as a "redeemer race," while it associated whites with a series of unflattering characteristics with deep roots in the racial past. Suspicions about inherent racial differences persisted among black intellectuals during Reconstruction, with Martin Delaney and others not so much refuting the emerging racialism as turning it to their own uses.[47]

Bay's consideration of black postwar thought has joined other recent attempts within American intellectual history to include a wider range of perspectives, especially of those racial "others" typically considered as objects of thought rather than thinkers themselves. Compared to their white counterparts, the black intellectuals who have garnered recent attention during the Reconstruction period were relatively untroubled by national consolidation, making it hard to fit them into that particular narrative. African Americans knew the connections between the triumph of the nation-state and the eradication of slavery and were thus leery of diminishing federal authority. Faith in the national state, and commitment to the national project, could perhaps best be seen in the early postwar career of Frederick Douglass, whose Reconstruction-era thought has been usefully developed by both David Blight and Waldo Martin. While Douglass was the most prominent black thinker, there were others who more quickly despaired, as Wilson Moses writes in *The Golden Age of Black Nationalism* (1978). Still others transferred their energies to the work of extending "civilization" in Africa, as Moses explains in his biography of Alexander Crummell and Lamin Sanneh shows in *Abolitionists Abroad* (1999).[48] We know less at this point about black women during the Reconstruction period, though Nell Painter's *Sojourner Truth* (1996), scholarship on Charlotte Forten, and parts of Lyde Sizer's *The Political Work of Northern Women Writers* have all made an intriguing start.[49]

---

[47] Mia Bay, *The White Image in the Black Mind: African-American Ideas about White People, 1830–1925* (New York: Oxford University Press, 2000).

[48] David Blight, *Frederick Douglass's Civil War: Keeping Faith in Jubilee* (Baton Rouge: Louisiana State University Press, 1989); Waldo Martin, *The Mind of Frederick Douglass* (Chapel Hill: University of North Carolina Press, 1984); Wilson Moses, *The Golden Age of Black Nationalism* (New York: Oxford University Press, 1978), and *Alexander Crummell: A Study in Civilization and Discontent* (New York: Oxford University Press, 1989); Lamin Sanneh, *Abolitionists Abroad: American Blacks and the Making of Modern West Africa* (Cambridge, Mass.: Harvard University Press, 1999).

[49] Nell Painter, *Sojourner Truth: A Life, A Symbol* (New York: Norton, 1996); Brenda Stevenson, ed., *The Journals of Charlotte Forten Grimke* (New York: Oxford University Press, 1988); Carla Peterson, "Reconstructing the Nation: Frances Harper, Charlotte Forten, and the Racial Politics of Periodical Publication," *Proceedings of the American Antiquarian Society* 107 (1997):

Intellectual histories of race have been influenced not just by a broadening of voices but by a fundamental rethinking of how ideas about race related to the transformation of ideological and social structures after emancipation. Some have gone so far as to question the very usefulness of charting racial thinking as a transhistorical phenomenon—as Fredrickson did in *Black Image in the White Mind*—finding it more meaningful instead to see ideas as manifestations of particular struggles in the economy and politics. In her classic essay "Race and Ideology in American History," Barbara Fields influentially insisted that ideas about race had no autonomous existence and could never be abstracted from the social and economic realities in which they were generated or deployed, a line of analysis expressed in somewhat different terms by Thomas Holt. Fredrickson himself has been has been more carefully attuned to the relationship between ideas and social structure in his more recent analysis of racial thought.[50]

More specifically, scholars have investigated how the social and economic realities of emancipation corresponded with ideas about racial character or destiny. Applying the methodologies of J. G. A. Pocock and Paul Ricoeur to examine the way dominant discourses have made sense of black freedom, Demetrius Eudell has mined not classic intellectual history texts but dispatches from the American Freedman's Bureau (especially as it operated in South Carolina) and those of the Jamaican special magistrates. He argues, in *The Political Languages of Emancipation in the British Caribbean and the U.S. South* (2002), that these historically distinct experiences produced significantly similar responses, whether one considers debates over the structure of labor, efforts of former planters to regain local political autonomy, or, perhaps most important, the resolution of that "vexed question of original unity" involving the differences between blacks and whites. For Eudell, freedom paradoxically led to a hardening of intellectual distinctions based on race, an argument consistent with Thomas Holt's "Empire over the Mind" and Seymour Drescher's *The Mighty Experiment* (2002). These three scholars share the conclusion that the failure of emancipation to bear out social scientific theories about the superiority of free labor resulted in heightened misgivings about the abilities of black people.[51]

301–334; Hazel V. Carby, *Reconstructing Womanhood: The Emergence of the Afro-American Woman Novelist* (New York: Oxford University Press, 1987).

[50] Barbara Fields, "Ideology and Race in American History," and Thomas C. Holt, "'An Empire over the Mind': Emancipation, Race, and Ideology in the British West Indies and the American South" both in *Region, Race, and Reconstruction: Essays in Honor of C. Vann Woodward*, ed. J. Morgan Kousser and James McPherson (New York: Oxford University Press, 1982), 143–177 and 283–313; George Fredrickson, *The Arrogance of Race: Historical Perspectives on Slavery, Racism, and Social Inequality* (Middletown Conn.: Wesleyan University Press, 1988).

[51] Demetrius Lynn Eudell, *The Political Languages of Emancipation in the British Caribbean and the U.S. South* (Chapel Hill: University of North Carolina Press, 2002); Holt, "Empire over the Mind"; Seymour Drescher, *The Mighty Experiment: Free Labor versus Slavery in British Emancipation* (New York: Oxford University Press, 2002).

Slavery's end will no doubt continue to draw attention from intellectual historians of race. But as Elliott West has recently charged in his stimulating "Reconstructing Race," the focus on black-white racial issues may have come at the expense of understanding other racialized relationships, especially those involving Native American, Asian American, and Hispanic populations in the trans-Mississippi West. Given the current sophistication of our understanding of how emancipation coincided with the hardening of some racial categories, it seems worthwhile to push these insights further, and to link histories of other racial developments with the transformations of the late 1860s and 1870s, particularly with the consolidating state and the new organization of knowledge. Some of the newer work on "whiteness" might point the way toward making these linkages. For example, Matthew Jacobson, in both *Whiteness of a Different Color* (1998) and *Barbarian Virtues* (2000), has emphasized the cultural and intellectual roots of racial construction, grounding his analysis in a discussion of midcentury racial science, but he also explicitly connects such constructions to the role of the state, demonstrating the importance (if variability) of immigration law, the U.S. Census Bureau, and other governmental agencies in classifying people.[52]

Liberalism

The topic of American liberalism has lately become one of the most fertile areas of Reconstruction-era intellectual history. A number of reasons could plausibly account for liberalism's intensive reentry into historical debates: a reaction to its use as a foil in the "republican synthesis" scholarship of 1970s and 1980s; a post–Cold War willingness to reinvestigate a central American political language; or the political demonization of modern-day liberalism in cur-

---

[52] West, "Reconstructing Race"—a point anticipated in Brian Collins, "Presidential Reconstructions: Mark Twain's *Letters from Hawaii* and the Integration of Civil Society," *American Studies* 37 (1996): 51–62; Matthew Jacobson, *Whiteness of a Different Color: European Immigrants and the Alchemy of Race* (Cambridge, Mass.: Harvard University Press, 1998), and *Barbarian Virtues: The United States Encounters Foreign Peoples at Home and Abroad, 1876–1919* (New York: Hill and Wang, 2000). Though many of its themes were anticipated in studies of American nativism like John Higham, *Strangers in the Land: Patterns of American Nativism 1860–1925* (New York: Atheneum, 1973), and Barbara Solomon, *Ancestors and Immigrants: A Changing New England Tradition* (Cambridge, Mass.: Harvard University Press, 1956), historical "whiteness" studies can perhaps be said to have begun with David Roediger, *The Wages of Whiteness: Race and the Making of the American Working Class* (London: Verso, 1991), and have by now produced a steady stream of scholarship in all disciplines. For a trenchant critique of the methodological and conceptual shortcomings of some of this scholarship, see Eric Arnesen, "Whiteness and the Historians' Imagination," *International Labor and Working Class History* 60 (Fall 2001), 3–32.

rent political debate. Whatever the reason, the days of simply deriding Louis Hartz's "liberal tradition" seem to be over, with scholars taking up the "L-word" once more. This new scholarship represents less a return to Hartzian consensus, however, than a series of attempts to discern the complexities, connections, and contradictions in this ultimate "contested truth."[53] After decades of reducing liberalism to its supposed kernel of property rights and market freedom and of shunting aside the tradition's ethical, religious, and cultural features, political theorists and historians of political thought have begun to restore some conceptual nuance and historical specificity to our understanding of the term.[54] Historians seem to agree that something important happened to American liberalism on its way to the twentieth century, and that the forces unleashed by the Civil War and Reconstruction had something to do with the transformation. Here agreement ends, however, as a variety of phenomena have been put forth as explanations for liberalism's modification, contraction, expansion, or reconstruction in this era.

In the one of the most ambitious works of intellectual history in the past generation, James Kloppenberg has shown how two generations of philosophers and political theorists forged a "via media" between socialism and laissez-faire liberalism in their articulation of European social democracy and American progressivism. Beginning in the 1870s, radical philosophers in Britain, France, Germany, and the United States broke down the inherited epistemological and ethical distinctions between the idealist/intuitionist and empiricist/utilitarian traditions and adopted new understandings of knowledge and ethics based on history and the social nature of experience. William James and John Dewey represented the American wing of this transatlantic "discursive community," whose shared notion of uncertain and contingent pragmatic "truths" laid the philosophical foundation for the modern welfare state. Placing the progressive revision of American liberalism within this larger "western" conversa-

---

[53] Daniel T. Rodgers, *Contested Truths: Keywords in American Politics Since Independence* (New York: Basic Books, 1987); Louis Hartz, *The Liberal Tradition in America: Political Thought in America Since the Revolution* (New York: Harcourt Brace, 1955). For an overview of the varied history of liberalism, though one that primarily examines its economic manifestations, see Dorothy Ross, "Liberalism," in *Encyclopedia of American Political History: Studies of the Principal Movements and Ideas*, ed. Jack P. Greene (New York: Scribner's, 1984), 2:750–763.

[54] Two important exceptions to the normative view of liberalism as self-possessed individualism can be found in Gary Gerstle's examination of the dialectical relationship between "economic" and "cultural" liberalism in the twentieth century and in James Kloppenberg's exploration of the overlapping political languages at work in early America. Gerstle helpfully reminds us that "any effort to define the liberal community must be firmly located in time and space" in "The Protean Character of American Liberalism," *American Historical Review* 99 (October 1994): 1043–1073. Kloppenberg, "The Virtues of Liberalism: Christianity, Republicanism, and Ethics in Early American Political Discourse," reprinted in *The Virtues of Liberalism* (New York: Oxford University Press, 1998).

tion, Kloppenberg has established a philosophical basis for developments often depicted as a haphazard and conflicted series of reforms. *Uncertain Victory* does not look to the Civil War and Reconstruction as a causal force in this philosophical and theoretical revision of liberalism; Kloppenberg's comparative method and emphasis on the common international dimensions of this crisis of liberalism necessarily minimize the importance of peculiarly national events. But we can infer the impact of Reconstruction indirectly, as it unleashed and gave direction to the forces of consolidation, incorporation, and industrialization that transformed the United States, along with its European counterparts, into "urbanized and mechanized nation states."[55]

By contrast, other recent works have focused directly on Reconstruction as the crucial context for charting the development of liberalism between the Civil War and the twentieth century. Amy Dru Stanley's *From Bondage to Contract* (1998) details how emancipation forced a reconsideration of classic liberalism. The dilemmas of "contract freedom" expanded during the age of emancipation, a trend evident both in the struggles of leading thinkers and in such anomalous cases as the tramp who refused to enter labor contracts and the prostitute whose sexual commodification posed an affront to those "bonds" of matrimony that society had thoroughly disassociated from market relations. As these cases suggest, the importance of slavery's end went beyond the experience of masters and slaves, and even beyond the confines of the South. The destruction of bondage as a legitimate relation forced postwar Americans to grapple with nothing less than the matter of which sort of human relations should be governed by contract and exchange, and which should be placed on a more sacrosanct basis.[56]

Stanley emphasizes the limits of a contractarian liberalism based on self-possession and voluntary exchange in the market but also notes the power that contract freedom (with the self-possession it implied) could hold for the disempowered as both a language and an idea. Feminists invoked contract to make marriage equitable, and freedmen and freedwomen, aware of what it meant not to possess one's self, found in it a powerful language of political advocacy. The case of the freedwomen was especially important, Stanley has argued, in a separate essay that challenges the claim that former female slaves understood freedom in strictly collective, communitarian terms rather than individual ones.

[55] Kloppenberg, *Uncertain Victory*, 4.

[56] Amy Dru Stanley, *From Bondage to Contract: Wage Labor, Marriage, and the Market in the Age of Slave Emancipation* (New York: Cambridge University Press, 1998). Stanley's book provides a welcome addition to Daniel T. Rodgers, *The Work Ethic in Industrial America, 1850–1920* (Chicago: University of Chicago Press, 1978), which provides an inspired exploration of what happens to the "work ethic" when work itself is fundamentally transformed by intensive industrialization but does not consider the impact of slavery's end on ideas about labor in the North.

While black women cherished their kinship bonds and worked for collective free-dom, in Stanley's view they "were also keenly aware of their rights as individu-als—rights premised on possession of the self." Warning against an "uncritical celebration" of liberal self-possession, Stanley nonetheless notes the "emancipa-tory power" of the "ideal of self-ownership" and argues that if it were as hollow as historians have at times suggested, "it could not have disguised the existing coercions of free society" as well as it did.[57]

Nancy Cohen's *The Reconstruction of American Liberalism, 1865–1914* con-cerns two generations of liberal intellectuals, who she claims moved away from laissez-faire orthodoxy and embraced instead an "administrative mandate" that placed government regulation in the hands of experts removed from democratic control. Framing her work as a study of "political ideology, which is more about power and culture than the quality of ideas," Cohen has built on the earlier insights of David Montgomery's *Beyond Equality* (1967), arguing that early liberal supporters of Radical Reconstruction (men like E. L. Godkin, Francis A. Walker, and David A. Wells) grew alarmed at laborers' and agrarian radi-cals' challenges to property through an expanded, activist state. In response, and with the help of a set of younger liberals they coerced into allies, these lib-eral intellectuals foreclosed any redistributionist threats by articulating a ver-sion of liberalism that replaced the antebellum capitalism of small producers with a consumer-based corporate capitalism regulated and administered by an undemocratic cadre of experts. Liberals of the 1870s and 1880s, not those of the Progressive Era, were thus, according to Cohen, ultimately responsible for vitiat-ing liberal democracy in the United States. This revised declension narrative is more poignant as it involves the betrayal not just of a Progressive reform spirit but also of the revolutionary potential of Reconstruction.[58]

My own work, *Cultivating American Democracy*, focuses on a set of self-defined transatlantic liberals whose participation in the Civil War led to a distinctive and influential program of postbellum liberal reform on both sides of the Atlantic. A coterie whose members included George William Curtis, James Russell Lowell, Charles Eliot Norton, James Bryce, Goldwin Smith, and Leslie Stephen under-

---

[57] Stanley, *From Bondage to Contract*; Stanley, "The Right to Possess all the Faculties that God Has Given: Possessive Individualism, Slave Women, and Abolitionist Thought," in *Moral Problems in America: New Perspectives on Cultural History*, ed. Lewis Perry and Karen Hattunen (Ithaca, N.Y.: Cornell University Press, 1998), 123–143, quotation at 143. Though he does not deal explicitly with "liberalism" as an ideology, Sklansky, *The Soul's Economy*, seems similarly engaged in an effort to recover the emancipatory potential of liberal theory based in possessive individualism.

[58] Nancy Cohen, *The Reconstruction of American Liberalism, 1865–1914* (Chapel Hill: Uni-versity of North Carolina Press, 2002); David Montgomery, *Beyond Equality: Labor and the Radi-cal Republicans, 1862–1872* (New York: Knopf, 1967). Compare with Fine, *Laissez Faire and the General-Welfare State*.

stood emancipation and Union victory as a moment of opportunity for trans-atlantic liberalism, working in the war's aftermath to apply John Stuart Mill's understanding of democracy to constitutional change, political reform, and cultural stewardship. As men of letters, this group elevated the cultural aspects of liberalism over economic ones and probed how applying notions of self-possession to an enlarged electorate involved cultivating moral autonomy, political responsibility, and an appreciation for the civic virtues of aesthetic experience. In their view, liberal progress depended less on an expanding market (which actually threatened the liberal values they held dear) than on the education and cultivation of a reasoning and cosmopolitan citizenry.[59]

While liberalism has received a great deal of interest from intellectual historians, recent work has also investigated challenges to the liberal mainstream. Timothy Messer-Kruse's *The Yankee International* (1998) has examined American participation in the International Workingman's Association (IWA), revealing the importance of this era to the history of radicalism. The IWA was organized in Britain in 1864 and eventually fell apart in 1876. Representing the American wing of the movement was a curious mix of German and immigrant Marxists, former abolitionists, feminists like Victoria Woodhull, and Yankee labor radicals. Tensions between the orthodox Marxism of the immigrants and the native republicanism of the Yankees eventually grew too strong to overcome, Messer-Kruse argues, and the Yankees were purged in 1871, representing the removal of Marxism from the "liberal tradition" thereafter. A similar view of how Reconstruction witnessed a consolidating, but also a constricting, liberalism through the decline of other options has been offered by Dorothy Ross in her essay "Socialism and American Liberalism" (1978).[60]

A quite different response to the consolidating liberal nationalism of Reconstruction can be seen in the pivotal chapter of John McGreevy's *Catholicism and American Freedom* (2003), a study of the perennial tensions between Catholic orthodoxy and liberalism across American history. Catholic skepticism about the Republican Party began in the 1850s, when both politicians and intellectuals like Ralph Waldo Emerson, John Greenleaf Whittier, and Charles Eliot Norton linked slavery and popery as dual threats to republican freedom. President Grant intensified this concern in 1875, when he warned that a new struggle over "our national existence" might not be one based on the conflict between North and South but one "between patriotism and intelligence on the one side" and the Church's "superstition, ambition and ignorance on the other." Such hostility stemmed from Catholics' questioning of the liberal focus on the indi-

[59] Butler, *Cultivating American Democracy*.

[60] Timothy Messer-Kruse, *The Yankee International: Marxism and the American Reform Tradition, 1848–1876* (Chapel Hill: University of North Carolina Press, 1998); Dorothy Ross, "Socialism and American Liberalism: Academic Social Thought in the 1880s," *Perspectives in American History* 9 (1977–78): 7–79.

vidual, their notion of the family as the basic unit of social organization, and their emphasis on obedience over individual conscience. Fierce conflict between liberals and Catholics over education cooled during the 1880s, as political leaders sought Catholic votes and as "leading citizens" began to express a preference for "a predominantly Catholic working class to a potentially socialist one."[61] This recent work on liberalism (and its challengers) makes clear that we still, fifty years after Hartz identified it as the central American "tradition," have much to learn about the meanings Americans attached to some of their most basic political and cultural commitments. No less clear is that the Reconstruction era represents as crucial a chapter in this story as the Progressive Era, the 1930s, or the 1960s.

International Connections

McGreevy's attention to Vatican history and to the reaction of European Catholics and non-Catholics to American developments sheds comparative light on struggles over Catholicism across the Atlantic. It was the First Vatican Council's pronouncement of papal infallibility in 1870 that provided the context for Reconstruction-era fears of Catholicism's incompatibility with American ideals of freedom. In McGreevy's rendering, Catholics and liberals alike drew parallels between the cultural and political struggles at home in the 1860s and 1870s and Germany's *Kulturkampf*.

McGreevy's international orientation is shared by several other American intellectual and cultural historians, who have earlier and at times more willingly crossed national boundaries than counterparts in other subfields. In 1982, David Hollinger urged scholars to pursue "distinctively American issues"—those ideas, myths, languages, and arguments that served Americans as Americans— but then to build as well upon the "insight that America is, for some purposes, part of Europe," and has participated in what Richard Rorty has called "the conversation of the west." As we have seen, Reconstruction offers a good instance of the importance (and difficulty) of balancing these two agendas, as the country was both experiencing a nationally particular set of challenges and participating with the rest of the Atlantic world in the enormous transformations of industrial capitalism, liberal nationalism, and scientific reorientation.[62]

---

[61] John T. McGreevy, *Catholicism and American Freedom: A History* (New York: Norton, 2003), 91, 123. Though it deals with a slightly later period, one might also include among the challengers to liberalism the antimodernism that T. J. Jackson Lears has so imaginatively outlined in *No Place of Grace: Antimodernism and the Transformation of American Culture, 1880–1920* (New York: Pantheon Books, 1981).

[62] David Hollinger, "American Intellectual History: Issues for the 1980s," *Reviews in American History* 10 (December 1982): 306–317, reprinted in Hollinger, *In the American Province*.

James Kloppenberg and Daniel Rodgers have provided the two most impressive examples of "connected history." Though Rodgers differentiates this kind of history from "comparative history," both he and Kloppenberg offer an expansive investigation of a set of ideas or dilemmas that social scientists or political theorists grappled with in Europe and the United States. Their approach, while it undoubtedly sacrifices some local particularity, attempts to reveal how the ideas and policies common to the northern Atlantic world were elaborated, enacted, or ignored in different national settings. Charles Cashdollar has employed a similar approach in his examination of the theological response to positivism in nineteenth-century Britain and the United States. Cashdollar, like Kloppenberg and Rodgers, presents a thorough examination of how ideas were actually transmitted across national boundaries, revealing, for example, that Americans came to know the writings of Auguste Comte largely secondhand, through Scottish translations, before Harriet Martineau published her own translation in 1853.[63]

Other scholars have taken a different approach, by working to situate their study of American thought in a larger international framework, but without attempting a comparative examination. These scholars have shared Michael O'Brien's conviction that "intellectuals, because they live in two places, their imaginations and places like Concord, live in more than two places" and historians who study them "likewise, must have a license to roam, if those imaginations are to be recaptured." Paying attention to what intellectuals read as well as what they wrote of necessity causes intellectual historians to cast their gaze across both spatial and temporal boundaries. A model for this kind of work is James Turner's study of Charles Eliot Norton, which puts the Harvard art historian in an appropriately international context, as an informal diplomat and friend to countless "eminent Victorians" and as a pioneering scholar of a version of cultural history (of art and literature) who corresponded with other scholars across Europe.

As Turner's discussion of Norton's postwar activities makes clear, a transatlantic framework can fruitfully be combined with an explicit focus on the Civil War and Reconstruction. Norton not only grappled with the meanings of emancipation and national union in a context of international correspondence, travel, and publication; he also understood these national events to have significant meanings for the international community. My own work argues that the Civil War and its aftermath represented the pivotal moment in the development of an extensive Anglo-American network of friendship, authorship, and

[63] Daniel T. Rodgers, *Atlantic Crossings: Social Politics in a Progressive Age* (Cambridge: Harvard University Press, 1998), 4–5; Cashdollar, *The Transformation of Theology*. Work on religion and science in the age of Darwin has been particularly rooted in a transatlantic context, as shown in notes 30 and 34.

reform.[64] Richard Blackett's *Divided Hearts* (2001) reveals how Britons largely shared the American sense of the worldwide implications of the American war. In an examination of the wartime mission of the Confederate propagandist Henry Hotze, Robert Bonner reveals how the work of American thinkers was crucially shaped by diplomatic imperatives, especially the effort to influence international opinion about race. Insights and strategies from Blackett's and Bonner's work might fruitfully be extended into the postwar period.[65]

Finally, another interesting approach has involved examining how Americans responded to discrete European events or ideas. Messer-Kruse's study of "Yankee" participation in the short-lived IWA offers one example of this approach, while Gillis Harp's examination of American Comteans presents another. Philip Katz's *From Appomattox to Montmartre* (1998) explores American reactions to the French Commune of 1871, arguing that although some initial responses to the Commune were mutedly enthusiastic, if a bit confused, Americans came to fear and disapprove of this radical movement abroad as they increasingly faced their own labor troubles throughout the 1870s.[66]

Concluding Thoughts

Recent scholarship has established Reconstruction as a crucial turning point in American intellectual and cultural history. Such work has shown how this period's economic and political changes simultaneously enlivened institutions of American thought and transformed the questions posed, and answered, by American thinkers. During Reconstruction, persistent dilemmas of sectional distinctiveness, science and religion, self and society, national consolidation, liberalism, and America's place in the world began to assume a recognizably modern form.

---

[64] O'Brien, *Conjectures of Order*, vol. 1, 21; Turner, *The Liberal Education of Charles Eliot Norton*; Butler, *Cultivating American Democracy*, especially chaps. 2 and 3. Pioneering works in transatlantic intellectual history of the late nineteenth century, though they do not deal explicitly with the Civil War or Reconstruction, include Robert Kelley, *The Transatlantic Persuasion: The Liberal-Democratic Mind in the Age of Gladstone* (New York: Knopf, 1969) and David D. Hall, "The Victorian Connection," in *Victorian America*, ed. Daniel Walker Howe (Philadelphia: University of Pennsylvania Press, 1976).

[65] R. J. M. Blackett, *Divided Hearts: Britain and the American Civil War* (Baton Rouge: Louisiana State University Press, 2001); Robert E. Bonner, "Slavery, Confederate Diplomacy, and the Racialist Mission of Henry Hotze," *Civil War History* 51 (September 2005), 288–316. The vast scholarship on British responses to the Civil War, far too extensive to cite here, can be found in Blackett's helpful bibliography.

[66] Messer-Kruse, *Yankee International*; Harp, *Positivist Republic*; Katz, *From Appomattox to Montmartre: Americans and the Paris Commune* (Cambridge, Mass.: Harvard University Press, 1998).

Yet even with this new work, there is room for much more. The development of ideas in the Reconstruction South deserves greater attention, especially that which might move the conversation beyond sectional themes to address how notions of self and society evolved in a place transformed by war, defeat, and emancipation. Drew Faust and Michael O'Brien have both offered tantalizing suggestions about how the region's elite whites (especially women) established distinctive modes of selfhood during the war, but no study has followed these insights through the Reconstruction era or framed a comparable agenda for a wider spectrum of southerners, black and white.[67] In a different area, works by Faust and Franny Nudelman have shown the promise of attending to how Americans—intellectuals, ordinary civilians, and soldiers alike—made sense of the unprecedented encounter with mass death. As the theme of wartime violence and death evolves as a matter for intellectual historians to consider, religion will deserve to be a part of this story, in the formal theodicy of postwar ministers and in the grappling of everyday Americans with the problem of suffering. Charles Royster's brilliant *The Destructive War* (1991) offers ruminations on sacrifice and the nature of war more generally that stand out for their insight and perspective.[68] There are undoubtedly other ways for historians of American thought to reckon with such themes, especially as these themes relate to Darwinian perspectives and to the varied transmutations of American liberalism. Further work on the South, and on death and war-making, may also draw attention to the distinct varieties of American conservatism that developed in a period notably absent from such canonical treatments as Russell Kirk's *The Conservative Mind, from Burke to Eliot*. This "conservative tradition" is something we know a lot less about than any liberal tradition, but if the recent work on liberalism offers any guidance, it might be to suggest the postwar era as a particularly fertile field for investigation.[69]

While there is room for new areas to be developed, so, too, are there opportunities to put the distinct themes of Reconstruction-era thought in conversation with one another. Links between consolidation and liberalism, for instance, or between African-American freedom and the agencies of intellectual life could do much to illuminate this period's role in the development of American ideas. Works that cross national boundaries should continue, especially if they build

[67] Faust, *Mothers of Invention: Women of the Slaveholding South in the American Civil War* (Chapel Hill: University of North Carolina Press, 1996), especially chaps. 7 and 11; and the discussion of Augusta Jane Evans in O'Brien, *Conjectures of Order*, vol. 1, chap. 22.

[68] Drew Faust, "The Civil War Soldier and the Art of Dying," *Journal of Southern History* 67 (2001): 3–38; Franny Nudelman, *John Brown's Body: Slavery, Violence, and the Culture of War* (Chapel Hill: University of North Carolina Press, 2004); Charles Royster, *The Destructive War: William Tecumseh Sherman, Stonewall Jackson, and the Americans* (New York: Random House, 1991).

[69] Russell Kirk, *The Conservative Mind, from Burke to Eliot* (New York: Regnery, 1972).

upon those studies that have succeeded in this approach. Seymour Drescher's important investigation of the post-emancipation course of British social science and racial thought might be extended to the postwar American scene. It is also worth considering how the example of southern emancipation reverberated across the world, and to what extent these reverberations resembled the international response to slavery's end in the Caribbean.[70] American confrontations with postwar questions of nationalism and federalism might also usefully be placed in a larger context. Especially intriguing connections might be made, for instance, of Reconstruction-era ideas about government in the United States to the contemporaneous dilemmas of British governance over Ireland, Canada, and its other dominions, or to the political restructuring of Italy and of the Austro-Hungarian and Prussian empires.[71]

Intellectual histories that focus on the Reconstruction period will likely remain split between those consciously attuned to the American Civil War's aftermath and those working in frameworks that attribute little intrinsic importance to this conflict. There is nothing wrong with exploring those social, economic, scientific, and religious influences on mid-Victorian American thought that were independent of the transformation of the antebellum republic to a free-labor nation-state unified by war. As work progresses toward a synthesis of this period's intellectual preoccupations, it should become clearer how Reconstruction per se did or did not matter to American thought, and also how ideas operated in the process of establishing a second American republic. Skeptics might continue to question how thoroughly those wrenching events of the postwar years penetrated intellectual life of this period. Others might agree with Mill, however, and wonder how the American mind could have emerged from its wartime "concussion" without being changed fundamentally, permanently, and in every conceivable manner.

[70] Drescher, *The Mighty Experiment*.

[71] See, for example, Joseph M. Hernon, "The Use of the American Civil War in the Debate over Irish Home Rule," *American Historical Review* 69 (July 1964): 1022–1026.

8

CIVIL WAR REMEMBRANCE
AS RECONSTRUCTION

THOMAS J. BROWN

Reconstruction centered on questions of how to remember the
Civil War. Etymology underscored that memory defined the issue
of amnesty for ex-Confederates, which characterized the prosecutorial forbear-
ance of the federal government as an act of forgetting. Other problems of the
period similarly revolved around the continuing meanings to be attached to
wartime events. The United States made crucial decisions about the governance
of states previously in rebellion, the rights of African Americans formerly held
in slavery, and the entitlements due to military veterans. If forward-looking in
its essence, the process of Reconstruction was also a process of retrospection.

Memory of the war went far beyond policy-making channels. Many Americans regarded the war as the most momentous period of their lives and looked
back to it constantly. Shortly before Walt Whitman died in 1892, a friend asked
if the poet ever returned in his mind to the war years. Whitman replied, "I have
never left them."[1] Explicitly postbellum forms of culture and society began to
multiply while the war was still underway. Civil War stories quickly emerged as
a major American literary genre, flexible enough to explore and connect a wide
range of public and personal crises. Civic monuments, military cemeteries, and
battlefield parks made the war a prominent feature of the national landscape,
and community rituals in honor of fallen soldiers and in celebration of emancipation made the war a prominent feature of the national calendar. Several
different Civil War commemorative associations ranked among the most important voluntary social organizations of the postwar era. All of these initiatives
envisioned the war as a part of the past that remained a part of the present. This

---

[1]Daniel Aaron, *The Unwritten War: American Writers and the Civil War* (New York: Knopf,
1973), 72.

reorientation of American imagination around the reference point of the war was a vital aspect of Reconstruction.

The pervasiveness of Civil War remembrance in the postbellum United States links the study of Reconstruction to one of the most striking trends in historical literature of the past twenty years, the outpouring of scholarship on historical memory. A historical account of historical interpretations of historical memory of the Civil War might even describe the recent stream of research on the topic as an offshoot of the wider phenomenon, examining Eric Hobsbawm's "invention of tradition" and Pierre Nora's "lieux de mémoire" in such contexts as the origins of Memorial Day and the preservation of former battlefields.[2] That account would be misleading. Work on Civil War memory has certainly gained momentum from the broad academic interest in historical memory. But the more specific influence of that international scholarship has been limited. The Civil War research has additional origins that have raised separate sets of questions. The study of American folklore and American religion have been key points of departure. Longstanding attention to literary representations of the war has produced a large body of scholarship that can only be noted selectively in a brief overview of work on commemorative practices. Many studies of Civil War remembrance respond directly to Reconstruction historiographical debates about the extent of social change in the South and the explanation for the northern retreat from reform. As research has proliferated, however, it has increasingly intersected with the writing about collective memory by historians of other countries and other eras. That scholarship suggests some new dimensions for the concept of Reconstruction.

Like Reconstruction more generally, remembrance of the Civil War is an unfinished process. The prominence of the war in contemporary popular culture is one of the main sources for the surge of academic interest in the history of its commemoration. Many authors have sought to contribute to current political discussion by suggesting connections between early and ongoing Civil War remembrance. At the same time, like other aspects of Reconstruction, remembrance of the war has a periodization. It, too, began almost immediately upon secession and can be extended to a variety of dates. Historians have most frequently traced the lines of memory emanating from the war to the Spanish-American War or into the Civil War semicentennial or through World War I. The dedication of the Lincoln Memorial in 1922 provides a terminal point that encompasses the substantial research to date on the first cycle of Civil War remembrance while setting aside for present purposes the growing number of studies focused on more recent commemorative activities. This span of

<hr />

[2] Eric Hobsbawm and Terence Ranger, eds., *The Invention of Tradition* (Cambridge: Cambridge University Press, 1983); Pierre Nora, ed., *Les Lieux de Mémoire*, 3 vols. (Paris: Gallimard Press, 1984–92).

more than half a century obviously reaches well beyond working definitions of Reconstruction as a period, but it allows for a full examination of the retrospective tendencies that historians have found in that era.

The spotlight that the study of collective memory places on the continuing uses of the past complements the well-established alertness of Reconstruction scholarship to the political implications of historical interpretation. Recognition of the creativity and force with which Americans made Civil War remembrance a medium of everyday life, including but not limited to politics, suggests that historical writing about that process should be examined as carefully for the insights it provides into today as for the effectiveness with which it describes the late nineteenth and early twentieth centuries. Certainly scholars might advance more or less persuasive explanations for patterns of Civil War commemoration. Often, however, a choice must be made between equally plausible interpretations that do not contradict each other so much as they differ in allocations of emphasis informed by competing ideas about the current significance of the topic. Historians who probe the ways that earlier generations drew on the past to respond to the pressures of the present presumably invite the same scrutiny of their own work.

Remembrance as Religion

Long before historians took an interest in the idea of social memory, a literature began to develop that examined remembrance of the Civil War as an example of folklore, myth, or religion. For some commentators, these labels amounted to an observation that certain stories of the war enjoyed lasting currency that did not depend on their verification. Other historians applied the concepts more rigorously to analyze commemorative practices and evaluate the influence of Civil War remembrance in the wider context of American belief systems. These approaches have not been rendered obsolete by more recent formulations. They continue to inform the scholarship on memory of the war and to frame opportunities for further research.

Interest in Civil War stories as folklore or mythology shared in concerns that animated the American studies movement in the mid–twentieth century. Studies of Lincoln as a legendary figure or of the Lost Cause as a regional myth sought to demonstrate that United States history had spawned indigenous traditions.[3] Although suggestive, these works were less ambitious than other exam-

---

[3] Roy P. Basler, *The Lincoln Legend: A Study in Changing Conceptions* (1935; reprint, New York: Octagon Books, 1969); David Donald, "The Folklore Lincoln," *Journal of the Illinois State Historical Society* 40 (December 1947): 377–396; Susan Speare Durant, "The Gently Furled Banner: The Development of the Myth of the Lost Cause, 1865–1900" (Ph.D. diss., University of North Carolina, 1972); Sharon Elaine Hannum, "Confederate Cavaliers: The Myth in War

ples of their genre. No scholar systematically collected folktales about Lincoln or explained precisely how his image fit into American oral and popular literature. Theoretical frameworks of folklore and mythology scholarship received little attention after Lloyd Lewis's application of Sir James Frazer's *The Golden Bough* to legends of the Lincoln assassination.[4] The work on the postwar era that answered George Tindall's call for examination of southern mythology amply described the central motifs of the Lost Cause, but it generally lacked the sort of analytic energy that Ericksonian psychology provided in William Taylor's parallel study of antebellum myths of sectional identity.[5] Despite the aim of some authors to expose the racial implications of Confederate commemoration, the research did not situate the development of the Lost Cause firmly in its social and political contexts.

Studies of Civil War remembrance as myth intertwined with a more expansive scholarship that had separate roots in the concept of civil religion. Robert Bellah prominently featured Civil War commemorative practices in his famous 1967 essay on the dynamics of national religious culture. Bellah pointed out that Civil War remembrance had installed the violent sacrifice of citizens at the heart of American identity in the scriptural status accorded to the Gettysburg Address, the reliance on Christian archetypes for honoring the martyred Lincoln, and the institution of Memorial Day rites and the Arlington National Cemetery shrine. At the same time, Bellah also saw the legacy of Lincoln more optimistically as expanding the American model of a prophetic figure able to stand outside the entrenched sins of the country and recall it to a sense of mission.[6]

Edmund Wilson's *Patriotic Gore* (1962) connected the militarization of American civil religion to nineteenth-century shifts in church life. His reading of Unionist literature as an illustration that "the minds of nations at war are invariably dominated by myths" suggested that the Civil War application of the axiom reflected upheavals in the New England religious tradition. The book opened with a chapter on *Uncle Tom's Cabin* in which Wilson stressed that Harriet Beecher Stowe's central subject was the crisis in Calvinist theology

and Defeat" (Ph.D. diss., Rice University, 1965); Rollin Osterweis, *The Myth of the Lost Cause* (Hamden, Conn.: Archon Books, 1973).

[4]Lloyd Lewis, *Myths after Lincoln* (New York: Harcourt, Brace, 1929). See more recently C. Wyatt Evans, *The Legend of John Wilkes Booth: Myth, Memory, and a Mummy* (Lawrence: University Press of Kansas, 2004).

[5]George B. Tindall, "Mythology: A New Frontier in Southern History," in *The Idea of the South: Pursuit of a Central Theme*, ed. Frank Vandiver (Chicago: University of Chicago Press, 1964), 1–15; William R. Taylor, *Cavalier and Yankee: The Old South and American National Character* (New York: Braziller, 1961). Wolfgang Schivelbusch, *The Culture of Defeat: On National Trauma, Mourning, and Recovery*, trans. Jefferson Chase (New York: Holt, 2003), 1–35, is a suggestive recent attempt to incorporate the Lost Cause in a psychological interpretation of common mythic structures.

[6]Robert N. Bellah, "Religion in America," *Daedalus* 96 (Winter 1967): 1–21.

prompted by the rise of liberal Protestantism. He then proceeded, in the style of Perry Miller, to the converse crisis of a liberal Protestantism that lacked the emotional intensity of Puritanism. Filling this void was the apocalyptic nationalism of Julia Ward Howe's "Battle Hymn of the Republic" and Lincoln's conception of the Union, which, in the oft-quoted words of Alexander Stephens, "in sentiment rose to the sublimity of a religious mysticism." *Patriotic Gore* concluded with what Wilson considered the most substantial alternative conjunction of religion and Civil War memory, the "soldier's faith" of Oliver Wendell Holmes Jr., a New England atheist one generation removed from the Unitarian elite typified by Howe and two generations removed from the Calvinist clergy depicted by Stowe.[7]

Comparable work on Confederate memory has detailed the Lost Cause ideology, rituals, and symbols that "sacralized the Southern way of life."[8] This literature has asked how white southerners reconciled their confidence in God's favor with their crushing defeat in the war. The answer has often been a readiness to view the calamity as the appointed suffering of a chosen people. Such reassurance made failure no less real, and several authors have emphasized that a sense of human limitation and tragedy was integral to the original Lost Cause, only to fade as Confederate remembrance was adapted into a national story of success and progress. For Thomas Connelly and Barbara Bellows, "the Lost Cause was a realization of mortality existing in an America that reached for the gnostic immortal."[9] Charles Reagan Wilson has observed that this pattern served the institutional interests of specific churches, noting that "to Southern preachers, the Lost Cause was useful in keeping Southerners a Christian people." He suggests that in some respects the culture of commemoration especially benefited the Episcopal Church, though his interest is in the broad construction of regional identity rather than in particular denominational strategies.[10]

Current studies have continued to identify Civil War remembrance as a significant force in the development of postbellum religious institutions and the religious dimensions of nationalism. Daniel Stowell stresses that interpretations of the war played an important role in the growth of racially and

---

[7]Edmund Wilson, *Patriotic Gore: Studies in the Literature of the American Civil War* (New York: Oxford University Press, 1962), 91, 97.

[8]Lloyd Arthur Hunter, "The Sacred South: Postwar Confederates and the Sacralization of Southern Culture" (Ph.D. diss., Saint Louis University, 1978), x. See also Hunter, "The Immortal Confederacy: Another Look at Lost Cause Religion," in *The Myth of the Lost Cause and Civil War History*, ed. Gary W. Gallagher and Alan T. Nolan (Bloomington: Indiana University Press, 2000), 185–218.

[9]Thomas Connelly and Barbara L. Bellows, *God and General Longstreet: The Lost Cause and the Southern Mind* (Baton Rouge: Louisiana State University Press, 1982), 108.

[10]Charles Reagan Wilson, *Baptized in Blood: The Religion of the Lost Cause, 1865–1920* (Athens: University of Georgia Press, 1980), 33.

regionally distinct evangelical denominations, and Kathleen Clark has examined the strategy of the AME Church in promoting a race narrative centered on emancipation.[11] Perhaps the most widely read book on Civil War memory, Garry Wills's *Lincoln at Gettysburg* (1992) highlights the theological ideas in the Gettysburg Address and the Second Inaugural Address, which have received further elaboration in the recent tide of monographs on Lincoln as an intellectual.[12] To be sure, the concept of civil religion has continued to draw debate. W. Scott Poole has lately criticized it as too inclined to envision a politics of inclusion and insufficiently attentive to division and conflict. But Poole's study of the Lost Cause as a sanctification of southern society, which supports many of the arguments of Charles Reagan Wilson and Thomas Connelly, illustrates the persistent interest in Civil War remembrance as a blurring of the sacred and the secular.[13]

Robert Bonner's *Colors and Blood* (2002) is an especially powerful exploration of this process. While focused on the Confederacy, his study is one of several to demonstrate that the distinctive American reverence for flags originated in the Civil War.[14] This research supplements Robert Bellah's analysis by tracing the emergence of the central icon of American nationalism through a historically contingent process shaped by the military tactics and Victorian emotional conventions specific to the mid–nineteenth century. At the same time, Bonner highlights a primal production of religious sentiment independent of the appropriation of biblical archetypes that Bellah emphasized. He argues that bloodshed transformed flags from symbols of ideological commitments into totems of remembered experiences, so that the Southern Cross came to derive its sacred aura less from its invocation of Christianity than from its reminder of a consecrating violence. The parallel rebirth of the United States flag as a site of mem-

[11]Daniel W. Stowell, *Rebuilding Zion: The Religious Reconstruction of the South, 1863–1877* (New York: Oxford University Press, 1998); Kathleen Ann Clark, *Defining Moments: African American Commemoration and Political Culture in the South, 1863–1913,* (Chapel Hill: University of North Carolina Press, 2005).

[12]Garry Wills, *Lincoln at Gettysburg: The Words That Remade America* (New York: Simon and Schuster, 1992). See also, e.g., Kent Gramm, *November: Lincoln's Elegy at Gettysburg* (Bloomington: Indiana University Press, 2001); James Tackach, *Lincoln's Moral Vision: The Second Inaugural Address* (Jackson: University Press of Mississippi, 2002); Ronald C. White Jr., *Lincoln's Greatest Speech: The Second Inaugural* (New York: Simon and Schuster, 2002).

[13]W. Scott Poole, *Never Surrender: Confederate Memory and Conservatism in the South Carolina Upcountry* (Athens: University of Georgia Press, 2004), 3, 53.

[14]Robert E. Bonner, *Colors and Blood: Flag Passions of the Confederate South* (Princeton: Princeton University Press, 2002). See also Alice Fahs, *The Imagined Civil War: Popular Literature of the North and South, 1861–1865* (Chapel Hill: University of North Carolina Press, 2001), 68–72; Stuart McConnell, *Glorious Contentment: The Grand Army of the Republic, 1865–1900* (Chapel Hill: University of North Carolina Press, 1992), 228–230; Cecelia O'Leary, *To Die For: The Paradox of American Patriotism* (Princeton: Princeton University Press, 1999), 20–22, 26–27.

ory for fallen soldiers would be ritualistically renewed long after flags had largely disappeared from battlefields. This interpretation not only illuminates a reconstruction of national culture, through which veneration of flags would make them frequent flashpoints of controversy over individual rights of free expression, but also provides a stimulating reflection on the ways in which religious attachments can arise from social remembrance.

The Politics of the Lost Cause

A largely distinct body of scholarship has examined Confederate remembrance as a forum for the negotiation of power relations among the principal groups in southern society. Although this research has sometimes drawn on studies of the Lost Cause as myth or religion, it has focused on the role of commemoration in the definition of class, race, and gender lines in the postwar South.

Gaines Foster's *Ghosts of the Confederacy* (1987) introduced this approach in a well-crafted analysis of the ties that C. Vann Woodward had identified between white southern remembrance and New South boosterism.[15] In the period immediately after the war, Foster's southerners mourned their dead and buried their active loyalty to a cause that, unlike failed rebellions in many other parts of the world, did not inspire another attempt. A Virginia-dominated clique centered on the Southern Historical Society and the Association for the Army of Northern Virginia sought to channel bitter memories of the war into southern hostility toward industrialization and urbanization, but Foster argued that this circle enjoyed little popular influence. He attached more significance to the veterans' associations that proliferated in the 1880s, leading to the founding of the United Confederate Veterans in 1889. According to Foster, these organizations attracted members from a relatively broad range of social classes by offering camaraderie, relief from the anxieties of economic upheaval, and a patriotic sense of reintegration into the nation rather a program of resistance to modernization and the North. The resulting "Confederate celebration" stabilized as it mobilized ordinary white people in the New South. "Praise for discipline and respect for private property within the Confederate ranks, commendation of the veterans' role in rebuilding the South, and acclaim for the soldiers' sacrifice of self for the good of society served indirectly to protect the New South," Foster observed. While eschewing any allegation that elites had deliberately manipulated remembrance

---

[15]C. Vann Woodward, *Origins of the New South, 1877–1913* (Baton Rouge: Louisiana State University Press, 1951), 154–158. See also Paul M. Gaston, *The New South Creed: A Study in Southern Mythmaking* (New York: Knopf, 1970), chap. 5, which stands between early approaches to the Lost Cause and Foster's themes.

as an instrument of social control, he concluded that the Lost Cause had established a cultural foundation for the conservatism that would long characterize
southern politics and labor relations.[16]

Much of the recent writing on Confederate memory responds directly to
Ghosts of the Confederacy. Many scholars have supported Foster's interpretation.
Carol Reardon has reported that the reputation of Pickett's Charge as the central turning point of the war reflected in part the triumph of the New South
faction of Virginia veterans over Jubal Early's band of unreconstructed Confederates. David Currey has found that residents of Franklin, Tennessee, relied on
commemoration to address qualms about urbanization, placing a Confederate
statue in the town square as a moral counterweight to the commerce and vice
associated with the site, and Court Carney has shown that businessmen in turn-
of-the-century Memphis burnished a genteel, conciliatory image of Nathan
Bedford Forrest that differed sharply from the defiant folk hero later celebrated
by the Southern Renascence. Edward Ayers's synthesis *The Promise of the New
South* (1992) typifies the acceptance of the view that "the Lost Cause was not
simple evidence of Southern distinctiveness, Southern intransigence, but was
also ironic evidence that the South marched in step with the rest of the country."[17] Some historians have carried Foster's arguments further than he did.
Wallace Hettle points out that even the quintessential unreconstructed polemi-
cist Robert L. Dabney promoted the values of the emergent market society in his
biography of Stonewall Jackson. Fred Arthur Bailey bluntly describes southern
schoolbooks as an attempt to maintain patrician political dominance in a period
of economic and social transformation.[18]

Ghosts of the Confederacy has also drawn challenges from several directions.
Charles Holden and W. Scott Poole maintain that Foster's two-stage narrative
underestimates the effectiveness of the irreconcilable Confederates. They report
that the first two decades of postwar commemoration in South Carolina successfully renewed deference to planter elites and rejected the bourgeois tenden-

[16]Gaines M. Foster, *Ghosts of the Confederacy: Defeat, the Lost Cause, and the Emergence of the
New South* (Baton Rouge: Louisiana State University Press, 1987), 124.

[17]Edward L. Ayers, *The Promise of the New South: Life after Reconstruction* (New York:
Oxford University Press, 1992), 334; Court Carney, "The Contested Image of Nathan Bedford
Forrest," *Journal of Southern History* 67 (August 2001): 601–630; David Currey, "The Virtuous
Soldier: Constructing a Usable Confederate Past in Franklin, Tennessee," in *Monuments to the
Lost Cause: Women, Art, and the Landscapes of Southern Memory*, ed. Cynthia Mills and Pamela
H. Simpson (Knoxville: University of Tennessee Press, 2003), 133–146; Carol Reardon, *Pickett's
Charge in History and Memory* (Chapel Hill: University of North Carolina Press, 1997), chap. 4.

[18]Wallace Hettle, "The Minister, the Martyr, and the Maxim: Robert Lewis Dabney and
Stonewall Jackson Biography," *Civil War History* 49 (December 2003): 353–369; Fred Bailey,
"The Textbooks of the 'Lost Cause': Censorship and the Creation of Southern State Histories,"
Georgia Historical Quarterly (Summer 1991): 507–533.

cies of the North. This position overlaps, particularly in Poole's account, with depiction of the Lost Cause as a sacralized alternative to a national faith in progress.[19] The claim that the early Lost Cause established an antimodern tradition that retained cultural vitality long after losing political power calls for closer examination of that critique and its heirs. Poole and Holden build shrewdly on scholarship that has placed South Carolina at the center of antebellum southern intellectual history, but the influence of the state in postbellum antimodernist southern thought is less clear. At the least, their focus on South Carolina points out that studies of Confederate commemoration have often centered on the Upper South and invites further investigation of local variations in regional remembrance.

A second challenge to Foster's interpretation has argued that the expansion of Confederate commemoration owed less to tensions of industrialization and urbanization than to efforts to consolidate white supremacism. Like the first critique, this approach proposes to adjust the relative weights of the Lost Cause elements identified by Foster, who acknowledged that the Confederate celebration reinforced racial hierarchy but saw less fluidity and social pressure in that situation than in the condition of farmers and urban workers.[20] In contrast, David Blight, W. Fitzhugh Brundage, Catherine Bishir, and other scholars depict considerable white anxiety over the public presence of African Americans and the potential for interracial coalition. The Confederate memory they describe is more racially virulent, especially in its remembrance of Reconstruction as a regime of corrupt tyranny overthrown by "redemption."[21] As alternative primary explanations for the overall pattern of the Lost Cause, the themes make different claims to significance. Foster offers an ironic story of the conflicted, sometimes nostalgic manner in which white southerners adjusted to a new social order at the cost of a clearer awareness of the interests advanced by the

[19]Poole, *Never Surrender*; Charles Holden, "'Is Our Love for Wade Hampton Foolishness?' South Carolina and the Lost Cause," in Gallagher and Nolan, *Myth of the Lost Cause*, 60–88.

[20]Foster, *Ghosts of the Confederacy*, 86–87.

[21]See, e.g., Bruce E. Baker, "Devastated by Passion and Belief: Remembering Reconstruction in the Twentieth-Century South" (Ph.D. diss., University of North Carolina, 2003); Catherine W. Bishir, "Landmarks of Power: Building a Southern Past in Raleigh and Wilmington, North Carolina, 1885–1915," in *Where These Memories Grow: History, Memory, and Southern Identity*, ed. W. Fitzhugh Brundage (Chapel Hill: University of North Carolina Press, 2000), 139–168; Catherine W. Bishir, "'A Strong Force of Ladies': Women, Politics, and Confederate Memorial Associations in Nineteenth-Century Raleigh," *North Carolina Historical Review* 77 (October 2000): 455–491; David W. Blight, *Race and Reunion: The Civil War in American Memory* (Cambridge, Mass.: Harvard University Press, 2001), 80–84; W. Fitzhugh Brundage, *The Southern Past: A Clash of Race and Memory* (Cambridge, Mass.: Harvard University Press, 2005), 28–36. Kirk Savage, *Standing Soldiers, Kneeling Slaves: Race, War, and Monument in Nineteenth-Century America* (Princeton: Princeton University Press, 1997), chap. 5, adroitly integrates the themes of economic modernization and race relations.

transformation. The rival interpretation describes a more purposeful strategy of racism, contested vigorously and sometimes successfully by African Americans but spreading beyond the South to influence the views of whites across the country. To a greater extent than Foster's tale of transition, this scholarship brings history to bear directly on contemporary political controversies over the racial meaning of Confederate remembrance.

The most varied challenges to Foster's framework have focused on the gender dynamics of the Lost Cause. While previous scholarship had devoted little attention to this topic, *Ghosts of the Confederacy* thoughtfully examined it but saw few new developments. Foster indicated that defeat briefly threatened Confederate veterans' sense of masculinity but that loyal white southern women helped to restore male self-confidence and authority by earning a reputation for continued antagonism toward northern men. Women's memorialization of the dead in the first years after the war set mourning in an apolitical realm of sentiment, building up a cultural capital in white southern memory but giving it no ideological direction except to ease relinquishment of allegiance to secession. The dynamic phase of the Lost Cause came with the mobilization of veterans. Indeed, for Foster, one measure of the declining importance of the Lost Cause was that primary responsibility for it passed not to the Sons of Confederate Veterans but to the United Daughters of the Confederacy (UDC), which he described as an outlet for high society with relatively little impact on the South as a whole.[22]

Recent studies have attached more significance to women's role in remembrance. Considerable research has documented the activities of women's Lost Cause organizations and the participation of women writers in the commemorative culture. UDC historian-general Mildred Lewis Rutherford alone has been the subject of three substantial essays.[23] In the fullest assessment of women's leadership position, including but not limited to the Lost Cause, W. Fitzhugh Brundage concludes that women's organizations deserve primary credit for the creation of a regional institutional infrastructure for dissemination of collec-

[22]Foster, *Ghosts of the Confederacy*, 26–33, 38–46, 131–139, 169–178.

[23]In addition to the works discussed hereafter, see especially Karen L. Cox, *Dixie's Daughters: The United Daughters of the Confederacy and the Preservation of Confederate Culture* (Gainesville: University Press of Florida, 2003), and Sarah E. Gardner, *Blood and Irony: Southern White Women's Narratives of the Civil War, 1861–1937* (Chapel Hill: University of North Carolina Press, 2004). On Rutherford, see Fred Bailey, "Mildred Lewis Rutherford and the Patrician Cult of the Old South," *Georgia Historical Quarterly* 78 (Summer 1994): 509–534; Sarah H. Case, "The Historical Ideology of Mildred Lewis Rutherford: A Confederate Historian's New South Creed," *Journal of Southern History* 68 (August 2002): 599–628; and Grace Hale, "'Some Women Have Never Been Reconstructed': Mildred Lewis Rutherford, Lucy M. Stanton, and the Racial Politics of White Womanhood, 1900–1930," in *Georgia in Black and White: Explorations in the Race Relations of a Southern State, 1865–1930*, ed. John Inscoe (Athens: University of Georgia Press, 1994), 173–201.

tive historical memory. Their success played an important role in the eventual decline of their influence, he adds, for as the celebratory, archival, and educational ventures of women gained recognition of remembrance as an appropriate field of state action, men tended to take control of it.[24]

Despite the agreement on the magnitude of women's commemorative effort, Jane Turner Censer has recently noted that historians remain "perplexed" about its place in the reconstruction of white southern gender patterns. Foster depicts stasis by emphasizing that the mourning practices of Ladies Memorial Associations and the sociability of the UDC overlapped with traditional realms of women's activity. Drew Gilpin Faust has written that women of the Lost Cause engaged in a "rehabilitation of patriarchy" propelled by eagerness to reassert class order. William Blair and John Neff describe women's leadership role as merely a tactic adopted by white southerners when northerners restricted men's commemoration of the Confederacy.[25] Other historians have been more impressed by the extent to which the Lost Cause expanded white southern women's opportunities to engage in public life. For Anastatia Sims and Rebecca Montgomery, the initiatives of the UDC and similar organizations were important steps toward woman suffrage.[26] Jane Turner Censer suggests instead that women carved out a public space they largely controlled in the early postwar era but that their autonomy and ambition faded as veterans' organizations came to the fore in the late 1880s.[27] That male ascendancy, several studies have

[24]W. Fitzhugh Brundage, "White Women and the Politics of Historical Memory in the New South, 1880–1920," in *Jumpin' Jim Crow: Southern Politics from Civil War to Civil Rights*, ed. Jane Dailey, Glenda Elizabeth Gilmore, and Bryant Simon (Princeton: Princeton University Press, 2000), 115–139.

[25]Jane Turner Censer, *The Reconstruction of White Southern Womanhood, 1865–1895* (Baton Rouge: Louisiana State University Press, 2003), 191; Drew Gilpin Faust, *Mothers of Invention: Women of the Slaveholding South in the American Civil War* (Chapel Hill: University of North Carolina Press, 1996), 247; William Blair, *Cities of the Dead: Contesting the Memory of the Civil War in the South, 1865–1914* (Chapel Hill: University of North Carolina Press, 2004); John R. Neff, *Honoring the Civil War Dead: Commemoration and the Problem of Reconciliation* (Lawrence: University Press of Kansas, 2005). See also Poole, *Never Surrender*, 25–29, 67–73, 128–131, 156–157; Anne Sarah Rubin, *A Shattered Nation: The Rise and Fall of the Confederacy, 1861–1868* (Chapel Hill: University of North Carolina Press, 2005), 230–239.

[26]Rebecca Montgomery, "Lost Cause Mythology in New South Reform: Gender, Class, Race, and the Politics of Patriotic Citizenship in Georgia, 1890–1925," in *Negotiating the Boundaries of Southern Womanhood: Dealing with the Powers That Be*, ed. Janet L. Coryell, Thomas H. Appleton, Jr., Anastatia Sims, and Sandra Gioia Treadway (Columbia: University of Missouri Press, 2000), 174–198; Anastatia Sims, *The Power of Femininity in the New South: Women's Organizations and Politics in Georgia, 1880–1930* (Columbia: University of South Carolina Press, 1997), chap. 4.

[27]Censer, *Reconstruction of White Southern Womanhood*, 190–203. See also Thomas J. Brown, "The Monumental Legacy of Calhoun," in *The Memory of the Civil War in American Cul-*

agreed, included strenuous attempts to install a depoliticized image of Confederate womanhood.[28]

The institutional infrastructure of historical memory and the political authority of women are not the only issues at stake in examinations of women's contribution to the Lost Cause. Contrary to arguments that ex-Confederate women sought to restore patriarchy as much as circumstances permitted, some historians have found that women aimed to redefine social ideals of masculinity. Censer reports that white southern women's novels featuring sectionalized romantic rivalries presented a sharp critique of Confederate veterans, juxtaposing them with the discipline, energy, and thoughtfulness of modernized northern protagonists, but that by the 1890s women authors had lapsed into admiration for the assertive strength that they identified with the southern male.[29] LeeAnn Whites suggests that women achieved a more lasting success in shifting the essence of white southern manhood from slaveholders' demand for prerogatives to a self-sacrificing defense of home and family. She acknowledges that veterans' organizations took charge of the Lost Cause around 1890 but argues that their ideas of masculinity "had to incorporate the domestic transformation of their wartime experience that the Ladies' Memorial Association had promoted in the decade after the war." This transition extended beyond models for relations between individual men and women, she indicates, and informed a broader reconstruction of the public realm to promote the protection of dependents through government programs, charitable initiatives, and employment practices. Rebecca Montgomery similarly argues ably for the continued importance of Lost Cause ideology in campaigns for "public mothering" during the next quarter-century.[30] Such interpretations move the literature from recognition of the resourcefulness and tenacity of white southern women to the more provocative theme of the differences in values espoused by men and women.

While the publication of *Gone with the Wind* (1936) presents an obvious culmination for scholars focusing on the literary tradition of the Lost Cause, social

ture, ed. Alice Fahs and Joan Waugh (Chapel Hill: University of North Carolina Press, 2004), 130–156.

[28]Thomas J. Brown, "The Confederate Retreat to Mars and Venus," in *Battle Scars: Gender and Sexuality in the U.S. Civil War*, ed. Catherine Clinton and Nina Silber (New York: Oxford University Press, 2006), 189–213; Elise L. Smith, "Belle Kinney and the Confederate Women's Monument," *Southern Quarterly* 32 (Summer 1994): 6–31.

[29]Jane Turner Censer, "Reimagining the North-South Reunion: Southern Women Novelists and the Intersectional Romance, 1876–1900," *Southern Cultures* 5 (Summer 1999): 64–91. See also Brown, "The Confederate Retreat to Mars and Venus."

[30]Montgomery, "Lost Cause Mythology in New South Reform"; LeeAnn Whites, *The Civil War as a Crisis in Gender: Augusta, Georgia, 1860–1890* (Athens: University of Georgia Press, 1995), 203.

and political historians tracing Confederate commemoration from the war years onward have rarely extended their studies beyond 1920. One of the few major works to span the period from Fort Sumter to the present, John Coski's history of the Confederate battle flag, supports the consensus by contrasting early reverence for the Southern Cross with the cultures of youth and consumerism that took off in the twenties.[31] Other historians have offered different justifications for their breakpoints, including the maturation of the New South economy, the consolidation of Jim Crow, and the Nineteenth Amendment's redefinition of women's options for participation in politics. One common argument has been that in or around World War I, the Lost Cause crossed a threshold of sectional reconciliation that extended beyond acceptance of economic transformation. The notion of southern reconciliation has been applied in two ways. Some research has measured white southern national sentiment through support for American military undertakings or solicitude for the president or, less often, adoption of specific Civil War aspects of patriotic culture such as reverence for Lincoln or observance of federal Memorial Day. More frequently, southern reconciliation has meant the satisfaction of white southerners with the extent to which northerners honored remembrance of the Confederacy. That story of a late victory for the Lost Cause takes place primarily on the battleground of northern memory, and it establishes the principal connection between studies focused on opposite sides of the sectional divide.

Rebuilding the Nation through Commemoration

The literature on memory of the Union effort in the Civil War has in some respects followed a pattern of development similar to the scholarship on the Lost Cause. Building on studies of remembrance as myth or civil religion, authors began in the late 1980s to look at commemoration as a venue for the negotiation of race, class, and gender relations. If research on the white South has linked those themes to postwar assertions of regional distinctiveness, however, work on the federal side has focused on the problem of fostering Civil War memory in a country that incorporated the former Confederacy. This literature has given

---

[31] John M. Coski, *The Confederate Battle Flag: America's Most Embattled Emblem* (Cambridge, Mass.: Harvard University Press, 2005). Brundage, *The Southern Past,* which is not limited to Confederate remembrance but devotes substantial attention to it, similarly sees a divide around 1920, as does Sally Leigh McWhite, "Echoes of the Lost Cause: Reverberations in Mississippi from 1865 to 2001" (Ph.D. diss., University of Mississippi, 2002). For stimulating depictions of the Lost Cause in crisis during the 1920s, see Grace Hale, *Making Whiteness: The Culture of Segregation in the South, 1890–1940* (New York: Pantheon Books, 1998), 241–244, 251–268; and Micki McElya, "Commemorating the Color Line: The National Mammy Monument Controversy of the 1920s," in Mills and Simpson, *Monuments to the Lost Cause,* 203–218.

fresh meaning to the concept of the Union, a term long treated as an artificial antebellum forerunner to the more dynamic postwar idea of the nation. Historians have described sectional reconciliation after Appomattox as a process of re-membering with grave costs as well as impressive cohesive force, and they have found that the Union provided a resonant metaphor for Americans' deeply personal hopes for union. The scholarship on Union commemoration has also illuminated the postbellum expansion of the state, particularly at the federal level. These concerns have maintained a continuity with the writing on religious dimensions of nationalism and deepened understanding of the ways in which Civil War remembrance reconstructed the United States.

Recent scholarship on Unionist commemoration represents a diametric reversal from Paul Buck's *Road to Reunion, 1865–1900* (1937), which received the Pulitzer Prize during the seventy-fifth anniversary of the war. Buck's book wove political, economic, and cultural strands into a single narrative in which partisan manipulation of sectional discord gave way to business incentives for cooperation and emotional impulses for reconciliation. Buck rigidly followed the lead of the Dunning school in reporting that the United States cohered when white northerners accepted a subordination of African Americans that corresponded to the supposed natural inferiority of the race. More original was his coverage of the "web of national sentiment which selected from bygone feuds those deeds of mutual valor which permitted pride in present achievement and future promise." That emphasis on the link between commemoration of the Confederacy and consolidation of the nation fit *Road to Reunion* neatly into the regionalist movement of the 1930s. "One of Dixie's major contributions to the new patriotism was its insistence that a valid nationalism could be premised only upon respect for and conservation of properly integrated variations in regional culture," Buck maintained. "This in a sense had been the Southern cause in the Civil War."[32]

Buck's critics have agreed that what David Blight has felicitously called "the valorization of the veteran" facilitated admiration of Confederates understood to have fought for home and constitutional principle, rather than slavery, and fostered acceptance of the idea that the causes of the war were less important than the military feats it inspired.[33] But contrary to Buck's conclusion that mutual respect for martial virtue enabled "a union of sentiment" to become "a fact," the most thoughtful recent interpretations of Civil War remembrance have treated sectional reconciliation not as a "fact" but as a cultural narrative that achieved dominance in a vigorous contest with alternative narratives.[34] The dis-

[32]Paul Buck, *Road to Reunion, 1865–1900* (Boston: Little, Brown, 1937), 310, 318.

[33]David W. Blight, "'What Will Peace among the Whites Bring?' Reunion and Race in the Struggle over the Memory of the Civil War in American Culture," *Massachusetts Review* 34 (Autumn 1993): 400.

[34]Buck, *Road to Reunion*, viii.

tinction goes beyond the problem of measuring and dating a factual reconciliation defined as more than the cessation of warfare. The contrasting approaches
shape works with different purposes. Buck attached no beneficial value to the
only alternative commemoration of the Civil War he could imagine, Republican
exploitation of the bloody shirt to suppress a permanently disaffected South,
and his book both described and participated in a national celebration of peace
between North and South. Current scholarship hesitates to credit the reconciliation motif with salvation of the United States and often sympathizes with competing themes of Civil War remembrance.

Blight revives counter-memory of the war most eloquently in his *Race and
Reunion* (2001), which traces the eclipse of an egalitarian "emancipationist"
narrative of the war by a martial "reconciliationist" narrative from Lincoln's
new birth of freedom to D. W. Griffith's *Birth of a Nation*. Blight suggests that the
struggle between the two conceptions was a tragic conflict between incompatible values of justice and healing, though he clearly indicates that the reunion
saga might have avoided such complete capture by white supremacism, most
obviously through the space that martial memory opened for appreciation of
the African Americans who served in the Union army and navy. Most important, he carefully shows that the emancipationist and reconciliationist narratives were both available at every point in the half-century he surveys. If the
northern construction of apolitical Confederate gallantry began soon after the
war in the writings of Walt Whitman and Horace Greeley, the celebration of
black citizenship as the war-born realization of American ideals extended forward to W. E. B. Du Bois's *Star of Ethiopia* pageant for the semicentennial of
the Emancipation Proclamation. The implication is that the continuing contest
holds out hope yet for a more satisfactory view of the war.

This mapping of the revisionist Reconstruction synthesis onto the field of
memory has plotted many examples of Union commemoration on a grid of
race and reunion. Several have achieved landmark status in the scholarship.
Historians have argued about the levels of reconciliationist sentiment in the
landscapes of Gettysburg National Military Park and Arlington National Cemetery, and they have debated the levels of racial egalitarianism in the policies of
the Grand Army of the Republic and the design of Augustus Saint-Gaudens's
memorial to Robert Gould Shaw and the soldiers of the Fifty-fourth Massachusetts Regiment.[35]

[35]On Gettysburg, compare Amy J. Kinsel, "'From These Honored Dead': Gettysburg in
American Culture, 1863–1938" (Ph.D. diss., Cornell University, 1992), with Edward Linen-
thal, *Sacred Ground: Americans and Their Battlefields* (Urbana: University of Illinois Press, 1991),
chap. 3. See also Christopher Waldrep, *Vicksburg's Long Shadow: The Civil War Legacy of Race and
Remembrance* (Lanham, Md.: Rowman and Littlefield, 2005), for a nuanced, wide-ranging study
centered on another important battleground. For different views of the Confederate graves in
Arlington National Cemetery, see Blair, *Cities of the Dead*, chap. 7; Neff, *Honoring the Civil War*

The broadest challenge to the overall framework has been that the envisioned trade-off between reconciliation and racial progress neglects many northerners who spurned sectional detente but expressed little interest in the emancipationist legacy of the war.[36] In part this criticism adapts the common charge that revisionist scholars of Reconstruction have tended to overestimate the prospect for reform. That argument may have some corrective value, although surely the cross-sectional valorization of the Confederate veteran contributed to a decline in white northern sympathy for African Americans. Moreover, if detached from the problem of racial justice, the reasons for documenting the limits to federal commemoration of the Confederacy are unclear. John Neff concludes his informative monograph with an exhortation to carry forward "the struggle to establish an inclusive, nonsectional nationalism" as "one of the noblest ideals that this nation has ever embraced."[37] But it is difficult to stir passion for a campaign against region-based discrimination in the contemporary United States.

While accounts of the emancipationist tradition have stressed the moral vision and courage of the African Americans who were its most determined supporters, historians have also recognized that black remembrance of the war was not restricted to a dialogue with whites. William Blair, David Blight, W. Fitzhugh Brundage, Kathleen Clark, and Mitch Kachun report that observances of Emancipation Day framed disagreements among African Americans about norms of celebration and gentility as well as debates about black allegiance to the Republican Party and the extent to which racial identity should center on remembrance of slavery and emancipation.[38] Kachun's *Festivals of Freedom* (2003) offers a particularly stimulating complement to the well-estab-

Dead, chap. 6; and Michele A. Krowl, "'In the Spirit of Fraternity': The United States Government and the Burial of the Confederate Dead at Arlington National Cemetery, 1864–1914," *Virginia Magazine of History and Biography* 111, no. 2 (2003): 151–186. Mixed assessments of the racial views of Union veterans include Andre Fleche, "'Shoulder to Shoulder as Comrades Tried': Black and White Veterans and Civil War Memory," *Civil War History* 51 (June 2005): 175–201; McConnell, *Glorious Contentment*, 8–9, 213–218; and Donald Shaffer, *After the Glory: The Struggles of Black Civil War Veterans* (Lawrence: University Press of Kansas, 2004), chap. 6. For the debate over the Shaw Memorial, see Martin H. Blatt, Thomas J. Brown, and Donald Yacovone, eds., *Hope and Glory: Essays on the Legacy of the Fifty-Fourth Massachusetts Regiment* (Amherst: University of Massachusetts Press, 2001).

[36]See especially Blair, *Cities of the Dead*, and Neff, *Honoring the Civil War Dead*. Ann Fabian, *The Unvarnished Truth: Personal Narratives in Nineteenth-Century America* (Berkeley: University of California Press, 2000), chap. 4, makes a complementary argument that racism pervaded the narratives written by survivors of Confederate prisons, a genre often regarded as incompatible with reconciliation sentiment.

[37]Neff, *Honoring the Civil War Dead*, 241.

[38]Blair, *Cities of the Dead*; Blight, *Race and Reunion*, chap. 9; Brundage, *The Southern Past*, chap. 2; Clark, *Defining Moments*; Mitch Kachun, *Festivals of Freedom: Memory and Meaning in African American Emancipation Celebrations, 1808–1915* (Amherst: University of Massachusetts Press, 2003).

lished white marginalization of the emancipationist legacy. In addition to the divisions among African Americans evident on Emancipation Day, and the fragmentation that resulted from its observance on the various dates that local communities experienced freedom, Kachun stresses that black withdrawal from the commemorative tradition also reflected the rise of a modern society—influenced in many ways by African Americans—that replaced retrospective civic rituals like Emancipation Day with new urban entertainments and new political structures. For Kachun, the decline of freedom festivals is not something to lament but a step toward a different culture in which African Americans exercised increasing autonomy and authority. The continuing importance he sees in "Juneteenth" lies less in the late-twentieth-century resurgence of interest in the Texas emancipation festival than in the impressions that earlier twentieth-century observances left on the young Ralph Ellison.

The reasons for the countervailing ascendancy of reconciliationist memory in the North remain somewhat puzzling despite all of the attention it has received. The group most committed to valorization of the veteran, former Union soldiers, often criticized any equation of Union and Confederate service, though there were conspicuous exceptions. Buck attributed much of the conciliatory impetus to northern business interests in sectional harmony, an argument some recent scholars have echoed with less enthusiasm for those commercial influences.[39] Matthew Grow rightly notes that the scholarship has not systematically analyzed the northern constituency for the conciliatory movement or fully explained its ties to the partisan dynamics of the retreat from Reconstruction, just as the scholarship situating the Lost Cause in the economic transition to the New South has not pinpointed those connections.[40] *Race and Reunion* and similar works have made their contribution less by suggesting illegitimacy in the forces behind northern adoption of the reconciliation motif than by documenting and extending an alternative commemorative tradition.

An important context for northern recognition of Confederate veterans was the broader emergence of the soldier as a figure in late-nineteenth-century American culture. Stuart McConnell, Nina Silber, and Gerald Linderman emphasize that the selfless ideal of the Union soldier provided an antidote to northern anxieties about Gilded Age materialism, a point that parallels Gaines Foster's interpretation of the Confederate celebration in the New South. McConnell's

[39] See Nina Silber, *The Romance of Reunion: Northerners and the South, 1865–1900* (Chapel Hill: University of North Carolina Press, 1993); Jay Weeks, *Gettysburg: Memory, Market, and an American Shrine* (Princeton: Princeton University Press, 2003).

[40] Matthew J. Grow, "The Shadow of the Civil War: A Historiography of Civil War Memory," *American Nineteenth Century History* 4 (Summer 2003): 97. For a thorough examination of the partisan dynamics of Union remembrance at a key juncture, see Patrick J. Kelly, "The Election of 1896 and the Restructuring of Civil War Memory," in Fahs and Waugh, *The Memory of the Civil War in American Culture*, 180–212.

examination of the Grand Army of the Republic provides the most detailed and subtle account of the ways veteranhood provided a critique of rampant capitalism but also a vehicle for participating in it. Similarly, David Blight observes that the proliferation of antimaterialistic soldiers' memoirs in the 1880s reflected a commodification of Civil War memory.[41] Scholars focusing on the North have also noted the overlap between turn-of-the-century controversies over immigration and the rise of the soldier as the embodiment of American patriotism. Craig Warren illustrates the usefulness of this approach in an essay describing the process by which the legend of the Irish Brigade obscured Irish Americans' wartime ambivalence about the Union effort and incorporated the ethnic group more solidly into the Civil War narrative of the nation.[42]

The historiography of Union and Confederate remembrance has developed differently in tracing the meanings for women of the valorization of the veteran. In contrast with the outpouring of research on women of the Lost Cause, only a few works explore the predicament faced by commemoration organizers who sought to exemplify women's citizenship amid the heightened status and influence of triumphant veterans.[43] Elizabeth Young's *Disarming the Nation* brilliantly illuminates the ways in which a long line of women writers, southern as well as northern, found in the war an elastic imaginative framework for testing gender conventions that overlapped with the issues of race, slavery, and political power at the center of the sectional conflict. Nurses' narratives are the most frequently scrutinized remembrances of Union women. Young and other authors show that in their determination to recall the importance of the nursing initiative and the difficulties it faced, women competed with and in some cases compromised with an alternative commemoration that tended to identify wartime nursing as a simple extension of conventional antebellum gender roles.[44] Meanwhile,

[41]Blight, *Race and Reunion*, 176; McConnell, *Glorious Contentment*; Silber, *Romance of Reunion*; Gerald Linderman, *Embattled Courage: The Experience of Combat in the Civil War* (New York: Free Press, 1987), 284–290.

[42]Craig A. Warren, "'Oh, God, What a Pity!': The Irish Brigade at Fredericksburg and the Creation of Myth," *Civil War History* 47 (September 2001): 193–221. See also Thomas J. Brown, "Reconstructing Boston: Civic Monuments of the Civil War," in Blatt, Brown, and Yacovone, *Hope and Glory*, 130–155.

[43]O'Leary, *To Die For*, chaps. 5–6, is the only scholarly examination of the Women's Relief Corps, the leading Union women's commemorative organization. On the tension between women's citizenship and veterans' status in African-American commemoration, see Clark, *Defining Moments*; and W. Fitzhugh Brundage, "Race, Memory, and Masculinity: Black Veterans Recall the Civil War, 1865–1915," in *The War Was You and Me: Civilians and the American Civil War*, ed. Joan Cashin (Princeton: Princeton University Press, 2002), 136–156.

[44]Elizabeth Young, *Disarming the Nation: Women's Writing and the American Civil War* (Chicago: University of Chicago Press, 1999); Jane E. Schultz, *Women at the Front: Hospital Workers in Civil War America* (Chapel Hill: University of North Carolina Press, 2004), chap. 7; Lyde Cullen Sizer, *The Political Work of Northern Women Writers and the Civil War, 1850–1872* (Chapel Hill: University of North Carolina Press, 2000), chaps. 6–7.

as Alice Fahs has demonstrated, the partnership between Union soldiers and women on the home front—fervently publicized during the war—disappeared from northern popular literature during the subsequent decades, despite the resistance of some women writers. Nina Silber offers the fullest treatment of the ways in which the postwar acceleration of feminism contributed to the increasingly problematic image of northern women and to the advent of an assertive, strenuous ideal of masculinity epitomized by the soldier.[45]

Silber's focus on romances of reunion also deftly connects the commemorative reconstruction of masculine ideals with the motif of sectional reconciliation. The presumed power dynamics of Victorian marriage form a consistent backdrop for the shift from the upright Union veteran subduing a rebel belle in John W. DeForest's *Miss Ravenel's Conversion from Secession to Loyalty* (1867) to the rough-and-ready Confederate veteran conquering a northern suffragist in Owen Wister's *The Virginian* (1902). Moreover, Silber's dissection of the marriage metaphor recovers crucial implications of the reconciliation theme in redefining American nationhood. The juxtaposition of marriage and nation offered something to each institution, Silber points out. It lent the prestige of nineteenth-century nationalism to the institution of marriage during a period of alarm over declining marriage rates and rising divorce rates. At the same time, it idealized political bonds in a personally immediate way that reinforced the increasing tendency to regard the nation as an organic entity animated by shared experiences and sentiments and by common blood.[46]

Silber's analysis of the marital metaphor is one of several secular additions to the scholarship on imagination of the postwar nation in religious terms. Timothy Sweet reports that poetry and photographs applied traditions of landscape imagery to represent the regenerated country; Alan Trachtenberg finds that poetry and photography linked the victorious Union to the triumphant march of mechanized industrialization. Franny Nudelman incorporates some of both perspectives in stressing that behind the imagined nation was the coercive state.[47] Alice Fahs and Kathleen Diffley provide penetrating studies of popular literature that break sharply from emphasis on remembrance of what the self-

---

[45]Silber, *Romance of Reunion*, 86–87, 117–119, 168; Alice Fahs, "The Feminized Civil War: Gender, Northern Popular Literature, and the Memory of the War, 1861–1900," *Journal of American History* 85 (March 1999): 1461–1494. On this ideal of masculinity, see also John Pettegrew, "'The Soldier's Faith': Turn-of-the-Century Memory of the Civil War and the Emergence of Modern American Nationalism," *Journal of Contemporary History* 31 (January 1996): 49–73.

[46]Silber, *Romance of Reunion*, 44–45, 55, 116–117.

[47]Franny Nudelman, *John Brown's Body: Slavery, Violence, and the Culture of War* (Chapel Hill: University of North Carolina Press, 2004); Timothy Sweet, *Traces of War: Poetry, Photography, and the Crisis of the Union* (Baltimore: Johns Hopkins University Press, 1990); Alan Trachtenberg, *Reading American Photographs: Images as History, Matthew Brady to Walker Evans* (New York: Hill and Wang, 1989), chap. 2.

sacrificing citizen could do for the wartime nation. Instead, they argue, popular literature increasingly focused on what the wartime nation could do for its citizens. Novels and short stories depicted mobilization as a state-sponsored adventure that included not only soldiers but also women and children authorized by the war to experience life beyond the boundaries of home.[48]

These themes of Civil War remembrance were not necessarily restricted to works of literature. Diffley suggests that Congressional debate over the Thirteenth, Fourteenth, and Fifteenth Amendments applied images of the war rehearsed in popular fiction. Recent work on the creation of the military cemetery, a notable commemorative innovation of the war, offers a ready example of convergence between literary and political culture. The promise of immortality that Lincoln addressed at Gettysburg was one way military cemeteries grounded national identity in remembrance of individual wartime deaths. Moreover, as several scholars have pointed out, the military cemetery was an important new federal institution. Its design projected a particular vision of the nation onto the landscape, which included a commitment to identify by name, if possible, each soldier who had died in the service of the United States. Responsibility for burial of citizens extended the state into a vital activity traditionally controlled by families and churches, and the additional option sometimes called for difficult decisions whether an individual should be buried among kin or among fellow soldiers. Commemorative practices could be as dramatic as postwar fiction in imagining the nation-state.[49]

The literature on remembrance of Abraham Lincoln encapsulates the main approaches to the study of Union memory. Informed by the same regionalism that influenced Paul Buck, early interpretations stressed the gradual resolution of a conflict between easterners like Josiah Holland who tried to tailor Lincoln's image to standards of Anglo-American gentility and westerners like William Herndon who portrayed him as a folk hero of the prairie frontier.[50] A newer scholarship has instead made Lincoln's changing image a prime example of the tension between race and reunion. This work points out the possibilities upon his death for a progressive commemoration of emancipation and shows that

[48]Kathleen Diffley, *Where My Heart Is Turning Ever: Civil War Stories and Constitutional Reform, 1861–1876* (Athens: University of Georgia Press, 1992); Alice Fahs, *The Imagined Civil War: Popular Literature of the North and South, 1861–1865* (Chapel Hill: University of North Carolina Press, 2001). See also Kathleen Diffley, ed., *To Live and Die: Collected Stories of the Civil War, 1861–1876* (Durham, N.C.: Duke University Press, 2002).

[49]See Neff, *Honoring the Civil War Dead*; Drew Gilpin Faust, "'The Dread Void of Uncertainty': Naming the Dead in the American Civil War," *Southern Cultures* 11 (Summer 2005): 7–32; Susan-Mary Grant, "Patriot Graves: American National Identity and the Civil War Dead," *American Nineteenth Century History* 5 (Fall 2004): 74–100; Catherine W. Zipf, "Marking Union Victory in the South: The Construction of the National Cemetery System," in Mills and Simpson, *Monuments to the Lost Cause*, 27–45.

[50]Basler, *The Lincoln Legend*; Donald, "The Folklore Lincoln."

those prospects largely failed of realization as white remembrance of Lincoln abandoned the theme of black freedom and presented him as a personification of the Union with roots in both the North and the South.[51] Finally, a third line of scholarship has stressed the importance of Lincoln to the growth of the state. This approach has emphasized the ways in which remembrance of Lincoln not only deepened citizens' loyalties, particularly through the spectacle of his funeral, but converged with an expansion of government activities and the scope of the presidency. Barry Schwartz correlates the turn-of-the-century apotheosis of Lincoln with hopes that a stronger state would alleviate the tribulations of the urban industrial order. C. Wyatt Evans identifies in legends of the Lincoln assassination fears that an uncontrollable bureaucracy would conspire against the people and their leader.[52]

These interpretations are not inconsistent and have been advanced jointly in some studies of Lincoln commemoration. But the approaches contrast in significant ways, as illustrated by the different readings of the Lincoln Memorial they advance. From the celebratory regionalist perspective, the debate stirred by Frank Lloyd Wright and other westerners who assailed Henry Bacon's neoclassical design as a bankrupt, misleading representation of Lincoln and America was one of the regional clashes that eventually led to a more inclusive national harmony. The temple on the Mall in Washington would eventually be balanced by western pendants like Mount Rushmore and recognized as a sanctuary for heartland American values by the homesick Senator Jefferson Smith in Frank Capra's film *Mr. Smith Goes to Washington* (1939). The revisionist scholarship laments the missed opportunity in Reconstruction to raise a progressive national monument to emancipation and exposes the moral backsliding involved in the determination to make the Lincoln Memorial, located at the entrance to the Memorial Bridge connecting Washington with Robert E. Lee's former estate at Arlington, the central point in a capital landscape of sectional reconciliation and martial memory. The emphasis of this interpretation on the continued vitality of emancipationist commemoration is dramatized by African Americans' successful use of the Lincoln Memorial as a key site in returning white attention to the black freedom struggle.[53]

Christopher Thomas's fine book on the Lincoln Memorial incorporates both of these points but devotes its chief energies to the third theme of state-building.

---

[51] Savage, *Standing Soldiers*, chaps. 3–4.

[52] Evans, *The Legend of John Wilkes Booth*, 207–210; Barry Schwartz, *Abraham Lincoln and the Forge of National Memory* (Chicago: University of Chicago Press, 2000), chaps. 3–4. On Lincoln's funeral and the postbellum state, see both of these books and also Neff, *Honoring the Civil War Dead*, chap. 2, and Merrill D. Peterson, *Lincoln in American Memory* (New York: Oxford University Press, 1994), chap. 1.

[53] Albert Boime, *The Unveiling of the National Icons: A Plea for Patriotic Iconoclasm in a Nationalist Era* (Cambridge: Cambridge University Press, 1998); Terree Randall, "Democracy's

He highlights not only the scale of federal funding for the Lincoln Memorial and the entire McMillan Commission remodeling of the national capital but also the ties between Lincoln remembrance and advocacy of new government responsibilities and an expanded presidency. Like several other scholars, he links the growth of the state to technological change. He shows that Bacon's archeologically informed design masked state-of-the-art construction techniques, and he emphasizes that the strongest alternative to the McMillan Commission plan for a shrine on the Mall was the proposal to build one of the first interstate paved highways as a tribute to Lincoln. This connection between the Lincoln Memorial and the social atomism of the onrushing automobile era is as close as any work in the field to Pierre Nora's conception of collective memory as a tragic site of transition from the continuity of folk tradition to the dislocations of accelerating time.[54] Several works that reach across the sectional divide in scholarship seek to connect study of Civil War remembrance more fully to other recent literature on memory and examine more explicitly the relationship between memory and modernity.

The Civil War and Modern Memory

For the most part, scholarship on Civil War commemoration has been closer to other writing on the Civil War era than to other writing on commemoration. Emphasis on the postbellum trajectory of issues that Union and Confederate supporters saw as the stakes of the war—sectional relations and the definition of the nation, the racial and gender orders, the social impact of economic change—has generally paralleled the priorities of the broader Reconstruction historiography. To be sure, these themes are pertinent to the broader historiography of American memory as well. Moreover, studies of Civil War commemoration have analyzed the same sorts of rituals and representations discussed in much of the international scholarship on memory and have foregrounded processes of social trauma, purposeful forgetting, counter-memory, and contestation that are often featured in that literature. But the research on collective memory that has proliferated so extensively since the late 1980s has also explored topics related much less directly to the politics of the sectional conflict. Several recent works suggest the possible benefits of examining Civil War remembrance through those lenses.

Passion Play: The Lincoln Memorial, Politics and History as Myth" (Ph.D. diss., City University of New York, 2002); Scott Sandage, "A Marble House Divided: The Lincoln Memorial, The Civil Rights Movement, and the Politics of Memory, 1939–1963," *Journal of American History* 80 (June 1993): 135–167.

[54]Christopher A. Thomas, *The Lincoln Memorial and American Life* (Princeton: Princeton University Press, 2002), 31–33, 51–54, 81–83.

Historians of Civil War commemoration have only begun to situate the topic in the broader patterns of American memory. Much of the scholarship implies that American culture scarcely had a retrospective dimension before the Civil War, an assumption now belied by a good deal of work on social remembrance in the early republic.[55] The notion that wartime experience led directly into postwar memory not only neglects the influence of antebellum models on postwar commemoration; it also neglects the influence of antebellum models on wartime experience. As Charles Royster has observed, in a study that shifts back and forth between the war and its aftershocks, the Americans who made the Civil War "surprised themselves, but the surprise consisted, in part, of getting what they had asked for."[56]

Current research is more carefully assessing the extent to which Civil War commemoration transformed American remembrance. Mitch Kachun achieves a thoughtfully nuanced analysis of postbellum emancipation commemorations by placing them in a tradition of freedom festivals dating back to anniversaries of the 1808 abolition of the Atlantic slave trade, which in turn adapted such precedents as July 4 celebrations, eighteenth-century Negro Election Day rituals, and African ceremonial practices. Jay Weeks's work on Gettysburg battlefield similarly offers a fresh interpretation of a much-studied manifestation of Civil War remembrance by contextualizing it in the development of American memory. He shows that promoters interested in the tourism potential of the battlefield initially sought to model it on genteel antebellum resorts like Saratoga Springs and, from a commemorative standpoint, rural cemeteries like Mount Auburn. The failure of that plan resulted largely from the intervention of veter-

[55]Michael Kammen, *Mystic Chords of Memory: The Transformation of Tradition in America* (New York: Knopf, 1991) is the most distinguished example of this position. The famous phrase quoted in the title is a reminder that Lincoln thought the United States had a strong sense of memory in 1861, but Kammen devotes only a small part of his magisterial synthesis to the antebellum period. The work tends to treat the Civil War as a special subtopic, mostly in separate sections focused on North-South dynamics, in contrast with the attention throughout the book to commemoration of early America. Essential titles on pre–Civil War commemoration include Blanche Linden-Ward, *Silent City on a Hill: Landscapes of Memory and Boston's Mount Auburn Cemetery* (Columbus: Ohio State University Press, 1989); Sarah J. Purcell, *Sealed with Blood: Sacrifice, War, and Memory in Revolutionary America* (Philadelphia: University of Pennsylvania Press, 2002); John Seelye, *Memory's Nation: The Place of Plymouth Rock* (Chapel Hill: University of North Carolina Press, 1998); Len Travers, *Celebrating the Fourth: Independence Day and the Rites of Nationalism in the Early Republic* (Amherst: University of Massachusetts, 1997); David Waldstreicher, *In the Midst of Perpetual Fetes: The Making of American Nationalism, 1776–1820* (Chapel Hill: University of North Carolina Press, 1997); Alfred F. Young, *The Shoemaker and the Tea Party: Memory and the American Revolution* (Boston: Beacon Press, 1999).

[56]Charles Royster, *The Destructive War: William Tecumseh Sherman, Stonewall Jackson, and the Americans* (New York: Knopf, 1991), xii. See Paul Christopher Anderson, *Blood Image: Turner Ashby in the Civil War and the Southern Mind* (Baton Rouge: Louisiana State University Press, 2002) for a creative application of this insight.

ans who incorporated some elements of the precedents but turned the premier site of postwar nationalism into a more actively stimulating, cross-class attraction comparable to the world's fairs of the era. From this perspective, the postwar use of the battlefield made it not only a vehicle for further negotiation of the political issues of the war but also a catalyst for unexpected reconstructions of American culture.[57]

Scholars interested in Civil War remembrance have also begun to incorporate more ideas from the international writing on war and memory. Wolfgang Schivelbusch has offered the most extended application of a comparative perspective, juxtaposing the Lost Cause with French and German responses to defeat in 1870–71 and 1918.[58] Many other parallels are available. To date, however, the Civil War literature has borrowed most fruitfully from scholarship on European remembrance of wartime mobilization and devastation, rather than commemoration of victory or defeat. Particularly valuable have been analogies with the rich literature on remembrance of World War I, which has developed differently from the Civil War scholarship. Postarmistice grappling over the specific issues underlying the conflict, the chief focus of research on Union and Confederate commemoration, figures less prominently in study of the aftermath of the Great War. Instead, the central theme has been the cultural impact of the traumas of combat.[59] The Civil War did not present participants with precisely the same nightmarish ordeal as World War I. It was, however, for mid-nineteenth-century Americans a similarly unprecedented mass mobilization in which new technology contributed to a shocking confrontation with death and destruction that reached in unexpected ways into the civilian population. Attention to that experience has led to a literature exploring the ways remembrance shaped a new postwar sensibility.

The most ambitious survey of war and memory in the United States, Kurt Piehler's *Remembering War the American Way* (1995), in some ways follows up on George Mosse's incisive account of the "myth of the war experience" that culminated in the frenzy among volunteers in European capitals in 1914.[60] Piehler, however, responds primarily to controversies over remembrance of the Vietnam

---

[57]Weeks, *Gettysburg*, chaps. 1–3.

[58]Schivelbusch, *The Culture of Defeat*.

[59]In addition to the works discussed hereafter, see especially Modris Eksteins, *Rites of Spring: The Great War and the Birth of the Modern Age* (Boston: Houghton Mifflin, 1989); Adrian Gregory, *The Silence of Memory: Armistice Day, 1919–1946* (Oxford: Berg, 1994); Rudy Koshar, *From Monuments to Traces: Artifacts of German Memory, 1870–1990* (Berkeley: University of California Press, 2000), chap. 2; Daniel J. Sherman, *The Construction of Memory in Interwar France* (Chicago: University of Chicago Press, 1999); J. M. Winter, *Sites of Memory, Sites of Mourning: The Great War in European Cultural History* (Cambridge: Cambridge University Press, 1995).

[60]George L. Mosse, *Fallen Soldiers: Reshaping the Memory of the World Wars* (New York: Oxford University Press, 1990); G. Kurt Piehler, *Remembering War the American Way* (Washington, D.C.: Smithsonian Institution Press, 1995).

War, and his aim is less to examine the career of the soldier as a cultural figure than to demonstrate that Americans have frequently disagreed in looking back at their wars. Certainly commemoration of the Civil War fits well into that thesis, though it is less consistent with Piehler's argument that one key ingredient of American war remembrance has been a perception of wars as aberrant incidents for a peace-loving society. Commemoration of the Civil War was also a notable forum for idealization of war as an unavoidable and exalted condition of life.[61] Closer to Mosse's concerns is Thomas Leonard's earlier analysis of Civil War remembrance as a template for American responses to the next half-century of wars. Leonard finds in this precedent much more than a simplistic glorification of war. He concludes that the pattern established by the Civil War systematically disguised the costs of war by discouraging soldiers from evaluating their moral decisions or probing their feelings about combat, by investing American identity in a violent ambivalence toward wartime enemies, and by encouraging faith in a solution to the tension between advancing military technology and traditional ideals of martial valor.[62]

Stuart McConnell's *Glorious Contentment* (1992) parallels outstanding work on World War I in tracing the reverberations among ex-soldiers of wartime experiences of mobilization and devastation.[63] His work shows that the study of Civil War remembrance has much to contribute to a neglected topic, the postwar development of ideas about democracy. Beginning with veterans' ambivalence toward civilian applications of military principles of rank and discipline, McConnell follows the elevation of the veteran into a leading position in American public life, not merely as a member of a voting bloc but as a quasi official with authority to arbitrate the meaning of patriotism. This important trend was potentially as dangerous for democracy as the glamorization of Civil War combat was for the soldiers who would fight in subsequent wars. In describing soldiers' response to the psychological trauma of the war, McConnell charts the transformation of the Grand Army of the Republic from an intensive support group for recovery from the ordeal of combat into a fraternal organization that responded to Gilded Age anxieties of masculinity, including middle-aged men's yearning for an idealized soldierly camaraderie.

[61] See, e.g., Pettegrew, "'The Soldier's Faith'"; Dennis Montagna, "Henry Merwin Shrady's Ulysses S. Grant Memorial in Washington, D.C.: A Study in Iconography, Content, and Patronage" (Ph.D. diss., University of Delaware, 1987).

[62] Thomas C. Leonard, *Above the Battle: War-Making in America from Appomattox to Versailles* (New York: Oxford University Press, 1978).

[63] See Charles Kimball, "The Ex-Service Movement in England and Wales, 1916–1930" (Ph.D. diss., Stanford University, 1990); Antoine Prost, *Les Anciens Combattants et la Societé Française, 1914–1939*, 3 vols. (Paris: Presses de la Fondation Nationale des Sciences Politiques, 1977).

These works on the meanings of veteranhood extend and sometimes redirect the observation that the valorization of the veteran provided a basis for a postwar culture of sectional reconciliation and racial relapse. Kirk Savage skillfully balances attention to the politics of memory and other legacies of warfare in his stimulating analysis of the generic Civil War monuments found throughout the North and the South. He argues that celebration of the common soldier as the new epitome of American citizenship disguised the ways in which mass conscription and technological innovation in the war had undercut the traditional ideal of the citizen-soldier. He neatly ties this point to race by stressing that soldier statues hid the growing resemblances between military service and slavery, in part by ignoring the many Union soldiers who had been slaves. That strategy converged with intersectional white refusal to acknowledge that African Americans had so abundantly satisfied the military expectations of citizenship. Savage's elegant formulation indicates that Civil War remembrance not only facilitated a retreat from Reconstruction but also furnished a refuge from postwar anxieties about new pressures on individual will.[64]

Reconstruction of the individual self is a key theme in the recent literature on memory of wartime trauma as a source of modern identity. This scholarship brings the Civil War into the framework of debate that Paul Fussell's classic *The Great War and Modern Memory* (1975) established in the context of World War I.[65] Studies by Alan Trachtenberg, Timothy Sweet, and Steven Conn analyze the shocking physical devastation of the Civil War as what Sweet has called a "crisis of representation," much as Fussell depicted trench warfare as shattering inherited British modes of perception and description and forging a new modern outlook. Conn's assessment of Civil War paintings typifies the judgment that the unprecedented experience of the war rendered previous forms of representation obsolete. Sweet and Trachtenberg sympathize with this view in their readings of photography, a medium closely associated with the modernity of Civil War memory, but they tend to be more impressed by the resilience with which artists adapted conventions of narrative and imagery to maintain a sense of continuity with the past that dovetailed with a faith in the renewal of the Union. Sweet, noting that collodion was used both in the photographic process and as a surgical dressing, calls the Civil War photograph

[64]Savage, *Standing Soldiers*, chap. 6. Annette Becker, "War Memorials: A Legacy of Total War?" in *On the Road to Total War: The American Civil War and the German Wars of Unification, 1861–1871*, ed. Stig Förster and Jörg Nagler (Washington, D.C.: German Historical Institute and Cambridge University Press, 1997), 657–680, offers a transnational examination of monuments as a consequence of the escalation of modern warfare.

[65]Paul Fussell, *The Great War and Modern Memory* (New York: Oxford University Press, 1975).

"a metaphorical bandage" that "attempted to hide and heal the wound even while marking it."[66]

Lisa Long and Lisa Herschbach imaginatively extend this line of inquiry by focusing on soldiers' bodies as a site of war remembrance. Their works most directly echo Fussell's argument that haunting memories of a new kind of war helped to constitute a modern sensibility. Long and Herschbach highlight the alienation, irony, and epistemological uncertainty introduced by the inability of doctors and even patients themselves to know exactly what the wounded felt, a problem dramatized by amputees' reports of sensations in a "phantom limb" remembered by the nervous system even after it had been removed. This attention to bodily memory, as well as similar developments like the wartime expulsion of nostalgia from the recognized set of mental illnesses, played an important part in the postwar emergence of neurology and later psychiatry. Long writes that "the seeds of a modern understanding of selfhood, in which the bodily economy is interpreted as out of control and in constant need of rehabilitation, were sown in Civil War hospitals."[67]

Civil War graves are also a fertile field for study of incipient modernism. Long argues that the pervasiveness and nature of death in the war prompted a reexamination of death that extended beyond attempts to align individual mortality with national immortality, presenting a more fundamental challenge to religious authority. Gary Laderman agrees, and adds that the importance of embalming in remembrance of the Civil War dead was crucial to the rise of a technocratic culture of death superintended by physicians and funeral directors. Franny Nudelman in turn stresses that the war legitimated dissection of the honored dead for medical study. Susan-Mary Grant sees in the uniformity of Civil War cemetery headstones and the high percentage of anonymous bodies a portent of an increasingly impersonal society. Drew Gilpin Faust, on the other hand, stresses that the determined efforts to preserve information about the dead, including their names whenever possible, expressed modern ideas about individual identity.[68]

[66]Sweet, *Traces of War*, 113; Trachtenberg, *Reading American Photographs*, chap. 2; Steven Conn, "Narrative Trauma and Civil War History Painting, or Why Are These Pictures So Terrible?" *History and Theory* 41 (December 2002): 17–42. See also Anne C. Rose, *Victorian America and the Civil War* (Cambridge: Cambridge University Press, 1992), chap. 6.

[67]Lisa Marie Herschbach, "Fragmentation and Reunion: Medicine, Memory and Body in the American Civil War" (Ph.D. diss., Harvard University, 1997); Lisa A. Long, *Rehabilitating Bodies: Health, History, and the American Civil War* (Philadelphia: University of Pennsylvania Press, 2004), quotation at 35.

[68]Long, *Rehabilitating Bodies*; Nudelman, *John Brown's Body*; Faust, "'The Dread Void of Uncertainty'"; Grant, "Patriot Graves"; Gary Laderman, *The Sacred Remains: American Attitudes Toward Death, 1799–1883* (New Haven: Yale University Press, 1996). See also Drew Gilpin Faust, "The Civil War Soldier and the Art of Dying," *Journal of Southern History* 67 (February 2001): 3–38; Faust, *"A Riddle of Death": Mortality and Meaning in the American Civil War* (Gettysburg, Pa.: Gettysburg College, 1995).

These works provide useful reminders that the metaphysical echoes of the war are important not only to appreciating the paintings of Winslow Homer and the poetry of Emily Dickinson but also to understanding everyday social relations.[69] Long, Herschbach, and Eric Dean argue that, to a greater extent than the literature has commonly depicted, an emotional gulf divided traumatized war survivors from other Americans.[70] This vein of scholarship also suggests that memory of the war more generally reshaped the interactions of Americans by introducing new views of the body. The authors' emphasis on medical dimensions of memory, so well attuned to the culture of the United States today, underscores that the postbellum reconstruction of power structures reached beyond the realm of government and included transformations in self-definition apart from political rights and social status. They offer a past that is valuable both for reviewing the public influence of science and for reexamining private philosophical commitments.

Has the Memory Theme Been Exhausted?

The scholarly literature on Civil War memory, less than an armful for a reader in the mid-1980s, has since multiplied to many items. Histories of the Civil War and Reconstruction era now routinely close on the theme of commemoration. The broader interest in memory, two leading scholars report, "has become almost an obsession."[71] A development of such rapid and conspicuous growth naturally invites questions about its solidity and durability.

The impulses that sparked the emergence of scholarship on Civil War remembrance have not faded. Historians are likely to continue to examine politics as pursued in such venues as public spectacles and popular media, longtime strongholds of commemoration, and to maintain a particular alertness to the degree of power that these forums provided to groups foreclosed from equal access to elections and legislation. The notion that consciousness of the past has engaged wide audiences and influenced the unfolding of the present

[69]The practical repercussions of Civil War modernism have often been explored through the concepts of law advanced by Oliver Wendell Holmes Jr. See, e.g., Louis Menand, *The Metaphysical Club: A Story of Ideas in America* (New York: Farrar, Straus and Giroux, 2001).

[70]Eric T. Dean Jr., *Shook over Hell: Post-Traumatic Stress, Vietnam, and the Civil War* (Cambridge, Mass.: Harvard University Press, 1997). Long emphasizes that noncombatants were also traumatized.

[71]Alon Confino and Peter Fritzsche, *The Work of Memory: New Directions in the Study of German Society and Culture* (Urbana: University of Illinois Press, 2002), 1. For the spread of this scholarship to college textbooks, see Thomas J. Brown, ed., *The Public Art of Civil War Commemoration: A Brief History with Documents* (New York: Saint Martin's, 2004); Michael Fellman, Lesley J. Gordon, and Daniel E. Sutherland, *This Terrible War: The Civil War and Its Aftermath* (New York: Longman, 2003), 374–382.

will doubtless remain appealing to historians. These authors must bear in mind that the place of the Civil War in American life is not what it once was, and the debate over the prospects for collective memory in contemporary culture is still unresolved. But remembrance of the Civil War retains a significant presence in the United States. It is foundational in American race relations, and recent controversies over representations of the Confederacy can be expected to continue and to foster interest in the history of those commemorations. More generally, the war remains embedded in the cultural heritage of the nation as a remarkably supple master narrative of inner conflict that should long sustain further examination.

The literature on Civil War remembrance has established a variety of research designs that invite further application. A large body of scholarship, including many literary studies, focuses on promoters of Civil War remembrance, but more work remains to be done on even the most prominent voices and organizations. A group as noteworthy as the Sons of Confederate Veterans, for example, remains almost entirely unstudied. Other research has centered on specific subjects of commemoration. Scholarship on the changing images of individuals and groups has concentrated heavily on a few topics, especially Lincoln and Lee. Historians have only begun to turn to remembrance of figures as central as John Brown and Ulysses S. Grant, and they have mostly neglected those whose fame was more short-lived, like Ben Butler and Sam Davis, as well as less powerful groups like Copperheads and white southern dissidents.[72] Remembrance of the major events of the war has also been a common focus. Commemoration of emancipation and the Battle of Gettysburg have attracted a good deal of work. Even an engagement as widely noted as the meeting of the *Monitor* and the *Merrimac* has not yet drawn much attention, however, despite the opportunity it provides to explore understandings of the war as a technological watershed. Similarly, little scholarship has focused on other passionately remembered events of the war, including Sherman's March and the Andersonville saga.[73] In addition to asking who has remembered the Civil War and what events they have remembered, scholars have often asked how Americans have remembered the war. Studies of Memorial Day observances, battlefield parks, military cemeteries, and public monuments have been standard frameworks of the scholar-

---

[72]Merrill D. Peterson, *John Brown: The Legend Revisited* (Charlottesville: University of Virginia Press, 2002); Joan Waugh, "'Pageantry of Woe': The Funeral of Ulysses S. Grant," *Civil War History* 51 (June 2005): 151–174. On Davis, see Wilson, *Baptized in Blood*, 52–54.

[73]See Douglas Gibson Gardner, "Andersonville and American Memory: Civil War Prisoners and Narratives of Suffering and Redemption" (Ph.D. diss., Miami University, 1998); Nancy A. Roberts, "The Afterlife of Civil War Prisons and Their Dead" (Ph.D. diss., University of Oregon, 1996).

ship. Yet one of the most significant forms of Civil War remembrance has been among the least explored: the collection and uses of war relics.[74]

The question of where Americans remembered the war has inspired less research than might be expected. Historians have focused on particular sites of memory like battlefields and on the regional significance of Civil War remembrance. But they have rarely looked at its workings on the community level. Some studies examine commemoration as an instrument in local rivalries and point out that the spotlight on the war competed with alternative historical identities fashioned by various cities.[75] Further work of this sort would be useful. Even in the most heavily studied case of Richmond, the scholarship does not identify the persistent constituencies for commemoration, and the relationship between Civil War remembrance and other themes of civic memory beckons for investigation in such cities as Charleston, New Orleans, and Philadelphia. The meanings of memory in smaller communities are more neglected. Historians have not often pursued Robert Penn Warren's observation that the Civil War owes part of its enduring appeal to the image of rootedness it has offered to a restless, mobile people.[76] It may not be coincidental that Civil War commemoration flourished during a peak in anxiety about the insularity and viability of small communities.

The motif of generational relations also calls for more attention. Many historians have noted that the Civil War defined a cohort group.[77] But no work in the current literature on remembrance has made generational relations as central as they were to Paul Buck's *Road to Reunion*, which argued that rising youth took the lead in preventing a self-perpetuating inheritance of sectional animosities. The brief glances at this topic in recent research raise doubts about Buck's claim that those too young to fight wholeheartedly acknowledged the centrality of the war while undermining their elders' bitterness, if only because that view ignores maturing men and women who regarded the ubiquitous remem-

[74]John M. Coski and Amy R. Feely, "A Monument to Southern Womanhood: The Founding Generation of the Confederate Museum," in *A Woman's War*, ed. Edward D. C. Campbell Jr. and Kym S. Rice (Richmond, Va.: Museum of the Confederacy, 1996), 131–163, is a starting point. For a lighthearted yet insightful look at artifacts, see Drew Gilpin Faust, "Equine Relics of the Civil War," *Southern Cultures* 6 (Spring 2000): 23–49.

[75]See, e.g., Brown, "Reconstructing Boston," in Blatt, Brown, and Yacovone, *Hope and Glory*; John Bodnar, *Remaking America: Public Memory, Commemoration, and Patriotism in the Twentieth Century* (Princeton: Princeton University Press, 1992), chap. 4; and Theodore J. Karawanski, "Memory's Landscape: Civil War Monuments in Chicago" *Chicago History* 26 (1997): 54–72.

[76]Robert Penn Warren, *The Legacy of the Civil War* (Cambridge, Mass.: Harvard University Press, 1961), 91–92. Evans, *Legend of John Wilkes Booth*, chap. 1, provides an excellent analysis of community dynamics of Civil War memory in Enid, Oklahoma.

[77]Censer, *Reconstruction of White Southern Womanhood*, is an especially thorough and thoughtful generational analysis.

brance of the war as a burden to be overthrown. Moreover, while Buck sought to use generational identities to explain historical memory, scholars familiar with the impact of World War II and the Vietnam War will be no less interested in reversing the equation and using historical memory to examine relations among people of different ages. That research would require examination of Civil War memory in fresh contexts, such as scholarship on family history and the construction of life cycles. Historical memory, a key constituent of generational relations, should be helpful in approaching a social category that American historians have generally handled much less successfully than race, class, or gender relations.[78]

The study of Civil War memory cannot be expected to maintain the same pace of production that it has experienced in the past two decades, but neither is it an academic fad that will disappear altogether. Remembrance of the war was one of the basic hallmarks of the postbellum era. It is also a topic of continuing importance for a nation so profoundly shaped by the selective remembrance and forgetting of its more recent military experiences. The era of Reconstruction remains the most instructive phase in the making of the self-consciously postwar cultures that have ever since characterized the United States.

[78]Jacquelyn Dowd Hall, "'You Must Remember This': Autobiography as Social Critique," *Journal of American History* 85 (September 1998): 439–465, offers a revealing glimpse of the interplay between Civil War memory and generational relations. Here again, work on remembrance of World War I offers useful models. See, e.g., Robert Wohl, *The Generation of 1914* (Cambridge, Mass.: Harvard University Press, 1979).

ACKNOWLEDGMENTS

This project was an initiative of the Institute for Southern Studies at the University of South Carolina. The contributors are grateful to Walter Edgar, director of the Institute, for his encouragement of the venture and to Robert McNair for his generous endowment of the fund that facilitated our efforts. Bob Ellis of the Institute staff assisted in countless ways, ranging from management of workshop logistics to indexing of the book, always with exemplary efficiency and good cheer. Page Putnam Miller amiably welcomed us into alliance with the Beaufort County Reconstruction Working Group, which has done valuable work toward enhancing the national visibility of that extraordinary historic landscape, and adeptly arranged for us to enjoy a stimulating visit to Beaufort. Marty Davis, Lawrence Rowland, and Steven Wise provided informative, engaging historical orientation to the surroundings. Marge Yanker and Jane Upshaw of the University of South Carolina, Beaufort, kindly permitted us to meet in the splendid and appropriate Beaufort College building, former office of the Freedmen's Bureau, and Nancy Scheider attended to us with gracious southern hospitality. We are also indebted to several other people who made the Beaufort workshop memorable, including Maxine Lutz of the Historic Beaufort Foundation, John Tucker of the National Park Service, Bernie Wright of the Penn Center, Cecily McMillan, and Dick Stewart. Steve Kantrowitz and Jane Dailey provided insightful counsel about planning the book. At Oxford University Press, Susan Ferber supported the project and arranged for helpful outside readings in addition to offering her own thoughtful editorial suggestions. Martha Ramsey and Rebecca Evans expertly copyedited and designed the book. Finally, the editor would like to thank the contributors for their professional collegiality and personal friendship. It is gratifying that so many pleasant working relationships have been involved in this survey of the collective enterprise of scholarship.

INDEX